MW01257424

# Racial Innocence

*America and the Long 19th Century*

GENERAL EDITORS
David Kazanjian, Elizabeth McHenry, and Priscilla Wald

# Racial Innocence

*Performing American Childhood
from Slavery to Civil Rights*

Robin Bernstein

NEW YORK UNIVERSITY PRESS

*New York and London*

NEW YORK UNIVERSITY PRESS
New York and London
www.nyupress.org

© 2011 by New York University
All rights reserved

LIBRARY OF CONGRESS CATALOGING-IN-PUBLICATION DATA

Bernstein, Robin, 1969–
Racial innocence : performing American childhood from slavery to
civil rights / Robin Bernstein.
p. cm. — (America and the long 19th Century)
Includes bibliographical references and index.
ISBN 978-0-8147-8707-6 (hardback : acid-free paper)
ISBN 978-0-8147-8708-3 (pbk.                )
ISBN 978-0-8147–8709-0 (e-book)
ISBN 978-0-8147-8978-0 (e-book)
1. United States—Race relations.   2. Slavery—United States—
History.   3. Racism in literature.   4. Children in literature.
5. United States—Civilization.   I. Title.
E185.61.B445   2011
305.800973—dc23

2011024713

References to Internet Web sites (URLs) were accurate at the time of
writing. Neither the author nor New York University Press is responsible
for URLs that may have expired or changed since the manuscript was
prepared.

New York University Press books

Manufactured in the United States of America
c 10 9 8 7 6 5 4 3 2 1
p 10 9 8 7 6 5 4 3 2 1

THE
AMERICAN
LITERATURES
INITIATIVE

A book in the American Literatures Initiative (ALI), a collaborative
publishing project of NYU Press, Fordham University Press, Rutgers
University Press, Temple University Press, and the University of Virginia
Press. The Initiative is supported by The Andrew W. Mellon Foundation.
For more information, please visit www.americanliteratures.org.

# Contents

# Acknowledgments

I wrote most of this book at Harvard University while I was an assistant professor in three extraordinary interdisciplinary programs: Women, Gender, and Sexuality; History and Literature; and the History of American Civilization. Just when the book went into production, I was honored to join the Department of African and African American Studies at Harvard. I gratefully acknowledge my colleagues and students in all these communities: their questions and provocations critically shaped this project, and their scholarship continues to inspire me. Harvard University generously supported my work with grants from the Faculty of Arts and Sciences Tenure-Track Faculty Publication Fund and the Clark Fund. I am also grateful for the Betsy Beinecke Shirley Fellowship in American Children's Literature and the Jay and Deborah Last Fellowship, which enabled me to conduct research at the Beinecke Rare Book and Manuscript Library at Yale University and the American Antiquarian Society, respectively. The David Keller Travel Grant and the Thomas F. Marshall Travel Grant enabled me to share my research at conferences of the American Society for Theatre Research. The Andrew W. Mellon Foundation, the John Perry Miller Fund, the Beinecke Rare Book and Manuscript Library, the John F. Enders fund, and the Graduate School of Arts and Sciences supported my studies at Yale University. Finally, a Donald D. Harrington Faculty Fellowship enabled me to complete the final stages of manuscript revision while in residence in the Department of Theatre and Dance at the University of Texas at Austin. I thank the Donald and Sybil Harrington Foundation for this honor, and I thank the many individuals at the University of Texas and Harvard whose creativity and commitment made it possible for me to accept this fellowship. On this point, I especially thank Charlotte Canning and Holly Williams, Brad Epps and Jill Lepore, and Deans Elizabeth Lambert and Heather Lantz.

This book developed in conversation with many scholars, and there is no way to overstate my appreciation for their acumen and heart. This book simply would not exist without them. I thank the members of my writing groups, which included, at different times, Renée Bergland, Vince Brown, Glenda Carpio, Cheryl Finley, Karen Flood, Jeanne Follansbee, Brian Herrera, Betsy Klimasmith, Kip Kosek, Sarah Luria, Elizabeth Dyrud Lyman, Ian J. Miller, Tavia Nyong'o, Sindhumathi Revuluri, Barbara Rodríguez, Laura Saltz, Adelheid Voskuhl, and Joanne van der Woude. Colleagues who read and commented on part or all of the manuscript, the book proposal, or the *PMLA* or *Social Text* essays that folded into this book include Colleen S. Boggs, Julie Buckler, Larry Buell, Wai Chee Dimock, Anna Mae Duane, Brad Epps, Ellen Gruber Garvey, Marah Gubar, Amy Strahler Holzapfel, Shannon Jackson, David Krieger, Jill Lane, Caroline Levander, Christie McDonald, Micki McElya, Afsaneh Najmabadi, Leah Price, Larry Rosenwald, Linda Schlossberg, Judith Surkis, Phyllis Thompson, and Patricia Yaeger. In addition, Patricia Crain, Julia Mickenberg, and Elizabeth Young reviewed the manuscript at different stages; their incisive readings clarified my vision and contributed crucially to the process of revision. My mentors, Julie Buckler and Alice Jardine, provided wise guidance throughout and beyond the process of writing this book. Two friends and colleagues, Brian Herrera and Ellen Gruber Garvey, deserve special mention. Brian has been one of my best and most present interlocutors since the beginning of this project. Our ongoing conversations about theater, performance, race, and U.S. history have made me a better scholar. Ellen read and very insightfully critiqued drafts of many parts of this manuscript; her unflagging enthusiasm continues to encourage me and propel me forward. And last, I thank those who were there first: Joseph Roach and Laura Wexler, my supportive, intellectually bracing, simply amazing doctoral advisers. No one paragraph can contain the magnitude of my appreciation for all Laura and Joe have taught me, so I will express my gratitude by conveying their lessons to my own students.

I developed my ideas about performance, race, and childhood in several scholarly communities. The Photographic Memory Workshop, founded and led by Laura Wexler, Cheryl Finley, and Leigh Raiford, revolutionized the ways in which I engage with visual materials; my participation in the PMW remains, to this day, one of the richest intellectual experiences of my life. The Mellon Seminar in Writing Performance History, convened by Joe Roach, galvanized some of the key ideas in this book. I am honored to be a member of the Nineteenth-Century American Women Writers Study Group, through which I have met many fabulous scholars.

I am especially grateful for the friendship and collegiality of Anna Mae Duane and Karen Sánchez-Eppler, whose insights into childhood fundamentally inform this book. The American Theatre and Drama Society has been one of my favorite organizational homes since 1998; I cherish that professionally supportive and heterogeneous community. I benefited from the comments I received when I presented my work at many conferences and at Brown University, Columbia University, Cornell University, Harvard University, the University of Connecticut at Storrs, the University of Pittsburgh, the University of Texas at Austin, Wellesley College, Williams College, and Yale University.

A researcher is only as good as her librarians, and it has been my good fortune to work with many brilliant archivists, curators, and other experts. I thank Annette Fern and Ric Wilson of the Harvard Theatre Collection and Barbara Burg and Sarah Phillips of Harvard's Widener Library. Louise Bernard, Patricia Willis, and Timothy Young provided crucial research support and stimulating conversation at the Beinecke. At the Harriet Beecher Stowe Center in Hartford, Connecticut, Dawn Adiletta spoke with me at length about the material culture of *Uncle Tom's Cabin*. That single conversation helped me frame some of the core ideas in this book. Professor Kimberly Wallace-Sanders of Emory University and Lowery Sims of the Museum of Arts and Design in New York generously discussed topsy-turvy dolls with me. Myla Perkins shared her knowledge of the National Negro Doll Company. Barbara Whiteman, Founder and Executive Director of the Philadelphia Doll Museum, spent the better part of a day discussing black dolls with me. Andy Kolovos of the Vermont Folklife Center and Jane Beck answered my many questions about Daisy Turner. David Coleman and Barbara Brown of the Harry Ransom Center at the University of Texas at Austin helped me date the collodion print that appears in Chapter 5. I am especially grateful to Joni Gruelle Wannamaker and Tom Wannamaker, who very generously allowed me access to Johnny Gruelle's papers and original artwork.

One month at the American Antiquarian Society, with support from the Jay and Deborah Last Foundation, utterly transformed this project. Many of the primary visual and literary sources for this book, especially in Chapters 1, 3, and 5, are archived at the AAS. I never would have found these sources without the expertise and camaraderie of Georgia Barnhill, Paul Erickson, Caroline F. Sloat, Laura Wasowicz, and other members of the AAS staff. I am tremendously grateful for these people and resources, and I cannot imagine what this book would have looked like without them.

Working with Eric Zinner and Ciara McLaughlin at New York University Press has been a great pleasure. I thank them for their enthusiasm for this project and their sound judgment at every turn. I also thank Tim Roberts and Teresa Jesionowski at the American Literatures Initiative for their support during production. Phyllis Thompson brought her expertise and level head to the enormous task of procuring and preparing the images, and she also co-created the index—thank you, Phyllis. Katie Brian, A. Robin Hoffman, Anna Lvovsky, Ioana Patuleanu, and especially Erin Dwyer provided superb research assistance. Parts of the Introduction and Chapters 2 and 5 appeared previously as passages in "Children's Books, Dolls, and the Performance of Race; Or, The Possibility of Children's Literature," *PMLA* 126, no. 1 (2011) and in "Dances with Things: Material Culture and the Performance of Race," *Social Text* no. 101 (2009). I thank the Modern Language Association and Duke University Press for their permission to reprint portions of these articles.

My parents, Joanne and Michael Bernstein, lovingly nurtured my mind while modeling a sense of humor with regard to academia. Even when I was a very young child, my mother affirmed my certainty that I would someday write books. My father, along with my grandparents, Florence and Leonard Bernstein, taught me how to make things with my hands, and these lessons ultimately became the foundation for my study of material culture. My in-laws, Janis and David Townsend, as well as Michael Townsend, Debi Lubawsky, and Stella and Len Moss, welcomed me with love into their warm, funny, smart family.

I am so grateful for my friends, many of whom I have already named. Additional people who have supported me in different ways and at different stages of this process include Andrea Becksvoort, Andy Bernstein, Elizabeth Bernstein, Chris Bobel, Kathy Coll, Steph Gauchel, Francoise Hamlin, Erica Jacobs, Lorrie Kim, Amy Kittelstrom, Caroline Light, Caryn Markson, Christianna Morgan, Susan Musinsky, Lesléa Newman, Robyn Ochs, Amy Parker, Victorine Shepard, Sara Warner, and Catherine Whalen. Lyn Swirda, acupuncturist extraordinaire, helped keep the writing flowing. My three dear friends—Elisa Michel, Nancy Grey, and Heidi Creamer—have sustained me since high school, college, and my early twenties, respectively. I especially thank Elisa for bringing my wondrous godson, Gavin Michel, into the world. Elisa, Nancy, Heidi: it was a treat to grow up with you, and I hope to grow old with you.

Most of all, I thank Maya Townsend, my beloved companion since 1995 and my spouse since 2004. Throughout this project, Maya provided unfailing love, support, laughter, play, and something like balance. I thank her for managing not to roll her eyes too much whenever I said, "No, really, *this* time it's impossible." Each impossible task became possible only because of Maya. Of course this book is dedicated to her. Maya, I love the life we have built together. Thank you for everything. *Matzati et she'ahavah nafshi.*

# Introduction

## *Playing Innocent: Childhood, Race, Performance*

In October 2009, Keith Bardwell, the justice of the peace in Louisiana's Tangipahoa Parish, refused to perform a wedding ceremony for Beth Humphrey, who is white, and Terence McKay, who is African American. "I don't do interracial marriages," Bardwell explained, "because I don't want to put children in a situation they didn't bring on themselves."[1] Bardwell, a white man, said that in his observation, "There is a problem with both groups accepting a child from such a marriage" and that therefore "the children will later suffer."[2] He asserted that his refusal to marry Humphrey and McKay did not constitute discrimination because he denied his services equally to a white woman and a black man. Bardwell claimed youth, not race, as his central concern: "I do it to protect the children. The kids are innocent and I worry about their futures."[3] Condemnation of Bardwell, as predictable as it was deserved, splattered from the Hammond, Louisiana, *Daily Star* to the *New York Times*, from CNN to CBS to Fox News, from the blogosphere to YouTube. Commentators decried the denial of civil rights to Humphrey and McKay (whom another justice of the peace did marry) and defended interracial families and children, often citing President Barack Obama as an example of a successful son born of an interracial marriage. The next month, Bardwell resigned, but he remained unrepentant: "I'm not a racist," he said. "My main concern is for the children."[4]

Throughout the uproar, one remarkable fact escaped mention: Bardwell refused to wed Humphrey and McKay in order to protect children *who did not exist*. Bardwell trumpeted his concern for "the children," but Humphrey and McKay had no children together in 2009.[5] The "children" whom Bardwell claimed to protect were wholly imagined. These figments competed with Humphrey and McKay: in Bardwell's view, imagined children deserve protection more than living adults deserve constitutional rights.

The needs of imagined children trumped even those of embodied children: Bardwell understood interracial children to "suffer" and said that therefore he "won't help put them through it."[6] Bardwell opposed interracial marriage, then, so as to protect imagined children from becoming flesh, to protect them from life itself. Thus Bardwell invoked "the children"—an abstract concept of childhood—not only to justify the denial of civil rights to adults, but also to excuse his attempt to prevent the birth of individual children those adults might choose to have.

Even Bardwell's most vigorous critics did not identify, much less probe, these incongruities, but instead largely accepted Bardwell's terms while contesting his conclusions: where Bardwell and his few supporters argued that interracial marriage hurts children, opponents responded that it benefits or at minimum does not harm children. Both sides, then, invoked abstract childhood to support their positions, while neither hesitated to accord rights to adults on the basis of imagined children's needs. And each side's argument was, to some, persuasive. The very fact that polar arguments used childhood to support diametrical claims seems to have struck no one as odd. But it should have. Why is abstracted childhood so flexible that it can simultaneously bolster arguments for and against interracial marriage? How did childhood acquire so much affective weight that the exhortation to "protect the children" seems to add persuasive power to almost any argument? How did the idea of "childhood innocence" become a crucial but naturalized element of contests over race and rights?

Answers to these questions root through the nineteenth century. An antecedent for Bardwell's antimiscegenation stance appears, for example, in Edward Williams Clay's 1839 engraving, *The Fruits of Amalgamation* (figure I.1). This image catalogs the supposedly alarming results of racial mixing: a white woman nursing an infant of color, an African American man and woman dressed in finery and being served by a white butler, and even a cat and a dog apparently defying nature by playing together.[7] However, the image's adults serve literally as backup to a mixed-race child in the foreground, upon whom the image's diagonal lines of sight converge. This child gives the image its visual focal point and title—he is literally the "fruit" of his parents' marriage—and thus delivers the image's political message. Such long-standing use of children in arguments against interracial marriage is well known; less familiar and more surprising are the nineteenth-century defenders of interracial marriage who also recruited childhood to their cause. In 1819, for example, Judge C. J. Parker ruled in the case of *The Inhabitants of Medway v. The Inhabitants of Needham* that

*Figure I.1.* Edward Williams Clay, *The Fruits of Amalgamation*, engraving, 1839. Courtesy of the American Antiquarian Society.

the commonwealth of Massachusetts, which outlawed interracial marriage, must recognize such a marriage performed legally in Rhode Island, so as "to avoid the great inconvenience and cruelty of bastardizing the issue of such marriages."[8] In 1833, Lydia Maria Child also argued against bans on interracial marriage on the basis that they hurt children: as Child pointed out, interracial couples "*will* make such marriages, in spite of the law," and the children of these extralegal unions are often deprived of their rightful inheritance "because the law pronounces them illegitimate."[9] The pluripotence that childhood held in 2009—its ability to imbue arguments against and for interracial marriage with at least some credence—has been in evidence, then, for almost two centuries.

This book explains how these strange cultural phenomena—the invocation of imagined children within directly opposing racial arguments, the use of abstract childhood to justify granting or withholding the rights of living adults and children—became so familiar as to appear unremarkable. I show how childhood figured pivotally in a set of large-scale U.S. racial projects: slavery and abolition, post-Emancipation enfranchisement and disenfranchisement of African Americans, and, by the turn of the twentieth century, antiblack violence, New Negro racial uplift, and the early civil rights movement.[10] I argue that performance, both on stage and, especially, in everyday life, was the vehicle by which childhood suffused, gave power to, and crucially shaped these racial projects. Childhood in performance enabled divergent political positions each to appear natural, inevitable, and therefore justified. I call this dynamic "racial innocence."

## *Racial Innocence*

The connection between childhood and innocence is not essential but is instead historically located.[11] During the colonial period, Calvinists did not believe that children were innocent; to the contrary, they lived with the terrifying idea that children, who were born with original sin, could die before they experienced Christian salvation, in which case they would endure eternal damnation. According to this "doctrine of infant depravity," children were inherently sinful and sexual—even more so, potentially, than adults, who had learned, through rationality and self-discipline, how to control their damnable impulses.[12] In the late eighteenth and early nineteenth century, however, a competing doctrine entered popular consciousness. In this emergent view, children were innocent: that is, sinless, absent of sexual feelings, and oblivious to worldly concerns. This view of the innocent child assumed a variety of complex and ever-shifting forms, including the Lockean tabula rasa and the Rousseauian youth who was at essence an uncorrupted element of nature.[13] American sermons and child-rearing manuals widely quoted and thus circulated William Wordsworth's representations of children as innocent, holy, and able to redeem adults.[14] By the mid-nineteenth century, prevailing beliefs about childhood inverted the doctrine of infant depravity: children were not sinful but innocent, not depraved souls risking hellfire but holy angels leading adults to heaven. By the mid-nineteenth century, sentimental culture had woven childhood and innocence together wholly. Childhood was then understood not as innocent but as innocence itself; not as a symbol of innocence but as its embodiment.[15] The doctrine of original sin receded, replaced by a doctrine of original innocence.

This innocence was raced white. Little Eva, the emblematic child-angel of the nineteenth century, was a spectacle of phenotypical and chromatic whiteness: in *Uncle Tom's Cabin*, Harriet Beecher Stowe interlaid descriptions of Eva's racially marked "golden-brown" hair and "deep blue eyes" with references to the girl's habit of dressing only in white.[16] Eva's death,

*Figure I.2.* "Little Eva Song, Uncle Tom's Guardian Angel," handkerchief printed for John P. Jewett, late 1852 or early 1853. Courtesy of the American Antiquarian Society.

arguably the best-known scene in all sentimental literature, occasioned a blizzard of whiteness: everything in Eva's bedroom, from statuettes and pictures, to the bed and bedside table, to the girl's corpse itself, was draped in white; and throughout the room, white flowers drooped in baskets and vases.[17] The paleness of Little Eva's body, especially her skin and hair, was not incidentally decorative but was instead crucial to Stowe's plot, as when one of Eva's "golden tress[es]" twined around Simon Legree's fingers, and the "fair hair" terrified the slaveholder and compelled him to refrain, if only for one night, from sexually assaulting an enslaved woman.[18] Little Eva was neither isolated nor unique but was instead, as Ann Douglas notes, the archetype of "innumerable pale and pious"—one might say white and sinless—"heroines" of nineteenth-century sentimental fiction.[19] Little Eva was a hub in a busy cultural system linking innocence to whiteness through the body of the child.

The white child's innocence was transferable to surrounding people and things, and that property made it politically usable.[20] This transmission occurred, for example, when Little Eva and Uncle Tom cuddled ecstatically in book illustrations, dramatic stagings of *Uncle Tom's Cabin*, games, advertisements, and household items such as handkerchiefs (figure I.2).[21] In these images, the propinquity between the sentimental white child, foundationally defined by innocence, and the enslaved adult caused the white child's aura of innocence to extend to an African American character.[22] Eva's and Tom's embrace made Tom, and by extension abolition itself, seem righteous, but the inverse political effect was equally possible: the white child's embrace could confer innocence upon not abolition but slavery, as became the case three decades later when plantation writer Joel Chandler Harris posed an unnamed white "Little Boy" on the knee of the happily enslaved Uncle Remus.[23] In each case, propinquity between a white child and an African American adult transferred innocence from white childhood to a political endeavor: abolition or post-Reconstruction romanticization of slavery, respectively.

To be innocent was to be innocent *of* something, to achieve obliviousness. This obliviousness was not merely an absence of knowledge, but an active state of repelling knowledge—the child's "holy ignorance," in the phrase of an 1822 article in *Blackwood's Magazine*.[24] James Kincaid echoes that idea in his characterization of Victorian childhood as a "wonderfully hollow category" in which "purity" is "figured as negation," a "ruthless distribution of eviction notices."[25] Individual nineteenth-century children, like all people, forgot and remembered, but to be legibly childlike—to perform "childhood innocence"—was to manifest a state of holy ignorance. However, not just any obliviousness constituted innocence: to be childlike was not to forget one's name or one's manners, and was certainly not to forget hymns or Him. Rather, sentimental childlike innocence manifested through the performed transcendence of social categories of class, gender, and, most importantly for this book, race.[26] Of course, no nineteenth-century children existed outside race (or gender or class), nor were any children perceived as unraced. Innocence was not a literal state of being unraced but was, rather, the performance of not-noticing, a performed claim of slipping beyond social categories. Little Eva loves everyone, of every race and age and gender and class, because she transcends the adult world; she is already halfway to heaven. In the iconic "arbor scene" reprinted on the handkerchief in figure I.2, artist Hammatt Billings positioned Eva's hand upon Uncle Tom's hand and thigh and thus visualized Eva ignoring racial prohibitions and not-imagining sexual congress. This illustration, arguably the best-known and most widely circulated image of Stowe's characters, represented Eva in the act of not-thinking about race, gender, age, or sexual desire.[27]

This association between innocence and forgetting exists in paradoxical tension with the tendency of the culture of childhood to retain past practices. Historians have shown that the materials and practices that surround living children, as well as historically located representations of children, have unique abilities to recapitulate adult culture while seeming to deflect it. Fragmentary images or gestures often linger, altered yet recognizable, in the culture of childhood after they have receded or even disappeared from adult culture: one century's proverb becomes the next century's nursery rhyme; a woman's mobcap of the eighteenth century adorns the head of a girl in a best-selling print of the late nineteenth century.[28] Today, riddles such as "Why did the chicken cross the road?" and "Why does a fireman wear red suspenders?" are fixtures in children's popular culture, but these riddles originated in nineteenth-century minstrel shows created by and for adults.[29] Anyone who can correctly answer these riddles has memorized a part of a minstrel script—and the transmission of that script probably occurred during the individual's childhood. Because the culture of childhood so often retains and repurposes that which has elsewhere become abject or abandoned, the study of childhood radically challenges many established historical periodizations. Sentimentalism or minstrelsy may have peaked in the lives of adults in the nineteenth century, but the popular cultures of childhood, this book shows, delivered, in fragmented and distorted forms, the images, practices, and ideologies of sentimentalism and minstrelsy well into the twentieth century.

Nineteenth-century childhood's ability to assert a state of holy obliviousness while retaining and recapitulating cultural memory was uniquely useful to the construction and maintenance of whiteness. Whiteness, as Richard Dyer and many other scholars have argued, derives power from its status as an unmarked category. George Lipsitz notes that "whiteness never has to speak its name, never has to acknowledge its role as an organizing principle in social and cultural relations."[30] This "silence about itself" is, for Ann DuCille, "the primary prerogative of whiteness, at once its grand scheme and its deep cover."[31] Childhood, I argue throughout this book, is a primary material in the historical construction of that cover. Childhood innocence—itself raced white, itself characterized by the ability to retain racial meanings but hide them under claims of holy obliviousness—secured the unmarked status of whiteness, and the power derived from that status, in the nineteenth and into the early twentieth centuries. Childhood innocence provided a perfect alibi: not only the ability to remember while appearing to forget, but even more powerfully, the production of racial memory through the performance of forgetting. What childhood innocence helped Americans to assert by forgetting, to think about by performing obliviousness, was not only whiteness but also racial difference constructed against whiteness. Racial binarism—understanding race in terms of white and nonwhite, or a "black and white" polarization that erases nonblack people of color—gained legibility through nineteenth-century childhood.

## *A New Method of Historical Analysis: Reading "Scriptive Things"*

The influence of childhood upon U.S. racial formation has been greatly underestimated because a crucial part of this influence occurred, this book will show, through lived behaviors—performances in everyday life. To scholars trained in the study of written and visual texts, these performances may seem ephemeral and untraceable. Past performances of everyday life can, however, be recovered. This book proposes a new method by which to analyze items of material culture in order to discover otherwise inaccessible evidence of past behaviors. The method entails using archival knowledge and historical context to determine the documented, probable, and possible uses of a category of object. This horizon of known and possible uses then informs a close reading of an individual artifact. The operative questions are, "What historically located behaviors did this artifact invite? And what practices did it discourage?" The goal is not to determine what any individual did with an artifact but rather to understand how a nonagential artifact, in its historical context, prompted or invited—scripted—actions of humans who were agential and not infrequently resistant. I detail this method in Chapter 2 and then use it in Chapters 3 through 5 to recover and analyze past performances that installed ideas about childhood in large-scale racial projects.[32]

The handkerchief shown in figure I.2 provides a useful example of a material item that invited historically located behaviors. The handkerchief is one of thousands of "Tomitudes," or items of material culture representing Stowe's characters, that proliferated during the nineteenth and early twentieth centuries. Lists of Tomitudes, from dolls and card games to statuary and embroidery to jam jars and tobacco tins, often appear in scholarship on *Uncle Tom's Cabin*. Scholars have been able to say almost nothing, however, about what people actually *did* with these items. The handkerchief frequently receives a highlighted mention within lists of Tomitudes, which suggests that scholars find the handkerchief interesting but inexplicable. One scholar writes, for example, "As testament to [Stowe's characters'] popularity, manufacturers on both sides of the Atlantic produced collectors' plates, statuettes, porcelain mugs, and even muslin handkerchiefs that depicted Tom and Eva."[33] As in this example, the handkerchief often appears last in a list of Tomitudes, punctuated by the word "even." Thus scholars mark the handkerchief as a puzzling curiosity, a strange little beacon that signals how much we do not know about the extensive material culture of *Uncle Tom's Cabin* and therefore about bodily experiences of nineteenth-century domesticity.

We do know a good deal about the handkerchief's provenance. John P. Jewett, Stowe's first American publisher, created the handkerchief in late 1852 or early 1853: Jewett commissioned John Greenleaf Whittier to write the poem about Little Eva and hired Manuel Emilio to set that poem to music. The illustration, by Hammatt Billings, of Eva and Tom in the arbor is reprinted from Jewett's first edition of *Uncle Tom's Cabin*. The handkerchief united these elements—illustration, poem, music, and material— and therefore capped a great deal of work on Jewett's part. But according to Claire Parfait, Jewett seems not to have sold the handkerchief, but rather to have given it away to customers.[34] The handkerchief, then, was an advertisement, an object whose purpose was to produce and channel consumerist desire.[35]

The handkerchief did not, however, produce meaning only through its component texts—visual, poetic, and musical. The difference between the handkerchief and a leaf of paper bearing an identical imprint is three-dimensional materiality and the uses prompted through that materiality. To understand the Jewett handkerchief, we must think about it as a thing in use. We must recover the historically located practices the handkerchief invited and discouraged.

One use was verboten: nose-blowing. To blow one's nose upon these

Christ-like characters was physically possible—and someone, somewhere, may have done it—but such an action would have been socially inappropriate at best and blasphemous at worst (for a contemporary analogy, one might think of a small American flag: it is physically possible to blow one's nose into it, but that action would be shockingly offensive). Nineteenth-century handkerchiefs for nose-blowing, which resembled what one now calls "bandanas," were typically red or brown, never white, and they included broad patterns that were designed to mask stains in an era when laundering was among the most time-consuming and exhausting of domestic chores.[36] A handkerchief such as Jewett's, featuring delicate designs printed on white cloth, was indisputably intended "for show, not blow."[37]

But *how* would a person show it? Use of the handkerchief as a doily or home decoration was physically possible but contra mid-nineteenth century custom. Handkerchiefs adorned the body, not the parlor: mid-nineteenth century women and men displayed artfully folded handkerchiefs in sleeves or pockets. This handkerchief, like other decorative handkerchiefs, was probably also carried in the hand, where it accented the bearer's physical grace and served as an important element of sentimental fashion. Women commonly waved handkerchiefs at political rallies. But what could one do with this handkerchief that one could not do with another?

The answer appears in the print on the handkerchief itself. Whittier's poem begins, "Dry the tears for holy Eva" and continues with a description of the imperative fulfilled: "tears are wiped." Jewett had the poem printed on a square of cloth that could wipe and dry tears. The text and form of the handkerchief therefore work together to prompt not nose-blowing but tear-drying. Before one can wipe one's eyes, however, one must produce tears. Jewett prompted this prerequisite weeping when he imprinted the handkerchief with Hammatt Billings's illustration of the "arbor scene" in which Eva predicts her death and apotheosis. Billings illustrates the moment in Stowe's text when Eva points and says, "I'm going *there* . . . to the spirits bright"—that is, to heaven.[38]

The poem, the hymnlike music, the illustration of Eva predicting her death and ascendance, and the novel the handkerchief advertised all coordinated to overdetermine the linked actions of weeping and tear-daubing. Henry James famously wrote that Stowe's novel was the "irresistible cause" of crying, but it was the handkerchief, as linked to but distinct from the novel, that channeled those tears literally onto and *into* the absorbent bodies of Little Eva and Uncle Tom. "We lived and moved," James wrote figuratively, "*in* Mrs. Stowe's novel"; and the handkerchief encouraged its user to shed a part of his or her bodily self and to mingle that substance with the materialization of Eva and Tom.[39] In an uncanny literalization of the empathy so prized by sentimentalists, the handkerchief user's tears flowed into the capillaries of the fabric, plumping and weighting the characters, thus inserting the reader bodily and affectively into the story.

The act of weeping itself then prompted a secondary action: using a handkerchief to hide (and thus flag) one's expressions of sympathy, the signs that one "feel[s] right."[40] Two of Stowe's most positively portrayed white characters, Mrs. Bird and Mrs. Shelby, model this sentimental gesture at key moments in the novel. In the first instance, Eliza, who is in the process of escaping slavery, explains her desperation to Mrs. Bird by asking, "Have you ever lost a child?"[41] This question's explicit equalization of Mrs. Bird's and Eliza's children, and the assertion of a universal and therefore raceless experience of mothering, causes Mrs. Bird to "show . . . signs of hearty sympathy" by keeping "her face fairly hidden in her pocket-handkerchief."[42] In another pivotal moment, Mrs. Shelby enters Uncle Tom's and Aunt Chloe's cabin to inform the couple that Tom has been sold. Mrs. Shelby, unable to speak the terrible news, "cover[s] her face with her handkerchief" and "beg[ins] to sob."[43] An 1852 consumer who obtained the handkerchief from the publisher of Stowe's novel, who was aware of the handkerchief's imperative not to blow but to show, who was prompted by the vision of Eva's death to cry, and who was instructed by Whittier's poem to "dry the tears," might well have spread the handkerchief across the face, hiding and calling attention to those treasured tears of sympathy. The handkerchief in this scenario masked the weeping eyes, covering the user's face with the representations of Little Eva and Uncle Tom. A person who wore the handkerchief-mask, and who saturated Eva and Tom with tears, affectively and effectively mingled with the characters.[44]

The handkerchief scripted this performance in that it issued explicit directions ("dry the tears") in combination with cultural prompts (the image of a dying child) in the historical context of normative behaviors (show, don't blow; weep, but mask crying eyes). In the absence of corroborating evidence, one cannot determine how any individual responded to these prompts. The method of reading material things as scripts aims to discover not what any individual actually did but rather what a thing invited its users to do. This act of scripting, this issuing of a culturally specific invitation, is itself a historical event—one that can be recovered and then analyzed as a fresh source of evidence.

The term *script* denotes not a rigid dictation of performed action but

rather a set of invitations that necessarily remain open to resistance, interpretation, and improvisation. I use the term *script* as a theatrical practitio-
ner might: to denote an evocative primary substance from which actors,
directors, and designers build complex, variable performances that occupy real time and space. A playscript, whether it be George Aiken's 1852
dramatization of *Uncle Tom's Cabin* or Robert Alexander's 1990 *I Ain't Yo'
Uncle: The New Jack Revisionist Uncle Tom's Cabin,* combines properties
of elasticity and resilience so that the play remains recognizable even as
it inspires a unique live performance each night.[45] A scriptive thing, like
a playscript, broadly structures a performance while allowing for agency
and unleashing original, live variations that may not be individually predictable. Items of material culture *script* in much the same sense that literary texts *mean*: neither a thing nor a poem (for example) is conscious or
agential, but a thing can invite behaviors that its maker did and did not
envision, and a poem may produce meanings that include and exceed a
poet's intentions. To describe elements of material culture as "scripting"
actions is not to suggest that things possess agency or that people lack it,
but instead to propose that agency emerges through constant engagement
with the stuff of our lives.

W. B. Worthen points out that a powerful current within performance studies contrasts "archival" memory—written and material text
that can be housed in an archive—with the "repertoire"—embodied
memory of traditions of performance including "gestures, orality, movement, dance, singing."[46] Diana Taylor and others call for "shifting the focus from written to embodied culture, from the discursive to the performative" because the archive "sustains power" whereas the repertoire often enacts social agency and resistance, especially of oppressed peoples
in the Americas.[47] Taylor describes the "relationship between the archive
and the repertoire" as "not by definition antagonistic or oppositional";
the two forms of knowledge "usually work in tandem" (as in the wedding ceremony, which requires "both the performative utterance of 'I
do' and the signed marriage license").[48] However, a model of interaction,
or even of harmonious cooperation, reifies a polarity between the two
forms of knowledge.

The heuristic of the scriptive thing explodes the very model of archive and repertoire as distinct-but-interactive, because the word
*script* captures the moment when dramatic narrative and movement
through space are in the act of becoming each other. The handkerchief
is both an artifact of and scriptive prop within a performance—that is,

simultaneously archive and repertoire, with neither form of knowledge preexisting the other. Within each scriptive thing, archive and repertoire are one. Therefore, when scriptive things enter a repository, repertoires arrive with them. Within a brick-and-mortar archive, scriptive things archive the repertoire—partially and richly, with a sense of openness and flux. To read things as scripts is to coax the archive into divulging the repertoire.

## *Uncle Tom's Cabin Is an Archive of Repertoires*

Most scholars have problematically characterized *Uncle Tom's Cabin* as either a novel—that is, a text, an archival fixture—or a cultural phenomenon. To read *Uncle Tom's Cabin* only as a novel is to impose, in a presentist mode, an isolation that did not exist in the nineteenth century: there was, in fact, no historical moment in which *Uncle Tom's Cabin* existed only as a novel. Even before Stowe sent her manuscript pages to the *National Era*, the newspaper that originally serialized the novel, she read many of those pages aloud to her children.[49] Scenes from *Uncle Tom's Cabin* existed, then, as parlor performances before they became serialized chapters. Before Jewett published Stowe's novel in the form of a book, he commissioned Hammatt Billings to create illustrations for *Uncle Tom's Cabin*; and Jewett circulated Billings's images in advertisements in March 1852—the same month in which he released Stowe's book. From its beginning, then, *Uncle Tom's Cabin* existed in multiple genres (parlor performance, prose, poetry, visual art, and material culture) and physical practices (reading, looking, singing, showing, weeping, drying tears, and masking, to name only the actions scripted by the handkerchief). It is therefore a mischaracterization to identify Stowe's prose as the "original" and the theatrical performances, illustrations, and Tomitudes as "adaptations." In an attempt to grapple with ever-proliferating genres and texts, many scholars have alternatively described *Uncle Tom's Cabin* as a cultural phenomenon. This characterization is equally inaccurate, however, because this term misleadingly implies a unity or coherence among the disparate parts. Leslie Fiedler's related term, "inadvertent epic," usefully signals political reversals between Stowe's novel and its reverberations in literature and films such as *Birth of a Nation*, but Fiedler overprivileges authored texts that in fact constituted but one aspect—and not necessarily the most influential aspect—of *Uncle Tom's Cabin*.[50]

In contrast to the characterizations of *Uncle Tom's Cabin* as a novel or a phenomenon, Henry James got it right when he described it as

> much less a book than a state of vision, of feeling and of consciousness, in which [people] didn't sit and read and appraise and pass the time, but walked and talked and laughed and cried and, in a manner of which Mrs. Stowe was the irresistible cause, generally conducted themselves.[51]

James, along with many of his contemporaries, experienced *Uncle Tom's Cabin* as neither a book nor a theatrical production in isolation (in this passage, James discusses both a stage performance and the novel) but as a set of practices such as walking, talking, laughing, and crying. In other words, *Uncle Tom's Cabin* existed in the nineteenth century as a repertoire. This repertoire shaped performances in everyday life, the ways in which people "generally conducted themselves." These repeated stylized gestures produced a "state of vision, of feeling and of consciousness"—that is to say, subjectivization.

*Uncle Tom's Cabin* is best understood as a repertoire, and the stuff of *Uncle Tom's Cabin*—books and illustrations, handkerchiefs and dolls, playscripts and stage props, photographs and statues—were in the nineteenth century, and remain today, scriptive things that archive that repertoire. A repertoire is by definition in constant flux, always being re-made. These re-formations occur deliberately, with the exercise of agency, as well as accidentally, on a small and large scale, through authored and unauthored actions. A repertoire is by definition relational; it exists among people, over time, and, I argue throughout this book, through people's everyday physical engagements with things.

By interpreting *Uncle Tom's Cabin* as a repertoire, this book offers a new understanding of *Uncle Tom's Cabin* as profoundly and uncomfortably collaborative—as neither a sprawling-yet-coherent phenomenon nor a multiply-authored "inadvertent epic," but instead as a formation of influence and cross-influence that is internally contentious and surprisingly tightly woven without ever becoming unified; that constantly transposes among theatrical, visual, literary, and, crucially, material genres; and that is not always authored.

As a repertoire, *Uncle Tom's Cabin* circulated practices of performance between the theater and the home. The Howard family theatrical troupe, one of the first companies to stage *Uncle Tom's Cabin*, provides a good example of how this bidirectional transmission occurred. The Howards exported practices of performance from the theater to the home when they sold souvenirs from their theater lobbies, including statuettes and a songbook that enabled audience members to restage at home the songs that the Howards sang in their production of *Uncle Tom's Cabin*. But the Howards also imported gestures *from* the home *to* the theater, and material culture conveyed these performances as well. The Howard family used a script by George Aiken that is well known to have lifted dialogue directly from Stowe's novel. As I show in Chapter 3, however, Aiken also embedded in his script tableaux that restaged each of the six illustrations that Billings created for Jewett's first American edition of *Uncle Tom's Cabin*—including the arbor scene imprinted on the handkerchief and so many other items of material culture. These illustrations, materialized in three-dimensional things such as handkerchiefs and books, scripted domestic performances. The Howards, then, quoted not only Stowe's prose and Billings's images but also the gestures and feelings that coordinated through the material culture of *Uncle Tom's Cabin*—even as they sold domestic knickknacks in their theater lobbies. Thus the Howards connected the parlor and the stage. These performances domesticated the theater and theatricalized the home to create what Lauren Berlant has called an "intimate public"—one centered not on women, but on children.[52]

The repertoires of *Uncle Tom's Cabin* were crucial to the installation of childhood innocence in large-scale racial projects. Stowe did not invent racial innocence, but through her iconic child-characters, especially Little Eva (and the young George Shelby, who receives extended attention in Chapter 3), Stowe captured and refracted the practices of racial innocence from existing sentimental culture, and transmitted those practices back into the popular culture in a newly focused, vivid, potent, and usable form.

In one of its most important functions, *Uncle Tom's Cabin* installed a black-white logic in American visions of childhood. This installation occurred primarily through the characters of Eva and Topsy. In creating Topsy, Stowe drew upon existing minstrel humor (which is visible in Topsy's comic violence and dancing of breakdowns), but Stowe combined that tradition of performance with a sophisticated argument that Topsy was an essentially innocent child who has been brutalized—hardened and made "wicked"—by slavery.[53] Stowe configured Topsy and Eva as a polarized dyad, the "two extremes of society": the "fair" child with a "golden head," and the "cringing" black child who had been viciously beaten by her previous owners.[54] This polarization contrasted the two children but simultaneously asserted that both *were* children, that Eva's innocence was also Topsy's. The violence of slavery, Stowe suggested, constituted an attack on Topsy's natural innocence, which could be partially restored— transmitted—through the loving touch of a white child.

Polarity is a form of connection. For Stowe, the polarity of Topsy and Eva reflected their underlying equivalence and mutuality, but the repertoire slurred polarity into contrast, into difference alone. When Little Eva appeared in nineteenth-century visual, theatrical, and material culture, she remained an emblem of child innocence. Topsy's stagers, however, cultivated the seeds of minstrelsy that Stowe had sowed in the character while exterminating the innocence that Stowe had insisted was Topsy's birthright. This refracted Topsy, emptied of innocence, became the prototype for the pickaninny, an imagined dehumanized black juvenile and a staple of U.S. popular culture from advertising images (such as the Gold Dust Twins) to children's literature, animation, and film (such as *Little Black Sambo*, Bosko, or the Little Rascals, respectively). The pickaninny—Topsy's "fearful progeny" in Montgomery Gregory's famous phrase—ultimately reconfigured the Topsy-Eva polarity itself.[55] The dehumanized pickaninny, contrasted with an angelic white child, argued in a polygenetic vein for irreconcilable differences between black and white youth. Thus the repertoires of *Uncle Tom's Cabin* configured childhood itself as what Linda Williams calls a "melodrama of black and white."[56]

In many cases, angelic white children were contrasted with pickaninnies so grotesque as to suggest that only white children *were* children. This is the flip side of the well-known libel of the "childlike Negro": the equally libelous, equally damaging, but heretofore underanalyzed exclusion of black youth from the category of childhood. Topsy was written within Stowe's argument that black children are innocent, but her reconstructed progeny defined black children out of innocence and therefore out of childhood itself.

## The Scripts and Repertoires of Dolls

This book engages two main archives of repertoires: one is *Uncle Tom's Cabin* and the other is dolls. Dolls, doll play, and literature about sentient dolls are crucial to this study because they weld childhood to slavery's most foundational, disturbing, and lingering question: What is a person? As Bill Brown has observed, this question has, from the antebellum period to the present, underlain anxieties so powerful as to constitute the "American Uncanny." *Uncle Tom's Cabin* encapsulated and shaped this anxiety because, as Philip Fisher argues, the Emancipation Proclamation combined with the Union's military victory and "the cultural work of *Uncle Tom's Cabin*" to "redesign" the "boundary" between human and thing (Stowe acknowledged this project when she originally subtitled her novel "The man that was a thing").[57] In other words, slavery legally defined some humans as things, and Emancipation legally redefined all humans as humans. Antebellum abolitionist culture, including *Uncle Tom's Cabin*, laid conceptual groundwork that made this legal change comprehensible and therefore possible. After Emancipation, however, "Lost Causers" and other white supremacists marshaled popular culture to undo this work and to redesign yet again the boundary between human and thing.[58] This effort appeared especially clearly in the post-Emancipation effort by the United Daughters of the Confederacy and other groups to freeze the imagined "faithful slave" in stone monuments.[59]

The cultural effort to objectify and later reobjectify African Americans found rich potential in doll play and doll literature, because all stories about sentient dolls reorganize the boundary between human and thing. As Lois Kuznets observes, sentient dolls in literature "embody human anxieties about what it means to be 'real'—an independent subject or self rather than an object or other."[60] Around the time of the American Civil War, books about sentient dolls increased in popularity,[61] and dolls in these books discuss their racial status, their duties to their owners, and even their relationship with enslaved people of African descent. The doll narrator of Julia Charlotte Maitland's *The Doll and Her Friends* (published in 1852, the same year as *Uncle Tom's Cabin*) describes dolls as "a race of mere dependents; some might even call us slaves."[62] The narrator pointedly informs the reader, however, that she is "not a negro doll, with wide mouth and woolly hair."[63] In this children's book and many others, dollness *itself* is a racial category that denotes servitude.[64] White-authored dolls in literature asserted their race's natural servitude exactly as abolition and later Emancipation challenged the belief that African Americans were constitutionally enslaveable. In the anonymously published *A Doll's Story* (also published circa 1852), two dolls, one of whom has just been purchased, discuss their relationship to American slavery.

"It is not pleasant to be sold, is it?" said little Minna; "so like slaves, of whom Emilie often tells me tales as I sit on her lap."

"I never heard much about slaves. To be sure, you don't mean *blacks*?" said Fanny. "I hope you don't mean to compare pretty wax dolls to negroes? There was a doll or two of that sort in the Exhibition, but we never took any notion of them."

"Did you not? Why, they were made of wax, I suppose, just like ourselves, and Emilie says black slaves are made of flesh and blood just like herself, and that no one has the right to buy or sell a fellow creature"

"You have some very odd notions," said the Exhibition doll.[65]

This dialogue's connection between the ownership of sentient dolls and the ownership of human beings is unusual only in its explicitness. From the mid-nineteenth century through the early twentieth, ideas and anxieties about racial slavery flowed as a steady, ominous undercurrent through much doll literature and through the physical properties of specific dolls. Dolls, as signs of childhood and property of many children, create propinquity between the idea of childhood and the racial project of determining who is a person and who is a thing; thus dolls tuck racial politics beneath a cloak of innocence. Chapter 4 delves deeply into one such instance: Raggedy Ann. Johnny Gruelle, the newspaper cartoonist who created Raggedy Ann in 1915, espoused racial egalitarianism (he wrote an unpublished didactic story that advocated race-blindness), but he loaded Raggedy Ann, as both a doll and a character in three dozen children's books, with blackface imagery. Gruelle styled Raggedy Ann after the minstrelized role of the Scarecrow, as performed by the blackface star Fred Stone in L. Frank Baum's 1903 staged extravaganza based on *The Wonderful Wizard of Oz*, and Gruelle also drew on the performances of stage Topsies and the British Golliwogg doll, which was based on American minstrel performances. Raggedy Ann was a racially saturated character: her white skin represented not racial whiteness but rather the complicated black-and-whiteness of the face-painted minstrel performer, and her stories imagined faithful servitude to her "Mistress," a human girl named Marcella, as free play and fun.

I argue throughout this book that the idea of childhood innocence and the bodies of living children have historically mystified racial ideology by hiding it in plain sight. Thus blackface imagery, which has long been banished from polite society, thrives under the light cover of children's culture and its penumbra of racial innocence. Minstrelsy lingers, too, in contemporary adult culture (the structure of *Saturday Night Live* is roughly that of a minstrel show); but children's culture has a special ability to preserve (even as it distorts) and transmit (even as it fragments) the blackface mask and styles of movement, which persist not only in Raggedy Ann and the Scarecrow but also in the faces and gloved hands of Mickey Mouse and Bugs Bunny.

Dolls provide especially effective safe houses for racial ideology because dolls are emblems of childhood that attach, through play, to the bodies of living children. Thus dolls refer in two distinct ways to childhood innocence (and when a doll represents a child, it gains a third level of reference). Dolls' ability to appear innocent was understood by the Confederate military, which recruited white girls to act as smugglers: Confederate soldiers stuffed dolls with quinine, calomel, and morphine; and white girls held these dolls and passed by northern soldiers unchallenged.[66] This literal, conscious act of smuggling drugs to support the system of slavery was possible only because dolls, the childhood they referenced, and the girls holding the dolls contained historical memory while performing innocence, performing obliviousness to history and to race. Dolls are crucial props within the performance of childhood because they are contrivances by which adults and children have historically played innocent.

Analyzing the historical formation of racial innocence through the repertoire of dolls enables me to foreground girls and girlhood without excluding other formations of gender or generalizing about girls' practices in an exceptionalist or identitarian mode. Boys did and do play with dolls; some individual boy doll-enthusiasts appear in Chapter 5 (and it is important to remember that the prohibition against boys playing with dolls was less viciously enforced in the nineteenth century than it is today). Nevertheless, dolls have, for more than two centuries, been understood as the defining feature of girls' culture and a metonym for girlhood itself. By considering dolls not as objects or texts that contain racial meanings but instead as things that script a repertoire of behaviors, I demonstrate the importance of dolls—*and therefore girls and girlhood*—to large-scale racial projects. Thus this book makes a case for the centrality of girls and girlhood to U.S. racial formation.

*Overview*

Chapter 1, "Tender Angels, Insensate Pickaninnies: The Divergent Paths of Racial Innocence," charts the racial polarization of childhood innocence in the second half of the nineteenth century. I argue that pain, and the alleged ability or inability to feel it, functioned in the mid-nineteenth century as a wedge that split white and black childhood into distinct trajectories. The white, tender, vulnerable angel-child co-emerged with (and depended on) the "pickaninny," who was defined by three properties: juvenile status, dark skin, and, crucially, the state of being comically impervious to pain. I take the pickaninny seriously not only because the figure abominably denigrated African Americans but also because it hinged the category of childhood to the libel that African Americans are insensate. As childhood was defined as tender innocence, as vulnerability, and as the pickaninny was defined by the inability to feel or to suffer, then the pickaninny—and the black juvenile it purported to represent—was defined out of childhood. African Americans understood these stakes, and writers such as Harriet Wilson and Frederick Douglass asserted black children's ability to feel pain so as to argue, in Douglass's words, that "SLAVE-children *are* children."[67]

Chapter 2, "Scriptive Things," develops the analytical tool of the scriptive thing and then uses it in a case study of one historical artifact: the "topsy-turvy doll." The topsy-turvy doll comprised two dolls in one: a black and white doll joined at the waist and shared a skirt. A child flipped the skirt over the head of the white pole to play with the black doll, and vice versa. As Karen Sánchez-Eppler and other scholars have argued, the doll's fusion of black and white referred to racial mixing, sex, and rape within the plantation system. African American women, the most likely creators of this doll-form, stitched politically volatile ideas into the children's toy and thereby made those ideas appear innocent. The toy's softness invited acts of cuddling on the part of white slaveowning children who possessed the doll; through this thing, enslaved women scripted performances in which children and dolls unwittingly smuggled enslaved women's thoughts and anger into the inner sanctum of southern domesticity.

Each of Chapters 3 through 5 uses the heuristic of the scriptive thing, as detailed in Chapter 2, to examine closely one segment of the distinct arcs of black and white childhood, as charted in Chapter 1. In Chapter 3, "Everyone Is Impressed: Slavery as a Tender Embrace from Uncle Tom's to Uncle Remus's Cabin," I show how an imagined loving touch between a slaveholding child and an enslaved adult (as pictured, for example, by Hammatt Billings in the Jewett handkerchief) traveled through and beyond the repertoires of *Uncle Tom's Cabin* and ultimately changed from an abolitionist critique of slavery to a Lost Cause defense of it. This reversal occurred, I argue, through performances scripted by material culture. Henry James described Stowe's characters as "wonderful 'leaping' fish," but in fact, the characters "flew" only when consumers literally moved the characters, that is, when people used scriptive things, including Tomitudes and illustrated editions of the novel, that materialized the narrative.[68] Performance, then, accounts for the alation that James observed but did not explain. Eva, Topsy, and other characters, uncontained by Stowe's abolitionist novel, traveled through the popular imaginary—from which they were appropriated by proslavery writers such as Joel Chandler Harris. Harris used Uncle Tom and his diminutive owner to invent memories of slaveowning as love and enslavement as the innocent embrace of a white child.

Chapter 4, "The Black-and-Whiteness of Raggedy Ann," delves deeply into one American icon. I show how Raggedy Ann—as a 1915 doll, 1918 children's book character, and 1923 theatrical performance—repackaged blackface minstrelsy and the pickanninized Topsy to imagine slavery as racially innocent fun. Johnny Gruelle marketed racially complex Raggedy Ann dolls in combination with Raggedy Ann children's books, which provided the doll with plot scenarios that were dense with references to slavery. Together, Raggedy Ann dolls and books co-scripted play scenarios in which faithful slaves cheerfully submitted to violence.

The final chapter, "The Scripts of Black Dolls," concludes the argument, begun in Chapter 1, regarding the libel that black children did not experience pain, by showing how black dolls functioned as a special site through which nineteenth-century white children and adults articulated this libel. White makers of black "Topsy" or "Dinah" dolls encouraged—and often explicitly instructed—children of all races to beat, throw, soil, burn, and hang black dolls. At the turn of the century, however, African American children and adults began using black dolls as a point of resistance. African American girls refused the violent scripts embedded in black dolls, and throughout the second and third decades of the twentieth century, New Negro adults attempted to script performances of tenderness through those same dolls. In 1939, psychologists Kenneth and Mamie Clark began their famous "doll tests" in which African American children were asked to designate either a black or a white doll "nice" or "bad." A majority of African American children preferred the white doll, and these results were widely understood to reveal internalized racism. The Clarks' findings figured influentially in *Brown v. Board of Education* (1954), in which the Supreme Court ruled against segregation in public schools. I argue that the doll tests staged a performance of black children's pain, and this performance of pain asserted that black children are innocent and are therefore children. This spectacular performance helped desegregate not only public schools but also the popular imagination of childhood innocence.

## Childhood Is a Performance

These chapters, taken together, intervene in a central problem in the field of childhood studies: the relationship between young people ("children") and the cultural construct of "childhood." Is childhood a category of historical analysis that produces and manages adult power, as Caroline Levander, Lee Edelman, Jacqueline Rose, James Kincaid, Anne Higonnet, Carolyn Steedman, and many others have argued? Conversely, do the complicated lives of young people constantly deconstruct and reconstruct abstract idealizations of "childhood," as is suggested by the work of Karin Calvert, Howard P. Chudacoff, and Steven Mintz, among others?[69] Literary scholars who study "the child" conjured in texts as well as historians and social scientists who focus on the lived experiences of young people have reached an unsatisfying détente with a model in which "imagined" childhood shapes the lived experiences of "real" juveniles, who respond by unevenly colluding in or resisting their construction as "children." Childhood, in this model, is abstract and disembodied, whereas children are tangible and fleshy. The model may declare superficially, with the requisite nod to Judith Butler, that "real" children cannot preexist "imagined" childhood; however, the model persistently suggests that constructed childhood and juvenile humans exist in tension with if not in opposition to one another. Because this model embeds opposition into the very foundation of childhood studies, the field has difficulty accounting for the simultaneity and mutual constitution of children and childhood. The field struggles to narrate the processes by which children and childhood give body to each other.

That act of embodiment is a performance. More specifically, that embodiment—the historical process through which childhood and children coproduce each other—occurs through surrogation, which Joseph R. Roach defines as the process by which "culture reproduces and re-creates itself."[70] Roach notes that the common definitions of performance, including repetition with a difference and restored or twice-behaved behavior, "assume that performance offers a substitute for something else that preexists it"; a performing body "stands in for an elusive entity that it is not but that it must vainly aspire both to embody and to replace."[71] This practice of standing-in defines surrogation, and the body that stands in is called an "effigy."[72] A performer's body is an effigy as it bears and brings forth collectively remembered, meaningful gestures, and thus surrogates for that which a community has lost. Children often serve as effigies that substitute uncannily for other, presumably adult, bodies and thus produce a surplus of meaning.[73] For example, four-year-old Shirley Temple engaged in surrogation when she adopted Mae West's swagger and purr to play a prostitute in the 1933 short, "Polly Tix in Washington."

Children's ability to surrogate adulthood is well noted, often with dismay. Childhood *itself*, however, is best understood as a process of surrogation, an endless attempt to find, fashion, and impel substitutes to fill a void caused by the loss of a half-forgotten original. In this form of surrogation, the lost original doubles upon the construction of childhood itself as a process of loss and forgetting. The Wordsworth-influenced romantic and later sentimental child was defined by the experience of being catapulted, through birth, out of God's presence and hurtled toward a lifetime of increasing separation from God. Immediately after Wordsworth declares that "Heaven lies about us in our infancy!," the poet laments the loss of that aura: "Shades of the prison-house begin to close / Upon the growing Boy." That growing boy travels from the light of Heaven but remains within its radiance: he "still is Nature's Priest." Only the onset of adulthood blunts the senses to God's light: "At length the Man perceives it die away, / And fade into the light of common day."[74] It's all downhill from the first breath: to grow is to lose sacred childhood innocence, and each day the young person develops, the essential child dies off a little. As Carolyn Steedman has shown, by the twentieth century, childhood became an emblem of a lost past, of a lost self, and of memory itself.[75]

Performance, like childhood, is by definition always in the act of disappearing; performance and childhood are both paradoxically present only through their impending absence. As Peggy Phelan has influentially argued, live performance disappears as soon as it appears, and for this reason, mourning and loss necessarily infuse performance.[76] The childhood constructed by romantics and sentimentalists, too, is defined by loss and consternated memory. If surrogation is an attempt to "fit satisfactory alternates" into "the cavities created by loss through death and other forms of departure,"[77] then, in the case of childhood, that cavity is constructed through the "departure" of growth rather than death. Both romanticism and sentimentalism constructed the death of a child not as dispossessive but as preservative, as a freezing that paradoxically prevents the essential child-quality from ever dying through maturation. Childhood is therefore best understood as an act of surrogation that compensates for losses incurred through growth.

A young person's body is the most frequently used effigy, or vehicle, by which that surrogation occurs. Juvenile bodies are not, however, the only effigies that surrogate childhood; mature bodies can, as well. For example, in 1924, Clarence Darrow, attorney for convicted murderers Nathan Leopold and Richard Loeb, convinced the court to imprison rather than execute his clients with a statement that referred to the defendants as "boys," and often as "these poor boys," no fewer than fourteen times. Despite the fact that Leopold and Loeb were both adults past the age of majority, Darrow was able to construct them as innocent "lads"—a substitution that saved their lives.[78] Nonhuman things, too, can surrogate childhood, as is frequently the case with dolls. James Kincaid is correct when he asserts that any available body (juvenile human, mature human, nonhuman) can be "thrust into the performance" of childhood. Kincaid errs, however, when he argues that juvenile actors play no special role in the performance of childhood because "[a]ny image, body, or being we can hollow out, purify, exalt, abuse, and locate sneakily in a field of desire will do for us as a 'child'" and that therefore the "child is not, in itself, anything."[79] Kincaid mistakes the possibility of an alienated fit between effigy and surrogation (that is, a body other than a juvenile human's performing "childhood") for absence of a relationship between the actor and the performance. The relationship between effigy and surrogation is flexible—not incidental, as in Kincaid's model, but often perverse.

The issue is that of casting. No body—juvenile, adult, or thing—can perfectly surrogate the ideals of childhood. No act of surrogation fully succeeds in restoring the half-remembered, imagined original, but different bodies partially succeed and yet fall short in importantly different ways. Juvenile bodies cast in the surrogation of childhood have the special ability to naturalize childhood, to assert an essential correspondence between childhood and the young human body—that is, to blur any distinction between children and childhood. Nonjuvenile bodies have other uses and abilities, and such effigies are not necessarily miscast in the surrogation of childhood. A visual mismatch between a mature body and a performance of childhood can, for example, redefine a group out of adulthood and the rights associated with that categorization. This was the case, for example, in 1844, when the abolitionist Reverend Orville Dewey argued that African American "nature is singularly childlike, affectionate, docile, and patient," and that such "inferiority" was "but an increased appeal to pity and generosity."[80] Romantic racialists' casting of "the Negro" as "childlike" was anything but accidental; it strategically sutured abolition to white supremacy.[81] Within such casting, however, a nonjuvenile actor may exert agency to undermine or at least complicate the production of meaning; thus the performance may produce multiple and often self-contradictory meanings.

Juvenile, nonjuvenile, and nonhuman bodies serve, then, as imperfectly useful and usefully imperfect effigies in the surrogation of childhood. A recent television performance demonstrates how these three kinds of effigies coordinate with each other. In 2006, Dakota Fanning, a blonde child actress who was then twelve years old, presented Shirley Temple Black with the Screen Actors Guild (SAG) Life Achievement Award (figure I.3). In the televised awards ceremony, Fanning held a Shirley Temple doll and explained,

> This doll was a part of my mom's doll collection when she was my age. The day I was born, it became mine, and has always sat in my room. My mom loved her, I love her, and I know someday, my daughter will, too. . . . I'm the fourth generation in my family who's loved [Shirley Temple's] films and admired her career of generous public service that followed.[82]

Lifetime achievement awards mark longevity; they are by definition that which a child cannot receive. A child therefore seems an odd choice to present such an award. Fanning, however, was appropriate in her inappropriateness. As a white, blonde, dimpled child actress who excites excessive desire, Fanning refilled Shirley Temple's particular mold of girlhood and thus gave life to the award recipient's greatest past achievement.[83] The speech (scripted, certainly, by a professional writer) repeatedly located Fanning as Shirley Temple's heir: the Shirley Temple doll, Fanning's speech claimed, descended from mother to daughter, and with that effigy Fanning inherited a tradition of performance and four generations' "love." As Temple's blonde surrogate, Fanning made "Shirley Temple-ness" present in a way that Shirley Temple Black, the adult, could not. Shirley Temple's extraordinary performance of girlhood resounded through Dakota Fanning,

*Figure I.3.* Dakota Fanning and a Shirley Temple Doll co-present a Screen Actors Guild Life Achievement Award to Shirley Temple Black, 29 January 2006. Photograph by Kevin Winter, Getty Images Entertainment, Courtesy of Getty Images.

and Fanning, in turn, resurrected that bluest eye of girlhood in the pale, never-quite-sufficient yet always excessive shadow of Shirley Temple Black, who is and always has been brown-eyed.

Even as Dakota Fanning gave life to Temple's greatest achievement—the Depression actress's performance of girlhood—she also marked Temple's greatest failure: the inability to remain a child. Fanning, then twelve years old, teetered between childhood and adolescence and thus referenced both childhood and its loss. Her costume reflected that liminal status: the dress sported childish bows and a Peter Pan collar, and the tight bodice highlighted Fanning's board-flat chest, but the dress's elegant long sleeves and floor-length skirt (a contrast with Temple's famously short peek-a-boo pinafores) suggested young womanhood. Fanning's scripted references to her own infancy and her imagined future maternity called attention, too, to Fanning's lost babyhood and impending exit from childhood. In but a few years, Fanning literally announced, she would be able to surrogate Shirley Temple no better than Shirley Temple Black could, and it would be time to bequeath the doll along with the tradition of performance.[84]

The ever-growing juvenile body—Dakota Fanning's or Shirley Temple's—is an unstable and therefore permanently inadequate effigy for childhood. That inadequacy in no way impedes the process of surrogation, which *relies* on failure. Shirley Temple's disappearance into Shirley Temple Black necessitated the emergence of someone like Dakota Fanning—much as Shirley Temple substituted for her now-forgotten predecessors, including the child star Cordelia Howard, who originated the stage role of Little Eva and who receives in-depth attention in Chapter 3.[85] The process of surrogation is one of repeated attempts at substitution, and these repetitions-with-differences are necessitated by each iteration's inexact fit with the imagined original. Each ill fit compels yet another performance. The juvenile body is a naturalistic effigy through which to surrogate childhood, but that body continually grows, incrementally and inevitably losing the state of childhood. Therefore, the most naturalistic effigy is also, in its very nature, a vexingly inadequate one, and this inadequacy urgently feeds the process of surrogation. A reciprocal action emerges in which the ever-growing and therefore inadequate effigy of the juvenile body continually surrogates childhood, but cannot contain that surrogation. The surrogation overflows into other effigies, including nonjuvenile bodies and nonhuman things such as dolls.

At the SAG Awards, each of three bodies—those of Shirley Temple Black, Dakota Fanning, and the doll—substituted differently, and differently imperfectly, for Shirley Temple, the award's true recipient (Temple Black's service as Republican dignitary and ambassador to Czechoslovakia and Ghana notwithstanding). Of these three effigies, only one will never grow and therefore never lose childhood. The doll, even more than Fanning or Temple Black, memorialized the doll-like perfection of Shirley Temple herself. The doll retained that which Temple Black lost and that which Fanning displayed herself in the act of losing. The doll, juxtaposed with Temple Black, constituted "before and after" shots and thus measured the distance between Shirley Temple and Shirley Temple Black; it, even more than Fanning, emblematized Temple's achievement and Temple Black's failure in the surrogation of childhood.

Throughout her performance at the SAG Awards, Fanning clutched the Shirley Temple doll by the calves and thus assumed the posture of an actor receiving an Academy Award. Recruited into the role of "Oscar," the doll surrogated not only Shirley Temple but also the sign of virtuoso acting itself. By simultaneously surrogating for Temple, girlhood, and achievement in acting, the doll articulated the performative foundation of girlhood. And as the doll doubled with Oscar, Fanning stepped into the role of Oscar recipient. Fanning's lines bestowed the Life Achievement Award upon Shirley Temple Black, but the girl's posturing body claimed Shirley Temple's legacy—including Temple's Oscar—for herself.[86]

Most children—not just famous ones—are virtuoso performers of childhood, because most children understand with precision the behaviors that children's things script. Toni Morrison fictively describes the development of this competency in *The Bluest Eye*: her narrator, a black girl named Claudia, receives the gift of a Shirley Temple–like white doll and momentarily wonders, "What was I supposed to do with it? Pretend I was its mother?" However, Claudia "learn[s] quickly," she says, that she is "expected" to "rock it, fabricate storied situations around it, even sleep with it."[87] Literary and visual culture are key to Claudia's certainty: she knows that she is "expected" to sleep with her doll because "[p]icture books were full of little girls sleeping with their dolls"—white girls and white dolls, that is.[88] Literary and visual culture (in Morrison's example, picture books) combine with material culture (dolls) to script performances, and children expertly perceive these scripts, which they then respond to in many ways, including resistance.

An understanding of children as experts in the scripts of children's culture, as virtuoso performers, challenges the position, espoused by Jacqueline Rose and James Kincaid, that children's culture is created by one, empowered group (adults) and given to or forced upon another, disempowered group (children). The problem with this top-down understanding of children's culture is that things, including books and toys, coordinate with an infinitely complex field of visual, material, theatrical, and literary culture so as to script performances whose meanings cannot be easily contained or controlled. Children do not passively receive culture. Rather, children expertly field the co-scripts of narratives and material culture and then collectively forge a third prompt: play itself. The three prompts then entangle to script future play, which continues to change as children collectively exercise agency.

Toni Morrison's fictive black girl, Claudia, understands that she is expected to "treasure" white baby dolls, but she resists the script and disembowels them instead (she also rejects "Raggedy Ann dolls [because she is] physically revolted by and secretly frightened of those round moronic eyes, the pancake face, and orangeworms hair"—all terms suggestive of Raggedy Ann's blackface ancestry).[89] The ultimate object of Claudia's aggression is not Shirley Temple dolls, or even, exactly, the white girls they represent, but the "secret of the magic" that white girls "weaved on others." Claudia asks, "What made people look at them and say, 'Awwwww,' but not for me?"[90] That "what," Morrison suggests, is the bluest eye of girlhood—an imagining of white girls as tender, innocently doll-like, and deserving of protection, and black girls as disqualified from all those qualities.

*Racial Innocence* historicizes the cultural formation that Claudia suffers and Morrison attacks. "Awwwww" is the sound of unspeech; it is noise that covers and distracts from the absence of articulated thought. It is ideology rendered so inarticulate that no rational argument can counter it. This book is about where that "Awwwww" came from, what its components were, and how it functioned within the history of race in the United States. I uncover the scripts, hidden in material things, that prompted everyday performances of that "Awwwww." And I show how, by the midtwentieth century, African Americans unmasked racial innocence—how they resisted and reconfigured racial ideologies that the glowing aura of childhood had, for a century, mystified.

# 1

## Tender Angels, Insensate Pickaninnies

### *The Divergent Paths of Racial Innocence*

In an advertising trade card from the 1890s, an African American girl smiles as she cuddles an armful of cotton (figure 1.1 and plate 1).[1] She advertises Cottolene, a lard substitute made out of cottonseed oil and animal fat.[2] The girl is well dressed and also well fed, as her chubby face and limbs attest. A yellow flower decorates her pigtail. The girl replicates the qualities of cuteness that coalesced at the turn of the twentieth century: her eyes are large in proportion to her head, her nose is small, her face is broad, her lips are plump but not to the point of caricature, and her expression is serene.[3] Dimples lightly accentuate her round cheeks and elbows. The girl holds the cotton as if it were a baby; the cotton seems almost to snuggle against the girl, to return her embrace. Everything—the girl, the cotton, the countryside—is soft and clean. It is hard to imagine a more tender, appealing image of child labor.

A 1916 photograph of a white girl picking cotton (figure 1.2) pictures the pain and poverty that the Cottolene trade card screens out.[4] The photograph is attributed to Lewis Hine, a documentary photographer in the tradition of Jacob Riis. Hine was a social reformer who used his camera to reveal the lives of laborers. Beginning in 1907, Hine worked for the National Child Labor Committee (NCLC), for which he is believed to have produced this photograph of Callie Campbell, age eleven. Callie Campbell is as thin as the Cottolene girl is plump, and the photograph's caption makes plain the white girl's feelings about her labor: "No, I don't like it very much." The Cottolene girl, in contrast, has no cause for discontent: in her fantasy milieu, cotton bolls puff out of the plants; they seem to give themselves up, almost to pick themselves. In contrast, the cotton plants that surround Callie Campbell are straggly and low to the

*Figure 1.1.* An African American girl cuddles a puff of cotton. Trade card for Cottolene, a lard substitute. N. K. Fairbank and Company, circa 1890s. Courtesy of the American Antiquarian Society.

*Figure 1.2.* Photograph of child laborer, taken for the National Child Labor Committee, attributed to Lewis Hine, 1916. The photograph's original caption reads, "Callie Campbell, 11 years old, picks 75 to 125 pounds of cotton a day, and totes 50 pounds of it when sack gets full. 'No, I don't like it very much.'" Courtesy of the Library of Congress, Prints and Photographs Division, National Child Labor Committee Collection.

ground; she must stoop to pick them. The Cottolene girl stands front and center, meeting the viewer's gaze; like the cotton plants behind her, she withholds nothing from the consumer. Campbell, however, crosses one arm in front of her body and lowers her head, frowning suspiciously at the photographer. Hine carefully includes signs of Campbell's suffering within his frame: a bonnet inadequately defends against the sun; long sleeves fend off the plants' prickles; and Campbell drags a sack that is longer than she is tall.[5] The caption specifies the bag's weight and juxtaposes the high poundage with the girl's young age: "Callie Campbell, 11 years old, picks 75 to 125 pounds of cotton a day, and totes 50 pounds of it when sack gets full." In contrast, the Cottolene girl's puffy cotton seems weightless, even cloud-like. The black girl's labor is unlabored; the white girl suffers under her burdens. Hine's image protests the use of an innocent white child as labor; the Cottolene advertisement sells a black child's labor as innocent.

Together, these two images emblematize the flexibility of ideology at the conjunction of childhood and innocence. Childhood in combination with innocence was able to figure, by the turn of the century, in sharply differing political agendas (for and against child labor, in this example) because of the ways in which the concept of childhood innocence changed during the nineteenth century. This chapter charts those changes, arguing that in the second half of the nineteenth century, pain functioned as a wedge that split childhood innocence, as a cultural formation, into distinct black and white trajectories. White children became constructed as tender angels while black children were libeled as unfeeling, noninnocent nonchildren (and this dyadic divergence, a "melodrama in black and white" in Linda Williams's term, largely erased nonblack children of color from popular representation). Through this polarization, racial innocence—that is, the use of childhood to make political projects appear innocuous, natural, and therefore justified—emerged.

Neither black nor white childhood was monolithic in representation, and certainly not in lived experience, during this period. Representations of white children especially diversified during the second half of the nineteenth century—so much so that Catherine Reef characterized the period of 1860 to 1905 as an "age of contrasts" in the lives and depictions of (white) children.[6] Books about angelic white children shared shelf space with books about bad boys and hoydens, and middle-class children became "priceless," in Viviana Zelizer's term, while working-class and poor children sweated in factories and fields.[7] Representations of African American children were less diverse, but variation existed here, too. Most depictions of African American children were denigrating, but some authors, white and black, produced fictional black child characters that were complex and mostly or fully realized; examples include Jacob Abbott's Rainbow and Harriet Wilson's Frado, to be discussed later in this chapter.[8]

Representations of white and of black children each varied, then, but not in equivalent ways. White child characters were depicted as innocent (even the "bad boy" that emerged in the final quarter of the nineteenth century in the work of Thomas Bailey Aldrich and Mark Twain was mischievous or wild, a "good-bad boy," in Leslie Fiedler's term, rather than truly wicked).[9] Only the rarest of white child characters was wholly lacking in innocence, and when such a character appeared, he or she usually met a terrible fate and thus invited the reader to identify against rather than with the character.[10] Representations of black children, in contrast, were increasingly and overwhelmingly evacuated of innocence. As Karen Sánchez-Eppler has argued, innocence defined nineteenth-century childhood, and not vice versa; therefore, as popular culture purged innocence from representations of African American children, the black child was redefined as a nonchild—a "pickaninny."[11]

The pickaninny was an imagined, subhuman black juvenile who was typically depicted outdoors, merrily accepting (or even inviting) violence.[12] The word (alternatively spelled "picaninny" or "piccaninny") dates to the seventeenth century, at which time it described any child of African descent; in the nineteenth century, the word was used pejoratively and in reference mainly to black children in the United States and Britain, but also to aboriginal children of the Americas, Australia, and New Zealand (in this case, the black-white dyad erases the specificity of nonblack children of color by absorbing them into blackness).[13] The word's origins are disputed, but the term may derive from the Portuguese word "pequenino," meaning a tiny child.[14] Characteristics of the pickaninny include dark or sometimes jet-black skin, exaggerated eyes and mouth, the action of gorging (especially on watermelon), and the state of being threatened or attacked by animals (especially alligators, geese, dogs, pigs, or tigers). Pickaninnies often wear ragged clothes (which suggest parental neglect) and are sometimes partially or fully naked. Genitals or buttocks are often exposed, and not infrequently targeted for attack by animals. In some of the most degrading constructions, pickaninnies shit or piss in public. Of course, no individual pickaninny image includes all these characteristics; and some pickaninnies are constructed as clean, well-dressed, and engaged in domestic chores (this is especially true of pickaninny images emblazoned on kitchenwares such as dishtowels). Some pickaninny figures are nonindividuated and doltish as cows, but others are clever as monkeys. When threatened, pickaninny characters might ignore danger or quake in exaggerated fear; when attacked, they might laugh or yelp, but in either case, they never experience or express pain or sustain wounds in any remotely realistic way. For example, in E. W. Kemble's 1898 alphabet book (see Chapter 2), two pickaninny characters play with a gun that accidentally fires.[15] As the characters are flung violently through the air, they look angry but not frightened or pained, much less wounded or killed. It is this absence of pain that unifies the construction of the pickaninny across differences. The pickaninny may be animalistic or adorable, ragged or neat, frightened or happy, American or British, but the figure is always juvenile, always of color, and always resistant if not immune to pain.

The pickaninny was a major figure in U.S. cultural history and as such must be taken seriously. Because pickaninnies were juvenile yet excluded from the exalted status of "child," they seemed not to matter. If, as Kirk Savage has argued, a granite monument declares its own necessity and inevitability, then a trade card emblazoned with a pickaninny claimed to be ephemeral, transitory, consumable, and discardable.[16] The pickaninny appeared to be, in all senses of the word, minor. That appearance of insignificance provided cover for a justification of violence against African American children. A focus on the pickaninny intervenes in the scholarly argument that U.S. popular culture has fetishized and commodified the pain of African Americans. Debra Walker King writes that "the pain-free, white American body exists easily in the cultural imagination," whereas "the black body is always a memorial to African and African American historical pain."[17] Examination of adult-oriented culture amply supports this perspective, but the lens of childhood inverts it. The unfeeling, unchildlike pickaninny is the mirror image of both the always-already pained African American adult and the "childlike Negro."

Today, the Cottolene girl might seem adorably childlike and not at all like the dehumanized pickaninnies in Kemble's alphabet book. At the close of the nineteenth century, however, a different mode of vision dominated, and in this context, a representation of a black child could seem adorable but not innocent, childlike, or even human. The writer William Cowper Brann made exactly this point when he wrote shortly before his death in 1898, "There is probably nothing on earth 'cuter' than a nigger baby; but, like other varieties in the genus 'coon,' they are not considered very valuable additions to society."[18] For Brann, cuteness in no way contradicted or mitigated the categorization of a "nigger baby" as a variety of the animalistic "genus 'coon,'" nor did the infant's cuteness imbue it with value. This chapter restores cultural context to make sense of this apparent non-sense, revealing the stakes in representations of black children in the second half of the long nineteenth century. In the context of the history that this chapter maps, the Cottolene girl's baby-shaped pile of white cotton emerges as arguably more childlike, more innocent, and more deserving of protection than its black, juvenile reaper.

Pain, and the ability to feel it, is what separated Callie Campbell from the Cottolene girl, and pain is what divided white childhood from black childhood in U.S. popular culture. The respective images suggested that

Callie Campbell's labors pained her; she belonged not in the field but in school or at home. The Cottolene girl, in contrast, felt no pain; she belonged exactly where she was. Thus the two images made agricultural labor seem, respectively, unjust for white children because it caused them to suffer and natural for black pickaninnies, who did not suffer. These turn-of-the-century images could function in this way because over the previous half-century, pain became a wedge that split one idea—childhood innocence—into diverging paths that produced opposing meanings in black and white. Pain divided tender white children from insensate pickaninnies. At stake in this split was fitness for citizenship and inclusion in the category of the child and, ultimately, the human.

## The Emergence of Childhood Innocence

Human societies have long acknowledged differences between juvenile and mature people (as in the biblical verse, "When I was a child, I spake as a child, I understood as a child, I thought as a child: but when I became a man, I put away childish things"[19]). However, the characterization of that difference as innocence versus experience—that is, children's sinlessness, asexuality, and obliviousness to politics versus adults' sexuality and worldliness—originated, as historian Philippe Ariès famously showed, with the European Enlightenment.[20] In North America, the belief that children are innocent did not become widespread until the late eighteenth century. Before that time, the Calvinist doctrine of infant depravity—the belief that people are born with original sin—dominated. According to this doctrine, children are inherently sinful and sexual and are therefore vulnerable to the worst fate imaginable: if they should die before they achieve Christian salvation, they are doomed to eternal hellfire.[21] High child mortality rates motivated parents to limit children's sinful behaviors by any means, and as early as possible, because a child's soul literally depended on control of the body. As Karin Calvert has shown, colonial material culture, including swaddling and walking stools, compelled infant bodies into upright positions and thus, parents hoped, hurried children out of uncontrolled, vulnerable infancy and toward mature piety.[22] Children were "better whipt, than damned," as Cotton Mather wrote; and parents who believed similarly sought to extinguish sexual and other misbehaviors through swift corporal punishment.[23] Eighteenth-century minister John Wesley famously called upon parents to

> Break their [children's] wills.... [B]egin this work before they can run
> alone, before they can speak plain, perhaps before they can speak at
> all. Whatever pains it costs, break the will, if you would not damn the
> child.... If you spare the rod, you spoil the child; if you do not conquer,
> you ruin him. Break his will now, and his soul shall live, and he will prob-
> ably bless you to all eternity.[24]

Pain, then, was a crucial tool by which to save a child's soul. Salvation depended upon two co-factors: the parents' administration of
pain and the child's reception of it. Despite these measures, however,
infant depravity and damnation remained terrifyingly beyond parents' physical control: no matter how often or vigorously parents applied the rod, they could never be certain that their children were not
damned.

In the late eighteenth and early nineteenth centuries, however, Calvinism and the doctrine of original sin gradually declined, child-rearing
practices changed dramatically, and the belief that children were inherently innocent proliferated.[25] The change registers in the contrast between
Anne Bradstreet's and William Wordsworth's respective takes on birth.
The verse "Childhood" from Bradstreet's 1650 poem, "The Four Ages of
Man," described the infant as

> . . . conceiv'd in sin, and born in sorrow,
> A nothing, here to day, but gone to morrow.
> Whose mean beginning blushing cann't reveale,
> But night and darkenesse, must with shame conceal.[26]

Bradstreet's seventeenth-century association of childhood with original sin, sex, birth-pains, and vulnerability to death contrasts with Wordsworth's 1807 "Ode: Intimation of Immortality." For Wordsworth, birth is
neither a result of sin nor an exercise in sorrow; rather,

> Our birth is but a sleep and a forgetting:
> The Soul that rises with us, our life's Star,
> Hath had elsewhere its setting,
> And cometh from afar:
> Not in entire forgetfulness,
> And not in utter nakedness,
> But trailing clouds of glory do we come

From God, who is our home:
Heaven lies about us in our infancy![27]

In the century and a half that separated Bradstreet's and Wordsworth's poems, conception transformed from "sin" and a "mean beginning" of "shame" to a disembodied, heavenly launch of the soul. Birth was no longer a woman's "sorrow" but an infant's "sleep" and "forgetting" of its recent "home" in God's realm. And the infant itself, in the seventeenth century "a nothing" that may die "to morrow" became by the nineteenth century a sacred comet "trailing clouds of glory" and ushering heaven itself into the home to surround the baby. Wordsworth's poem reflected cultural changes already under way throughout the Western world and also extended those changes, especially in the United States. As Barbara Garlitz has documented, references to Wordsworth's ode surfaced widely in poems, sermons, and child-rearing manuals in both Great Britain and the United States throughout the nineteenth century.[28] With this proliferation, Americans quoted Wordsworth's ode to express their own thoughts, and burgeoning mass culture metabolized and circulated these quotations as part of the literary formation of the "romantic child."[29]

The decline of the notion of original sin and the emergence of romantic childhood—the child as tabula rasa, or uncorrupted element of nature—gave rise to a new concept: childhood sexual purity. From the mid-nineteenth century until the early twentieth, when Sigmund Freud upset the applecart, Americans largely regarded children as innately devoid of sexual desire. This pre-Freudian belief, which has become profoundly unfamiliar, gains clarity through a brief consideration of nineteenth-century views regarding childhood masturbation and privacy. In the late nineteenth century, advice manuals frantically warned parents to prevent childhood masturbation and the degeneracy the practice supposedly caused. A crucial way to prevent masturbation, according to doctors, was to sequester each child in an individual bedroom. That privacy would prevent, rather than abet, masturbation seems counterintuitive today, but the advice makes sense within the context of a belief in fundamental childhood sexual purity. Essentially innocent children by definition lack any impulse that could cause them independently to discover or to invent masturbation. However, an innocent child, exposed to a corrupted child or a servant who masturbated, could imitate the practice. In this sense, masturbation was considered a sexually transmitted disease. The common practice of children sleeping together, or of children sleeping with servants, was understood to spread the contagion of masturbation, and therefore doctors and reformers called ardently for individual sleeping arrangements.[30]

As the example of beliefs about masturbation shows, the child was viewed as fundamentally innocent of sexual desire unless corrupted by an outside force. This child was not defined by absence (asexuality or pre-sexuality) but rather by sexual innocence: a fully present, embodied state of purity. This pure child was the sentimental angel-child, which became, by the mid-nineteenth century, a dominant formation within American childhood. In the words of Karin Calvert, (white) children of the second half of the nineteenth century were considered "virtually angels incarnate who, should they die in infancy, would transmute back into their angelic state."[31] The emblematic angel-child was, as many scholars have noted, Stowe's Little Eva.

The sentimental child, as a sexually pure angel of the house, functioned as a crucial figure in what Barbara Welter has called the cult of true womanhood and Aileen Kraditor has called the cult of domesticity.[32] The cult of true womanhood, as Welter famously argued, was built upon four pillars: piety, purity, submissiveness, and domesticity. Nancy Cott revised and deepened Welter's notion of "purity" when she introduced the concept of "passionlessness": for Cott, passionlessness, a "central tenet of Victorian sexual ideology," was a "view that women lacked sexual aggressiveness, that their sexual appetites contributed a very minor part (if any part at all) to their motivations, that lustfulness was simply uncharacteristic."[33] Cott and Welter agree that the cardinal virtues of womanhood presented an ideal that no historical women fulfilled perfectly. *Woman* may have been passionlessly pure, pious, submissive, and domestic, but historical *women* always experienced a gap between themselves and the ideal.

Some scholars have problematically read the sentimental child as an apparent bridge over this gulf—that is, as the ultimate fulfillment of the cult of true womanhood. In this view, children, especially girls, make better women than women do. Deborah Gorham argues this point most strongly: in her view, the "ideal of feminine purity is implicitly asexual," and this pillar of the cult of true womanhood created a paradox for Victorian wives and mothers who were assumed to be fulfilling their duties as sexual partners to their husbands. A girl, however, was assumed not to be engaging in sex, and therefore "could be perceived as a wholly unambiguous model of . . . sexual purity."[34] A girl "could represent the quintessential angel in the house"—above and beyond her mother.[35] The problem with this argument is that the primary texts suggest far greater complexity. For example, when Grace Greenwood (Sara Jane Clarke) wrote in 1846 that "true feminine genius" is "perpetual childhood,"[36] she described adult femininity as a form of childhood, not vice versa.[37] In 1842, Elizabeth Oakes Smith described an adult character named Eva (who may have informed Stowe's character of the same name) as a "true woman" because she combined a "woman's love and gentleness" with "childlike simplicity."[38] The suggestion that Victorian girls, or children more generally, fulfilled the virtues of true womanhood better than women did implies dynamics of competition and unidirectionality (children as women, not women as children) that the primary texts do not support.

I argue, in contrast, that the sentimental child presented an exceptionally credible vessel to contain the idea of passionlessness. To recast this argument in Joseph Roach's terms: the child presented an exceptionally capacious *effigy* through which to *surrogate*, or perform, passionlessness.[39] I am arguing not that children made better women than women did— nor that women made better children than children did—but rather that women, girls, and boys, as effigies, or bodies in performance, possessed different abilities to surrogate, or perform, the elements of domesticity— including "purity" or "passionlessness." One might think about the fit between actor and performance in terms of theatrical casting. Different actors might produce differently compelling performances within a single role. For example, in a contemporary stage performance of *The Wizard of Oz*, a director might consider casting in the role of Dorothy a young girl, a legibly gay man, or Diana Ross. Each one of these actors' bodies, these performing effigies, possesses a special capacity for bringing forth a particular aspect of the story and the role: a young girl might ratify and naturalize the play as a "children's classic"; an identifiably gay man might both nod to and burlesque the film's significance to gay history; or Diana Ross might prompt audiences to view *The Wizard of Oz* through the lens of *The Wiz* (and not, for once, vice versa) and might therefore make visible the whiteness that was unmarked in the original Oz books, plays, and films. Each of these casting decisions is differently compelling and productive; none of the choices is "correct" or "incorrect." Similarly, a mid-nineteenth-century woman, prepubescent girl, and prepubescent boy each possessed different abilities in varying performances of purity or passionlessness. A woman might assert the possibility of maintaining passionlessness within a marriage, and therefore in close proximity to a man's passions and in coexistence with sexual acts. A girl might naturalize feminine passionlessness most seamlessly. For boys, the performance of femininity was, paradoxically, useful to the construction of masculinity. Claudia Nelson argues that through "novelistic mechanisms[,] the ideals of womanliness were presented to Victorian boys as the ideals of manliness."[40] In other words, Victorian boys surrogated femininity as part of a historicized process of becoming manly. It is not the case, then, that girls made better women than women did, but rather that women, girls, and boys presented differently credible and differently useful vehicles for the performance of sexual innocence.

Where Welter sees purity and Cott sees passionlessness, I see innocence—an active state of purity that is manifested through embodied performances of passionlessness. Sexual innocence is not a state of absence (asexuality or presexuality) but is instead a state of deflection: a constantly replenishing obliviousness that causes sexual matters to slide by without sticking. As I argued in my Introduction, the nineteenth-century white child—boy or girl—possessed a special ability to appear to repel markings of gender, class, or sexuality. Little Eva's father, Augustine St. Clare, describes his daughter's innocence as deflection rather than absence when he notes that "evil rolls off Eva's mind like dew off a cabbage-leaf,—not a drop sinks in."[41] Because Eva's skills in deflection maintain her purity, she may mingle with Topsy without danger of becoming corrupted—sexually *or* racially. That is, Eva is not only sexually innocent but also racially innocent. Racial innocence is a form of deflection, a not-knowing or obliviousness that can be made politically useful. It is racial innocence that might make the Cottolene girl's viewer see her adorableness and notice her labor only later, if at all. Sexual innocence was a fundamental aspect of both the cult of true womanhood and sentimental childhood.[42] Contra Gorham, the cult of domesticity did not invent children as the ultimate women, nor women as hyperbolic children. Rather, the cult of domesticity demanded performances of sexual innocence within the home. Women and children—girls especially, but also boys—supplied these performances differently, at different times, and with different strengths.

Racial innocence, as much as sexual innocence, was fundamental to the cult of domesticity. Hazel Carby and Ann DuCille argue persuasively that the cult of true womanhood was an inherently racial political project. In Carby's view, the cult of true womanhood posited white women alone as sexually pure; the cult united white women across differences of class by excluding black women from purity and therefore from the category of womanhood.[43] DuCille takes up Nancy Cott's argument that the concept of passionlessness empowered white women. As Cott notes, "The ideology of passionlessness favored women's power and self-respect" by "elevat[ing] women above the weakness of animal nature" and "allowing more intellectual breadth."[44] In DuCille's view, passionlessness was especially useful to black women writers, "whom the dominant culture continued to construct as inherently licentious and 'always already sexual.'" For black women novelists of the 1890s, the ideology of passionlessness "negated a negative"; that is, it constituted a form of resistance rather than capitulation to middle-class values.[45] Together, Carby and DuCille suggest that sexual innocence, as an ideal for white women, excluded black women who were defined as sexual (or even hypersexual), and that black women's reclamation of sexual innocence should be viewed as resistance.

Innocent childhood resembled the cult of true womanhood in that each discourse attached sexual innocence to white children and women, respectively. Antebellum black children, like black women, were assumed to be ineligible for sexual purity: as Mary Niall Mitchell notes, the sale of enslaved prepubescent girls calculated "their sexuality, or at the very least their anticipated fertility," into their pricing.[46] During and after the Civil War, stage Topsies performed what Elizabeth Young calls "excessive female sexuality" and "promiscuous heterosexuality."[47] And this figure of Topsy, as Mitchell shows, suffused and clouded white people's visions of freed African American girls: white teachers of African American children often described their female pupils as "Topsies," and when a *New York Times* correspondent visited Port Royal in 1862, he reported seeing "curly-headed picaninnies" and a "swarm of happy Topseys [*sic*]!"[48] Enslavement and the construction of Topsy-like slatterns excluded African American girls, along with their mothers, from the realm of passionlessness and the empowerment that passionlessness could confer.[49]

Sexual innocence, then, divided white and black children in much the same way it did white and black women. Unique to the polarization of black and white children, however, was the libel, which emerged in the second half of the nineteenth century, that black juveniles did not—could not, even—experience pain. As Anna Mae Duane has argued persuasively, "vulnerability, suffering, and victimhood" defined nineteenth-century American childhood.[50] The libel that African American juveniles were invulnerable, did not suffer, and were not victims, then, defined them out of childhood itself.

## Pain and Black Childhood through the Mid-Nineteenth Century

When the concept of angelic childhood innocence first coalesced, it did not necessarily exclude children of color. Romantic poets, including William Blake, allowed black children—especially boys—into the garden of natural childhood. "The Little Black Boy," a very complex poem that Blake included among his *Songs of Innocence*, describes black and white children, at least on one level, as similar beneath their differences: "I am black, but O! my soul is white," declares the narrator.[51] Early abolitionist literature often connected innocence to the pain of slaves. For example, the anonymously authored poem "Negro Boy," published in the 1821 *Poems: Moral and Religious, for Children and Youth*, deployed the figure of an innocent Negro child to expose the outrage of slavery. In this poem (which may have been influenced by Blake's "The Little Black Boy"), the child narrator mourns his previous life in Africa, where he remembers being his "parents' joy" and their "darling Negro boy."[52] Enslavement decimates this ideal childhood: the child narrator must now "labour day by day," which causes sleepless nights of "pain."[53] Even under slavery's oppression, however, this child remains childlike: he misses his mother, and her absence pains him as much as his physical oppression does. "No mother's ear" can hear his "groans," so he is "cold and lonely"—a three-word phrase that conjoins physical and psychic pain.[54] The poem suggests, then, that slavery can assault but ultimately cannot eradicate this "darling" Negro boy's childlike nature: the narrator continues to miss his mother. Furthermore, the narrator remains certain that "Good Heav'n" will someday "receive the Negro boy."[55] For this poem's anonymous author, black children are children; they love and are loved by their parents; they experience physical and emotional pain; they can enter Heaven; and these facts are all evidence in a political argument against slavery.[56]

The narrator of "Negro Boy" experiences slavery, as would any child of any race, in relation to his family; thus the poem's author suggests an essential commonality between black and nonblack children. At the mid-nineteenth century, however, as romanticism sugared over into sentimentalism, writers began to polarize black and white childhood—a configuration that largely disappeared nonblack children of color.[57] *Uncle Tom's Cabin* crystallized the polarization of white and black childhood in this often-quoted description of Eva and Topsy:

There stood the two children, representatives of the two extremes of society. The fair, high-bred child, with her golden head, her deep eyes, her spiritual, noble brow, and prince-like movements; and her black, keen, subtle, cringing, yet acute neighbor. They stood the representatives of their races. The Saxon, born of ages of cultivation, command, education, physical and moral eminence; the Afric, born of ages of oppression, submission, ignorance, toil, and vice![58]

Many scholars view Stowe's Topsy as a minstrel-influenced caricature, an essentialized manifestation of Stowe's white supremacy.[59] These scholars are not wrong. However, Topsy's minstrel antics coexist with Stowe's powerful paeans to the enslaved girl's essential childhood innocence. In the passage cited above, for example, Stowe casts the differences between Eva and Topsy as biologically embedded but ultimately not entirely essential: the "two children," as "representatives of their races," are the respective products of "ages of cultivation" and "ages of oppression." Eva owes her "deep eyes" and "noble brow" to generations that were "high-bred," while Topsy's body results from generations of "ignorance" and "vice." Thus Stowe argues in the mode of monogenesis, the view that all people descend from a common ancestor and that racial differences stem from environment (particularly climate and "civilized" society or lack thereof); and she rejects polygenesis, the belief, embraced by many of Stowe's contemporaries, that different races are of different species.[60] For Stowe, bodily habits layer over Topsy's and Eva's inherited racial traits: Eva's "prince-like movements" contrast with Topsy's "cringing" posture. Inherited and learned differences, then, polarize Topsy and Eva—but these differences, Stowe suggests here, are more the bodily effects of culture than the cultural effects of biology. Topsy is therefore the site of some of the deepest contradictions in Stowe's novel and racial politics.

The life experiences of enslaved children especially fired Stowe's imagination. Topsy, whom Stowe viewed as a "representative of a large class of the children who are growing up under the institution of slavery," arrives at the St. Clare household hardened by past abuse.[61] This hardening renders the girl thinglike: before Topsy's conversion, Stowe describes Topsy as a "statue" and emphasizes the character's hardness in her doll-like "glassy eyes."[62] Ophelia echoes this objectification when she calls Topsy a "thing."[63] Topsy often declares that she feels no pain (Ophelia's whippings "wouldn't kill a skeeter," Topsy taunts[64]), but Stowe carefully shows that the opposite is true. Not only does Topsy feel pain, but it is her agonized screams that initially bring St. Clare to the restaurant in which Topsy works, where the owners of the restaurant beat and swear at Topsy every day.[65] St. Clare buys Topsy in part because he is disturbed by her screams and wants to end her abuse—that is, the expression of her pain provokes his empathy and desire to intervene. Topsy's hurt-ability is confirmed when Ophelia undresses the "neglected, abused child" and discovers that the "back and shoulders of the child" are marked with "great welts and calloused spots, ineffaceable marks of the system under which she had grown up."[66] The enslaved child's body is scarred, but even worse, her soul is "burnt . . . by the branding iron of cruel and unchristian scorn, that is a sorer and deeper wound than all the physical evils of slavery altogether."[67] For Stowe, then, Topsy is not only *a* child, but, as Richard Brodhead has argued, she is "*the* child"— that is, a "paradigmatic case" of the physically hurt sentimental child.[68]

Stowe confirms Topsy's essential childhood through a social "experiment" that St. Clare sets up when he gives Topsy to his cousin, Ophelia.[69] In St. Clare's view, the system of slavery "harden[s]" both slaves and slaveholders; the system causes "sensibilities to decline" among all people involved in slavery.[70] Once such desensitization occurs, an enslaved person may become governable "only by the lash"—and when the hardening becomes so thorough and the person so insensate that even the lash has no effect ("a very common state of things down here," St. Clare interjects), "how are they to be governed?"[71]

"It is your system makes such children," says Ophelia.[72] St. Clare's reply echoes and thus ratifies the constructed, nonessential nature of hardened slaves: "I know it; but they are *made,*—they exist,—and what is to be done with them?"

"Well," Ophelia replies, "I can't say I thank you for the experiment."[73]

In St. Clare's "experiment," then, Topsy tests whether a person "made" hard by the system of slavery can be returned to sensibility—that is, whether the essential child within Topsy is recoverable. Stowe argues that Topsy can be healed, but only through Eva's moral, loving influence— what Richard Brodhead calls "disciplinary intimacy." Stowe builds incrementally toward the touch that restores Topsy to humanity, natural Christianity, and childhood. At first, Eva speaks kindly to Topsy but does not touch her. In this scene, Eva pleads with Topsy not to steal, and offers to "give you anything of mine, [rather] than have you steal it."[74] Eva's are the

first word[s] of kindness the child [Topsy] had ever heard in her life; and the sweet tone and manner struck strangely on the wild, rude heart, and

*Figure 1.3.* Tailpiece illustration by Hammatt Billings for *Uncle Tom's Cabin; or, Life Among the Lowly*, by Harriet Beecher Stowe, illustrated edition (Boston: John P. Jewett, 1853). Eva touches Topsy and thus restores feeling in the hardened slave. Billings's illustration, like Stowe's text, emphasizes the contrast between Topsy and Eva while suggesting an underlying connection and even equivalence: Billings marks differences in the girls' skin color and dresses (Eva's floats ethereally while Topsy's is appropriate for work), but the girls are of roughly equal size. Neither girl's face is caricatured; of the two, Topsy's is the more individualized. This image, like Stowe's prose, argues for Topsy's fundamental humanity. Courtesy of the American Antiquarian Society.

a sparkle of something like a tear shone in the keen, round, glittering eye; but it was followed by a short laugh and habitual grin. No! the ear that has never heard anything but abuse is strangely incredulous of anything so heavenly as kindness.[75]

Eva's tender words partially penetrate Topsy's hardened exterior and cause

"something *like* a tear" (emphasis added) to well in Topsy's beadlike, "glittering eye." At this point in the narrative, Topsy has not shed a true tear—sentimentalism's supreme sign of empathy and therefore of humanity. Because her ear is hardened by verbal abuse, her eyes can respond to kindness only with not-quite tears. Topsy's conversion occurs only when Eva combines words of love with gentle touch (figure 1.3):

> "[Miss Ophelia] can't bar me, 'cause I'm a nigger!—she'd soon have a toad touch her! There can't nobody love niggers, and niggers can't do nothin'! I don't care," said Topsy, beginning to whistle.
>
> "O, Topsy, poor child, *I* love you!" said Eva, with a sudden burst of feeling, and *laying her little thin, white hand on Topsy's shoulder;* "I love you, because you haven't had any father, or mother, or friends;—because you've been a poor, abused child! I love you, and I want you to be good. . . ."
>
> The round, keen eyes of the black child were overcast with tears;—large, bright drops rolled heavily down, one by one, and fell on the little white hand. Yes, in that moment, a ray of real belief, a ray of heavenly love, had penetrated the darkness of her heathen soul! She laid her head down between her knees, and wept and sobbed,—while the beautiful child, bending over her, looked like the picture of some bright angel stooping to reclaim a sinner.
>
> "Poor Topsy!" said Eva, "don't you know that Jesus loves all alike? . . . He will help you to be good; and you can go to Heaven at last, and be an angel forever, just as much as if you were white."[76]

In this passage, Stowe first emphasizes Topsy's hardened character: upon calling herself a "nigger," likening herself to a toad, and declaring herself unlovable, Topsy proclaims herself unhurt ("I don't care") and whistles. Only the touch of Eva's "white hand" combined with declarations of love for Topsy as a "poor, abused child" transforms "the black child." At that moment, a "ray of real belief, a ray of heavenly love" penetrates Topsy, and for the first time in the novel, she weeps. It is in this scene that Topsy is converted into sensation, into humanized childhood, and even, Eva promises, potential angelhood—"just as much as if you were white."

The next scene demonstrates the success of Topsy's conversion and links that conversion explicitly to innocence. Topsy picks flowers, a crime for which Marie, Eva's mother, slaps Topsy and calls her a "good-for-nothing nigger."[77] Because these words issue from Marie, a wholly unsympathetic character, they invite the reader to believe the opposite. Topsy insists that she picked the flowers not out of mischief, but out of desire to decorate Eva's sickroom. Eva—and Stowe's ideal reader—recognizes the truth that Marie cannot: that Topsy is innocent of any crime; that "Topsy is different from what she used to be" and is "quite unlike" her former self.[78] By promising that "Topsy could become an angel," Eva names the enslaved girl's conversion into Christian innocence and thus into sentimental childhood itself.[79] Stowe, too, acknowledges Topsy's new status as a childlike innocent: from the moment of Topsy's conversion, Stowe's references to Topsy's eyes as "glittering" and "glassy" disappear. Topsy, now a feeling figure of sentimental domesticity, cries frequently and sincerely. By the time Eva dies, Topsy's "callous indifference [is] gone."[80] Stowe, through St. Clare, explicitly names Eva's touch as the reason for the positive outcome of the "experiment": "if we want to give sight to the blind, we must be willing to do as Christ did,—call them to us, and *put our hands on them.*"[81]

Before the mid-nineteenth century, then, black juveniles such as the 1821 "Negro Boy" were not uncommonly associated with innocence and the ability to feel pain; thus romantic childhood included black youth. At midcentury, Stowe created in Topsy an extraordinarily sophisticated and powerful argument for enslaved children's essential innocence and their susceptibility to suffering; thus Stowe configured Topsy as not only *a* child but, as Brodhead argues, *the* child of sentimentalism. Even as Stowe accomplished this feat, however, she loaded Topsy with contradictions and internal schisms. Topsy may have been a—or the—"neglected, abused child," but she was also a minstrel-infused comic darky. She screamed and scarred, but she constantly declared herself unhurt—and for many readers, her memorable protestations ultimately drowned out the counter-testifying evidence Stowe so carefully planted in the novel.

These contradictions rendered Topsy vulnerable to selective readings and re-presentations. A reader, illustrator, or stager of *Uncle Tom's Cabin* could—and often did, as we shall see—focus on Topsy's comic antics and her claims to feel no pain while editing out the screams that St. Clare heard and the wounds that Ophelia saw. Stowe's interpreters could remember the contrasts between Topsy and Eva while forgetting that for Stowe, the characters' differences overlaid fundamental connections. This pattern of editing reversed the resolution of St. Clare's experiment and with it, a sheaf of Stowe's arguments: that slavery hardens otherwise sensate people, that this hardening can be reversed, and that all this is true because black children are essentially children.

## Insensate Pickaninnies

One of the first and most influential people to stage elements of *Uncle Tom's Cabin* selectively and thus alter Stowe's politics was George L. Aiken. In 1852, Aiken penned a stage play of *Uncle Tom's Cabin* for performance by the Howard family troupe of actors (Aiken was a cousin of the troupe's leading players). This play—a "Tom show," as the popular stagings of *Uncle Tom's Cabin* came to be known—maximized the minstrel aspects that Stowe had already embedded in Topsy. In Aiken's script, Topsy arrives in the St. Clare household without welts and calluses, without any history of abuse legible on her body.[82] Asked to sing and dance, the actress Caroline Fox Howard, who first played Topsy, belted out a catchy tune that highlights the stage character's signature lines, "I was never born," and "I's so wicked" (see figure 4.14 in Chapter 4):

> Oh! White-folks I was never born,
> Aunt Sue raise me on de corn,
> Send me errands night and morn,
> Ching a ring a ring a ricked.

> She used to knock me on de floor,
> Den bang my head agin de door,
> And tare my hair out by de core,
> Oh! Cause I was so wicked.[83]

This song merrily, blithely reverses Stowe's assertion of Topsy's pain—and the political argument based on that assertion. Stowe's Topsy reports that her former mistress "used to pull my har, and knock my head agin the door"; Howard's song quotes these lines but attributes the violence to a black caretaker, not a white slaveholder.[84] Aiken's Topsy responds to violence not by becoming physically and emotionally damaged, but by laughing and singing about her invulnerability. Stowe's Topsy falsely believes herself to be "never born" because the system of slavery has imposed ignorance and godlessness upon her, but Aiken's Topsy transforms "never born" into a catchphrase, an automatic laugh line emptied of meaning. Perhaps the most telling reversal occurs along the axis of the word "wicked." Stowe's Topsy initially believes herself to be wicked because she has been emotionally abused. After Topsy's conversion via Eva's touch, however, the word "wicked" in reference to Topsy disappears simply and suddenly from

Stowe's novel. After the conversion, none of Stowe's characters, including Topsy herself, ever again calls the enslaved girl wicked. In contrast, Aiken's Topsy calls herself wicked immediately *after* her conversion: in response to Eva's exhortation to be good, Aiken's Topsy, sobbing, promises, "I will try; but den, I's so wicked!"[85] Topsy's signature song, "I'se So Wicked," similarly declares Topsy immune to Eva's efforts at conversion: "'Tis Little Eva, kind and fair, / Says if I'se good I will go dere, / But den I tells her, I don't care, / Oh! ain't I very wicked?"[86] Sentimental childhood, as Anna Mae Duane has argued, is founded on the child's suffering as it invites the adult reader or viewer to weep with and for the child.[87] Aiken stages Topsy weeping at her conversion, but within this pathos, he plants the laugh line, "I's so wicked." Aiken's script, then, invites the audience to laugh while Topsy cries. This invitation turns sentimentalism itself topsy-turvy.

When the Howard-Aiken version of *Uncle Tom's Cabin* configured Topsy as invulnerable to pain and invited audiences to laugh at the sight of Topsy's tears, the show not only reversed Stowe's individual politics, but also counteracted one of abolitionism's most organized, long-standing, and successful arguments: that slaves feel pain, and that this ability to feel pain demonstrates African Americans' fitness for freedom. Slavery had been legitimized in part by widespread claims that African Americans were impervious to pain. Thomas Jefferson, for example, wrote in 1781 in *Notes on the State of Virginia* that Negroes' "griefs are transient."[88] Southern doctors claimed that people of African descent carried a hereditary disease called "dyaesthesia Aethiopis," or an "obtuse sensibility of body" that supposedly rendered black people invulnerable to corporal punishment.[89]

At stake in pain was not only justification for violence but also eligibility for citizenship and humanity. Visible pain, or what Lauren Berlant calls the "trumping power of suffering," established individuals' and groups' subjectivity—and therefore, Linda Williams adds, their "worth as citizens."[90] Elizabeth B. Clark has shown that abolitionists understood the libel of black insensateness to disqualify African Americans from what Elaine Scarry has called the world-making properties of pain. Abolitionists understood a century and a half before Scarry that "the story of *physical pain*" is "a story about the expansive nature of human *sentience*, the felt-fact of aliveness."[91] The stakes of pain are nothing less than the stakes of sentience, of humanity itself. To combat the libel of black insensateness, abolitionists showcased the physical, emotional, and spiritual suffering of enslaved people. When abolitionists dramatized slaves' pain—indeed, when sentimental writers such as Stowe provoked readers sympathetically to *feel* slaves' pain—they based an argument for human rights on the ability to suffer. The refutation of the libel of black insensateness was one of abolitionism's most effective strategies and greatest triumphs.

When abolitionists succeeded, at mid-century, in circulating a counterdiscourse of African American pain and therefore sentience and humanity, the libel of insensateness did not disappear, but instead took up new residence in the juvenile form of the pickaninny. As this book argues throughout, when a racial argument is effectively countered or even delegitimized in adult culture, the argument often flows stealthily into children's culture or performances involving children's bodies. So located, the argument appears racially innocent. This appearance of innocence provides a cover under which otherwise discredited racial ideology survives and continues, covertly, to influence culture.

Throughout the second half of the nineteenth century, Topsy constituted an especially powerful vehicle for the newly juvenilized libel of black insensateness. Stowe had configured Topsy within the larger abolitionist project of asserting and showcasing slaves' pain: for Stowe, pain, as a fundamental aspect of the system of slavery, hardened Topsy *because* she felt it. In other words, Stowe's Topsy unnaturally *became* unfeeling exactly because by nature she *could* feel. Topsy's conversion *back* into feeling, into sensation, into weeping, is, for Stowe, crucial to Topsy's fitness for freedom. (Similarly, in the 1821 poem "Negro Boy," the narrator's suffering at losing his family constitutes the core of an abolitionist argument.) Popular culture however, erased both Topsy's hardening through abuse and her conversion into sensation. The Topsy of popular culture was therefore permanently, essentially unfit for citizenship.[92] It was this unfeeling Topsy—the one scripted by Aiken and performed by Caroline Fox Howard—that "flew," as Henry James put it, out of Stowe's context to devolve into the pickaninny.[93] The Howard-Aiken production toured the United States and England for over thirty years and attracted hundreds of imitations. During these years, the Howard-Aiken vision of Topsy became a fixture in popular culture. This Topsy spawned "fearful progeny" in the pickaninny, as Montgomery Gregory wrote in 1925 and as contemporary scholars Jayna Brown, Tavia Nyong'o, and Patricia A. Turner have recently affirmed.[94] The inability to feel pain is the thread of DNA that connected the Howard-Aiken Topsy to all pickaninnies.

A series of advertisements that ran in the juvenile magazine the *Youth's Companion* from October 1893 through December 1894 makes explicit the slippage between Topsy and the pickaninny at the axis of unfelt violence. Arnold Print Works, a company in North Adams, Massachusetts, advertised a variety of printed cloth dolls, including animals, Little Red Riding Hood, and "Pickaninny." In the eyes of the copywriter, the "Pickaninny" doll answered—and commodified—a national desire to commit violence against a representation of an African American child:

> What child in America does not at some time want a cloth "Nigger" dollie—one that can be petted or thrown about without harm to the doll or anything that it comes in contact with[?] "Pickaninny" fills all the requirements most completely.[95]

By October 1894, the Arnold Print Works revised the advertisement to list the doll under the name "Topsy" as well as "Pickaninny."[96] Topsy may be interchangeable with the pickaninny, these advertisements suggested, but either is a "Nigger" that any (white) "child in America" naturally wants to pet or throw about. This advertisement thus exemplifies the merging of Topsy, the pickaninny, and dollness as varieties of racist denigration (the word "nigger"). These ideas and identities merge at the point of unhurtability: what makes this doll a pickaninny, a Topsy, a "nigger" is not only its color, but also, crucially, the fact that it can be "thrown without harm." That is, it cannot be hurt. This invulnerability allows or even instructs a presumably white child to play violently with the doll. The copy suggests that every (white) child in America wants to abuse a black doll, and the virtue of this particular black doll is that it can endure that practice without shattering. The doll itself, in its materiality, is seen to invite its own abuse.[97]

Unrestrained violence against representations of black juveniles was, by the turn of the twentieth century, normalized in American popular culture. In advertisements, stage plays, film, material culture, and children's books such as E. W. Kemble's *A Coon Alphabet*, pickaninnies were beaten, scalded, attacked by animals, neglected, and dismembered—all without significant suffering. The libel that black youth cannot feel pain appears with horrifying vividness in Booth Tarkington's *Penrod*, which was the seventh-best-selling novel of 1914.[98] *Penrod*'s eponymous protagonist was seen to emblematize the white boy adolescent, but two other characters in the novel—Herman and Verman—emblematize, with equal force, the pickaninny. Herman and Verman are African American brothers who move into a ramshackle cottage not far from Penrod's home (their older brother, Sherman, is dead—a loss that no one ever explains or mourns).

The brothers are young, but their ages are never specified. When Penrod meets the brothers, Herman shows off his right hand, which lacks a forefinger. Herman explains eagerly that he had invited Verman to chop off the finger, and so Verman, whose name likens him to a small, vicious animal, had happily obliged by "chop[ping] 'er right spang off up to de roots!"[99] "What *for*?" Penrod asks with justified astonishment. "Jes' fo' nothin'," Herman replies. Penrod repeats his question, and again Herman replies that he did it for "Nothin'. I jes' said it 'at way—an' he jes' chop 'er off!" The brothers "looked pleased and proud" of the mutilation.[100]

Today, this episode is shocking, but in 1914, no critics remarked on the story's allegations that dismemberment does not pain black children and that violence is a "nothing" that pickaninnies comically visit upon each other. Indeed, *Penrod* was perceived as a novel that reproduced the care-free innocence of boyhood: "The book is deliciously whimsical, clever, and filled with innocent fun," commented one reviewer.[101] If a review mentioned Herman and Verman, it typically did so in appreciation of the characters' humorous antics. Violence against these child characters in no way diminished or polluted the pleasure they delivered to white consumers, as one reviewer of a stage adaptation acknowledged by calling Herman and Verman an "unalloyed delight."[102]

*Penrod* could be celebrated as "innocent fun" because by the time the novel was published, the pickaninny, defined by insensitivity to pain, was among the most common libels against African Americans. By the early twentieth century, manufacturers had slapped the image of the pickaninny on products including soap, postcards, sheet music, games, dolls, tobacco, matches, ashtrays, crackers, soda, menus, letter openers, figurines, brooches, farm produce, textiles of all sorts, and much, much more.[103] The repetitious ubiquity of the insensate pickaninny itself de-sensitized white readers and other consumers to African American pain. Throughout this proliferation of pickaninny images, Topsy remained a central figure in the libel that black children were physically invulnerable. In the 1933 animated short, "Mickey's Mellerdrammer," Walt Disney's characters stage a production of *Uncle Tom's Cabin*. Before the play begins, Mickey costumes himself as Topsy by donning a ragged sack and a wild wig, and then lighting a stick of dynamite in his mouth. The dynamite explodes and blackens Mickey's face; the mouse grins at his dressing-room mirror, delighted with the explosion's effect. Thus unfelt violence literally constitutes the blackness of Topsy—and, by implication, all her fearful progeny.[104]

The concept of African American insensateness had existed in Jefferson's eighteenth century, but the pickaninny compressed the libel into the icon of a juvenile body. As a compact and instantly recognizable emblem of black insensateness, the pickaninny was uniquely useful in advertising, as we saw in the Cottolene trade card: the Cottolene girl appears to feel no pain or even discomfort in her labor, and this absence of pain configures the production of cotton, Cottolene's definitional ingredient, as innocent—a sharp contrast with Hine's photograph of Callie Campbell, which pictures a white girl's pain and thus critiques the use of child labor in the production of cotton. When laminated to commodities, the pickaninny, as that-which-cannot-be-hurt, masked the exploitative and even violent aspects of industrialization. Topsy's hardness, her insensateness, was, for Stowe, a constructed and pathological result—and therefore indictment—of the violence inherent in the system of slavery. But the pickaninny's essentialized insensateness *resolved* ethical problems of violence: viciousness against African American juveniles was not immoral if it did not hurt. Thus the pickaninny transformed Stowe's critique of racist violence into an apology for it.

This history of Topsy's polarity with Eva, of Topsy as the pickaninny's progenitor, and of the politics of insensateness explains not only how the trade card sold Cottolene but also how Hine's photograph protested child labor through the dynamic of defamiliarization. Many scholars have gestured toward Hine's use of defamiliarization when they have noted that Hine photographed children's bodies where an adult body was expected: Hine showed children dwarfed by machines, and this juxtaposition asserted a mismatch between children and labor.[105] We see this well-known dynamic in figure 1.2 in the disproportion between Callie Campbell and her sack, which makes a visual case against so small a child bearing so great a burden.[106] Hine also employed, however, a second and heretofore unacknowledged mode of defamiliarization: in this photograph and many others, Hine substituted not only a child for an adult, but also a white child for an African American of any age. In the era of Jim Crow, the naturalized body picking cotton was black. By the time Hine photographed Callie Campbell, U.S. popular culture had swelled for at least six decades with images of de-childed pickaninnies and childlike black adults picking cotton. From advertisements and book illustrations to sheet music and stage shows, images of happy African Americans laboring in the fields justified and naturalized slavery and later sharecropping. The Hine photograph interrupted this field of vision when it placed a white child, topsy-turvy, where a black child (or adult) was expected.[107] Callie

Campbell's white innocence, her essential childhood that her labor threatened and that Hine's photograph asked its viewer to protect, depended on the logic of the pickaninny, on the evacuation of innocence from African American children.

The pickaninny, as a de-childed juvenile, ultimately reserved infanthood for black adults. The libelous, de-childed pickaninny was interdependent with the libel of the "childlike Negro."[108] At stake in the refutation of the pickaninny image was not only black childhood but also black adulthood. African Americans, both adults and children, widely understood what was at stake in the insensate pickaninny, and they resisted.

## "SLAVE-*children* are *children*"

When U.S. culture began, at mid-century, to libel black children as unhurtable and unchildlike, African Americans—both children and adults—began asserting that black children were, of course, children and did, of course, feel pain. In 1863, for example, in Corinth, Mississippi, an African American girl named Nell fought back against white adults who insisted on likening her to the insensate, minstrelized vision of Topsy. Nell's teacher claimed that the girl "testifie[d] to the genuineness and reality" in Stowe's "portrait of 'Topsy.'" When the teacher "dressed her up and kept her about to do little errands" and to "sing, dance, and act quite as comically as Topsy ever did," she cast Nell in a performance of Topsy.[109] Costuming, singing, dancing, and comedy are all important to the performance of Topsy, but the core element, as I have argued, is unfelt violence. A clerk attempted to impose this element on Nell when he "got in the habit of tapping [Nell] upon the head . . . just to see her roll up her eyes at me" in a "comically-deprecating" gesture of minstrelsy. The clerk said that he "tapped her pretty hard sometimes" on the head because it amused him to do so, and because he believed that "Her wool is thick" and that therefore he could "rely . . . upon its softness to protect her." That is, the clerk read Nell's racial markings as evidence that his "tapp[ing] her pretty hard" could not hurt her.

Of course, Nell was no minstrel darky, and the clerk's blows did pain her. The girl found a way to protect herself: she tucked an ounce of pins into her hair with the points out. The clerk soon "tapped" her as usual, "so hard as to get a dozen [pins] right through [his] hand," which became "covered with blood."[110] Nell's action was practical and immediately effective, certainly, but it also intervened brilliantly (although probably not consciously) on a textual level. Nell's teacher and the clerk together con-figured the girl as an unhurtable Topsy, a comic pickaninny rather than a human child. Nell's strategy was not simply one of self-protection, which she could have enacted by tucking padding rather than pins into her hair. Nor did Nell reach simply for revenge—quite unlike Stowe's preconver-sion Topsy, who often arranged for "some inconvenient accident" such as a "libation of dirty slop" to fall on anyone who "cast an indignity" upon her.[111] In lieu of simple self-protection or revenge, Nell caused reciprocal pain to penetrate the clerk at the precise moment of his blow. She caused the clerk's blow to hurt *him*. Thus Nell simultaneously restored and signi-fied on the sentimental sympathy that stage Topsies had evacuated from black childhood. She forced the clerk to feel her pain; she made him, in Stowe's famous phrase, "feel right."[112]

African American adults, too, fought for recognition of black children's pain. Harriet Wilson, author of the 1859 novel *Our Nig; or, Sketches from the Life of a Free Black*, reimagined *Uncle Tom's Cabin* toward this end. *Our Nig* tells the story of Frado, the free daughter of a white mother and black father in the North, who is forced to labor for the vicious Mrs. Bell-mont and her family. Mrs. Bellmont and her daughter Mary torture Frado physically and emotionally, as the novel describes with agonizing speci-ficity. In several especially brutal scenes, Mrs. Bellmont wedges Frado's mouth open with a block of wood or a towel, thus silencing the girl while the woman beats her. Carla Peterson, Elizabeth Ammons, and other schol-ars have identified parallels and inversions between *Our Nig* and *Uncle Tom's Cabin* that suggest that Wilson was familiar with Stowe's novel, that it influenced her, and that she may have envisioned her novel as a partial response to Stowe's.[113] Ammons, for example, maps "mirror imaging" be-tween Stowe's Marie St. Clare and Wilson's Mrs. Bellmont, between Little Eva and James (Bellmont's saintly son who tries to protect Frado and who ultimately dies), and between Tom and Frado.[114] Two characters, however, are notably absent from Ammons's pairings: Stowe's Topsy and Wilson's Mary. These major characters, I argue, actually figure at the center of Wil-son's rereading of—and attack on—Stowe.

Stowe's novel, we recall, argues that Topsy was naturally feeling, but that slavery hardened her, and that Topsy could be at least partially re-deemed through the loving touch of an angelic white girl. Wilson's novel argues, in contrast, that the absence of African Americans' tears is a per-formance that white people impose and maintain, fully aware that the tearless African American face masks agony. Topsy's absence of tears prior to conversion is, for Stowe, a *symptom* of white-on-black violence, but Frado's absence of tears is, for Wilson, a *mode* of white-on-black violence. Unlike the hardened Topsy, Frado does not stop crying because Mrs. Bellmont beats her; rather, Mrs. Bellmont and her daughter Mary beat Frado to force her to stop the spectacle of black pain. In scene after scene, Mrs. Bellmont whips Frado for the "act of disobedience" of having "wept aloud."[115] For Frado, showing pain is a crime, so she endeavors "not to be seen . . . in tears."[116] The excruciating scenes of gagging literalize Frado's enforced self-gagging in which she "choke[s]" her tears to evade further violence.[117]

By choking, gagging, and beating Frado, Mrs. Bellmont and Mary produce an appearance of black insensateness that even Mrs. Bellmont knows to be illusory: as Bellmont's son James notes, his mother "*pretends* to think she [Frado] don't know enough to sorrow for anything."[118] Mrs. Bellmont wants to see Frado as a pickaninny who is too stupid to sorrow, but Bellmont can only "pretend" to believe in the essentiality of the performance she coerced. Frado dons a tearless mask, an appearance, only, of the absence of feeling. The strain of withholding tears, of performing insensateness, becomes an integral part of the torture. By exposing this dynamic, Wilson brilliantly deconstructs the libel of black insensateness, showing it to be neither a symptom of black inferiority (as per proslavery writers) nor a pathological response to violence (as per Stowe), but rather a black performance that white people coerce out of their own pathological desires simultaneously to cause pain and to deny that they are doing so.

In her defense of black childhood, Wilson singles out the white angel-child, especially as emblematized by Stowe's Eva, for trenchant attack. Stowe's Eva and Wilson's Mary occupy parallel places in the family structure: each is the daughter of the white couple that holds a black girl (either as a slave or an extralegally indentured servant). While Eva embraces Topsy through the act of converting the black girl, Mary locks into a grim embrace with Frado through the act of torturing her. James does, as Ammons notes, partially resurrect Eva in boy form, but Mary is Eva's evil twin, and Frado is Topsy's true redeemer.

Wilson begins her bold attack on the figure of the white angel-child in the novel's first paragraph. The novel opens with Mag, who is identified in the first chapter's title as "My Mother," giving birth to an illegitimate baby. The reader might reasonably suppose this baby—the daughter of "my mother"—to be the narrator, who is in that case telling the story of her own birth. By the end of the first paragraph, however, that expectation is thwarted: the baby dies, and Mag, a ghoulish parody of what Elizabeth Ammons calls the sentimental "mother-savior," exults. The deceased baby, the reader learns, is not the "Free Black" of the novel's subtitle, but is instead a white baby—that most conventional sentimental sign of angelic innocence. However, this dead white baby girl is sin-stained, not heaven-bound. The white children of women such as Mag, the narrator comments, may "inherit a wicked heart of their own" that requires "lifelong scrutiny and restraint."[119] The angelic qualities that Stowe might ascribe to the white baby, Wilson assigns ironically to Mag's white seducer, whose voice "*seemed* like an angel's."[120] Wilson purges a dead, white baby girl of her expected angelic qualities and assigns the *illusion* of them to a rake who ventriloquizes an angel's voice as a means by which to ruin Mag. These events, all of which occur within the novel's first three hundred words, signal a narrative strategy of using racial flip-flops to decimate sentimental notions of childhood innocence. The baby whom the reader expected to become the "Free Black" narrator turns out to be a white infant; the dead white baby is no angel; and the only apparent angel deserves suspicion rather than reverence.

Later in the novel, Wilson uses racial flip-flops to skewer the white angel-child again, but even more forcefully: when the malevolent Mary Bellmont dies, Frado comments, "S'posen she goes to hell, she'll be as black as I am."[121] To appreciate the full force of this extraordinary line, it is necessary to contextualize it within abolitionist conversations about white children, black children, and angels. As Elizabeth Clark has shown, white abolitionists argued tenaciously, and to great effect, that African Americans could and did feel pain. In the context of childhood, this assertion raised a question: if black youth could feel pain (because they were black, not because they were children), could they, like white children, complete the sequence of suffering, dying, and becoming angels? A few decades earlier, abolitionists such as the author of the 1821 poem "Negro Boy" readily answered "yes." At midcentury, however, as white and black childhood began to split, this question acquired a nervous edge. Black and white childhood had begun differentiating from each other along the polarity of tender white angel/insensate black pickaninny, and to allow for black angels was to mix the poles and thus potentially to threaten the emerging nature of *white* sentimental childhood. At this moment, stories began to appear in which characters engaged in lengthy and often unresolved debates over whether black children who piously endured pain could become angels.

A representative example of this anxious debate appears in Lynde

Palmer's 1862 antislavery story "Poor Black Violet." The story accentuates the pain that Violet, an enslaved girl, feels as she hauls bricks: "Poor little Violet was much bruised, but she could not rest long, for the overseer called her name, and told her 'not to be lazy.' So she went slowly on as if in a dream, toiling painfully over the weary way."[122] Even as the story affirms the abolitionist argument that slaves feel pain, however, the narrative dances nervously around the question of whether black children can enter heaven and become angels. In one very disturbing scene, Violet discusses death and angelhood with a white slaveholding girl named Carrie. Violet asks,

> "[W]hen we goes to Canaan, that old Sambo sings about, may I be your little slave *then*, Miss Carrie, 'cause you's allus so kind?"
>
> "I don't think there will be any slaves there," said Carrie, slowly, pondering over the matter.
>
> "Why, what will the black people do, then?" cried Violet, with curious round eyes.
>
> "Maybe," replied Carrie hesitatingly, "maybe there won't *be* any black people—you know, Violet, our bodies are covered up in the ground,"—Violet shivered,—"but our souls go to heaven, and they must all be white."
>
> "*All* of 'em?" asked Violet, eagerly.
>
> "Yes, mamma told me that no soul can go till it is washed *white* in Jesus' blood."
>
> "And can my *soul* be white?" whispered Violet.
>
> "Yes," said Carrie, "if you ask God."[123]

Soon after this dialogue, a poisonous snake attacks Carrie's brother Frank, who, earlier in the story, had threatened Violet and called her a nigger. Violet saves her tormentor from the snake, but in the process it bites her. As Violet dies, Carrie prays, "Please, Jesus, give Violet a white soul."[124] The story ends without resolving the question of whether Violet will enter heaven and become an angel, and the closing line calls attention to that absence of closure.

> Frank shuddered violently as he thought of the terrible fate he had escaped, and his heart was full of remorse as he remembered his cruelty to the patient, forgiving little slave, who had been so much more noble than he. His father, with a heart full of thanksgiving for the life of his only son, looked tearfully upon the motionless little form, and said, tenderly,—"Poor little

black Violet!" And Carrie, sobbing bitterly, forgetful of the new white soul, echoed,—"Poor little black Violet!" But no one knew what the angels said.[125]

Wilson, writing in 1859, could not have read Palmer's 1862 story, but she was clearly aware of abolitionist writing and culture, including but not limited to *Uncle Tom's Cabin*, in which Palmer's story was located.[126] And she certainly seems to have been aware of white abolitionists' tedious and condescending conversations about whether black children could become angel-children, and if so, whether they would have to become white first. Stowe might have considered herself quite the racial progressive when she wrote Eva's line reassuring Topsy that the black girl "can go to Heaven at last, and be an angel forever, just as much as if you were white."[127] But Wilson turns the entire debate topsy-turvy. Against Stowe's and Palmer's simpering characters who long for heaven, Frado turns her thoughts toward hell. If Mary "goes to hell," Frado declares fearlessly, "she'll be as black as I am." Frado follows immediately with an even more shocking coda: "Would n't mistress be mad to see her a nigger!"[128] With this ugly racial flip-flop, the shocking image of a white girl—Little Eva's structural parallel in the Bellmont family—going to hell, turning black, and being *seen*, spectacularly, by her own mother as a "nigger," is an attack on the midcentury's most cherished ideologies of white childhood. Wilson, through Frado, tells the entire abolitionist debate over angel-children to go to hell. With this malediction, Wilson attacks nothing less than the racial innocence that was, in 1859, rapidly becoming the new foundation of white childhood.

Whereas Harriet Wilson asserted a black child's pain as a means by which to damn white childhood, Frederick Douglass took a different tack. In *My Bondage and My Freedom*, Douglass asserted, in the most explicit language and typographic emphasis available, "SLAVE-children *are* children."[129] Douglass, like Wilson, coupled his defense of African American children as children and as sensate with an attack on the foundations of white childhood. Wilson targeted the white angel-child as a major figure of sentimentalism, but Douglass uprooted sentimental childhood itself and planted black boys—including and especially himself—in the landscape of romantic childhood.[130] Douglass, like Wilson, tucked his assertion that enslaved children are children within descriptions of black children's vulnerability and pain—in this case, emotional pain:

Children have their sorrows as well as men and women; and it would be well to remember this in our dealings with them. SLAVE-children *are* children, and prove no exception to the general rule. The liability to be separated from my grandmother, seldom or never to see her again, haunted me. . . . I look back to this as among the heaviest of my childhood's sorrows."[131]

Douglass's argument that black children are children suspends between and depends on his assertions of black children's sorrows. However, Douglass hastens in the next paragraph to add that it "is not even within the power of slavery to write *indelible* sorrow, at a single dash, over the heart of a child."[132] Douglass, like Stowe, suggests that no amount of abuse can obliterate an enslaved child's essential childhood. Stowe argues that black and white childhoods are connected even as they polarize; her Topsy and Eva are both inversions of each other and quasi-siblings (and later, when Ophelia adopts Topsy, and after Eva dies, the girls posthumously become second cousins).[133] Although Eva and Topsy do not share paternity, Stowe raises through them the specter of black and white children being literal half siblings. Douglass makes this point more explicitly and infinitely more trenchantly: "The first seven or eight years of the slave-boy's life," Douglass tells his reader, "are about as full of sweet content as those of the most favored and petted *white* children of the slaveholder."[134] By italicizing the word *white*, Douglass implies the possibility of other, nonwhite children of the slaveholder. The next sentence asserts not the possibility but the reality of differently raced siblings coexisting: "The slave-boy," Douglass writes, "escapes many troubles which befall and vex his white brother."[135]

The troubles that befall the slaveholder's *white* children are those of the overcivilized, feminized boy who is forced to "act like a nice little gentleman" or "swallow pretty little sugar-coated pills, to cleanse his blood, or to quicken his appetite."[136] This nice, sugary, appetite-less boy is the passionless child of sentimentalism. Douglass ridicules this child and embraces instead his rugged, romantic ancestor. It would be wrong to say that Douglass resurrected romantic childhood, because it never went away (indeed, traces of it remain today in summer camps and other cultural structures that suggest that no childhood is complete without contact with the wilderness). Romanticism, we recall, had long included black children, and especially black boys. What is new in Douglass's autobiography, however, is his use of romantic childhood to argue that black boys make *better* boys than their white brothers do. Douglass accomplishes this feat in one massive paragraph which, in the book's original edition, spanned three full pages. The enslaved boy, writes Douglass, seldom has to listen to lectures on propriety of behavior, or on anything else. . . . He never has the misfortune, in his games or sports, of soiling or tearing his clothes, for he has almost none to soil or tear. He is never expected to act like a nice little gentleman, for he is only a rude little slave. Thus, freed from all restraint, the slave-boy can be, in his life and conduct, a genuine boy, doing whatever his boyish nature suggests. . . . He literally runs wild; has no pretty little verses to learn in the nursery; no nice little speeches to make for aunts, uncles, or cousins, to show how smart he is. . . . [O]ur sable boy continues to roll in the dust, or play in the mud, as bests [*sic*] suits him, and in the veriest freedom. If he feels uncomfortable, from mud or from dust, the coast is clear; he can plunge into the river or the pond, without the ceremony of undressing, or the fear of wetting his clothes. . . . His days, when the weather is warm, are spent in the pure, open air, and in the bright sunshine. He always sleeps in airy apartments; he seldom has to take powders, or to be paid to swallow pretty little sugar-coated pills, to cleanse his blood, or to quicken his appetite. . . . In a word, he is, for the most part of the first eight years of his life, a spirited, joyous, uproarious, and happy boy, upon whom troubles fall only like water on a duck's back. And such a boy, so far as I can now remember, was the boy whose life in slavery I am now narrating.[137]

Slavery, this passage argues, paradoxically frees a slave-boy to be "a genuine boy" who runs unfettered in nature, breathing clean air, sporting without fear of dirt, or plunging into a swimming hole. The enslaved boy, Douglass argues, is not only *a* boy but *the* ideal boy—not of sentimentalism, but of romanticism. Unlike the slaveholder's *white* son, who needs medicine to achieve a normal appetite, the enslaved child is "a spirited, joyous, uproarious, and happy boy." Douglass's reclamation of romantic childhood, over and above sentimental childhood, marks a critical intersection of gender with race and age.

Abolitionists sometimes struggled to include suffering black girls such as Topsy or Violet within sentimental childhood, often with internally contradictory or ambiguous results; but white writers' efforts to envision black boys as sentimental children were extremely rare and even more awkward. This failure of imagination registers, for example, in Harry Harris, the son of Eliza and George Harris in *Uncle Tom's Cabin* (and many scholars agree that Douglass both mirrored and refuted Harry in *My Bondage and My Freedom*).[138] Harry appears at Stowe's novel's outset, where he answers to the name of "Jim Crow" and performs, upon request, "a wild, grotesque song" and "scamper[s]" after raisins that the slaveholding Shelby scatters on the floor.[139] Harry's beauty and minstrel skills motivate the slave trader Haley to buy the boy. Eliza learns of the sale and flees with Harry—an action that launches the rest of the novel's plot. After Stowe locates Harry at the heart of her novel, however, she demotes him from a full-fledged if minstrelized character to a plot device. Harry, who seems so full of vigor and talent in the opening scene, never again says or does anything individuated or interesting, never again exerts anything resembling agency. His main actions, for the rest of the novel, are to be fed seedcakes, to be petted as characters exclaim over his glossy curls, and to sleep. He is something beloved to look at and protect, a feminized object who passively accepts being cross-dressed as a girl during one portion of the escape. No wonder that in Tom shows, Harry was often played by a doll in Eliza's arms.[140]

Douglass rejected such constructions of African American childhood by banishing *girls,* as well as feminine sentimental boys, from his vision of ideal childhood. Douglass shows little interest in a black boy like Harry who performs piety, purity, submissiveness, and domesticity—even as an element, as Claudia Nelson suggests, of sentimental manliness. He does not demand space within sentimentalism for a beautiful black boy like Harry who "makes" a "pretty girl."[141] Instead, Douglass rejects sentimentalism in favor of a masculinist romanticism. In this landscape, the enslaved boy becomes not a timid or grateful visitor to the realm of childhood, but instead its worthiest citizen. "And such a boy," Douglass tells the reader pointedly, is none other than "the boy whose life in slavery I am now narrating"—that is, Douglass himself, not a boy, but a man. At stake in black childhood, Douglass well understood, is black adulthood, black manhood—for the black boy is the father of the black man.

### Different Trajectories, Different Destinations

Different trajectories of white and black childhood during the second half of the nineteenth century resulted, by the turn of the twentieth, in sharply bifurcated visions of American childhood. In the second half of the nineteenth century, white childhood, and especially white girlhood, became laminated to the idea of innocence; to invoke white childhood was to invoke innocence itself. In contrast, images of nonsuffering black pickaninnies emptied black childhood of innocence. Even when a pickaninny was

*Figure 1.4.* A white girl advertises Cottolene, a lard substitute. Trade card for Cottolene, manufactured by N. K. Fairbank and Company, Chicago, circa 1890s. Collection of the author.

well-dressed and adorable, as in the Cottolene advertisement that opened this chapter, this icon of insensateness did not call for protection. Whereas the white child manifested innocence, the pickaninny deflected it: the pickaninny made not itself, but its violent context, appear innocent. Carefree innocence suffused Penrod, that icon of white boyhood; but what was innocent about the mutilated Herman was not himself, but the unfelt violence against him. Hine's photograph of an innocent white girl called on the viewer to protect its subject by opposing child labor, whereas the pain-free figure in the Cottolene card made child labor and its product—cotton—seem innocuous, naturalized, and beyond criticism. The bifurcation of childhood innocence, through pain and its alleged absence, imbued racial innocence—that is, the pivotal use of childhood innocence in racial politics—with an uncanny flexibility and therefore the power to support opposing agendas.

The divergence between black and white childhood by the end of the nineteenth century can ultimately be measured and marked in the contrast between the Cottolene card depicting a black girl and a second one, also of the 1890s, which features a white girl with long blond hair (figure 1.4 and plate 2). The black Cottolene girl presents her tender puff of cotton as she might a baby. This gesture of showing in fact hides and mystifies the means of cotton production by making the Cottolene girl's labor seem innocent. The black Cottolene girl labors, shows, and hides; the white Cottolene girl, in contrast, is not shown in the midst of any action: she is neither producing an ingredient for, cooking with, nor consuming food containing Cottolene. She only hovers, cloud-like, with a facial expression of passive contentment. This white girl exists as a decoration—an emblem, perhaps, of Cottolene's white color, or of the product's "Purity!," as the trade card's verso exclaims. If the black Cottolene girl is Topsy's "fearful progeny," the white Cottolene girl is Eva's. She is the pure, white angel-child whom popular culture retained long after sentimentalism lost currency (and who still lingers, today, in the tender faces of blond girls from Shirley Temple to Jon-Benet Ramsay to Dakota Fanning). Defined, always, in relation to this white angel-child, the black Cottolene girl painlessly labors so the white angel might rest placidly. In contrast to both the naturally cotton-picking pickaninny and the white angel-child, Callie Campbell seems like an angel with unjustly clipped wings. And a cloud-like puff of white cotton seems to deserve the tender care that the black girl who tirelessly picks it for Cottolene never needs.

One final image measures the distance traveled—and not—between the mid-nineteenth century and the early twentieth. In 1908, Reilly and Britton, publisher of L. Frank Baum's Oz series, produced a volume that contained both Helen Bannerman's *The Story of Little Black Sambo* and an anonymously authored revision of *Uncle Tom's Cabin* titled "The Story of Topsy." John R. Neill, Baum's most famous illustrator, signed the illustrations for *Little Black Sambo*, and there is no reason to doubt that he also illustrated Topsy's story.[142] One of the illustrations (figure 1.5 and plate 3) accompanies the scene in which Eva converts Topsy—the same scene that Hammatt Billings illustrated in 1853 (figure 1.3). The similarities and contrasts between the 1853 and 1908 illustrations track the divergent paths of the white angel-child and black pickaninny.

From Billings's 1853 to Neill's 1908, Eva has changed relatively little. In each image, the white girl shows her profile to the reader while her eyes focus on Topsy's face. The hand of each white girl touches the enslaved girl's shoulder. Eva's hair, in both images, is soft and light; her feet are slippered and small. Eva's dresses differ according to the fashion of the day, but both the 1853 and 1908 dresses puff, cloudlike, around her body. Each image provides a reference point to emphasize Eva's smallness: Billings juxtaposes his Eva with a large table and Neill burdens his Eva with an oversized hat and ribbon, each of which makes the white girl seem delicate, even vulnerable.

As these two images exemplify, the white angel-child was preserved, largely unchanged, from 1853 to 1908. The black child, however, changed mightily in the half-century separating Billings's image from Neill's. In 1853, Billings orients Topsy's body away from Eva, but he turns Topsy's head toward the little evangelist. The mixed orientation in the image suggests not only the possibility of change but the moment of literal turning. Billings's illustration, like Stowe's prose, asserts the possibility of Topsy awakening to sensation, and thus argues for Topsy's essential humanity. In 1908, Neill burlesques this possibility: his Eva, too, touches Topsy, who faces Eva squarely and with full attention, but there is no hope that this cringing, muscular, big-footed, inhumanly lipped creature could ever be childlike, could ever be human. In Stowe's prose that pairs with Billings's illustration, Eva's touch makes Topsy feel and weep. In contrast, Neill's Topsy, upon receiving Eva's touch and kind words, "could only blink and rub her eyes."[143] The Topsy of Stowe and Billings converts to Christianity and eventually becomes a missionary. The Topsy that Neill pictures in the 1908 version, however, "soon learn[s] the ways of negroes of the

*Figure 1.5.* Unsigned illustration (most likely by John R. Neill) for "The Story of Topsy from *Uncle Tom's Cabin,*" published in *Little Black Sambo,* by Helen Bannerman (Chicago: Reilly and Britton, 1908). Eva converts Topsy, who is depicted as a pickaninny with inhuman lips, oversized feet, and unchildlike muscles. Courtesy of the Beinecke Rare Book and Manuscript Library, Yale University.

better class" but remains essentially mischievous, engaging in boisterous play with pillows and bedclothes long after the conversion that convinced Stowe's Topsy to be good.[144] When caught dressing a bolster in Ophelia's nightgown, Neill's Topsy asks to be whipped—much as *Penrod*'s Herman requests to be mutilated. At the dawn of the twentieth century, the perpetually dying Eva lingered, while Topsy, the damaged child, was overpowered, redefined, and replaced by her fearful spawn. Innocence had become the exclusive property of the vulnerable white child, while the pain-free pickaninny was exiled from innocence and with it, from childhood—and humanity.

# 2

# Scriptive Things

In about 1855, more than three decades before Frances Hodgson Burnett wrote the best-selling children's book *Little Lord Fauntleroy*, she was a child—Frances Eliza Hodgson—and she read Harriet Beecher Stowe's *Uncle Tom's Cabin*. She found Stowe's novel, like all the stories she encountered, to be "imperfect, unsatisfactory, filling her with vague, restless craving for greater completeness of form."[1] The form the girl craved—that is, the material she believed she needed to complete the narrative—was a black doll. Burnett obtained a black rubber doll with a "cheerfully hideous grin," named it Topsy, and used it to "act" out the parts of the novel that she found most "thrilling."[2] Casting a white doll she already owned as Little Eva, Burnett played out ever-repeating scenes of Eva laying hands on Topsy and thus awakening the hardened slave girl to Christian love. Burnett also kept the Eva doll "actively employed slowly fading away and dying," and in these scenes Burnett played the role of Uncle Tom.[3] At other times, Burnett performed the scene of Eva's death, casting the white doll as Eva and herself as "all the weeping slaves at once."[4] And at least once she redesignated the black doll as Uncle Tom and cast herself as Simon Legree. For this play-scenario, the girl bound the doll to a candelabra stand (figure 2.1). "[F]urious with insensate rage," she whipped her doll. Throughout the whipping, the rubber doll continued to grin, which suggested to the girl that Uncle Tom was "enjoying the situation" of being "brutally lashed."[5]

Burnett's performance of whipping responded to two distinct cultural prompts: Stowe's narrative and the materiality of the doll itself. For Burnett and many children like her, literature and material culture appeared to invite engagement with each other: as Burnett later wrote, stories in the absence of dolls were "imperfect," and dolls "seemed only things stuffed with sawdust" until "literature assisted imagination and gave them character."[6] Burnett's selection of one particular doll to play Topsy and later Uncle Tom was not random, but was prompted by the doll's physical

At the end of the entrance hall of the house in which she lived was a tall stand for a candelabra. It was of worked iron and its standard was ornamented with certain decorative supports to the upper part. What were the emotions of the

Small Person's Mamma, who was the gentlest and kindest of her sex, on coming upon her offspring one day, on descending the staircase, to find her apparently furious with insensate rage, muttering to herself as she brutally lashed, with

*Figure 2.1.* Illustration by Reginald B. Birch in Frances Hodgson Burnett, *The One I Knew Best of All: A Memory of the Mind of a Child* (New York: Charles Scribner's Sons, 1893), 55. Courtesy of the American Antiquarian Society.

properties: its blackness in combination with its composition of gutta-percha, a form of resilient rubber used in nineteenth-century dolls to enable them to survive rough play that would destroy a doll made of porcelain or wax.[7] No evidence suggests that the doll's manufacturer intended for a girl to name the black doll "Uncle Tom" or to whip it, but the plaything did script broadly violent play: black rubber dolls were manufactured, as patent applications for such dolls often specified, to withstand rough use, and this doll's smile suggested that violent play was acceptable, even enjoyable.[8] Tavia Nyong'o rightly suggests that the materiality of black ceramic figurines proposes "blackness as a hardened form of subjectivity,"[9] but in contrast, the materiality of black rubber dolls configures blackness as an elastic form of subjectivity that can withstand blows without breaking. This elasticity enables the fun of roughhousing with rubber dolls to extend through practices that would shatter ceramic figures and thus terminate play. Burnett's material doll converged in its historical context with the plot scenario provided by *Uncle Tom's Cabin* to prompt, inspire, and structure one child's performance of racial violence, a scene of subjection.[10] That is, the doll-in-context scripted Burnett's practice of play.

To say that the doll *scripted* behavior is to describe a set of prompts that the plaything issued. I understand a script as theater directors do: a script is a dynamic substance that deeply influences but does not entirely determine live performances, which vary according to agential individuals' visions, impulses, resistances, revisions, and management of unexpected disruptions (as when Burnett's mother discovered the child attacking the doll and a self-conscious Burnett terminated the performance). Burnett's ritual of whipping her black doll was far from unique, but it was not compelled: other children played with similar things in dissimilar ways, and even Burnett played with her doll in different ways at different times. Rubber dolls in general prompt rough play, but the specific physical properties of Burnett's doll—its blackness, its grin—combined with *Uncle Tom's Cabin* to script Burnett's historically located performance of whipping.[11] Burnett's act was one of many performances that installed childhood innocence as a powerful component of large-scale racial projects, including slavery and other forms of organized violence against African Americans. Many of these performances, including Burnett's, coordinated through a device, a contrivance, that I call a "scriptive thing," an item of material culture that prompts meaningful bodily behaviors. The set of prompts that a thing issues is not the same as a performance because individuals commonly resist, revise, or ignore instructions. In other words, the set of prompts does not reveal a performance, but it does reveal a *script* for a performance. That script is itself a historical artifact. Examination of that artifact can produce new knowledge about the past.

### Dances with Things

Things, but not objects, script behaviors. Martin Heidegger and more recent scholars of "thing theory" define an object as a chunk of matter that one looks through or beyond to understand something human.[12] A thing, in contrast, asserts itself within a field of matter. For example, when an amateur cook uses a knife to chop an onion, the knife might function as an object that the amateur barely notices; in this scenario, the knife is only a tool used to obtain the chopped onion that the human desires. For a trained chef, however, a knife can never be an object: for such a person, each edge of a knife glitters individually with potential and stubbornness, with past, present, and future motions of slicing and chopping.[13] The trained chef's knife is therefore a thing with which a chef negotiates, while an amateur's knife is an object to the extent that it is only a means to an end. If the amateur's knife should slip and cut a finger, however, that knife suddenly becomes a thing that has leaped up and asserted itself, a thing that demands to be reckoned with.[14] The difference between objects and things, then, is not essential but situational and subjective.

The distinction between object and thing parallels Roland Barthes's distinction, in photography, between *studium* and *punctum*. The *studium* consists of a photograph's general visual field; it openly displays what the photographer photographed and thus enables the viewer to encounter the photographer's conscious intentions.[15] The *punctum* is a small detail in the photograph that punctures the *studium*. In a photograph by Lewis Hine of two institutionalized children, for example, Barthes glances past the *studium* of the children's faces to be captivated by the *punctums* of the boy's oversized collar and the girl's bandaged finger. Seldom or never inserted intentionally by the photographer, the *punctum* is an "element which rises from the scene, shoots out of it like an arrow, and pierces" an individual viewer.[16] In other words, a patch in what would have been *studium* becomes *punctum* at the moment in which it leaps forward to pierce the spectator, much as a knife-object becomes a knife-thing when it slips and cuts a finger. The difference between *punctum* and *studium*, like the difference between thing and object, is subjective: Barthes was moved by the girl's finger-bandage, a detail that another person might not notice, and a knife may be a thing to a chef but an object to an amateur, or a thing to an amateur on one day and an object to that same person on another day. Both *studium* and object are orderly; each orients toward human thoughts and intentions. In contrast, *punctum* and thing are unruly, unpredictable rogues.

A thing, like a *punctum*, demands that people confront it on its own terms; thus a thing forces a person into an awareness of the self in material relation to the thing. When a thing makes a human body a "thing among things," it upsets the boundary between person and object.[17] The thing and person are unmoored from their binarized positions, twirling in sudden mutual relationship. Thus the thing "names less an object than a particular subject-object relation."[18] The destabilizing interaction between human and thing constitutes what Arjun Appadurai called the "social life of things," or "the things-in-motion that illuminate their social context."[19] An object becomes a thing when it invites a person to dance.

Things are not alive, but people "behave," as W. J. T. Mitchell notes, "as if works of art had minds of their own, as if images had a power to influence human beings, demanding things from us, persuading, seducing, and leading us astray."[20] Thing theorists have eloquently explored the ways in which this animative power derives from the psychological investments of people or from a thing itself. However, things also literally shape human behaviors. A chef's knife, a rubber doll, and, we shall see, a children's alphabet book all invite—indeed, create occasions for—repetitions of acts, distinctive and meaningful motions of eyes, hands, shoulders, hips, feet. These things are citational in that they arrange and propel bodies in recognizable ways, through paths of evocative movement that have been traveled before. In this way, objects become things when they trigger what Joseph Roach calls "kinesthetic imagination" as a "faculty of memory"—as when a knife cuts a finger and the person to whom that finger is attached (or was attached, in the worst case) performs a dance of pain that is stylized through its citation of gender, class, age, race, and other categories of analysis.[21] Kinesthetic memory is a way of "thinking through movements—at once remembered and reinvented—the otherwise unthinkable, just as dance is often said to be a way of expressing the unspeakable."[22] Stylized bodily performances in everyday life are utterances of thoughts that cannot be expressed in words. These thoughts are neither conscious nor unconscious, neither wholly voluntary expressions of intention nor compulsory, mechanical movement. Things invite us to dance, and when we sweep them onto the dance floor, they appear to animate.

At the deepest ontological level, then, performance is what distinguishes an object from a thing. In J. L. Austin's terms, objects are "constatives" in that what is most important lies beyond the material or the utterance (an amateur's knife is a means to a diced onion; a constative describes something beyond itself), whereas things are performatives in that they *do* something: they invite humans to move.[23] Dances with things, too, are performative in that they constitute actions: they *think*, or more accurately, they *are the act of thinking*. Things script meaningful bodily movements, and these citational movements think the otherwise unthinkable. In the case of Burnett, a black rubber doll prompted a performance that cited *Uncle Tom's Cabin* and, through that narrative, an ongoing history of racist viciousness and oppression. The white girl's action of whipping performed ideas that the girl could not utter in words, as became clear when her mother asked her daughter to explain her actions. In reply, the normally articulate girl could but stammer, "I was—only just—pretending something."[24]

### Determined and Implied Scripts

Things script performances in two ways: through orders and blandishments. Orders issue through *determined* actions that are necessary for the thing to function. For example, a novel's determined actions include opening the covers and reading English print from left to right. Although it is possible not to open a book's covers and to use a novel as, say, a doorstop, that use redesignates the novel functionally as something other than a novel. To use an English-language, printed book as a book, one must open the covers and read words from left to right. These actions are broad and necessarily stable across time and geography.

The force of determined actions becomes clear through a close reading of E. W. Kemble's 1898 *A Coon Alphabet*.[25] Kemble was a white artist and writer who remains best known for his advertising logos (including his creation of the Gold Dust Twins for the N. K. Fairbank Company, which also manufactured Cottolene), as well as his illustrations of the first edition of Mark Twain's *Huckleberry Finn,* an 1892 edition of Stowe's *Uncle Tom's Cabin,* and works by Joel Chandler Harris, Thomas Nelson Page, and Paul Laurence Dunbar. Kemble wrote and illustrated *A Coon Alphabet,* a ferociously violent alphabet book in which African American characters are scalded, stung by bees, bitten by alligators, pummeled and battered. In this book, Kemble directs violence particularly at African American characters who reach toward social advancement. For example, Kemble opens his book with the rhyme, "A is for Amos / what rides an ole mule / so he can be early / each monin ter school."[26] The final line of the verse is accompanied by an illustration of the mule pitching Amos toward a building marked "Gramer Schole." Thus the book ridicules African Americans' education and connects their learning and by extension their social advancement to violence.

This literary-visual content combines crucially with the book's physical properties and the sequential actions that those properties script for the reader. Kemble formatted his alphabet book as an "alphabet array" or "worldly alphabet"; that is, one based on the repetition of the phrase "is for," as in "A is for Apple."[27] During the nineteenth century, this format became dominant over other types of alphabet books, such as the "body alphabet" in which contorting human figures represent each letter, or the "swallow alphabet" in which letters eat other letters or are eaten by children or animals. By listing objects from apple to zither, or people from archer to zany (jester), "alphabet arrays" seem to index the world, rendering it, in Patricia Crain's words, "graspable, and, most strikingly, obtainable."[28] As such, the alphabet book "initiates the individual into that world."[29]

Crain uses the terms "grasp," "obtain," and "initiate" figuratively, but the physical configuration of Kemble's book literalizes the first two and sheds new light on the third. In Kemble's book, each letter of the alphabet receives two pages of illustration. On the first page, the reader encounters the first three lines of a rhyme. For example (figure 2.2), "D is for Didimus / what blew down a gun; / now he and his sister—." The incomplete rhyme and interrupted rhythm create a sense of tension and inevitability: the reader seeks the satisfaction of the rhyme's closure. The format of the book instructs the reader literally to grasp the page and turn it to obtain the missing portion of the rhyme. The next page (figure 2.3) completes the rhyme in a way that brings violence upon the African American characters—a process that repeats with differences twenty-four times in Kemble's book.[30] The reader's literal grasping-obtaining

*Figure 2.2.* "D is for Didimus." E. W. Kemble, *A Coon Alphabet* (New York: R. H. Russell, 1898), n.p. Courtesy of the Beinecke Rare Book and Manuscript Library, Yale University.

action doubles with the "worldly alphabet" book's figurative claim to render the world graspable and obtainable as knowledge; thus the reader physically causes the characters to meet their violent fate while the format of the "worldly alphabet" configures that fate as an objective, phenomenological part of the world, as apparently unconstructed and discoverable as an apple.

Kemble scripted this meaningful action for the reader. He could have included each full rhyme in a two-page spread; instead he chose, less obviously, to leave every left-side page blank. No evidence suggests that Kemble consciously thought about the history of alphabet books or that he aimed to inculcate child readers of any race with a psychological urge to attack African Americans. Regardless of his conscious or unconscious intentions, upon which the archive is silent, Kemble designed the book so as to impel the reader's grasping-obtaining, to conflate that action with the perpetration of violence against African American child characters, to substitute satisfaction at a completed rhyme for any other emotion one might feel while participating in violence—and to repeat that sequence twenty-four times.

The act of turning the page of Kemble's alphabet book, which Crain might describe as "initiation" into a world of alphabetically indexed, naturalized violence against African Americans, I would call "enscription"—that is, interpellation through a scriptive thing that combines narrative with materiality to structure behavior. Scriptive things such as Kemble's alphabet book hail human actors as distinctly as a police officer crying out, "Hey, you there!"[31] Like the police, scriptive things leap out within a field, address an individual, and demand to be reckoned with. The ontological distinction between things and objects is that things *hail*. And they do so persistently, constantly, when we are alone and when we are in groups; when we think about them and when we do not; when we respond obediently and when we resist; and when we individually or collectively accept the invitation to dance, refuse it, accept but improvise new steps; or renegotiate, deconstruct, or explode the roles of leader and follower. A hail demands bodily action: turning to face the police or turning the page of the book. By answering a hail, by entering the scripted scenario, the individual is interpellated into ideology and thus into subjecthood.[32] Interpellation occurs not only or even mainly through verbal demands followed by bodily actions, as in Althusser's scenario, but through encounters in the material world: dances between people and things.

Kemble's alphabet book determinatively scripts the reader's grasping-obtaining action and, through that ritualistic behavior (repeated twenty-four times), initiates or interpellates the reader into one specific version of the world—one in which violence against African Americans is as satisfying, inevitable, and banal as the act of turning a page in a book. To resist the script by, say, flipping the pages in reverse or random order is to interrupt linear alphabetization itself. Therefore, without executing the determined physical action, it is impossible to use Kemble's alphabet book as an alphabet book.

Things script behavior not only through determined actions that are required for function but also through *implied* or *prompted* actions. For example, *Uncle Tom's Cabin*, when published in book form in English, determines that the reader, regardless of historical context, must open the covers to read the print from left to right; one cannot defy this determined script and still use the novel as a novel. In Stowe's historical context of mid-nineteenth-century sentimental culture, however, the novel simultaneously cued or prompted a reader to weep at the death of Little Eva—a script that Frances Hodgson Burnett literally staged with dolls, casting herself as "all the weeping slaves at once."[33]

*Figure 2.3.* "—ain't havin' much fun." E. W. Kemble, *A Coon Alphabet* (New York: R. H. Russell, 1898), n.p. Courtesy of the Beinecke Rare Book and Manuscript Library, Yale University.

Burnett perceived the prompt to weep because she possessed what I call "performance competence," a parallel to Jonathan Culler's concept of "literary competence." Culler argues that literature functions as a system of signs; just as comprehension of an individual word depends on competence in a linguistic system, comprehension of a single text depends on a minimal understanding of literary genre (for example, the competent reader approaches a novel, a scholarly monograph, and a dictionary with different expectations).[34] Similarly, the competent performer understands how a book or other thing scripts broad behaviors within her or his historical moment—regardless of whether or how the performer follows that script. Competence differs from literacy in both reading and performance: a reader who possesses literacy but not literary competence might read a novel and a scholarly monograph and understand each individual sentence but fail to understand the conventions and functions of the respective genres. In parallel, a person who possesses performance literacy but not performance competence would understand that a chair exists, literally, as an object to accommodate sitting, but would not understand that a beanbag chair and a Hepplewhite, as things, prompt different styles of sitting, and that each of those practices of sitting embeds in a system of culture, in a *habitus*.[35]

Unlike an incompetent performer who cannot decode a thing's invitation to dance, a resistant performer understands and exerts agency against the script. Often, however, an action that appears to be resistant actually follows a secondary script within a thing's range of prompts. These prompts toward apparently resistant behaviors can be understood as "transgressive scripts." Oscar Wilde gestured toward transgressive scripting when he famously quipped, "One must have a heart of stone to read the death of Little Nell without laughing."[36] The humor in Wilde's observation depends partially on the fact that laughter, in the nineteenth century or today, *is* a possible response to sentimentalism. To laugh at the death (or life) of Little Nell or Eva is not to exile oneself to a lunatic fringe, but to indulge in an apparently resistant action that the text's script does permit—or even, covertly, invite (in contradiction, certainly, to the novelist's intention). Indeed, in November 1853, a young woman named Else Elisabeth Hysing Koren attended a theatrical production of *Uncle Tom's Cabin* and observed in her diary that the audience "laughed and clapped as loud as they could" at Little Eva's misfortunes.[37] This moment reveals a range of implied actions Stowe's novel scripted in its historical moment: it prompted actors to stage the work and audiences to pay to attend the show (Koren was clearly familiar with the novel, as she listed discrepancies between the book and the play in her journal). Within the theater, some audience members laughed at Little Eva, while Koren's reference to the revelers as "they" suggests that she did not share their mirth (her evening was not a washout, however: she noted that the scenery was "pretty" and "the theater itself was attractive").[38]

The scriptive thing is a tool for analyzing incomplete evidence—and all evidence is incomplete—to make responsible, limited inferences about the past.[39] A brief tabulation of the evidence already introduced in this chapter suggests the evidentiary gaps that the scriptive thing can bridge. In the case of Frances Hodgson Burnett's performance of doll play, the available evidence includes an adult's published reportage of her long-past thoughts, emotions, and actions; a narrative frame (*Uncle Tom's Cabin*) that structured the child's play; Burnett's description of the doll's appearance and composition; and contextualizing archival evidence relating to the manufacture of similar dolls and to other girls' practices with dolls in the 1850s. Burnett's actual gutta-percha doll, however, is not extant. E. W. Kemble's *A Coon Alphabet* presents an almost inverse configuration of evidence: in this case, evidence includes the material thing of the book; but no written archive, published or unpublished, attests to the producers' intentions. We have contextualizing information in the history of alphabet books, but we have no corroborating archival evidence—no journal entry, no letter, no photograph or film clip, no eyewitness account—to tell us how living children interacted with Kemble's book. We know Burnett's name, race, gender, and class, but we do not know the names or socioeconomic locations of any historical children who owned *A Coon Alphabet*. These disparities do not necessarily mean, however, that we can make more reliable inferences regarding performances involving Burnett's doll than those engaging Kemble's book. To the contrary, we can make more reliable inferences about the *latter*, because it is possible that Burnett misremembered, distorted, or flat-out lied in her memoir, but it is not possible that no child ever turned the pages of Kemble's alphabet book. By reading things' scripts within historically located traditions of performance, we can make well-supported claims about normative aggregate behavior: in the 1890s, competent performers turned pages of picture books; in the 1850s, competent performers cried (and laughed, as Koren observed) at the death of Little Eva.

Scriptive things contain massive historical evidence—evidence that is often unavailable from any other source. The evidence delivered through scriptive things is crucial to the histories of oppressed peoples, including enslaved African Americans. As James C. Scott and Saidiya V. Hartman have both argued, oppressed people often conceal "hidden transcripts" in performances in everyday life[40]—and the scriptive thing is a key cloaking device for these transcripts. Scriptive things were useful to enslaved people not only because of limited access to literacy or print technologies, but also, and more importantly, because of the properties of performance. Performance, more than writing, provides opportunities for misdirection, the skills and traditions of masquerade, and plausible deniability. Performance in daily life is often cheap and portable. Performances can usefully produce many meanings simultaneously, and can even tuck one meaning within another, opposing meaning: as Hartman notes, some enslaved people's "performances constituted acts of defiance conducted under the cover of nonsense, indirection, and seeming acquiescence."[41] Performance can appear to leave no trace (a gesture does not mark the air in the way that ink marks a page), but the repetition of performance—the repertoire—does habituate and thus deeply inscribe the body; for this reason, performance usefully appears ephemeral when it in fact lingers and haunts. The balance of this chapter delves deeply into one such haunting: the "topsy-turvy doll."

## The Topsy-Turvy Doll: Cloth and Code

The topsy-turvy doll is two dolls in one (figure 2.4 and plate 4). A black torso and a white one fuse at the waist, where a shared skirt fences the races. To play with the black half-doll, one flips the skirt over the head of the white half-doll, and vice versa.[42] Most scholars agree that this doll was originally sewn by enslaved African American women in the antebellum South, but very little corroborating evidence exists to document the process by which the doll was created or used before the Civil War.[43] The following analysis of the topsy-turvy doll as a scriptive thing recovers a provocative and otherwise invisible instance of enslaved women's agency, resistance, and, ultimately, humor.

A profoundly doubled and doubling object, the topsy-turvy doll has been read as enslaved women's polyvalent representation of their experiences of sexual violation. Karen Sánchez-Eppler, for example, argues influentially that the topsy-turvy doll is both "prudish" and obscene. The toy is prudish in that it "elides sexuality: there are no genitals underneath her skirt, not even hips or thighs." However, the doll's fusion of black and white nervously refers to racial mixing within antebellum plantations and to systematic rape of enslaved African American women by white slaveholding men. Sánchez-Eppler notes that "as one head emerges from the skirts of the other, she can be seen as enacting an interracial birthing (marked by past acts of miscegenation)."[44] As scholars from Elizabeth Young to Leland S. Person to Robert Leigh Davis have affirmed, the topsy-turvy doll symbolizes illicit sexual contact, including rape.[45] But the doll's symbolism is endlessly complicated, for in the mermaid-like absence of a crotch, African American women figured un-rape-ability, sexual safety. In another important interpretation, Kimberly Wallace-Sanders reads the topsy-turvy doll as enslaved women's meditation on their work of caregiving: "perhaps a slave mother [left, in the doll,] some personal testimony about her own fragmented life," in which she "divided . . . attention and affection between [her] own children and the white children [she] tended."[46]

These insightful and generative readings approach the doll as a

*Figure 2.4.* A mid-twentieth-century Vogart sewing pattern for a topsy-turvy doll. This image usefully shows the doll in three positions: with the skirt flipped to reveal the white doll and to hide the black doll (left), vice versa (right), and mid-flip (center). Collection of the author.

visual image and treat it much as one might a painting, photograph, or film clip. The advantage of such analysis is that it enables us to regard topsy-turvy dolls as artifacts of African American women's intellectual history. In this mode, topsy-turvy dolls emerge as texts through which enslaved African American women reflected on their experiences of forced labor and sexual violence. As Patricia Hill Collins notes, "A rich intellectual tradition exists" among African American women, but it has "remained virtually invisible."[47] Perceiving and understanding this intellectual history, writes Hill Collins, "involves searching for its expression in alternative institutional locations and among women who are not commonly perceived as intellectuals."[48] Such women include those enslaved, and the alternative locations by which we must seek their intellectual work include the material products of their labors. As enslaved women sewed dolls, we must look to these things for hidden transcripts.[49]

Looking for thoughts in stitches does not and should not equate sewing with writing. Some symbolic systems did appear in enslaved African American women's cloth arts; for example, the manner of folding a kerchief could indicate a woman's birth in a particular region of Africa. Some quilts, too, retained and transmitted African imagery.[50] However, claims that quilts constituted enslaved women's "personal and communal history, recorded not on *paper* but on *fabric*" misleadingly configure sewing as a direct substitute for writing.[51] Jacqueline L. Tobin and Raymond G. Dobard have pushed this claim furthest, arguing that enslaved people's quilts contained a complex code that transmitted information regarding the underground railroad, including signals regarding the tools, methods, routes, and timing of escapes.[52] Many scholars have cast doubt on Tobin and Dobard's work, largely because the study overrelies on the oral testimony of one informant and therefore does not provide a breadth of evidence commensurate to the scope of the claims. David Blight attacked the concept of the "quilt code" with exceptional vitriol, calling it "a myth, bordering on a hoax"; and a debate about the book on an H-Net discussion network threatened to "degenerate into an episode of 'Historians Gone Wild.'"[53]

The fundamental problem with Tobin and Dobard's book was that it read enslaved women's quilts as transmitters of what Joan N. Radner and Susan S. Lanser call "complicit coding."[54] In an influential essay, Radner and Lanser distinguish among different kinds of coding. In "complicit" coding, meaning travels through "collectively determined" signals that appear, to the uninitiated, to be insignificant.[55] To exemplify complicit coding, Radner and Lanser cite Frances Harper's 1892 novel *Iola Leroy*, which opens with a scene of enslaved African Americans using verbal code to communicate information about the Civil War: "If they wished to announce a victory of the Union army, they said the butter was fresh," Harper wrote. "If defeat befell them, then the butter and other produce were rancid or stale."[56] Complicit code differs from a second, "explicit" type of code such as military or Morse code, in which someone who cannot read the code nevertheless understands that a message is coded. Complicit and explicit codes are similar, however, in that in each, *only* the submerged meaning is significant. In the example from *Iola Leroy*, the code depended on the recipient understanding that the speaker conveyed *no* reliable information about whether the butter was indeed fresh or rancid, and in Morse code, the recipient understands that any aesthetic quality produced through the dashes and dots is purely coincidental.

*Pace* Tobin and Dobard, very few quilts or other fabric arts are known to contain enslaved African Americans' complicit (much less explicit) code. Enslaved women did, however, widely employ a third type of code, which Radner and Lanser call "implicit." Implicit code differs from both complicit and explicit code in that the latter two forms communicate a single meaning in reference to a mutually understood key. Implicit coding, in contrast, communicates through multifaceted cultural references and thus opens manifold and often contradictory meanings. In a single-key code such as Morse, only the submerged message is important; in implicit coding, however, all layers of meaning—including those conscious and unconscious—matter. Implicit coding is improvisational, creative, and expressive, often playful or joyful, and it creates a sense of control.[57] The "context for implicit coding exists when there is a situation of oppression, dominance, or risk for a particular individual or identifiable group; when there is some kind of opposition to this situation that cannot safely be made explicit; and when there is a community of potential 'listeners' from which one would want to protect oneself"; and for this reason, implicit code is especially common among people of color and women of all races.[58] Because implicit code produces meanings on many levels at once, it often emerges accidentally: the coder may not realize she or he was producing code until the receiver decodes it.

Implicit code figures in *Iola Leroy* in the plot device of a hymn passed through generations.[59] Iola, a freed slave who has been separated from her family, nurses Robert, a Union soldier from a Colored Regiment. To soothe the wounded soldier, she sings a hymn she recalls from her childhood. Robert recognizes the hymn as one that his mother used to sing, and this recognition leads the characters to discover that they are uncle and niece. Later in the novel, the hymn's implicit code, which the characters discovered by accident, is deployed in a purposeful context: Robert and Iola, searching together for more relatives, attend a church meeting for freed people who seek their loved ones. Robert sings the hymn to the congregation, and in response, "a dear old mother [rises] from her seat."⁶⁰ The woman does not say that she recognizes the hymn, but it inspires her to speak of her own lost son and daughter, who immediately become recognizable as Robert and his sister, Iola's mother. Robert's singing of the hymn functions as a coded broadcast that most of the listeners receive—not incorrectly— as a heartfelt paean to Christ, but that reaches one sought-after auditor with additional meaning, and that produces, in this transmission, a powerfully desired result. This example includes many key qualities of implicit code: it signifies on multiple levels to distinct audiences (and all these levels are meaningful); it may emerge accidentally or deliberately; it may be deployed consciously, unconsciously, or semi-consciously; and it often appears in situations that are emotionally charged and where the stakes are high. Most significantly, implicit code is often both performative and performed. In the case of *Iola Leroy*, Robert performs the hymn, and that performance does not merely *transmit* the code; it *is* the code. In other words, no code exists in the absence of the performance—the singing—of the code.

The performative nature of implicit code enables a new understanding of intentionality. Earlier in this chapter, I characterized dances with things as neither wholly voluntary expressions of human intention nor rigidly imposed movements that bear no relationship to interiority, but instead as movement-thoughts or kinesthetic imagination; as manifestations of thought that cannot adequately manifest in words. The concept of implicit code confirms and expands this paradigm. Implicit code is used in situations in which other forms of communication are dangerous or impossible, and implicit codes have no single key (unlike complicit or explicit codes). For this reason, implicit coding seldom pairs with clear statements of intention. In *Iola Leroy*, for example, Robert never states that he sings the hymn to the congregation in hopes that his mother will respond to his call. Had the character conceived this idea in words, he could have advanced his cause by announcing, "I will now sing a hymn my mother used to sing; if you recognize this hymn, please step forward." In the context of the church gathering, Robert *could have* made such a statement without endangering himself, and such an articulation might have helped him to reach his goal of finding family members. The absence of such a statement, therefore, suggests that the character did not consciously articulate the thought to himself in words. The *singing* of the hymn *was* the articulation of Robert's idea; the singing was not an expression of a separately conceived, worded thought.

The performative nature of implicit coding enables attention to shift from the production of code (and the coder's intention as it is assumed to exist prior to or separate from the code itself) to the enactment of coding in a context of reception. This shift revises what qualifies as a statement of intentionality. For Meir Sternberg, intentionality is "a shorthand for the structure of meaning and effect supported by the conventions that the text appeals to or devises."[61] In the case of *Iola Leroy*, Robert attends the church meeting to find lost relatives, and he sings a hymn as a sub-action within that super-action. One can reasonably infer that Robert sings the hymn with the intention—conscious, unconscious, or semiconscious— of finding loved ones, because *everything* that Robert does in the church serves that goal. Intentionality, then, refers to what Radner and Lanser call "assumptions inferable from the *performance-in-context*, which includes what we know of the performer and her circumstances but does not rely on the performer's own words for its guarantee."[62] In other words, the fictional Robert's intention is best understood not through some corroborating statement (which does not exist), but through the *context* of the church meeting and through the *response* of the woman who received the code. When Radner and Lanser speak of "intention-as-contextually-realized,"[63] they speak of performances *as* thoughts rather than as deferred expressions of thoughts. In implicitly coded performances, intention is inseparable from action.

The example of implicit coding in Frances Harper's fiction clarifies historically contextualized coding in the topsy-turvy doll. Karen Sánchez-Eppler and Kimberly Wallace-Sanders both interpret the topsy-turvy doll as a source of implicit code, although neither employs that term. Both these scholars, and those influenced by them, analyze how the topsy-turvy doll looked, both still and in motion, and what meanings this visual configuration might have produced in historical context. Because implicit code emerges through performance, however, it is crucial to consider the topsy-turvy doll not only as a visual text but as a scriptive thing. To do so, one begins by asking, what behaviors—both determined and implied— did the topsy-turvy doll script for its historically specific users, who included both black and white children, mainly girls, in the antebellum South?

## *The Scripts of the Topsy-Turvy Doll*

The topsy-turvy doll determinatively scripts one action: any user, regardless of age, race, gender, or historical context, necessarily obscures one character pole to play with the other character pole. The contemporary literary scholar Shirley Samuels and the turn-of-the-century poet Rebecca Deming Moore observe the same phenomenon from very different vantage points when they write, respectively, "The topsy-turvy doll can be only one color at a time" and "When Topsy comes, Miss Turvy goes."[64] The thing also determinatively precludes actions. For example, the doll is typically too stiff to allow the black and white characters to bend sufficiently at the waist to face each other. The user therefore can never stage the two figures talking with each other or playing with each other (had Frances Hodgson Burnett owned a topsy-turvy doll, she could not have used it to stage the scene of Eva laying hands on Topsy to convert her to Christianity—a scene Burnett frequently performed with her black guttapercha doll and her white doll). Nor can the user stage herself or himself playing with both character poles at once. The thing determines that the black and white poles never interact, and that one character always obliterates the other.

This determined estrangement balances, however, against the doll's implied script. While the scriptive thing determines that the character poles can never talk or play together, the script simultaneously invites the playing child to alternate between the poles, to flip the skirts. It is physically possible to expose permanently one pole or the other, but to do so is to forgo the doll's unique pleasures. The doll urges its user to flip the skirts—at least occasionally. Rebecca Deming Moore gave voice to this implied instruction in her poem, "The Topsy-Turvy Doll":

> Now you see her, cheeks of red,
> Muslin cap upon her head,
> Bright blue eyes and golden hair,
> Never face more sweet and fair.
> Presto! change! She's black as night,
> Woolly hair all curling tight.[65]

An advertisement for a postbellum, commercially produced topsy-turvy doll read similarly, "Turn Me Up / Turn Me Back / First I'm White / Then

I'm Black."[66] Moore's poem and the advertisement each verbalized the instruction that the doll uttered scriptively. A child who minimally followed the implied script by incorporating the skirt-flip into play felt the balance of the doll, the fact that the poles weighed equally in the hands as the doll rotated. The thing scripted its user to position neither black nor white permanently on top; the competent user received the thing's message that the hierarchy could—and *should*—flip. With this thing, enslaved African American women scripted racial flip-flops, a performance of black and white in endless oscillation rather than permanent ranks of dominant and oppressed.

However, the flipping skirts constituted only one of the doll's scriptive elements. An equally important script is embedded in the cloth topsy-turvy doll's physical softness. To understand the scriptive property of the softness, it is useful to imagine a topsy-turvy doll made of wood and fitted with a cloth skirt. Enslaved African Americans did carve wooden dolls, and did sometimes dress those wooden dolls in cloth (such dolls are extant).[67] Nothing physical prevented an enslaved person from creating a wooden topsy-turvy doll with a flexible cloth skirt. Such a wooden thing would have created precisely the same symbolic meanings as the cloth version, and the cloth skirt of the wooden doll would have scripted meaningful actions identical to those of the skirt on the cloth topsy-turvy doll. In other words, all the insights that Karen Sánchez-Eppler and Kimberly Wallace-Sanders offer regarding soft topsy-turvy dolls would apply equally well to a hard topsy-turvy doll. Yet there is no evidence that a non-cloth topsy-turvy doll existed in the antebellum South. The softness of the doll's body is therefore a deliberate choice on the part of the doll's makers. And when the dollmakers chose cloth—exclusively—rather than wood, they also chose the actions scripted by softness—exclusively—rather than the actions scripted by hardness. Those scripted actions are hidden transcripts, movement-thoughts that enslaved women scripted for children to dance forth.

An action that a cloth doll invited, but a doll made of wood would have repelled, is cuddling.[68] African American women sewed a doll that referred symbolically to rape, racial mixing, and racial hierarchy. By making the doll soft, enslaved women scripted black and white children to cuddle that politically and sexually volatile thing. When an enslaved woman sewed a topsy-turvy doll for her enslaved child, typically a daughter, she offered that child an opportunity to own and to have complete power over a representation of a white girl.[69] The doll's constitutive skirt always gendered both poles of the doll as girls or women. The single shared skirt gendered the poles of the dolls equally; it asserted, long before the declaration attributed to Sojourner Truth, that if white women are women, then black women are also women. The dollmaker scripted a performance of equal gendering stitched to racial resistance, of play in which the skirt that genders white girls simultaneously and equally genders black girls (or, in the case of some topsy-turvy dolls, a white girl and a black woman), of play in which white domination is always temporary.

But when an enslaved African American woman sewed a topsy-turvy doll for a slaveholding white child, the script that emerged was not only intellectually brilliant but also angry and bitterly witty. In this script, the African American dollmaker sent that child to bed with a sign of systematic rapes committed by members of that child's race, if not that child's immediate family. She tucked beneath the child's blanket—which she may have washed—a sign of the child's enslaved half-sibling, either literal or symbolic. This script delivers trenchant political critique through humor: if an enslaved woman sews an obscene doll and gives it to a glorified, white slaveholding child, who cuddles and kisses and adores it and takes it into bed while slaveholding adults look on in obtuse approval, *that's funny*. It is a bitter joke, a shocking joke, even a tragic joke; but it is a joke and it is funny. By constructing the doll as cuddly, the dollmaker scripted an ironic performance (to which she and other slaves were the privileged audience) in which the white child nuzzled and adored a thing that was explicitly prudish (in the lack of a crotch) and implicitly obscene (in the reference to rape, illicit sex, and resultant birthing). This private performance was not unlike the one African Americans witnessed when white slaveholders ate food in which enslaved cooks had spat. In each of these instances, enslaved women inserted something inappropriate and disgusting into a product of forced labor (food or textile). Many scholars have correctly identified the corruption of food as a form of resistance. However, the insertion of filth (saliva or rape imagery) into a product only *begins* this act of resistance. The act continues when a slaveholder incorporates the item and its filth (by eating or playing), and concludes when the oppressed person directly or indirectly witnesses this incorporation. When slaveholders involved themselves bodily with corrupted products, they unknowingly performed comic acts before those whom they enslaved. By tricking slaveholders into performing, enslaved people transformed themselves into privileged spectators. Beneath the topsy-turvy skirts, we find not only a chastely genitalless, polarized doll, but also a demurely murmured "fuck you."

The softness of the topsy-turvy doll instructed the child to carry the thing into the spaces in which cuddling occurred: the home, the bed. The thing functioned as a Trojan horse that smuggled an enslaved woman's emotions, analyses, and critiques into white slaveholders' homes. Thus the enslaved African American woman transformed the slaveholding white child from exalted innocent to smuggler's mule, a beast of burden dragging the Trojan horse. Topsy turvy, the slaveholding child became the conscripted laborer on behalf of the enslaved adult.

Racial innocence enabled the dance between the topsy-turvy doll and a child to perform these complex meanings. Five hundred years earlier, a young person's caress would not have seemed innocent and therefore would not have provided a protective vehicle for an oppressed person's thoughts, emotions, and humor. By the mid-nineteenth century, however, sentimental visions of white childhood innocence had achieved dominance in U.S. culture; and through the topsy-turvy doll, enslaved women appropriated white childhood innocence, transforming it into a tool to be deployed for their own political purposes. When Little Eva caressed Uncle Tom, propinquity between the white child and the African American adult caused the child's aura of innocence to extend to Tom and, in Stowe's novel, to abolition itself. Similarly, when the slaveholding white child caressed the soft topsy-turvy doll, that child's aura of innocence— that performance of innocent-of, of obliviousness—suffused the doll and thus masked the political ideas that its enslaved maker stitched into it. The white child who followed the topsy-turvy doll's script made the dollmaker's thoughts appear innocent.

The stakes of this alibi become clearest when one imagines what would have happened if an enslaved woman had created an object that represented parallel thoughts but that did not attach itself to the idea or body of any child. If she had carved, say, a wooden sculpture of black and white characters fused—a noncuddly item designed to be looked at rather than touched, a frankly political object that scripted adults' contemplation in open air rather than children's play in intimate domestic settings—the slaveholders' retribution against her would surely have been violent or even lethal. It is racial innocence that enabled a soft topsy-turvy doll to penetrate the slaveholders' home, whereas a sculpture lacking the aura of racial innocence would have brought destruction to itself and its maker. As the following three chapters show, racial innocence, as coordinated through scriptive things, provided cover beneath which dominant groups dominated and oppressed groups resisted—all the while denying they were doing any such thing.

# 3

## Everyone Is Impressed

*Slavery as a Tender Embrace from Uncle Tom's to Uncle Remus's Cabin*

To the modern nose, much nineteenth-century literature might seem to stink of pedophilia. Uncle Tom spies Little Eva on the steamboat and "cut[s] cunning little baskets out of cherry-stones" to "attract" the child. Little Eva is initially "shy," and Tom finds it "not easy to tame her." But the girl "bashful[ly]" accepts Tom's gifts, and soon the two get "on quite confidential terms." In this reading, the seduction culminates when Eva "whisper[s] softly . . . 'I want him.'"[1] In a later best-selling tale of interracial, cross-generational love, Joel Chandler Harris's Uncle Remus "initiates" a white, unnamed Little Boy by taking him into Remus's cabin, "stroking the child's hair thoughtfully and caressingly" while holding the Boy on his lap, and murmuring tales of Brer Rabbit's mayhem into his ear.[2]

For scholars who read in this mode, Little Eva's and the Little Boy's status as children provides a vessel for adult sexual desires. Hortense J. Spillers argues that Harriet Beecher Stowe constructed Little Eva as a "temptress" who directed "lush sensuality" toward Uncle Tom; this sensuality "stands in" for unruly female sexuality, including white women's desire for black men. Had Stowe written Eva as an adult, this argument suggests, the tender caresses between Eva and Tom would have seemed overtly sexual or romantic; Eva's childhood is therefore an alibi that allows Stowe to disavow cross-racial sexual desire even as she covertly (and perhaps inadvertently) represents it.[3] In contrast, James Kincaid argues after Michel Foucault that the figure of the child does not represent adult sexuality so much as produce it. In Kincaid's view, signs of nineteenth-century children's innocence—repetitious descriptions of cherubic visages and clear, trusting eyes and artless declarations of love—obsessively detail the sexually unthinkable; thus the disavowal of desire actually constructs it.[4] Performing the homoerotic gesture that birthed nothing less than American literature itself, Uncle Remus invites the Little Boy to come back to the cabin again, honey—an essay Leslie Fiedler never wrote.[5]

Such arguments that Little Eva and the Little Boy either reflect or produce eroticism inevitably fall short because they seek sexual content in Stowe's and Harris's prose—and that content is, in truth, sparse. Physical contact, as one important measure of intimacy, provides an illuminative index. In Stowe's text, Little Eva and Uncle Tom touch exactly four times, and then only fleetingly. The first touch occurs in chapter 14, when Tom saves Eva from drowning ("he caught her in his arms").[6] In chapter 16, Eva "sat down on his knee" while "hanging a wreath of roses round his neck."[7] In chapter 18, Eva "catch[es] his hand."[8] And finally, in chapter 26, Tom delights in carrying the dying Eva's "little frail form in his arms."[9] Spillers reads sensuality and "intimate contact" between Tom and Eva especially in the so-called arbor scene of chapter 22; but in fact, Stowe neither describes nor implies any touching between Tom and Eva anywhere in that chapter.[10]

The occasional and limited touches between Eva and Tom contrast with Eva's unrestrained embraces with a nursemaid called Mammy: when Eva returns from her steamboat voyage, she cries out, "O, there's Mammy!" and then "fl[ies] across the room; and, throwing herself into her arms, she kisse[s] her repeatedly." Later, Eva "thr[ows] her arms around" Mammy and "thrust[s]" a diamond-encrusted box "into [Mammy's] bosom, and, kissing her, r[uns] down stairs."[11] On her deathbed, as Eva hands out locks of her hair, she embraces Mammy while keeping Tom physically distanced.

> "Here, Uncle Tom," said Eva, "is a beautiful [lock of hair] for you. O, I am so happy, Uncle Tom, to think I shall see you in heaven,—for I'm sure I shall; and Mammy,—dear, good, kind Mammy!" she said, fondly throwing her arms round her old nurse,—"I know you'll be there, too."[12]

As this representative passage shows, Eva's physical engagement with Tom is chaste in comparison to the unbridled sensuality between Eva and Mammy. Never does Eva throw her arms around Tom or kiss him, much less thrust jewels into his bosom. Yet no scholar has read forbidden eroticism into the Eva/Mammy relationship. Nor should one. Many nineteenth- and twentieth-century readers did respond erotically to *Uncle Tom's Cabin*, as Sigmund Freud and Richard Krafft-Ebing observed; but scholars who dowse for sex in Stowe's prose come up, at best, damp.[13] The submerged spring in the repertoires of *Uncle Tom's Cabin* and Harris's books about Uncle Remus and the Little Boy is not sex but polymorphous sensuality, a relentless focus on white children and African American adults touching each other.[14] These caresses did not simply attest to slaves' Christian humanity (as Stowe may have hoped) or imagine loving relationships between individuals within the system of slavery (as the most sympathetic interpreter might understand Harris's fiction). Rather, as Saidiya V. Hartman, Ann Laura Stoler, Laura Wexler, and others have argued, physical tenderness can function as a necessary component of racial domination and violence.[15] Intimacy does not mitigate subjection, but instead constructs it at the deepest levels.

Uncle Tom's Cabin codified racially powerful touches—some contained within literature, many more extending outward, into cultural repertoires. Hortense Spillers and other readers recall a "lush sensuality" between Eva and Tom that is difficult to find in Stowe's prose, and they forget passionate embraces that Stowe did write between Eva and Mammy. This chapter shows how material culture and performance were crucial to this process of remembering and forgetting. In performances, both onstage and in everyday life, Eva and Tom and their descendants *did* caress each other tenderly, endlessly. By century's end, that embrace became as useful to slavery's apologists as it had once been to abolitionists.

## Touching and Being Touched by Uncle Tom's Cabin

Even before *Uncle Tom's Cabin* was published in book form in 1852, artists and entrepreneurs began to peel the characters out of Stowe's narrative and to install them in visual, material, and theatrical culture. Little Eva, Uncle Tom, and other *Uncle Tom's Cabin* characters adorned hundreds of inexpensive products that appealed to the rising middle class. The characters filled consumers' hands and homes in the form of handkerchiefs, decorative plates that could be collected by the dozen, vases, pitchers, spoons, candlesticks, sheet music, ceramic plaques, needlepoint, scarves, jigsaw puzzles, jars, mugs, and other "Tomitudes."[16] In December 1852, only nine months after Stowe's novel was published in book form, a reviewer proclaimed that *Uncle Tom's Cabin* "is everywhere: drawing room, nursery, kitchen, library."[17]

This suffusion of characters and story lines—beyond the printed text and into the domestic living space—atomized *Uncle Tom's Cabin*, reconfiguring it, in Henry James's words, as "much less a book than a state of vision, of feeling and of consciousness."[18] James called Stowe's creations "wonderful 'leaping' fish," but the characters did not, in fact, have any powers of self-propulsion.[19] Writers transported Little Eva, Uncle Tom, and other characters into new literary sites such as poetry and anti-Tom novels. But the characters also leaped physically via the bodies of consumers, who literally moved the characters when they used Tomitudes. In other words, performances—quotidian practices—involving domestic items such as card games, book illustrations, handkerchiefs, and figurines provided the motions that transformed Stowe's characters into leaping fish. When the characters leaped, via Tomitudes in everyday use, out of the water of Stowe's novel and into the air of mass culture, they transplanted some memories, created others, and forgot a lot. The characters, uncontained in Stowe's abolitionist novel, floated in the popular imaginary—where, by the end of the nineteenth century, they were easy game for proslavery writers such as Joel Chandler Harris. Harris netted Uncle Tom and his juvenile owner and sealed them in Uncle Remus's cabin. There, he set them to the labor of reconfiguring slaveholding as love and enslavement as the innocent embrace of a white child.

Tender touches between Eva and Tom materialized through many of the Tomitudes cluttering the drawing room, nursery, kitchen, and library. In one nineteenth-century metal statuette, for example, Tom inclines toward Eva and encircles her with his arms, while Eva balletically arches her back and reaches toward Tom's face and neck.[20] This statuette depicts an embrace between Tom and Eva, but many other mass-produced goods connect Eva and Tom through the body of the consumer. In these cases, physical tenderness between Eva and Tom materializes not in the Tomitude itself, but through a person's *use* of a Tomitude. For example, an 1852 card game published by V. S. W. Parkhurst "direct[ed]" the consumer to "hold" Little Eva and Uncle Tom, literally to enfold the cards within the hands: the "winner of the game is the one who holds Uncle Tom, Little Eva, and Justice."[21] The individual cards representing Eva and Tom (figure 3.1 and plate 5) contain signs of their inevitable union. Eva sits outside, on a rustic bench, with an open book (presumably a Bible) on a footstool. She looks into the distance in a partial recapitulation of Stowe's "arbor scene," as illustrated by Hammatt Billings in the first American edition of *Uncle Tom's Cabin* (figure 3.2). The influence of Billings on the Parkhurst cards

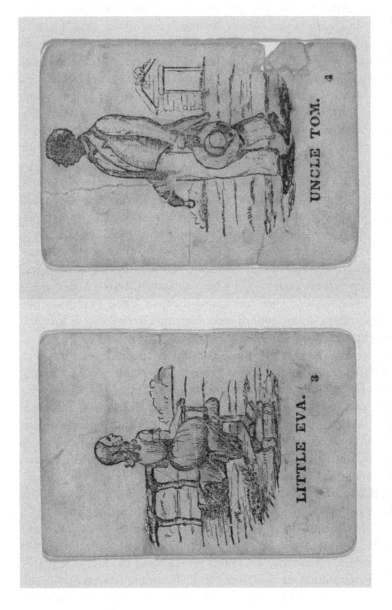

*Figure 3.1.* Playing cards representing Little Eva (left) and Uncle Tom (right). "Game of Uncle Tom and Little Eva," card game, Providence: V. S. W. Parkhurst, 1852. Courtesy of the American Antiquarian Society.

registers in the back of Eva's bench, which is nearly identical in the two images.[22] Another echo appears in the Parkhurst card's image of Uncle Tom, which nearly traces the profile of Billings's Tom in the arbor (the brows and chins of the two Toms are especially striking in their similarity). Also telling is the repetition of Tom's straw hat: Stowe never associated Tom with a hat, but Billings gave Tom a hat in the arbor scene. The straw hat then became standard to representations of Uncle Tom—and a testament to the influence of Billings's arbor scene. The Parkhurst Eva looks into the distance, but in the absence of Tom she appears to look for her companion. Tom's card, in contrast, locates its subject not in the arbor, but in front of a cabin. If players understand that cabin to represent the domicile of the novel's title, then they gaze at Tom before he meets Eva. But he, like Eva, looks into the distance, and the sign of what he seeks appears in his hand: he holds one of the "cunning little baskets" he carves "out of cherry-stones" on the steamboat on which he meets Eva. Tom's card therefore contains a sign of a future event—the meeting of Tom and Eva. Tom is both at his cabin and searching for someone he *will* meet with the assistance of the cunning little basket he *will* carve. Thus the Eva and Tom cards contain signs of each other and of the characters' longing toward each other, and the user seeks to pair the cards in order to win the game. The more the game "is played," an advertisement of October 23, 1852, promised, "the more it is desired."[23] The cards in play thus circulate longing and belonging, enfolding and holding.

Consumer items such as the Parkhurst cards exemplify what Lori Merish calls "sentimental materialism" in that they sutured ownership to sentimental structures of feeling. Through this process, the commodities constructed feelings and cultural norms that were useful to capitalism. Merish persuasively shows how sentimental culture and "feminine consumer 'subjectivity'" co-developed and were mutually dependent.[24] However, Merish's narrative skips the step of scripting. More precisely: commodities structured feelings that emerged from and scripted *identifiable bodily practices*—performances in everyday domestic life—that were useful to a range of systems of power including capitalism. Merish shows that sentimental culture figured crucially in the historical process by which ownership of mass-produced goods became an overwhelmingly important form of personal expression, as well as the shorthand by which people categorized themselves by gender, class, and race. This process occurred, however, not only because one could show what one owned but also because what one owned arranged one's body. In other words, people

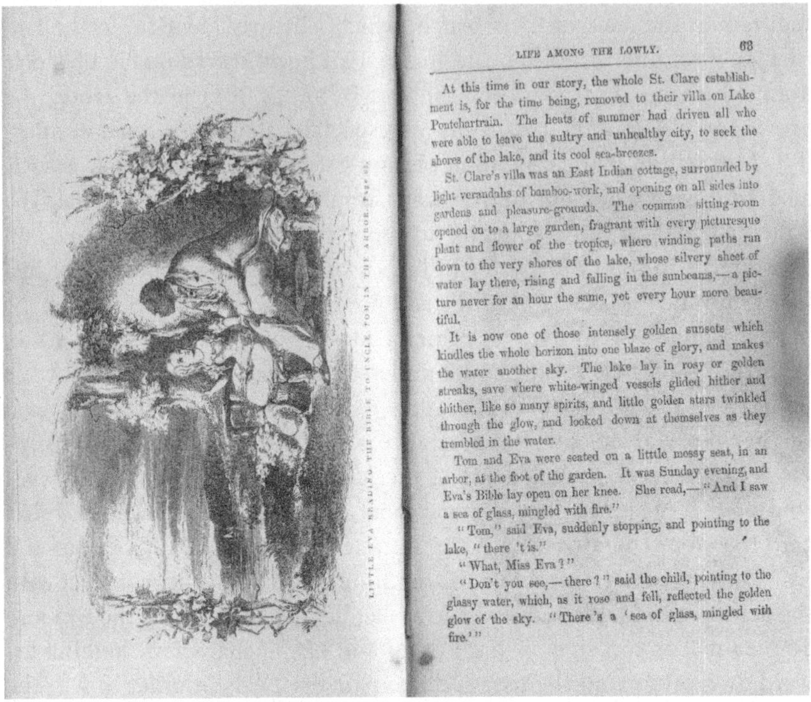

LIFE AMONG THE LOWLY.    63

At this time in our story, the whole St. Clare establishment is, for the time being, removed to their villa on Lake Pontchartrain. The heats of summer had driven all who were able to leave the sultry and unhealthy city, to seek the shores of the lake, and its cool sea-breezes.

St. Clare's villa was an East Indian cottage, surrounded by light verandahs of bamboo-work, and opening on all sides into gardens and pleasure-grounds. The common sitting-room opened on to a large garden, fragrant with every picturesque plant and flower of the tropics, where winding paths run down to the very shores of the lake, whose silvery sheet of water lay there, rising and falling in the sunbeams,—a picture never for an hour the same, yet every hour more beautiful.

It is now one of those intensely golden sunsets which kindles the whole horizon into one blaze of glory, and makes the water another sky. The lake lay in rosy or golden streaks, save where white-winged vessels glided hither and thither, like so many spirits, and little golden stars twinkled through the glow, and looked down at themselves as they trembled in the water.

Tom and Eva were seated on a little mossy seat, in an arbor, at the foot of the garden. It was Sunday evening, and Eva's Bible lay open on her knee. She read,— "And I saw a sea of glass, mingled with fire."

"Tom," said Eva, suddenly stopping, and pointing to the lake, "there 't is."

"What, Miss Eva?"

"Don't you see,—there?" said the child, pointing to the glassy water, which, as it rose and fell, reflected the golden glow of the sky. "There 's a 'sea of glass, mingled with fire.'"

LITTLE EVA READING THE BIBLE TO UNCLE TOM IN THE ARBOR. Page 66.

*Figure 3.2.* "Little Eva Reading the Bible to Uncle Tom in the Arbor. Page 63." Two-page spread containing Hammatt Billings's "arbor scene" as it appeared in the first American edition of Harriet Beecher Stowe's *Uncle Tom's Cabin, or, Life Among the Lowly,* Vol. 2 (Boston: John P. Jewett, 1852). Courtesy of the Beinecke Rare Book and Manuscript Library, Yale University.

chose and displayed the goods that they owned, but goods also framed and displayed the body in ways that did not simply reflect (or resist) the intentions of the things' producers or consumers. Objects of sentimental culture could not self-propel, but scriptive things could instruct the user to move them. Scriptive things such as the Parkhurst cards issued directions for their manipulation, and these movements—when executed compliantly, altered, *or* refused—performed gender, class, and race. Thus sentimental consumer products "moved" in both the motional and the affective sense of the word: the Parkhurst cards posited Tom and Eva as emotionally moving, and they asked the user to move. Tom was touching; Eva was touching; Tom and Eva touched each other; and the player who followed the game's directions touched them touching each other, embraced their embrace literally within the hands.

Performance is crucial to sentimental materialism because the movements involved in using a product can create meanings beyond—and sometimes counter to—those embedded in the images a product contains. Through performance, the Parkhurst cards create an embrace (and, the advertisement promises, ever-increasing desire) that exists in neither the individual cards nor in Stowe's prose. Performance can detach characters from one context and transplant them to another. Henry James made this point vividly, if quixotically, in the words quoted earlier from his 1913 memoir, *A Small Boy and Others*. In this book, which has become a touchstone for Stowe scholars, James recalls his childhood encounter with the novel and dramatization of *Uncle Tom's Cabin*.[25] This passage is worth reconstituting and examining as a block.

> We lived and moved at that time, with great intensity, in Mrs. Stowe's novel. . . . [*Uncle Tom's Cabin* was,] for an immense number of people, much less a book than a state of vision, of feeling and of consciousness, in which they didn't sit and read and appraise and pass the time, but walked and talked and laughed and cried and, in a manner of which Mrs. Stowe was the irresistible cause, generally conducted themselves. . . . Uncle Tom, instead of making even one of the cheap short cuts through the medium in which books breathe, even as fishes in water, went gaily roundabout it altogether, as if a fish, a wonderful "leaping" fish, had simply flown through the air. This feat accomplished, the surprising creature could naturally fly anywhere. . . . If the amount of life represented in such a work is measurable by the ease with which representation is taken up and carried further, carried even violently furthest, the fate of Mrs. Stowe's picture was conclusive: it simply sat down wherever it lighted and made itself, so to speak, at home; thither multitudes flocked afresh and there, in each case, it rose to its height again and went, with all its vivacity and good faith, through all its motions.[26]

Here, James describes two seemingly contrary phenomena. First, he claims that people "lived and moved" in Stowe's novel. "Living" in the novel, James explains, means inhabiting "a state of vision, of feeling and of consciousness." "Moving" in the novel entails a repertoire of bodily actions: walking, talking, laughing, crying, and conducting daily life and manners. The second phenomenon appears to invert the first: James describes not the reader's immersion *in* the novel but rather the extraction *from* the novel of its eponymous character, whom James likens to a "wonderful 'leaping' fish" that can jump out of one environment of water and fly into the unlikely, even impossible environment of air. The fish, having accomplished this first impossibility, can then "fly anywhere."

These apparently oppositional movements—immersion and extraction—were in fact mutually dependent. Extraction occurred when artists and entrepreneurs conducted characters out of Stowe's novel and into the scriptive material culture of everyday life. When iconic images of Stowe's characters leaped into Tomitudes, they also leaped into consumers' physical practices involving those things. Thus the characters, in James's words, flew into the "manner" by which consumers "generally conducted themselves." James's observation that "Mrs. Stowe's picture . . . sat down wherever it lighted and made itself, so to speak, at home" is literally true in that images of Stowe's characters, laminated to the material culture of domesticity, lodged in the home, where they scripted everyday behaviors—thus the "picture" went "through all its motions." As consumers used Tomitudes, the things moved, and the people moved; this repertoire produced a "state of vision, of feeling and of consciousness." The dynamics of extraction and immersion, then, intersected at the site of domestic material culture that scripted performances in everyday life. Eventually, the characters flew from Uncle Tom's cabin into Uncle Remus's cabin, where the wonderful leaping fish "made itself, so to speak, at home."[27] First, however, they leaped into consumers' vision, alighted on consumers' flesh—and burrowed in.

## Impressing the Flesh

Stowe imagined *Uncle Tom's Cabin* in visual terms—a fact that has attracted extensive scholarly attention.[28] Stowe's consistent link between visuality and tactility, however, has escaped notice. In fact, Stowe connected visuality to the author's, characters', and readers' acts of touching, being touched, and trying to touch; thus Stowe merged image (archive) and movement (repertoire). This connection between sight and touch is manifested, for example, in a well-known narrative of the novel's conception. The introduction to the 1878 edition of the novel described Stowe "sitting at the communion-table in the little church in Brunswick" when the death of Uncle Tom "presented itself almost as a tangible vision."[29] The

assignment of the word "tangible" to a vision—a picture that is by definition intangible—is peculiar, and the modifier "almost" marks the gap
between the impulse to touch and the ability to do so. Upon receiving this
nearly palpable vision, Stowe

> was perfectly overcome by it, and could scarcely restrain the convulsion
> of tears and sobbings that shook her frame. She hastened home and wrote
> [the scene in which Uncle Tom dies], and her husband being away she read
> it to her two sons of ten and twelve years of age. The little fellows broke out
> into convulsions of weeping.[30]

In this narrative of the novel's inception, a received vision and the impossible impulse to touch it prompted bodily actions: writing, reading aloud
(in James's term, they "talked"), and weeping (as James put it, "cried").

Stowe consciously aimed to link vision and bodily practices to produce
changes in affect. Stowe articulated her intentions in an 1851 letter to Gamaliel Bailey, editor of the *National Era* newspaper that originally serialized *Uncle Tom's Cabin*. In this letter, Stowe described herself as

> a painter, and my object will be to hold up in the most lifelike and graphic
> manner possible Slavery, its reverses, [and] changes. . . . There is no arguing
> with *pictures*, and everyone is impressed by them, whether they mean to be
> or not.[31]

Scholars often cite this letter as the Rosetta Stone of Stowe's literary strategy
of creating vivid word pictures.[32] The passage, however, actually describes
ekphrasis not as an end but as a means to something else: scripting. Stowe
wanted her readers to engage bodily, affectively, with her novel, and she
posited vivid visual description as a tool by which to achieve that goal.
The bodily performance she names—the action she wants her pictures to
script—is that of being "impressed." Given the centrality of this quotation
to scholars' understanding of Stowe, the word "impression" merits close
examination, especially as the term relates to performance.

"Impression," in both the nineteenth century and today, possesses multiple meanings, two of which reverse each other: an "impression" refers,
on the one hand, to a superficial, generalized notion and, on the other
hand, to an indentation or depression that marks the penetration of a
deep, specific, and lasting influence. This second meaning, which has been
associated with printing since the sixteenth century, likens "impressing"

to stamping another's mind; in this vein, to be "impressed" means to receive that pressure and bear its permanent mark. Throughout *Uncle Tom's Cabin* and *The Key to* Uncle Tom's Cabin, Stowe pointedly exercised the term's denotation of either superficiality or penetration. For example, Marie St. Clare's inability to sympathize—the worst failure for a woman in sentimental culture—manifests in her use of the term's superficial meaning: "Men are constitutionally selfish and inconsiderate to woman," Marie complains. "That, at least, is my impression."[33] In contrast, Stowe twice lauds Tom's "impressible" nature, his plastic receptivity to Christian influence.[34] This valorized, printerly meaning of "impression" is both physical and emotional, as Stowe makes clear through Augustine St. Clare's bitter pun regarding Topsy. "I've seen this child whipped with a poker, knocked down with the shovel or tongs," St. Clare says to Ophelia, "and, seeing that she is used to that style of operation, I think your whippings will have to be pretty energetic, to make much impression."[35] Violence has callused over Topsy's natural impressibility, so Ophelia's whippings fail to mark Topsy's skin or soul.

Stowe told Bailey that she wanted her verbal pictures, her printed text, to press into the souls of her readers, and she wanted readers to respond plastically, to be "impressed by them, whether they mean to be or not." This does not mean that Stowe (or Ophelia) wanted her message's recipient to cede agency and accept her stamp passively. Indeed, Stowe parodies such rote obedience and the superficial appearance of change when Topsy, ordered by Ophelia to confess to a theft, cheerfully obeys by claiming she stole Eva's coral necklace—a crime that she did not commit, and that in fact did not even occur. Ophelia's beatings produce only the superficial impression—the generalized appearance of an effect—in Topsy, but the deep impression, true conversion and transformation, occurs through Eva's loving touch, the laying on of a white child's hands. It is this touch-borne, responsive, bodily, printerly, conversion-producing impression that Stowe called for her readers to experience—a touch that passes not between Eva and Tom, but between Eva and Topsy.

As St. Clare observes, a wound is, under normal circumstances, one kind of an impression. This categorization of wounds as a subset of impressions recalibrates Marianne Noble's important concept of "sentimental wounding." Noble argues that Stowe depicted emotional and physical violence against slaves so as to spark sympathetic pain—"sentimental wounds"—in her readers. Sentimental wounding confuses the boundaries of the individual (producing what Jessica Benjamin calls "intersubjectivity") while exciting an "ecstatic transcendence" in sexual terms. The result, in Noble's view, is readers' experience of sexual (specifically, masochistic) arousal.[36] Noble correctly notes that *Uncle Tom's Cabin*'s erotics lodge not only in the book's content but in the interaction between the content and the techniques of writing as they affect the experience of reading (here, Noble productively departs from Spillers). However, sentimental wounds constitute a subset within the larger category of impressions, and therefore the spectrum of erotic effects that Noble describes is one part of a larger sensual logic that Stowe deployed in the service of abolitionism.

The ultimate impression of slavery is the burn-wound, the brand.[37] Theodore D. Weld's 1839 antislavery tract, *American Slavery As It Is: Testimony of a Thousand Witnesses*, which Stowe claimed in *The Key to* Uncle Tom's Cabin as one of her source texts, included many incendiary descriptions of human branding.[38] Stowe drew this practice into *Uncle Tom's Cabin* through George Harris, whose right hand, branded with the letter "H," marked him as the property of Mr. Harris. By permanently disfiguring the body of George Harris, the brand declared him to be essentially a slave (and not a man who was enslaved) and simultaneously assisted in the practical continuation of that reality by making escape more difficult.

George Harris's branded hand recalls that of Jonathan Walker, a white sea captain who was prosecuted in 1844 for attempting to smuggle slaves to freedom in the Bahamas. After a lengthy pretrial imprisonment, Walker was found guilty and sentenced to a fine, an hour in the pillory, and, in a most unusual punishment, he was branded with the letters "SS"—slave stealer—below the thumb of his right hand. As Stowe surely knew, Walker transformed his wound into an abolitionist symbol by writing his story and disseminating mass-reproduced images of his hand in broadsides, periodicals, and children's books, where the image was often accompanied by John Greenleaf Whittier's ballad, "The Branded Hand" (figure 3.3).[39] On the abolitionist lecture circuit in 1848, Walker told his story, displayed his hand, and hawked souvenirs.[40] Walker's abolitionism, his status as a slave stealer, was literally seared, as text, into his hand, which he then displayed onstage; thus Walker united wounding, impression, and performance (George Harris, too, strategically concealed and then theatrically revealed his branded hand).[41] Stowe wanted her text to sear and scar her readers, to produce an impression that was perhaps less visible than Jonathan Walker's and George Harris's, but that was equally fleshy and permanent.

Stowe's readers confirmed that her text did, indeed, burn into their souls. The singer Jenny Lind wrote to Stowe in 1852, "You must know what

# THE BRANDED HAND.

Walker resided in Florida with his family from 1836 until 1841. He then removed to Massachusetts because he would not bring up his children among the poisonous influences of slavery. While in Florida, the colored people whom he employed were treated as equals in his family, much to the chagrin of the slaveholders of that region. In 1844 he returned to Pensacola in his own vessel. When leaving, seven of the slaves who had in former years been in his employ, and were members of the church with which he communed, begged to go with him. He consented. When out fourteen days, a Southern sloop fell in with and seized them. Prostrated by sickness, he was confined in a dungeon, chained on a damp floor without table, bed or chair. He was in the pillory for an hour, pelted with rotten eggs, branded S. S.—slave stealer—in the palm of his right hand, by Ebenezer Dorr, United States Marshal, fined $150, and imprisoned eleven months.

## THE BRANDED HAND.

### BY JOHN G. WHITTIER.

Welcome home again, brave seaman! with thy thoughtful brow and gray,
And the old heroic spirit of our earlier, better day—
With that front of calm endurance, on whose steady nerve, in vain
Pressed the iron of the prison, smote the fiery shafts of pain!

Is the tyrant's brand upon thee? Did the brutal cravens aim
To make God's truth thy falsehood, His holiest work thy shame?
When, all blood-quenched, from the torture the iron was withdrawn,
How laughed their evil angel the baffled fools to scorn!

*They* change to wrong, the duty which God hath written out
On the great heart of humanity too legible for doubt!
*They,* the loathsome moral lepers, blotched from foot-sole up to crown,
Give to shame what God hath given unto honor and renown!

Why, that brand is highest honor!—than it traces never yet
Upon old armorial hatchments was a prouder blazon set;
And thy unborn generations, as they crowd our rocky strand,
Shall tell with pride the story of their father's BRANDED HAND!

*Figure 3.3.* "The Branded Hand." Poem by John G. Whittier and anonymous woodcut representing the right hand of Jonathan Walker branded "SS" for "slave stealer," ca. 1845. Courtesy of the American Antiquarian Society.

a deep impression *Uncle Tom's Cabin* has made upon every heart that can feel for the dignity of human existence." The earl of Shaftesbury concurred that *Uncle Tom's Cabin* "has absolutely startled the whole world, and impressed many thousands."[42] Proslavery writers also acknowledged, with outrage, Stowe's power to impress her ideas upon readers' minds. The novel "will make [the] impression on the minds of most of its readers," one 1853 reviewer lamented, that slaveholders are "God-forsaken, heaven-daring, hell-deserving barbarians."[43] Stowe's word pictures, these readers confirmed, seared the spirit by provoking the fleshy action of being impressed. Stowe's earliest American publisher and illustrator, John P. Jewett and Hammatt Billings, respectively, soon expanded Stowe's strategy: they co-created physical pictures that choreographed bodily movements. These movements immersed consumers in *Uncle Tom's Cabin*—but not quite the same cabin that Stowe imagined.

## Turning the Page: Hammatt Billings's Scripts

Hammatt Billings's illustrations for Jewett's first edition of *Uncle Tom's Cabin* are usually understood as enormously popular interpretations or representations of Stowe's narrative. In this paradigm, Stowe's novel is the original that Billings adapted. As I will show, however, Billings's images were not objects contained within Stowe's book but were instead scriptive things that traveled beyond the novel into material culture, behaviors in everyday life, and theatrical performances.

Billings created his illustrations as one component of an extraordinary advertising campaign forged by Jewett. Before Jewett published Stowe's novel in book form in March 1852, he was a modestly successful bookseller and publisher whose offerings included Christian texts, readers, fiction, and some abolitionist works. As Claire Parfait notes, Jewett announced his publishing agreement with Stowe in the *National Era* on September 18, 1851, when barely a third of Stowe's novel had been serialized. Jewett therefore ventured significant capital on a product that did not yet fully exist (and which another publisher had refused, deeming a first novel by a woman on a polarizing subject to be "too risky").[44] As Stowe wrote more, Jewett's risk increased: the ever-lengthening story spilled into an expensive two-volume format—a tougher sale.[45]

Jewett's faith in the profitability of Stowe's novel (and, he later claimed, his abolitionist politics) motivated his brinkmanship. He published, by

Parfait's count, 310,000 copies of *Uncle Tom's Cabin,* in three different editions, from 1852 to 1853. The fact that he never republished after 1853, however, suggests that the inventory did not sell immediately.[46] Earlier publishing histories, most notably that of Thomas F. Gossett, envisioned consumers mobbing to buy *Uncle Tom's Cabin*; in this scenario, the novel itself generated excitement that motivated sales.[47] Examination of Jewett's enormous effort to move his inventory, however, reveals a story not of a spontaneously popular novel, but instead of a publisher who, in his feverish marketing of his product, used visual and material culture to script consumers' everyday practices. This combination enabled Jewett eventually to sell over 300,000 books, but in that process, it fundamentally altered the ontology of *Uncle Tom's Cabin.*

Jewett's advertising campaign was daringly expensive: Jewett placed a variety of editorials, brief notices, and partial- and full-page advertisements in northern newspapers, including the *National Era, Norton's Literary Gazette and Publisher's Circular,* the *Independent* (New York), the *Olive Branch* (Boston), and the *Literary World.* "Before a single copy of the book had been bound," Jewett wrote, "I had expended thousands of dollars for advertising—an enormous sum in those days to be spent in advertising a single book."[48] Because of these expenses, Jewett wrote, his associates considered his publicity campaign "insane."[49]

As part of this effort to stimulate desire for Stowe's book, Jewett contacted Hammatt Billings, a Boston-based illustrator who in 1850 had designed the third masthead for William Lloyd Garrison's abolitionist newspaper, the *Liberator.* Jewett commissioned Billings to create six full-page woodcuts, plus images for the cover and title page of the first U.S. edition of *Uncle Tom's Cabin.*[50] These illustrations figured immediately and prominently in Jewett's advertising frenzy. As early as March 4, 1852, Jewett's advertisements promoted the novel's inclusion of "six elegant designs by Billings"; and by late 1852, Jewett began inserting Billings's illustrations within print advertisements (figure 3.4).[51] Thus Billings's illustrations predated the book form (although not the newspaper serialization) of Stowe's novel. And from their inception, Billings's illustrations coordinated as much with Jewett's publicity as they did with Stowe's bound book.

This advertisement, like the handkerchief analyzed in the Introduction, features Billings's "arbor scene" in which Tom and Eva read the Bible by the shore of Lake Pontchartrain. Billings's biographer, James F. O'Gorman, calls the arbor scene "without doubt the most important

*Figure 3.4.* "An Edition for the Million." Hammatt Billings's image of Little Eva and Uncle Tom in the arbor, as contained in John P. Jewett's advertisement for Stowe's novel. *Norton's Literary Gazette* 2, no. 12 (1852): 248. Courtesy of the American Antiquarian Society.

image of the first edition," because it "was repeated over and over again for framing prints, sheet music covers, and other ephemera" (including, most likely, the Parkhurst cards) and because it influenced other artists including Robert Stuart Duncanson, Miguel Covarrubias, F. L. Jones, and George Cruikshank, all of whom subsequently singled out the same scene for illustration.[52] Even more significantly, however, the arbor scene scripted everyday behaviors when it materialized in things such as handkerchiefs and playing cards (as I have argued) and books (as I will argue). And perhaps most significantly of all, Billings's illustrations, especially the arbor scene, structured theatrical performances of *Uncle Tom's Cabin*—performances that played throughout the United States and Europe, and that eventually defined memories of the characters for Henry James and so many others.

Billings's arbor scene (figure 3.2) seats Tom and Eva side by side, with the Bible open on Eva's lap. Tom's hands rest on his own right knee, and Eva nestles her left hand between Tom's hands—a tender touch that Billings invented without any hint from Stowe. Eva points diagonally to her right, illustrating either of two moments in the chapter in which Eva points. In the first instance, Eva reads in Revelation 15.2 of a "sea of glass, mingled with fire," and exclaims, "*pointing* to the lake, 'there 'tis.'"[53] In the second instance, which appears a page later, Eva and Tom sing a "wellknown Methodist hymn" describing angels "robed in spotless white" that will "convey me home / To the new Jerusalem." After singing, Eva "*pointed* her little hand to the sky. . . . 'I'm going *there*,' she said, 'to the spirits bright, Tom; I'm *going, before long.*'"[54] Eva's two circumstances of pointing appear in rapid succession, but they are distinct: in the first, she points horizontally toward the lake; in the second, she points vertically toward the sky. Billings's Eva bends her elbow 45 degrees, midway between vertical and horizontal axes. This angle enables Billings's illustration to contain two of Stowe's textual moments simultaneously. This ability to flicker between two meanings extends to the actions that the illustration, in the context of Stowe's first edition, scripted for the reader.

Billings's illustration of Tom and Eva in the arbor appears sideways; to view the image properly, the reader necessarily passes through an ordered series of steps. First, the reader must realize that something is wrong with the image. Next, the reader must stop reading Stowe's prose and rotate the book (or the head and neck) 90 degrees. Regardless of how quickly or automatically the reader performs the action, the reader must first perceive that sideways image. Indeed, the sideways image crucially instructs the reader to manipulate the book; if the reader does not competently perceive the sideways image's script, the reader will fail to execute the necessary movement, and the "proper" image will never appear. The reader, in other words, encounters one image (the sideways one) and that image prompts the reader physically to coproduce a second image (the "proper" one). This scripted process causes Billings's illustration to function not as one image, but as two images in sequence. The reader first encounters the sideways image, which says to the reader, "Something is wrong. You must fix the problem." The competent reader comprehends the message and responds with the determined action of turning the book or the head.[55]

But exactly what problem manifests in the sideways image?

As the image appears in the novel, Tom hovers above Eva, looking down upon her. Eva gazes up at Tom. A fire appears to blaze beneath them. The image is lopsided, unbalanced: the characters could tumble into the fire. Tom and Eva's missionary position suggests both sexual contact and a reordering of racial hierarchy to place an African American "on top." The initial image thus enfolds within it racist anxiety about not only interracial sexual contact, but also the relative political positions of black and white.

The reader terminates the instability by turning the book. The reader topples Tom from the superior position and slides Eva out from beneath him; the reader empties the scene of sexuality by uncoupling the characters and repositioning them side-by-side. Tom's profiled face, which had gazed down upon Eva, becomes, in the "proper" image, an echo of familiar phrenological drawings that argued for Africans' biological inferiority (figure 3.5). The process of turning the page literalizes the "mingl[ing]" of a "sea of glass" and fire: what looked like hellish fire from below becomes, after the rotation, a heavenly sunset, the "spirits bright" to which Eva will travel. Meanwhile, the reader's movements cause Eva and Tom to retreat from the implication of sexual mingling. Each character, lopsided and unbalanced before, emerges as a near-equilateral triangle—the image of stability. The reader's act of turning the page, then, extinguishes the image's unsettled and potentially unsettling elements, replacing them with a restabilized affirmation of racial hierarchy.[56]

That stability does not last, however. The reader cannot maintain the "proper" image, because when the book turns 90 degrees, Stowe's text dissolves into illegible, vertical lines. To continue reading the novel, the reader necessarily resurrects the sexually suggestive, racially subversive sideways image. Thus the sequence of two frames becomes one of three

## V. NEGRO.

*Figure 3.5.* "Negro." Phrenological drawing from "Tableau to accompany Prof. Agassiz's 'Sketch.'" J[osiah] C[lark] Nott and Geo[rge] R[obins] Gliddon, *Types of Mankind; or, Ethnological Researches, Based upon the Ancient Monuments, Paintings, Sculptures, and Crania of the Races, and upon their Natural, Geological, Philological, and Biblical History,* illustrated by selections from the Inedited [*sic*] Papers of Samuel George Morton, M.D. (Philadelphia: Lippincott, Grambo, 1854), n.p. Courtesy of Harvard College Library, Widener Library, An358.54.

frames: sideways, upright, sideways again. The reader's actions, as scripted by Billings's illustration within Stowe's book, create this protofilmic narrative. Some scholars perceive pedophilic "intimate contact" between Eva and Tom in the arbor; but the mingling, the physical intimacy—sexual or otherwise—in fact emerges not from Stowe's prose or even from Billings's straightforward illustration, but from the *blur* that the *reader* creates through bodily interaction with the material book.[57]

Soon after Jewett published the first edition with Billings's six illustrations,

## CHAPTER XXII.

### "THE GRASS WITHERETH — THE FLOWER FADETH."

IFE passes, with us all, a day at a time; so it passed with our friend Tom, till two years were gone. Though parted from all his soul held dear, and though often yearning for what lay beyond, still was he never positively and consciously miserable; for so well is the harp of human feeling strung, that nothing but a crash that breaks every string can wholly mar its harmony; and, on looking back to seasons which in review appear to us as those of deprivation and trial, we can remember that each hour, as it glided, brought its diversions and alleviations, so that, though not happy wholly, we were not, either, wholly miserable.

Tom read, in his only literary cabinet, of one who had 'learned in whatsoever state he was, therewith to be con-

*Figure 3.6.* Hammatt Billings's second "arbor scene" as it appeared in Harriet Beecher Stowe, *Uncle Tom's Cabin; or, Life Among the Lowly. Illustrated Edition, Complete in One Volume, Original Designs by Billings; Engraved by Baker and Smith* (Boston: John P. Jewett, 1853 [1852]), 324. Courtesy of the Beinecke Rare Book and Manuscript Library, Yale University.

he commissioned Billings to create a second set of woodcuts for a more lavishly illustrated volume to sell for the Christmas season of 1852.[58] Billings responded with 117 images, plus a decorative letter to head each chapter. This volume (the "Illustrated Edition") reprinted none of Billings's images from the first edition, and in the new illustrations, Billings closely retained the composition of only one earlier image—that of Uncle Tom and Little Eva in the arbor (figure 3.6).

Billings's two arbor scenes are similar as two-dimensional pictures (although several scholars have noted that Billings's first Eva appears more physically mature and have argued that the second Eva's more childlike body submerges the possibility of sexual contact between Eva and Tom).[59] The two arbor scenes are very different, however, as things that script actions. The so-called Illustrated Edition (as opposed to the earlier edition, which was also illustrated) includes no full-page illustrations or sideways images. Whereas Billings's first arbor scene requires a swivel that disrupted Stowe's text, the second arbor scene is integrated within the chapter (indeed, the chapter's first, illuminated, letter merges illustration and text). The Illustrated Edition requires no rotation; the reader negotiates no protofilmic sequence of images that disrupts, then reinforces, and then redisrupts existing racial hierarchies. Instead, in Billings's Illustrated Edition, Eva and Tom pose statically, frozen forever as a sexual innocent and a phrenological diagram, respectively. Thus the Illustrated Edition conserves that which the first edition disturbs. The sideways illustration in the first American edition scripts a rotation that ruptures the narrative and potentially provokes a proto-Brechtian moment of consciousness of the self reading. In the Illustrated Edition, in contrast, pictures and text flow together, thus eliminating the need for rotation and facilitating a fully absorptive state in which a reader might forget the self that was reading—the self that existed in a world in which some humans legally owned others. Thus the Illustrated Edition, in its historical context, scripted a politically potent forgetting, a performance of racial innocence.

### "A play and to play were the same": How Billings's Scripts Traveled to the Stage

The material culture of *Uncle Tom's Cabin*—illustrated editions of Stowe's novel, handkerchiefs, playing cards, print advertisements, and countless knickknacks—arranged human bodies, recruiting consumers into acts of holding character cards, rotating pages, and weeping and drying tears. These home-based activities, scaled to the human hands and face, seem unconnected or even opposed to the public, sweepingly large tradition of the Tom shows, or staged performances of *Uncle Tom's Cabin*, which thundered through popular culture in the fall and winter of 1852 and which remained continuously on the boards, staged simultaneously by as many as five hundred Tom companies, until the 1930s.[60] In fact, however, material culture functioned as a *corpus callosum* that connected the home and the theater, allowing the spheres' mirrored differences to coordinate. Tom shows configured touching between Little Eva and Uncle Tom and then circulated that desirous impulse, as the following section shows, through Tomitudes, celebrity culture, and practices of audienceship. Acts of touching and desires to touch connected the parlor and the stage, thus domesticating the theater and theatricalizing the home.

A few scattered stagings of *Uncle Tom's Cabin* appeared as early as January 1852, but each of these closed after only a few nights.[61] The first Tom show to gain and retain traction in popular culture was that of the Howard family troupe, which opened in Troy, New York, on September 27, 1852. The play ran for one hundred performances before closing on December 1 of the same year.[62] After that, the Howards played in Albany before moving to Purdy's National Theatre in New York on July 18, 1853, where the play received critical acclaim and popular devotion.[63] The Howards performed *Uncle Tom's Cabin* for over thirty years, well into the postbellum era, and their production deeply and extensively influenced the hundreds of other Tom shows for close to a century. Many images from these Tom shows ultimately eclipsed Stowe's novel, replacing Stowe's characters with their theatrical counterparts in the popular imagination (the superannuated Uncle Tom of cultural memory, for example, traces his gray hairs more to stage wigs than to Stowe's picture of a "broad-chested, powerfully-made man" with young children).[64]

The Howard family produced *Uncle Tom's Cabin* less out of a commitment to abolitionist politics than out of desire to turn the troupe's junior member, four-year-old Cordelia Howard, into a star. According to theatrical lore, actor-manager George C. Howard discovered his daughter's histrionic gift in 1852 when the family produced *Oliver Twist*.[65] Unable to find a child to play Little Dick, Howard cast his toddling daughter in the role. Caroline Fox Howard, Cordelia's mother, whitened the girl's face to make her appear consumptive, taught her the minimal lines, plopped her onstage, and hoped for the best. Cordelia was to poke a spade into a pile of dirt (to signify the digging of a grave) and to exchange a few simple words with Oliver. The girl, however, reportedly became carried away with the emotion of the scene and improvised:

> "I'll come back and see you some day, Dick," said Mrs. Howard as Oliver.
> "It yont be no use, Olly, dear," sobbed the little actress. "When oo tum back, I yont be digging 'ittle graves, I'll be all dead an' in a 'ittle grave by myself."[66]

With this, Cordelia Howard reportedly burst into tears, and her father recognized talent—and better yet, financial opportunity. George C. Howard began searching for a script that would highlight his daughter's abilities at the very moment in 1852 when Jewett energetically infused U.S. popular culture with images of *Uncle Tom's Cabin,* particularly Billings's arbor scene. When Howard chose *Uncle Tom's Cabin* as his daughter's chariot to fame, he surely thought the character of Little Eva would showcase the lachrymal abilities that Cordelia had demonstrated in *Oliver Twist.* Even more significantly, however, *Uncle Tom's Cabin* was a sound financial bet because it benefited parasitically from Jewett's marketing campaign: Jewett's circulation of images from Stowe's novel translated into free publicity for any Tom play. George C. Howard commissioned his wife's cousin, an actor named George L. Aiken, to develop a Tom script that emphasized Little Eva. Aiken responded in less than a week with a script that lifted much of its dialogue directly from Stowe.

Members of the Howard family seem to have held moderate antislavery views that were unremarkable for New Englanders of the 1850s. In 1928 when Cordelia Howard MacDonald (her married name) penned a brief memoir, she subsumed politics to economics in her claim that "aside from believing that it [the dramatization of *Uncle Tom's Cabin*] would be a financial success, his [George C. Howard's] warm sympathies were enlisted in the Anti-Slavery Cause, and he felt that the play would be as powerful as the novel in forwarding the movement."[67] Aiken reflected these ordered commitments to cash and politics in a script that contained political ambiguities and contradictions. On the one hand, as Eric Lott and David Grimstead have noted, Aiken's versions of Stowe's black characters exaggerated their comedic aspects and diminished their agency.[68] And Bruce A. McConachie has influentially argued that Aiken masculinized Stowe's story by eliminating, minimizing, or burlesquing many of her women characters; thus Aiken disrupted Stowe's abolitionist address to women.[69] On the other hand, as Bluford Adams and Lott have made clear, a competing dramatization of *Uncle Tom's Cabin* by H. J. Conway cast itself as the "compromise" script in contrast to the supposed pro-Negro and anti-South aspects of the Aiken-Howard production.[70] P. T. Barnum, who staged Conway's dramatization at the American Museum in New York while the Howards played at the National Theatre in the same city, boasted that his production, unlike that of the Howards, did "not foolishly and unjustly elevate the negro above the white man in intellect or morals."[71]

These political contradictions within Aiken's script did not make the show appear incoherent because the Howard-Aiken production aimed more to produce fame and wealth for a girl and her family than to end slavery. In other words, the drama existed to produce, manage, and profit from desire circulating through Cordelia Howard. The nineteenth-century innocent child possessed unique abilities to manage memory and forgetting, to bear flickering meanings. Racial innocence flared when contradictory racial meanings coursed through the body of Cordelia Howard to ignite impulses toward sensual touch—impulses that made ideological content, unitary or not, seem natural, innocuous, or merely beside the point. The Howard-Aiken *Uncle Tom's Cabin* produced this effect in three ways: by incorporating key aspects of Billings's illustrations; by focusing audiences' desires on Cordelia Howard; and by circulating material culture, including Staffordshire figurines, that enabled audience members to take miniatures of Cordelia, and all the meanings she performed, home with them.

Many scholars have noted that Aiken's script took much of its dialogue directly from the archive of Stowe's novel. What has gone unnoticed, however, is the quotation of Billings's illustrations—and the performances they scripted—in both the Howard troupe's advertising and in Aiken's script. For example, an October 1859 broadside advertising the Howard family's production at the Pine Street Theatre in Providence, Rhode Island (figure 3.7), roughly copied Billings's illustration of George and Eliza kneeling, with baby Harry, in thanksgiving for their freedom (figure 3.8). On the simplest level, the repetition demonstrates that the Howards were aware of Billings and that they thought advertisements incorporating his images would sell theater tickets. More subtly, the Howards' use of Billings drew the dramatization of *Uncle Tom's Cabin* into the circulation of desire that Stowe, Jewett, and Billings had already set into motion. Henry James might say that when Jewett disseminated the Billings images in the form of advertising, he extracted Stowe's characters from the novel and

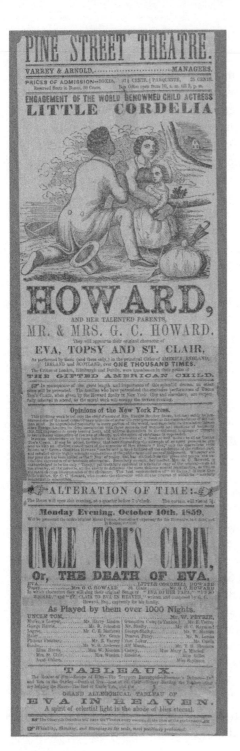

*Figure 3.7.* "Engagement of the World Renowned Child Actress Little Cordelia Howard, and her Talented Parents, Mr. & Mrs. G. C. Howard." Broadside advertisement for the Howard family production of *Uncle Tom's Cabin* at the Pine Street Theatre in Providence, Rhode Island, 10 October 1859. Courtesy of the Harvard Theatre Collection, Houghton Library, Harvard University.

*Figure 3.8.* "The Fugitives Are Safe in a Free Land." Hammatt Billings's illustration of (left to right) Harry, Eliza, and George Harris and Mrs. Smyth. From chapter 37 of the first edition of *Uncle Tom's Cabin,* Vol. 2 (Boston: John P. Jewett, 1852). Courtesy of the American Antiquarian Society.

transformed them into wonderful leaping fish. The Howards participated in and extended this process.

In this broadside (figure 3.7), an anonymous (and less talented) artist has copied Billings's composition but reversed the orientation and eliminated the figure of Mrs. Smyth (who has disappeared from popular memory, as have many of Stowe's characters who did not circulate visually). Billings represented George Harris's skin as slightly darker that that of his wife and child, but the broadside's artist exaggerated that difference. The advertisement trumpets the "world renowned child actress" Cordelia Howard as the play's primary draw, and the image appears between the girl's first and last names. This layout, combined with the exaggerated difference in skin tone, enables the illustration to represent simultaneously the Harris family and "Little Cordelia Howard"—that is, the actress in character as Little Eva, with Uncle Tom kneeling before her in worshipful servitude.[72] Thus the image produces contradictory meanings: happy freedom *and* happy slavery, an African American man kneeling before his son in gratitude to God *and* kneeling in submissive devotion to a slaveholding white girl.

Billings also influenced the script for the show the broadside advertised. Stowe's novel occupies forty-five chapters and hundreds of pages, and includes dozens of characters; each Tom show necessarily edited the story to make it stageable. Aiken, like every other Tom playwright, excised far more of Stowe's scenes and characters than he retained. Aiken's choices now seem inevitable (how could an adaptor not include Little Eva?), but at the time, they were not. The necessity of Eva was not self-evident to C. W. Taylor, whose 1852 Tom show omitted Eva, Topsy, and Ophelia.[73] Aiken, unlike Taylor, selected scenes and characters according to a unique principle: he used the sequence of Billings's images as a skeleton upon which to drape Stowe's prose. Aiken included only a small fraction of Stowe's material, but he pointedly staged all six of Billings's first-edition illustrations. The correspondence between the first set of Billings images and the Aiken script is one hundred percent, and there is no noticeable correspondence between the Aiken script and Billings's second set of images, that included in the Illustrated Edition, which was published after Aiken completed his script.

Aiken often used Billings's images to open and close scenes: for example, Act III, Scene 2 opens with a tableau of Billings's arbor scene—the same scene that Jewett impressed upon print advertisements and handkerchiefs:

> *The flat represents the lake. The rays of the setting sun tinge the waters with gold.—A large tree.—Beneath this is a grassy bank, on which* EVA *and* TOM *are seated side by side.—Eva has a Bible open on her lap.*[74]

Other Billings images close scenes, as in Act II, Scene 6, which ends with a restaging of the illustration that the Howards used in their broadsides (figures 3.7, 3.8): "GEORGE *and* ELIZA *kneel in an attitude of thanksgiving, with the* CHILD *between them. . . . Tableau.*"[75] Tableaux, by definition, use living bodies to stage works of visual art. In this case, the tableau of George, Eliza, and Harry simultaneously staged Billings's illustration and the Howards' own advertising; thus the performance connected theater to material culture (book and advertisements) seen and handled in daily life. As these extracted images circulated from book to periodical advertising to broadsides to handkerchiefs to the stage, they immersed consumers in *Uncle Tom's Cabin,* producing a stream of consciousness in which the meaning of slavery flowed always back and through a child's embrace.

Aiken beaded the full sequence of Billings's six images through his

TABLE 3.1

| Billings's illustrations as they appear in Stowe's novel, *Uncle Tom's Cabin* | Corresponding stage directions in Aiken's script for the play, *Uncle Tom's Cabin* |
| --- | --- |
| Chapter 5: "Eliza comes to tell Uncle Tom that he is sold, and that she is running away to save her child" (Stowe, 33). Billings depicts Eliza with Harry in her arms, Chloe in a white nightcap, and Tom holding a candle. | Act 1, scene 3: "UNCLE TOM'S *Cabin.* . . . *Enter* ELIZA *hastily, with* HARRY *in her arms.* . . . AUNT CHLOE *appears at window with a large white night-cap on.* . . . *The door opens and* CHLOE *enters, followed by* UNCLE TOM *in his shirt sleeves, holding a tallow candle*" (Aiken, 380). |
| Chapter 12: "The Auction Sale" (Stowe, 104). | Act 5, scene 1: "*An Auction Mart*" (Aiken, 420) |
| Chapter 17: "The Freeman's Defence" (Stowe, 171). Billings depicts George Harris on a rock, pistol drawn at Tom Loker and others. | Act 2, scene 6: "*A Rocky Pass in the Hills.—Large set rock and platform.* . . . LOKER *dashes up the rock.—*GEORGE *fires.—He staggers for a moment, then springs to the top*" (Aiken, 403, 405). |
| Chapter 34: "Cassy ministering to Uncle Tom after his whipping" (Stowe, 311). Billings depicts Cassy kneeling by Tom's side with a cup in her hand. | Act 6, scene 1: "TOM *is discovered in shed, lying on some old cotton bagging.* CASSY *kneels by his side, holding a cup to his lips*" (Aiken, 433). |

script. In addition to the two correspondences described above, the remaining four are shown in table 3.1.

All six of Billings's original illustrations appear in Aiken's script, but one of the six—the arbor scene—influenced the script beyond the corresponding tableau. Stowe wrote a few, fleeting touches between Eva and Tom; and Billings created an arbor scene that invented more touching between the characters—touch that complicated as the reader rotated the scene in Stowe's book. Aiken, charged by George Howard with stimulating public desire for Cordelia, scripted lengthy, rapturous cuddling between the white child actress and a white, blacked up, adult actor. These caresses, which Aiken's script specifies in almost every scene that includes both Eva and Tom, expand upon Billings to revise Stowe aggressively and alter her politics. For example, Aiken's second act opens with Eva and her father, Augustine St. Clare, returning to their plantation after a trip during which St. Clare purchased Uncle Tom. In Stowe's iteration of this scene of reunion, Eva kisses Mammy. Aiken, however, reassigns the embrace to Uncle Tom (see table 3.2).

By substituting Uncle Tom for Mammy, Aiken supplies an easy answer to Ophelia's question, "how can she [kiss a 'nigger']?" In Stowe's text, St. Clare does not answer Ophelia's question but instead responds with another question, and then laughs and touches Mammy and the other slaves. The question hangs nervously unanswered, calling attention

TABLE 3.2

| Stowe's novel *Uncle Tom's Cabin* | Aiken's script for the play *Uncle Tom's Cabin* |
|---|---|
| "O, there's Mammy!" said Eva, as she flew across the room; and, throwing herself into her arms, she kissed her repeatedly. | EVA: Uncle Tom! (*Runs to him. He lifts her in his arms. She kisses him.*) |
| This woman did not tell her that she made her head ache, but, on the contrary, she hugged her . . . and when released from her, Eva flew from one to another, shaking hands and kissing. . . . | TOM: The dear soul! |
| | OPHELIA (*Astonished*): How shiftless! |
| "Well!" said Miss Ophelia, "you southern children can do something that *I* couldn't! . . . Well, I want to be kind to everybody, and I wouldn't have anything hurt; but as to kissing—" | ST. CLARE (*Overhearing her*): What's the matter now, pray? |
| | OPHELIA: Well, I want to be kind to everybody, and I wouldn't have anything hurt, but as to kissing— |
| "Niggers," said St. Clare, "that you're not up to,—hey?" | ST. CLARE: Niggers! that you're not up to, hey? |
| "Yes, that's it. How can she?" | |
| St. Clare laughed, as he went into the passage. "Hulloa, here, what's to pay out there? Here, you all—Mammy, Jimmy, Polly, Sukey— glad to see Mas'r?" he said, as he went shaking hands from one to another.[a] | OPHELIA: Yes, that's it—how can she? |
| | ST. CLARE: Oh! bless you, it's nothing when you are used to it![b] |

SOURCE: [a]Harriet Beecher Stowe, *Uncle Tom's Cabin* (1852), Norton Critical Edition, ed. Elizabeth Ammons (New York: W. W. Norton, 1994), 143.
[b] George Aiken, *Uncle Tom's Cabin* (1852), in *Early American Drama*, ed. Jeffrey H. Richards (New York: Penguin, 1997), 388.

to St. Clare's unwillingness to confront his role in the system of slavery. In contrast, Aiken's St. Clare shrugs off the question by declaring kissing "nothing." Thus Aiken's script smoothed over Stowe's ironies and pointed critiques.

The reassignment of Eva's embrace from Mammy to Tom occasioned a sight never before seen on the U.S. stage: that of a white girl cuddling lovingly with a blacked-up white actor. Sentimental culture defined the white child as inherently innocent, and that aura of innocence extended, by propinquity, to whatever she touched. Therefore, the blackfaced adult actor, the character he performed, and the onstage embrace between girl and man and between the characters of Eva and Tom all became innocent. The appeal of this innocence helped the Howards transform Cordelia into a celebrity: "Never was greater concentration of childish simplicity and transparent innocence presented on the stage," gushed one reviewer of Cordelia Howard's performance.[76]

The Howards deployed innocence to plug their daughter into the culture of celebrity that coalesced in the mid-nineteenth century.[77] Although

Cordelia Howard's name is largely forgotten today, it is impossible to overstate the extent of her fame, which far outlasted her stage career. Later acknowledged as a forerunner to Shirley Temple, Cordelia Howard was then celebrated as "the life and soul" of Little Eva. Abraham Lincoln reportedly applauded her.[78] When the little girl walked down the street, large crowds gathered and followed her; she was recognized in public so frequently that she amused her family by commenting, "I wish I wasn't celebrated."[79] A reviewer for the *Liberator*—the very abolitionist newspaper for which Billings designed a masthead—wrote of the actress, "No one can see her without loving her, and feeling that his nature is improved after witnessing her perform."[80] Cordelia Howard exited the stage for the last time in 1870, but until her death in 1941, the public never lost interest in the most mundane aspects of her life. Well into the twentieth century, when Cordelia Howard MacDonald was in her seventies, eighties, and nineties, her birthday or an outing with her niece warranted newspaper coverage.[81] Obituaries published upon Howard MacDonald's death in 1941 were bountiful, but even before that year, some newspapers were hungry enough for stories about Howard MacDonald that they published articles announcing that the actress had *not yet* died: "First Little Eva Still Lives in Boston," declared the Boston *Sunday Globe* on what must have been a particularly slow news day in 1933.[82]

Cordelia Howard's celebrity rested upon her ability to move her audience in both the affective and the motional sense. The famous actor Edwin Forrest and the poet and literary critic William Cullen Bryan reportedly "we[pt] like children" at her performances.[83] Even Harriet Beecher Stowe, whose religious beliefs caused her to oppose all theater regardless of content, quietly attended one of Cordelia's performances in 1853, and was said to have been "moved to tears."[84] Adolphus M. Hart, a newspaperman, reported the frequent sight of "some demure looking gentleman" who "drew out his white pocket handkerchief"—perhaps even a Jewett handkerchief?—"and applied it to his eyes, as the black apostle of liberty, Uncle Tom, was reading the Bible, or Little Cordelia Howard was suffering perhaps her hundredth martyrdom."[85]

Cordelia Howard was a linchpin in a cycle of performances of desire. Aiken took the image that Billings and Jewett had embedded in a paper-based scriptive thing—the arbor scene on the page—and transformed it into a play script. But it was Cordelia Howard and G. C. Germon (the blackfaced actor who first played Uncle Tom) who fully peeled the paper away from the characters. Surrogated by Howard and Germon, Little Eva and Uncle Tom flew into the realm of pure flesh and motion. Germon did not, however, become a locus of desire on- or offstage (he died in 1854, and none of the subsequent actors who played Tom opposite Cordelia's Eva achieved any special fame). Audiences lavished their attention and adoration exclusively on Cordelia Howard, the wonderful *petite* who "vibrates to the innermost heart, and melts the *hardest adamantine* into a state of unwonted liquidity."[86] At curtain call, audiences threw dense, lace-edged bouquets—some strung with tiny gold rings—to the girl.[87] These sensual gifts addressed the child's hands and face: rings encircled her fingers; lacy bouquets invited contact with her nose and cheeks. These were gifts of touch—part of a larger impulse to caress Cordelia Howard, to be physically close to her. More than half a century after witnessing the little girl's performance, one spectator named Arden Seymour still felt compelled to share his bodily responses to the child.

> Cordelia was simply blindly worshipped by the boys who jammed the pit at the Chatham, and not to be one of the large "guard" which nightly escorted her to and from the temple of Thespis was to be outside the pale of the boyish four hundred of that day in lower New York; while to be one of her select "gang" that walked nearest to her sacred person, carried her umbrella when it rained . . . and even to speak to her and learn from her coral lips her wants and wishes, was for a boy to be as distinguished among his fellows . . . while, greatest of all, is to be admitted at the heels of our divinity, to the mystic realm of the stage, as I often was, and there, with blackened face, to mingle with the band of slaves which gathered about the dying Eva.[88]

Blackface, in Seymour's memory, functioned as an extension of physical longing. Seymour and boys like him "blindly worshipped" the child and competed to "walk nearest to her sacred person" and to catch the "wishes" of her "coral lips." However, the "greatest" way to get physically close to Cordelia Howard, the most intensely intimate experience to which a fan could aspire, was to cork up and join her onstage as a supernumerary. Blackface, for Seymour, was a performance of desire for Cordelia Howard—one that, like the Jewett handkerchief, enabled a material "mingl[ing]" with the beloved.

The language that reviewers and fans used to describe Cordelia Howard was undeniably sexual, but an understandable rush to identify and condemn pedophilia can obscure the fact that sexual desire functioned, in this case, not as its own end but as an aspect of a larger system of child-centered sensuality that used innocence, as invested in the bodies of white children, to imagine slavery as a form of love. Cordelia Howard's performance, and her parents' framing of that performance in star-making publicity, melded a slave's imagined love for a child owner with an audience member's love for a child actress at the precise moment when celebrity worship gained traction in U.S. culture. The Howards' broadside (figure 3.7) simultaneously depicts George Harris thanking God for freedom and Uncle Tom "worship[ing]" Eva in the arbor—but it also encloses its image within Cordelia Howard's name, and thus represents an actor in blackface as Uncle Tom, reaching toward the child actress.[89] If Arden Seymour (or one of his four hundred competitors for Cordelia Howard's affections) viewed this broadside, perhaps he saw neither the Harris family thanking God for freedom nor Uncle Tom slavishly worshiping Eva, but himself, Arden, a boy from the streets of lower New York, blacked up to "blindly worship" Cordelia Howard in the "temple of Thespis." The Howards doubled audiences' love for "Little Cordelia" upon Uncle Tom's love for Little Eva. Both in the use of supernumeraries and in their publicity, the Howards invited white audiences to mingle their perspectives, to attain intersubjectivity, with a black character as part of the production and management of Cordelia Howard's fame.

Material culture extended this surrogation by enabling audiences to take their idol home with them. Nineteenth-century theatrical troupes often sold or gave away souvenirs of their shows. One such memento was the Staffordshire figurine (figure 3.9 and plate 6), now a valuable collectors' item but in the 1850s an inexpensive knickknack. Staffordshire, a British company, manufactured many figurines of nineteenth-century actors in their roles: Charlotte Cushman, Edmund Kean, and David Garrick were all modeled in character.[90] Staffordshire produced *Uncle Tom's Cabin* figurines as blank, unpainted pottery for American markets. In the United States, working-class women, generally between the ages of eighteen and thirty, bought the blanks wholesale and painted them either at home or in large workshops. The figurines were then sold in theater lobbies as souvenirs of theatrical performances.[91] Staffordshire manufactured perhaps a dozen different representations of characters from *Uncle Tom's Cabin* for sale in theaters. Most of the figurines represented scenes that Billings illustrated and that Aiken staged: for example, figure 3.9, in which Eva and Tom sit side-by-side and read the Bible, stages yet again the arbor scene.

Because the painting of the figurines was decentralized, extant figurines

*Figure 3.9.* Staffordshire figurine depicting Uncle Tom and Little Eva in the arbor, mid-nineteenth century. Photograph courtesy of McKinley Hill Antiques.

vary widely in the selection and arrangement of color: Tom may have striped or solid pants; Eva's dress may be pink or blue or white, dotted or plaid or plain. Nearly universally, however, the painters colored Eva's hair dark brown, as is the case in figure 3.9 and plate 6. This choice is surprising, as Stowe described Eva's hair repeatedly as "golden" or sometimes "golden-brown." The lightness of Eva's hair figures in Stowe's plot: when Legree discovers that Tom has a lock of hair that Eva gave him on her deathbed, the "long, shining curl of *fair* hair" leaps, "like a living thing, [and] twine[s] itself round Legree's fingers."[92] Legree "scream[s]" as if the "golden tress" has "burned him."[93] Stowe's Little Eva has light hair, but Cordelia Howard, both onstage and offstage, was a dark brunette. All extant drawings, paintings, and photographs of Cordelia Howard, both in character as Little Eva and not, plainly show her dark hair. No evidence suggests that Howard was wigged when she appeared onstage in *Uncle Tom's Cabin*. That dozens of Staffordshire painters independently elected to paint Eva's hair dark brown, in opposition to Stowe's text but in accordance with Cordelia Howard's body, suggests that they were representing the "world-renowned child actress" (figure 3.7) in performance as Little Eva, rather than Stowe's character.[94] When the Howards hawked the Staffordshire figurine in their theater lobbies, they were selling not only a decorative knickknack but an opportunity for home-based "worship" of Cordelia Howard.

Other souvenirs, most notably a collection of "Hymns Sung By Little Cordelia Howard and Her Parents" (figure 3.10), further encouraged quasi-religious devotion to the little actress—this time, through the scripted action of singing hymns. Yet another redrawing of Billings's illustration graces the cover. The halo-like hat on the child, visible in Billings's original and in the broadside, is now larger and more distinct. The booklet's title lists two adult actors and one child actor, and the illustration depicts two adults and one child. Like the broadside, the hymnal simultaneously represents the Harris family thanking God (through the quotation of Billings's image), "Little Cordelia Howard and her parents" united in song (as per the booklet's title and content), and Uncle Tom worshipping Little Eva (in the depiction of a haloed, light-skinned child in proximity to both a dark-skinned adult man and in the name "Cordelia Howard").

This souvenir book enabled audiences to restage, at home, the image on the cover by singing the songs contained within the book. George C. Howard wrote songs—"hymns"—for *Uncle Tom's Cabin*, including "Eva to

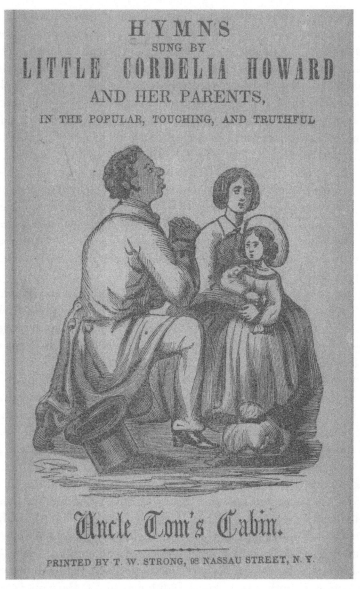

*Figure 3.10.* "Hymns Sung by Little Cordelia Howard and Her Parents, in the Popular, Touching, and Truthful Uncle Tom's Cabin." Souvenir songbook sold at performances of *Uncle Tom's Cabin* at Barnum's Museum in New York City (New York: T. W. Strong, 1853). Courtesy of the John Hay Library, Brown University.

Her Papa," "St. Clair [*sic*] to Little Eva in Heaven," "Uncle Tom's Religion," and Topsy's "Oh, I'se So Wicked." These songs became highlights in the show, and sheet music for each song was sold separately, often with cover engravings taken from photographs of the actors in character (see Chapter 4, figure 4.14 for sheet music with a cover image of Caroline Fox Howard, Cordelia's mother, performing the role of Topsy). The songbook shown in figure 3.10 included all of these songs and therefore enabled families to re-capitulate at home the experience of the theater, substituting their bodies for the ones they saw onstage—a "touching" experience, the songbook's cover promised.

Cordelia Howard's career failed to survive one great disruption of 1861—namely, the onset of the actress's puberty. As the body of a woman replaced that of the girl, Howard lost all appeal to audiences. None of Howard's contemporaries described explicit discomfort at watching the increasingly mature white girl embrace the blacked-up actor playing Uncle Tom, but the implication is inescapable: the appeal of Howard, like that of Shirley Temple three-quarters of a century later, depended on her ability to perform childhood. When she shed the visual markers of childhood, this capacity vanished. Later, as a married adult, Cordelia Howard MacDonald attributed her fall to her increasing age. "The worst thing about . . . prodigies is that they generally prove nonentities in their later years," Howard MacDonald wrote cheerfully in 1928, the same year Shirley Temple was born. "I am no exception to the rule!"[95] In 1861, when Howard proposed retirement at the age of thirteen, her parents acquiesced swiftly and with apparent relief. After that, Howard returned only briefly to the stage in an 1870 comedy titled *The Little Treasure*. A reviewer from the Howards' home town of Troy, New York, managed to revere Cordelia while acknowledging her performance's shortcomings: "There was, here and there," the *Northern Budget* hedged, "just the slightest bit of novice-y action, but it only served to improve her relations with the audience, and to render her all the more winsome."[96] There were no revivals.

After Cordelia Howard retired from "Tomming," another child actress replaced her, and the show went on—although now, Howard's mother, Caroline Fox Howard, received top billing for her role of Topsy. After the Civil War, then, Topsy, not Eva, served as the dramatic center of the Howard-Aiken production of *Uncle Tom's Cabin*. One might attribute this metamorphosis of "The Little Eva Show" into "The Topsy Show" to simple economic strategy: this arrangement enabled a member of the Howard family always to take the top billing. The Howards' recalibration fit into a larger trend, however, as Eva lost status as an obsessive attraction in shows across the country. After the Civil War, hundreds of Tom shows drifted away from sentimentalism, away from the character of Eva, and toward spectacle. By the late 1870s and early 1880s, spectacle engulfed the shows. In 1879, Jay Rial's Tom troupe thrilled audiences by sending live dogs in pursuit of Eliza as she crossed the Ohio River. Other shows quickly copied and expanded on the use of animals, and by the 1880s, Tom shows routinely, if inexplicably, featured not only dogs but also donkeys, ponies, and even elephants. Human actors also shed any claim to sentimental realism with the increasing practice of doubled casts.[97] Such "double mammoth" productions featured two of selected characters—two Topsies, for example, or two lawyers. The paired actors chimed their lines in unison, apparently pleasing crowds that found two Topsies twice as amusing as one.[98]

Even after Cordelia Howard retired and Tom shows became circus-like affairs, however, material culture continued to circulate practices of desire between the theater and the home. The memoir of the modernist poet H.D. (Hilda Doolittle) represented this circulation in prose so pulsingly vivid as to border on the psychedelic.[99] In 1892, when Doolittle was six years old, a Tom show visited Doolittle's small Pennsylvania town. Like many Tom shows of the 1890s, the one Doolittle witnessed featured live dogs and donkeys and a circus-like atmosphere. The encounter with the Tommers constituted, in the words of Susan Stanford Friedman, "the beginning point of her aesthetic awakening as a child."[100] It was, in other words, the first step in Hilda Doolittle's transformation into the poet H.D.

Before Doolittle attended the Tom show, she saw a parade in which wagons, each bearing an iconic scene from *Uncle Tom's Cabin*, rolled through town to entice audiences to the theater. The parade confused the six-year-old's sense of reality, and an adult had to explain the most basic conventions of public enactment:

> There was someone on the ice with a baby, but the baby, Ida [Drease, a white housekeeper] said, was a doll, and the ice was not real ice because it was summer and it would have melted, but Eliza, I think it was, was pulled along with the ice on wheels, like Uncle Tom's cabin. Then there were some horses and donkeys . . . and then there was the last and the best thing. It was a sort of golden cart or it was a chariot like *Swing low, sweet chariot,* and there was an angel, [which] was stretching out its wings and it was holding the wreath over the head of Little Eva who was the most important thing in the procession.[101]

As Doolittle realized that the doll and the ice were props that substituted for the "real," she also gained awareness that what Tracy Davis calls "performative time" differs from ordinary, linear time.[102] The parade's scenes played simultaneously, each on its own wagon, but they revealed themselves sequentially to a viewer who remained, as Doolittle did, in one place on the street. Thus the Tom parade, like all parades, functioned both synchronically and diachronically. The parade was modular in that each character remained isolated in an iconic setting or action: Tom in his cabin, Eva dying, Eliza crossing the ice with a doll-baby. This isolation and modularity, combined with synchronic and diachronic time, recalled the dynamic of the Parkhurst playing cards. The Parkhurst game domiciled each character in an individual card, and the consumer connected Tom and Eva through the movements of play. A parade's overall shape on the street, as a bird might see it, coheres as cards cohere in a deck; and as the Parkhurst game's dance of separation and touching emerged through play, the Tom parade's narrative was produced through acts of engaged watching from the curb. A parade viewer who stood still and witnessed, like the card player who followed the game's directions, linked dying Eva to cabined Tom. And much as the Parkhurst cards jumbled time—the Parkhurst Tom stands in front of his cabin and searches for the child he *will* meet while holding the basket he *will* carve—so, too, did the parade. When a group of "darkie" actors marched by, "roped together" to represent a coffle of slaves, Doolittle's older brother reassured her, "It's only a parade . . . they are as free as you are."[103] Doolittle processed the scene as a swirl of reality, fiction, and history, of distance and home, of difference and familiarity, of synchronicity and diachronicity: "The darkies tied together, were as free as I was, because our father and our Uncle Alvin had fought in the Civil War and now we all had the same flag that Betsy Ross made in a house in Philadelphia."[104] For Doolittle, the parade folded the Civil War and the American Revolution into her moment, 1892.

Later, when Doolittle went to the theater and saw *Uncle Tom's Cabin* as a play, the complex relationship between the play and the parade triggered a set of insights into art's ability to curl time.

> Little Eva died in a bed, we saw her die. It was a stage, Ida said. You call it the stage and this was our first time at the theater. . . . Now Little Eva died and it was just as if she had died, but then she came back again in a long night-gown. Little Eva was not really dead at all. She was the same little girl with the long gold hair who was driven in the chariot down the street, and

she would do it all over again in Allentown or Easton, Ida said. . . . That was how it was. Little Eva was really in a book, yet Little Eva was there on the stage and we saw her die, just like the book, Aunt Belle said, though we hadn't read it.[105]

Performance, Doolittle realized, can make something simultaneously true and false: Eva can die and the death can register as real ("it was just as if she *had* died"), but then she can get up, go into a theater or to another town, and die all over again. A character can exist simultaneously, living and dying, on a street and on a stage and in a book—and even if one has not read that book, the character can be forever busy living and dying between the unopened covers. This performance of *Uncle Tom's Cabin* altered, for Doolittle, the familiar space of the street:

Anyhow it was over. We went home. But the street would never be the same again, it would always be different, really everything would always be different. This street that we walked along . . . was the street down which, only yesterday, Uncle Tom had been pulled, complete with log-cabin; the hounds we had seen, less than an hour ago, chasing Eliza, had snuffled and shuffled their way along these very paving-stones.[106]

Upon re-experiencing the street that framed the parade, the six-year-old Doolittle discovered a phenomenon that performance theorist Marvin Carlson, a century later, would call "ghosting": the ability of a performance to linger in a site, thus affecting that space into the future. In H.D.'s words, "the street would never be the same again" because Uncle Tom had been pulled there, bloodhounds snuffled after Eliza there, and Eva died there. For Carlson, all theater "is as a cultural activity deeply involved with memory and haunted by repetition."[107] If performance is defined as action that makes meaning through repetition and difference, then a "ghost" is that which a performance repeats (and changes) to create memory (and forgetting). In Carlson's view, ghosting affects each aspect of a play: a dramatic text is haunted by previous performances (including rehearsals); actors are haunted by the previous roles they played; roles by previous actors who played them; and props by previous stage uses. What Friedman called Doolittle's "aesthetic awakening" was, more precisely, the child's glimpse of the uniquely powerful relationship between performance and memory, performance and forgetting. Doolittle realized that the parade disintegrated into fragments that then reassembled, differently, in the theater (as playing cards shuffle into chaos and then reassemble in orderly patterns through play, only to be shuffled again). Her epiphany was that this cycle of breakdown and nonidentical reconstruction, this haunting, was *Uncle Tom's Cabin*'s source of life, the way in which it "came true."

> Well, really there had been so much, you kept remembering bits of it [the parade]; in the light of the play itself, the details of the parade came into different perspective, everything came true—that is what it was. Everything came true. The street came true in another world.[108]

As the final element in Doolittle's initial coming to consciousness as an artist, the child realized that not only did the street "come true" in the other world of the theater, but that "it didn't stop there because when we got home, everything was like that. If you take down one side of a wall, you have a stage. It would be like the doll-house that had only three walls."[109] In other words, the public "truths" of performance in the theater and the street always come home; thus performance dissolves the conceit of separate public and private spheres. The particular contrivance that links public and private performance is, for Doolittle, a doll. The doll-prop, which H.D. twice singles out for mention in regard to both the parade and the play, ghosts into Doolittle's home when the girl reimagines her house as simultaneously a dollhouse and a theatrical set. At the parade, Doolittle's stream of consciousness had linked Eliza's doll-prop to the singing of *Swing Low, Sweet Chariot*. Later, at home, the ghostly prop of the doll, the materiality of sheet music, and the performance of singing combined to produce, for Doolittle, a transcendent experience of intersubjectivity and surrogation, of herself merging bodily with the character of Eva.

> Mama was sitting at the piano and it was still Mama and yet it was Little Eva's mother. . . . There would be someone else who was myself, yet who was the child of the Lady who Played the Piano; then I would be Little Eva and I would have an Uncle Tom who was not really an uncle, but it was like that. It was called a play, it was the first play we had been to. But *a play and to play were the same.* . . . You could . . . see how the room had only three sides and . . . although anyone could see that you had short hair with, at best, mousy duck-tails at the nape of the neck, yet you could toss your head and the golden curls.[110]

The parade "came true" in the theater, and "the street would never be the

same again," but "it didn't stop there, because when we got home everything was like that." Doolittle's home became both theater and dollhouse,
populated by ghostly doll-props and physical paper goods such as sheet
music, which enabled family performances of singing that repeated, with
differences, scenarios from the play. The Doolittle family sang together, as
did the actors onstage and the figures on the cover of the Howard family songster (figure 3.10). Material culture such as Billings's rotating arbor
scene threaded through theatrical scripts; material culture such as Eliza's
doll-prop shimmered on the stage and the street; and audience members
carried material culture home from the theater in the form of figurines,
sheet music, and songbooks. These goods transformed the home into a set
because, as H.D. realized, "a play and to play were the same." A Tom play,
doll play, and the playing of music all intersected through bodies in motion. From the Parkhurst cards of 1852 to the Cordelia Howard songbook
of 1853 to a doll in a Tom show of 1892, material culture coordinated behaviors that relentlessly performed slavery as intimate desire circulating
around and through white children.

But the more the Parkhurst card game "is played the more it is desired,"
as an advertisement ominously promised.[111] Tomitudes frustrated desire as
they scripted it, and this frustration motivated further restlessness, further circulation: as soon as a player held Little Eva, Uncle Tom, and Justice, the game ended. To continue play, to continue circulating desire, one
fractured the Eva/Tom embrace, shuffled the cards, and started over.[112] Arden Seymour competed, as he recalled, with four hundred other boys to
walk near Cordelia Howard, to hold her umbrella, and to "mingle" near
her, blacked up, onstage. If he ever touched the child actress, however, he
omitted that fact from his "memories of stageland." This unfinished business kept him returning "nightly" to the throng outside the theater, hoping each time to be the one who "walked nearest to her sacred person."[113]

Cordelia Howard and Little Eva were ultimately elusive: both the celebrity and the character appeared only to disappear amid cardboard
clouds or the turn of a page. Their piscine slipperiness paralleled that of
performance, of childhood, and of the performance of childhood. Performance is a process of loss: the instant a performance leaps into the air
of the present moment, it disappears forever into the sea of the past.[114]
Live performance recorded by any technology—writing, photography,
wax cylinder, film, binary data—becomes something other than live performance. Childhood, too, disappears as it materializes: to be a child is
to change, to grow out of childhood. For William Wordsworth, a major

*Plate 1*. An African American girl cuddles a puff of cotton. Trade card for Cottolene, a lard substitute. N. K. Fairbank and Company, circa 1890s. Courtesy of the American Antiquarian Society.

*Plate 2.* A white girl advertises Cottolene, a lard substitute. Trade card for Cottolene. N. K. Fairbank and Company, Chicago, circa 1890s. Collection of the author.

*Plate 3.* Unsigned illustration (most likely by John R. Neill) for "The Story of Topsy from Uncle Tom's Cabin," published in Little Black Sambo, by Helen Bannerman (Chicago: Reilly and Britton, 1908). Eva converts Topsy, who is depicted as a pickaninny with inhuman lips, oversized feet, and unchildlike muscles. Courtesy of the Beinecke Rare Book and Manuscript Library, Yale University.

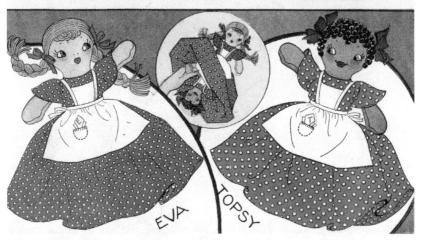

*Plate 4.* A mid-twentieth century Vogart sewing pattern for a topsy-turvy doll. This image usefully shows the doll in three positions: with the skirt flipped to reveal the white doll and to hide the black doll (left), vice versa (right), and mid-flip (center). Collection of the author.

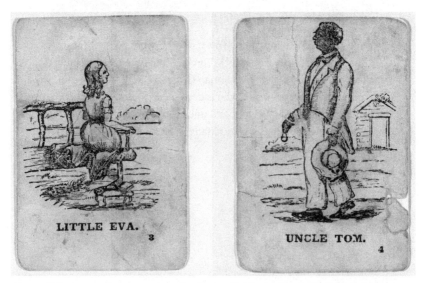

*Plate 5.* Playing cards representing Little Eva (left) and Uncle Tom (right). "Game of Uncle Tom and Little Eva," Providence, V. S. W. Parkhurst, 1852. Courtesy of the American Antiquarian Society

*Plate 6.* Staffordshire figurine depicting Uncle Tom and Little Eva in the arbor, mid-nineteenth century. Little Eva's brown hair echoes that of the brunet Cordelia Howard more than that of the "golden"-haired Eva of Stowe's novel. Photograph courtesy of McKinley Hill Antiques.

*Plate 7.* Golliwogg (seated) and three Dutch dolls. The Dutch dolls wear clothes fashioned from an American flag. Raggedy Ann inherited the Golliwogg's triangular nose, round eyes, and red, white, and blue clothes. Bertha Upton, *The Golliwogg's "Auto-Go-Cart,"* pictures by Florence Kate Upton (New York: Longman's, Green, 1901). Courtesy of the Houghton Library, Harvard University.

*Plate 8.* Raggedy Ann-Mammy Topsy-Turvy Doll, Kotton Kountry Kreations. Photograph by Phyllis Thompson.

*Plate 9.* Raggedy Ann hangs upside down by the crotch. Johnny Gruelle, *Raggedy Ann Stories* (Joliet, Ill.: P. F. Volland, 1918), 18.

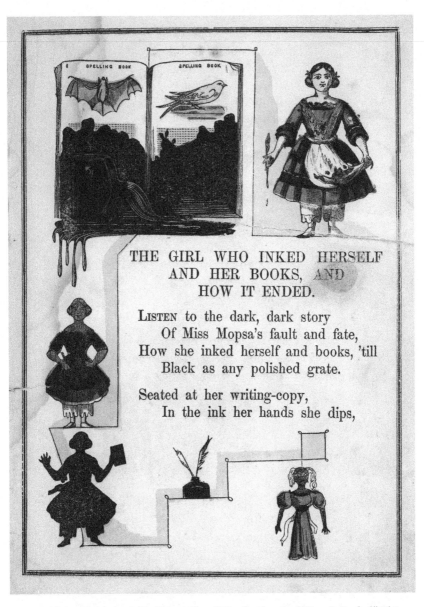

THE GIRL WHO INKED HERSELF
AND HER BOOKS, AND
HOW IT ENDED.

LISTEN to the dark, dark story
    Of Miss Mopsa's fault and fate,
How she inked herself and books, 'till
    Black as any polished grate.

Seated at her writing-copy,
    In the ink her hands she dips,

*Plate 10.* "The Girl Who Inked Herself and Her Books, And How It Ended." This first page of the story visually tells the entire tale: in the upper right corner, Miss Mopsa appears as a white girl. A line threads around the verse, leading the reader's eye first to the left, to the schoolbook Miss Mopsa defaces, then down, as Miss Mopsa turns gray and then black. Bottom center, the line becomes a shelf on which the inkwell rests, and finally, in the bottom right corner, the thread becomes the device by which Miss Mopsa, redefined and sold as a black doll, hangs. *Little Miss Consequence* ([New York:] McLoughlin Bros., between 1859 and 1862), n.p. Courtesy of the University of Florida Digital Collections.

architect of sentimental childhood, "Heaven lies about us in our infancy!" but "Shades of the prison-house begin to close / Upon the growing Boy."[115] For sentimentalists, growth entails the loss of childhood innocence: as an individual child grows, the Child withers. As Carolyn Steedman has shown, romantic and sentimental writers constructed childhood as a "lost realm"—that is, an emblem of a lost historical and personal past, a marker of the ebbs and flows of memory.[116] As such, childhood, especially as it intersected with performance-as-loss, offered a startling opportunity to proslavery writers such as Joel Chandler Harris who mourned antebellum southern culture as a "Lost Cause."

## From Abolition to Apology: Joel Chandler Harris's Impression of Stowe

Joel Chandler Harris, one of slavery's most effective and influential apologists, seems to have been engaging in wishful thinking when he called *Uncle Tom's Cabin* a "wonderful defense of slavery."[117] Harris registered this judgment in his 1880 introduction to his first book, *Uncle Remus: His Songs and His Sayings*, which launched a series of volumes featuring an elderly African American man named Uncle Remus who cuddles a white, unnamed Little Boy while telling folkloristic stories of Brer Rabbit. Harris's Uncle Remus books became best sellers of the nineteenth and early twentieth centuries; the books earned praise from Theodore Roosevelt and Andrew Carnegie, influenced writers from Mark Twain to Rudyard Kipling to Beatrix Potter, enraged Alice Walker, and ultimately served as the basis for Walt Disney's *Song of the South*.[118] Harris used Stowe to introduce and thus define his first book, which he described as a "curiously sympathetic supplement" to *Uncle Tom's Cabin*.[119] Harris understood that Stowe intended to "attack" the system of slavery, but in his interpretation, "her genius took possession of her and compelled her, in spite of her avowed purpose, to give a very fair picture of the institution she had intended to condemn."[120] For Harris, the "real moral that Mrs. Stowe's book teaches is that the . . . realities [of slavery], under the best and happiest conditions, possess a romantic beauty and a tenderness all their own."[121]

By reading *Uncle Tom's Cabin* as a defense of slavery, Harris did not simplistically misunderstand Stowe, nor did he merely impose or project his own proslavery politics onto her abolitionist novel. Rather, Harris read *Uncle Tom's Cabin* with a warped genius for selectivity and an impulse toward what Michael Rogin calls "motivated forgetting."[122] Harris, writing after the Civil War and Reconstruction, was motivated to forget southern defeat and the violence of slavery, to tuck history behind a screen memory of the "romantic beauty" and "tenderness" of the plantation South. This action located Harris within the project of the "Lost Cause," a term popularized in 1866 by the journalist Edward A. Pollard. Lost Cause ideology asserts that the antebellum South possessed a noble and chivalric civilization that was unique ("peculiar"), precious, and rightly self-enclosed. Military defeat and Emancipation caused this culture to become "Lost," but the greater "Cause" could be resurrected, Pollard argued, if writers and artists convinced the nation that southern culture ought to exist free of molestation from the North.[123] Harris accomplished this feat by extracting characters and scenarios from *Uncle Tom's Cabin* and relocating them to Uncle Remus's cabin, where he set them to labor toward reinventing slavery as the embrace of an innocent child.

I have argued that Stowe created vivid word pictures for the intended purpose of impressing her readers bodily—that is, she paired the literary strategy of ekphrasis with that of scripting fleshy engagement with the narrative. Stowe inadvertently made her book vulnerable to selective readings, however, when she combined the literary strategies of ekphrasis and scripting with a third technique: irony. Stowe's 1851 letter to Bailey revealed this three-part strategy in the description of herself as a "painter" who graphically depicted "slavery, its reverses, [and] changes"—that is, its ironies—so that "everyone is impressed by them."[124] These strategies of irony, ekphrasis, and scripting supported each other: for example, Stowe's ekphrasis enabled her vividly to render the interior of Uncle Tom's cabin, which made the reader all the more fleshily "impressed" with Tom's loss of that cabin—that is, the ironic reversal of Tom's fortune. Even as the intersecting strategies fortified the novel, however, they simultaneously rendered it vulnerable to selective readings. The ekphrasis vivified some scenes, characters, and plot elements but paled others. The ironic reversals cleaved the novel into discrete, contrasting units that could be individually re-presented or ignored. Thus Stowe enabled the pattern of spotlighting and screening, remembering and forgetting.

"There is no arguing with *pictures*, and everyone is impressed by them," Stowe claimed optimistically.[125] Harris echoed and affirmed the latter part of this statement on June 20, 1882, in a letter published in the *Atlantic Monthly* in honor of Stowe's birthday. Harris reported that he read *Uncle Tom's Cabin* in 1862, and that the novel "made a more vivid impression upon my mind than anything I have ever read since."[126] Stowe wanted "everyone" to be "impressed," and Harris reported that Stowe's novel made a "vivid impression" upon him—a neat knit indeed.[127]

Harris's actions, however, unraveled the first part of Stowe's claim—that "there is no arguing with *pictures*." Harris did indeed argue with Stowe's word pictures—not by criticizing or contradicting them, but by appropriating and restaging them in a new context so as to reverse their meaning. Harris acknowledged his repetition-with-a-difference in the description of his first book as a "curiously sympathetic supplement" to Stowe's novel: "sympathetic" suggests Harris's desire to duplicate or extend Stowe's project; "supplement" denotes Harris's intention to fill in that which Stowe omitted, to cut a jigsaw-puzzle piece with positive outcroppings to fill Stowe's negative spaces. The word "curious" is most curious of all, suggesting what Marianne Noble, quoting poet Lucy Larcom, calls the "weird curves" by which women "make accommodations in order to find pleasure and power within the cultural circumstances in which they find themselves."[128] To be a postwar white southerner who subscribed to Lost Cause ideology, as Harris was and did, meant to consider oneself a victim who had been stripped of the "right" to own slaves, a refugee from a noble and ruined civilization. This self-perception of victimhood may have caused Harris to write in "weird curves" for the same reason that women did: resistance. Harris credited Stowe's novel with making an impression on his mind, and Uncle Remus's cabin is indeed a curious "impression" of the cabin of Uncle Tom—that is, a negative like a woodcut that retains and reproduces the outline of a picture by reversing its foreground and background.[129] Harris's structuring device of Remus and the Little Boy cuddling in Remus's cabin retains and reproduces some structuring elements of Stowe's novel so as to reverse Stowe's abolitionism.

The first of Stowe's structures that Harris appropriated and curved weirdly was the cabin as a site for love between an enslaved man and a slaveholding child. Stowe begins and ends the story of her eponymous character in this eponymous built environment. Stowe introduces Tom and his cabin in her fourth chapter, where the reader encounters a happy, intact family and later a Christian community, all thriving under slavery. The vividly drawn cabin, filled with piety and ideal domesticity, glows ironically against the rest of the novel, which details the destruction of Tom's and other families. Tom's life ends in Simon Legree's shed—an emptied-out inversion of the cabin Tom once shared with Chloe and their children. As this ending came to Stowe chronologically first (it was this vision of Tom's death that motivated her to write her novel), she wrote the first forty chapters to build toward that climax.[130] What unites Tom's two cabins and bridges the ironic reversal is the presence of the young slave-holder, George Shelby. In chapter 4, George Shelby, still childish at thirteen, visits Tom and Chloe in their cabin, where he teaches Tom to write, enjoys Chloe's cooking, and participates in a Christian revival meeting. In Tom's final scene five years and thirty-seven chapters later, George, now eighteen and the master of his estate, reunites with the dying Tom in a shed. The opening and closing scenes of Tom's life thus triangulate the figures of Tom, George Shelby, and the cabin itself.

Harris reproduced Stowe's Tom-George-cabin triangle in his narrative device of Uncle Remus and the Little Boy cuddling in Remus's cabin as Remus tells the Boy stories of Brer Rabbit (this device is commonly called Harris's "frame"). As Harris replicated the triangle of Stowe's fourth chapter, however, he lopped off its ironic echo in Tom's death scene. By highlighting Tom's cabin and screening out Legree's shed, Harris resistantly read *Uncle Tom's Cabin* as a defense of slavery.[131] Harris mapped this reading in a 1904 article in the *Saturday Evening Post*.

> It seems to me to be impossible for any unprejudiced person to read Mrs. Stowe's book and fail to see in it a defense of American slavery as she found it in Kentucky. This defense will, of course, not be found in the *text* of the book, and it is useless to look for it there. It was far, very far, from the lady's intention to pay a tribute to slavery . . . [but] she had among her other possessions the spark of genius that is necessary to make the creations of fiction live and move, each in its place, and . . . that genius . . . would not permit her to smother or ignore the tender and romantic situation that she found in the home of her Kentucky friends. . . . And so, as it turns out, all the worthy and beloved characters in her book—Uncle Tom, little Eva, the beloved Master, and the rest—are the products of the system the *text* of the book is all the time condemning.[132]

Harris's reading, like the reminiscence Henry James would pen nine years later, contrasts Stowe's prose with the essence of *Uncle Tom's Cabin*. James describes *Uncle Tom's Cabin* as "much *less* a book than a state of vision, of feeling and of consciousness" (emphasis added); while Harris twice contrasts the book's meaning with its "text." Harris and James agree word-for-word that Stowe's characters "live and move" beyond the archive of Stowe's prose because of what James calls "the amount of life" in the novel, what

Harris calls Stowe's "genius," and what I call the "repertoire" of *Uncle Tom's Cabin*. Harris and James depart from each other, however, in their understanding of where the characters fly, and to what effect. For James, the characters can "fly anywhere" and can be "carried even violently furthest" from Stowe's purpose. In other words, James sees a range of possible flight paths, some of which "violently" depart from Stowe's intentions.[133] Harris, in contrast, reads Stowe's characters as unnaturally constrained within Stowe's abolitionist project. That is, Harris understands *Stowe* to have *diverted* her characters from their true path of happiness within plantation life. However, Stowe's "genius" would not permit her to "smother or ignore" the "tender and romantic . . . facts" of the antebellum South, which "spark" with life within the novel, constantly testifying against Stowe's "condemn[ation]" of slavery. For Harris, the tender love among Uncle Tom, Little Eva, and "the beloved Master"—that is, George Shelby—defends slavery in *contrast* to Stowe's "text." Whereas James envisions Stowe's characters flying beyond and sometimes violently far from Stowe's prose, Harris sees Stowe's characters flapping against the bars of the novel in which they find themselves caged, longing to fly to their true and happy home: "the system" of the antebellum South. In Harris's view, Stowe violently captured Tom, Eva, and the "beloved Master" *from* "the tender and romantic situation that she found" in slavery, and impressed them *within* her abolitionist novel.

Harris's fiction corrected this perceived displacement: Harris freed Stowe's white and black characters from their abolitionist servitude by relocating Stowe's Tom-George-cabin triangle to a happy plantation in the Lost Cause South. Harris accomplished this feat by restaging Stowe's first Tom-George-cabin scene but ignoring the ironic echo in Stowe's second Tom-George-cabin scene. Harris also edited out the blatant irony in the fourth chapter's coda, in which Stowe reveals that while George, Tom, and Tom's family and community enjoyed their evening in Uncle Tom's cabin, George's father sold Tom and Harry, Eliza's son.[134] Harris's impression of *Uncle Tom's Cabin* retained and reproduced Stowe's triangle but obliterated Stowe's irony—and with it, her abolitionism.

*Uncle Remus: His Songs and His Sayings* imagines what could have happened if Tom had never left the Shelby plantation. Stowe's novel ranges widely in its settings—from Kentucky to Ohio to Louisiana, upon and over the Mississippi, Ohio, and Red Rivers—and even more widely in its references to Vermont, Canada, Liberia, and other locations. This geographical range integrates with Stowe's political message because each time Tom travels, his tragedy deepens.[135] However, Harris's *Saturday*

*Evening Post* article referred only, and twice, to Kentucky, the site of the Shelby plantation and of Tom's cabin. In Harris's reading of Stowe's novel, and in his own writing, the enslaved adult and slaveholding child stay in the cabin forever, replaying over and over the scene of loving tenderness. Each Brer Rabbit story that Remus tells is new to the Boy, but the frame repeats endlessly, comfortingly, with only minor variations—like multiple strikes of a woodcut onto paper. Extracted from the "text" of Stowe's novel and replanted in "the system" of which Stowe's characters are "products," Remus and the Boy perform a fantasy of Stowe's fourth chapter, and the happy slavery it depicts, never ending.

Harris transformed Stowe's greatest strengths—her vivid word pictures, her power to impress, and her devastating irony—into exploitable vulnerabilities. Harris's ability to redirect Stowe's strengths against her purpose appears most poignantly in the twisting of Stowe's fourth chapter title, "An Evening in Uncle Tom's Cabin." The title of this chapter, unlike any other in *Uncle Tom's Cabin*, replicates and encloses the title of the novel. No other chapter title contains the word "uncle" or "cabin." The chapter's title suggests—falsely, pointedly falsely—that the entire novel may be found microcosmically within this chapter. Furthermore, the fourth chapter contains some of Stowe's most vivid ekphrasis ("we must daguerreotype [Tom] for our readers," Stowe wrote).[136] This resplendent wholeness can have the effect of making the topsy-turvy twin scene—the ironic echo of Tom's death in another cabin—all the more devastating in comparison. Or it can overpower the ironic echo and ultimately muffle it.

The title of the fourth chapter, "An Evening in Uncle Tom's Cabin," further facilitates the isolation of that chapter by framing the novel's title with the phrase, "An Evening in." The word "in" is crucial because it heralds Henry James's sense of immersion, of having "lived and moved . . . *in* Mrs. Stowe's novel"—an immersion, we have seen, that is interdependent with the dynamic of extraction.[137] Stowe opens her chapter with a one-paragraph description of the cabin's exterior, and then leads her second paragraph with the sentence, "Let us enter the dwelling."[138] Thus Stowe ushers the reader into the cabin, an intimate space lit warmly against the evening sky. But the chapter title's use of the word "in" also produces a pun. The "Uncle Tom's Cabin" in the chapter title refers both to the character's home and to the novel itself. With the addition of the word "in," the chapter title means "The Characters Are Spending an Evening Inside Uncle Tom's Dwelling" *and* "The Reader Is Spending an Evening Reading the Novel, *Uncle Tom's Cabin*." The word "in" refers to both physical enclosure

in a cabin and mental interiority—vision, feeling, and consciousness—
created by the absorptive act of novel-reading. Stowe reprises this pun
and again punctuates her ekphrastic scripting at the end of Tom's life,
at the close of her penultimate chapter, when she addresses her reader in
the imperative: "Think of your freedom every time you see UNCLE TOM'S
CABIN."[139] In this closing instruction, Stowe capitalizes the phrase "Uncle
Tom's cabin," thus setting it apart as the title of the novel and marking the
novel and something to "see," to experience visually. Both the novel's title
and the structure of the cabin, then, echo from the fourth chapter to the
end of the book, and Stowe posits the novel and the cabin both as dwell-
ings that the reader should "see" (through ekphrasis) and "enter" (through
performances of reading and of being bodily impressed).

Harris echoed Stowe when he titled the first chapter of his first book
"Uncle Remus Initiates the Little Boy." This chapter title, like Stowe's
fourth, is the only one to include the word "Uncle," the first word in the
books' respective titles. Where Stowe's chapter title names Uncle Tom and
his cabin but not George Shelby, Harris names Uncle Remus and the Little
Boy but not the cabin. However, the cabin is, for Harris, as important as
George Shelby is for Stowe. Harris's first chapter "initiates" the Little Boy
and the reader with the vision of a cabin lit warmly against the night sky.
In the book's opening paragraph,

> the lady whom Uncle Remus calls "Miss Sally" missed her little seven-year-
> old. Making search for him through the house and through the yard, she
> heard the sound of voices in the old man's cabin, and, looking through the
> window, saw the boy sitting by Uncle Remus. His head rested against the
> old man's arm, and he was gazing with an expression of the most intense
> interest into the rough, weather-beaten face, that beamed so kindly upon
> him.[140]

Harris, like Stowe, ushers the reader from the cabin's exterior to interior.
Unlike Stowe, however, Harris guides the reader into his narrative "frame"
through the eyes of Miss Sally, who focalizes the scene, as Gérard Gennette
would say.[141] Sally, along with the reader, looks through the cabin window
to witness the tender intimacy between the man and the boy. These characters are motionless, a tableau of idealized servitude. The window frames the
scene, simultaneously boxing the characters and opening them to Sally's
and the reader's visual inspection. Harris's night-lit cabin, his restaging of
the Tom-George-cabin triangle, is a diorama that invites appreciation and

therefore noninterference. And indeed, Sally, focalizing for the reader, does not interfere: her appreciation for the loving scene causes her to abandon her initial goal of fetching her son. Where Stowe, in her antebellum context, vivified scenes of slavery to incite abolitionist action, Harris, writing immediately after the end of Reconstruction in 1877, restaged "a romantic beauty and a tenderness . . . of the old plantation as we remember it"—that is, as *he* was motivated to remember it.[142] Thus Harris joined with other Lost Cause writers who described southern culture as unique, noble, and therefore deserving protection from northern interference. "Interference" was code for any effort to defend southern African Americans and their legal rights. Resistance against so-called interference constituted the most urgent goal of Lost Cause politics, because noninterference guaranteed that white southerners could resurrect slavery by what Douglas A. Blackmon has called "another name": forced labor in prisons and chain gangs, sharecropping, social rituals of submission, and disenfranchisement—all enforced through the terrorism of lynching.[143]

With his call for noninterference, Harris inverted Stowe. Harris retained and reproduced Stowe's triangle of "Uncle"-boy-cabin; he set that triangle, as did Stowe, against the beautiful evening sky. But he reversed Stowe's abolition along the axis of that little word "in." Stowe implicated her reader politically when she titled her chapter "An Evening in Uncle Tom's Cabin." The reader who accepts Stowe's invitation to "enter the dwelling" spends an evening "in" Uncle Tom's cabin when he or she spends an evening reading *Uncle Tom's Cabin*. By being "in" the novel— that is, by reading it—the reader enters the cabin—that is, not only Tom's freestanding dwelling, but also the full panorama of linked pictures, of subsequent cabins including Legree's shed. When Stowe ushers the reader into "An Evening in Uncle Tom's Cabin," her punning title says, "You are in (reading) my novel, *Uncle Tom's Cabin*. You are in (reading the scene set in) Uncle Tom's cabin. You are in (implicated in) the political system I condemn." The title of Harris's parallel chapter, "Uncle Remus Initiates the Little Boy," however, inverts Stowe. Whereas Stowe draws her readers into the cabin for the purpose of implicating them, spurring them to moral action, Uncle Remus initiates the Little Boy, draws him into Remus's cabin for the purpose of escaping into fantastical tales of Brer Rabbit's amoral antics framed by Remus's unchanging tenderness. Certainly, the word "initiate" can be read as shorthand for sexual activity, but more significantly, the word recruits sexual intimacy into a larger system of intimacy that ultimately facilitates subjugation.[144] As Remus initiated the

Boy, Harris immersed his reader in a state of consciousness known as the Lost Cause. Harris's impression of Stowe invited the reader, like Sally, to admire the romantic beauty and tenderness of slavery's innocent embrace—and, like Sally, to abandon any impulse to interfere. Through the figure of the child, Harris transformed Stowe's narrative into a love song to slavery.

## Coda: Lost Touch and the Lost Cause

At the turn of the twentieth century, the generation born after Emancipation came of age, and the older generation of Americans with firsthand knowledge of slavery began to die. Lost Causers such as Harris understood this generational change as a crisis in touch. Harris mourned the passing of his white generation that experienced physical "contact" and "intimate acquaintance" with "the old plantation and the old-time darky, who was its central figure."[145] He also mourned the African American "relics" of the same generation: "As for the old family servants, they are either gone or fast going, and we shall never behold their like again. May their souls repose in peace."[146] He feared the rising generation of African Americans, born after Emancipation, who had never "come in direct contact with the discipline of the plantation."[147] Most of all, he pitied and worried over the young white generation that had never felt the loving touch of a slave. Other white members of Harris's generation shared this concern for their postbellum descendants. Many white women tried to communicate the physical sensations of slaveholding in early twentieth century "mammy memoirs," often dedicated to their granddaughters, in which they rhapsodized about black women who partially raised them.[148]

In *Told by Uncle Remus* (1905), Harris tried to convey Remus's tender touch into the twentieth century. In this book, the Little Boy has grown up and has had a little boy of his own. However, this postbellum boy is "fragile" and too "polite." Overcivilized and effeminate, the boy is "like a girl in his refinement."[149] Remus "lure[s]" the boy into his lap, and the child instinctively molds his body into the proper position to re-create the "Uncle"-boy-cabin triangle that Sally saw through the window in the first paragraph of Harris's first book.[150] This new little boy

allowed his head to fall against the old negro's shoulder and held it there. The movement was as familiar to Uncle Remus as the walls of his cabin, for among all the children that he had known well, not one had failed to lay his head where that of the little boy now rested.[151]

Remus succeeds in influencing the new little boy somewhat (he gets the overly serious child to laugh, for example), but ultimately Remus's most tender caresses cannot produce deep change, because the "trouble with the boy was that he had had no childhood."[152] The "childhood" that this boy lacked was not a biological stage of development, but the historical experience of plantation slavery: the South, as the historian Alexander Saxton described it, "as a symbol of the collective rural past and of individual childhood."[153] Harris and other plantation writers succeeded in mapping the Lost Cause upon what Carolyn Steedman calls the "lost realm" of childhood: he hitched nostalgia for plantation slavery to nostalgia for childhood; thus he made slavery seem innocent and simultaneously associated childhood with a distinctly past period in U.S. history.[154] In Harris's view, young Americans, white and black, at the turn of the century had never known childhood because they had never known slavery as an innocent embrace.

Harris meditated upon this loss in his 1903 novel, *Wally Wanderoon and His Storytelling Machine*.[155] This novel awkwardly attempts to bring the Uncle Remus tales into the twentieth century by amalgamating the scene of storytelling and the content of African American folklore with the American fairyland conceit of L. Frank Baum's *The Wonderful Wizard of Oz* (1900). In *Wally Wanderoon*, Harris mourns the Lost Cause by positing Emancipation as a tragic estrangement between white child and storytelling slave, and by imagining modern technology as a mechanism of that separation.

*Wally Wanderoon* opens on the Abercrombie plantation after the Civil War. In an outrageous rewriting of postwar disenfranchisement, Harris describes the former Abercrombie slaves, apparently disillusioned with freedom, voluntarily returning to the plantation and "eager[ly]" asking to "take up their work where they had left off."[156] Because slavery had been outlawed, Mr. Abercrombie cannot grant their request, but he kindly installs them as sharecroppers. The novel's first chapter describes Drusilla, an African American girl, who is sad because when she was a slave, she lived close to the Abercrombies' home and played every day with the white children, Sweetest Susan and Buster John. Emancipation has estranged white from black and interrupted the innocent play of children, because sharecroppers, unlike slaves, must live by their fields. However, one day, as the three children enjoy a rare reunion, they chance to meet Wally Wanderoon, an elfin foreigner who wanders onto the Abercrombie plantation in search of "the Good Old Times we used to have."[157] Wally Wanderoon understands his search as a lost cause: he had "once hoped to find them [the Good Old Times] in a lump" but now has "given up that idea." He knows that "if I find them at all, I shall have to find them a piece at a time—an old song here and an old story yonder."[158] He recently found one fragment of the Old Times in the form of an "old-fashioned story-telling machine."[159] He stores the machine in his magical country, to which he and the children travel by touching a special tree.

Wally Wanderoon's description of the storytelling machine as a "relic"—the same word Harris used in the *Saturday Evening Post* to describe the "old time darky" who had known the "discipline" of slavery—might lead the reader to expect to find in the storytelling machine some sort of Uncle Remus automaton, a Baumesque Tin Woodman or Tik Tok in blackface.[160] When the children reach Wally Wanderoon's home, however, they discover that the storytelling "machine" is a fat white man imprisoned in a cabinet who tells stories through a hole in the box.[161] The cabinet claustrophobically shrinks Uncle Remus's cabin; no longer a container for intimacy, the wooden structure now chokes the storyteller and separates him from the child.

The cabinet parodies modern technology, and its contents—the fat storytelling artifact of the Good Old Times—caricatures the corpulent author himself. "I have caught and pickled this man," Wally Wanderoon explains, "because he is one of the old-fashioned story-tellers. He's the last of his kind so far as I know, and is one of the worst."[162] And indeed, when the storyteller attempts to meet the demand for tales, he bores his audience with academic excurses on the stories' origins. When the children try to tell each other stories, the machine ruins their fun by interjecting unsolicited critiques. Harris thus simultaneously parodies both his perceived self—an isolated relic of a lost civilization—and the pedantic version of himself that academics in the increasingly professionalized field of ethnography wanted him to be. Modern, scientific storytellers, Harris suggests, are overvalued humbugs, and the twentieth century requires a bearer of intimate touches to squeeze himself into a box. At the book's end, the children return to their postslavery plantation, where Drusilla leaves her friends to rejoin her sharecropping parents. Wally Wanderoon continues to mourn the Good Old Times, but even as he mourns, the knowledge of that which he misses is slipping away.

"What were you grieving about," inquired Sweetest Susan. . . .

"That is the trouble," replied Wally Wanderoon. "I don't remember; if I did, no doubt my mind would be easier on the subject."[163]

*Wally Wanderoon and the Storytelling Machine* received poor reviews when it was published, and it continues to be regarded as an artistic failure, a deflated imitation of Baum's Oz novels. However, Harris's book does not so much fail as it performs failure, as Peggy Phelan might say.[164] The book's graceless stories, wonderless wonderland, and unfulfilled intimacies produce in the reader an experience of disconnection, disappointment, and bewilderment as acute as that of the elf who seeks the Good Old Times. The story of a man in a box is a study in grief for lost touch, a jeremiad at generational change. Harris mourned what he perceived to be real physical tenderness between adult slaves and white children, and he performed, in *Wally Wanderoon*, the failure of literature to convey that caress into the twentieth century.

Joel Chandler Harris died in 1908, depressed by a world lacking the "romantic beauty and tenderness" of the antebellum plantation and dismayed by his generation's failure to impress twentieth-century children with visceral knowledge of slavery as a loving embrace.[165] Harriet Beecher Stowe lived until 1896—long enough to witness the 1892 publication of a new edition of *Uncle Tom's Cabin* illustrated by E. W. Kemble, creator of the Gold Dust Twins advertising logo, *A Coon Alphabet,* and other viciously racist works. Sentimental childhood receded (but did not disappear) as a new, modern childhood emerged—one that valued speed, science, and rough-and-tumble play. The Little Boy's little boy had no childhood, double mammoth Tom shows reinvented Stowe's novel as circus, and Little Eva and Uncle Tom lost much of their power to impress as they became, for many, kitschy banalities. The leaping fish of Stowe's characters had been swept away from Stowe, and even from Harris, in the currents of history.

Seven years after Harris's death, the United States celebrated the semicentenary of the end of the Civil War, and this anniversary demanded, with refreshed urgency, new patterns of remembering and forgetting slavery for the twentieth century. In that year, 1915, an artist named Johnny Gruelle picked up where Harris left off. Gruelle constructed a figure that united material and literary cultures of childhood so as to amalgamate touch, performance, blackness and whiteness, the wonderland of the imagined antebellum plantation, and even the American fairyland of L.

Frank Baum. And Gruelle, like Harris, extracted a child-character from *Uncle Tom's Cabin*—but Gruelle's extraction was neither George Shelby nor Eva, but Eva's inverted twin, Topsy. Topsy's mischief, not Eva's piety or George Shelby's nobility, animated Gruelle's creation: a doll named Raggedy Ann. Raggedy Ann channeled her cultural inheritance to script a new kind of play for the twentieth century: play that repackaged nineteenth-century racial ideologies and sentimentalism as modern vigor and optimism. These performances of play in everyday life stealthily reconfigured slaveholding and enslavement as racially innocent fun.

# 4

# The Black-and-Whiteness of
# Raggedy Ann

*I love 'er 'n spank 'er 'z much 'z I can,*
*But that never bothers my Raggedy Ann.*
—A. R. Quin, "My Raggedy Ann,"
*Chicago Daily Tribune,* 21 October 1920

In September of 1915, a young commercial artist named Johnny Gruelle seemed headed for a sustained if undistinguished career as a cartoonist and illustrator. The son of Richard Buckner Gruelle, a member of the Hoosier Group of impressionist painters, Johnny Gruelle had contributed incidental cartoons to the *Indianapolis Sun,* the *Indianapolis (Morning) Star,* the *Cleveland Press,* and other midwestern newspapers.[1] In 1910, while still in his twenties, he glimpsed fame when he bested 1,500 entries to win the *New York Herald's* competition for a new comic strip. The *Herald* ran Gruelle's eponymous strip about an elf, Mr. Twee Deedle, on the first page of the comics section, where it replaced Winsor McCay's "Little Nemo in Slumberland," when McCay absconded to a rival paper.[2] Many readers liked "Mr. Twee Deedle," but the strip inevitably suffered in comparison to its predecessor. The *Herald* manufactured and peddled a Mr. Twee Deedle doll, hoping for profits similar to those reaped by Rose O'Neill when she transformed her cartoon Kewpies into figurines, or by Palmer Cox when he plastered his cartoon Brownies on consumer goods ranging from dolls to soap advertisements to "Kodak Brownie Cameras." But Mr. Twee Deedle failed, as a cartoon or a doll, to create a sensation, and the *Herald* dropped both in 1915.[3] Gruelle then abandoned Mr. Twee Deedle but not the strategy of marketing characters simultaneously in print culture and dolls. In 1915 he trademarked several characters, each

*Figure 4.1.* J[ohnny] B[arton] Gruelle, patent 47,789, U.S. Patent Office, 7 September 1915.

intended to bridge toys and books. These characters included a pair of ducks named Quacky Doodles and Danny Daddles, who were destined for obscurity, and a cloth doll named Raggedy Ann, who was not.

Gruelle designed Raggedy Ann (figure 4.1) in part after a homemade doll that probably originally belonged to his mother, Alice Benton Gruelle, and he loaded the doll with references to American nostalgia and patriotism.[4] Raggedy Ann's red-striped stockings quoted the American flag, and her old-fashioned pinafore and homemade style gestured toward a pre-industrial past. Her name syncopated references to contemporary African American ragtime music with a portmanteau of two of midwestern poet James Whitcomb Riley's beloved characters: the Raggedy Man and Little Orphant Annie.[5] Raggedy Ann repackaged Riley's characters' references to rural America and piggybacked on the poems' popularity (Riley's were among the poems most often memorized and recited by American schoolchildren in the late nineteenth and early twentieth centuries).[6]

Gruelle's homage to Riley, which was easily recognizable in 1915, was personal: Riley had been a close neighbor and friend of Gruelle's parents when Johnny was growing up in the 1880s in Indianapolis (the Gruelles and Riley lived at 506 and 528 Lockerbie Street, respectively), and the boy had been entranced by the poet's verse recitations.[7] But the tribute was also a broader, nationalist one. Gruelle longed for the innocent American past imagined in Riley's poems, and he manifested this longing by explicitly rooting Raggedy Ann in neither his 1915 present nor his own 1880s childhood, but instead in the 1850s childhood of his parents' generation— the childhood of people like Alice Benton Gruelle, born in 1853, and Riley, born in 1849. Gruelle pointedly identified Raggedy Ann's antebellum origins in the introduction to his first book featuring the doll character: Raggedy Ann enters the narrative when a girl named Marcella (drawn after Gruelle's daughter of the same name) discovers Raggedy Ann in Grandma's attic, where the woman had abandoned the doll fifty years earlier.[8] With this introduction, Gruelle synchronized the timelines for his fictional character (a sentient doll owned by the grandmother of a character named Marcella) and material doll (a real toy owned in the 1850s by Alice Gruelle, grandmother of Marcella Gruelle), and he configured both as artifacts of the mid-nineteenth century.[9]

Raggedy Ann's concatenation of ruralism, patriotism, and nostalgia for antebellum America resonated powerfully in 1915, the semicentenary of the end of the Civil War. As historian David Blight has shown, the semicentenary of the Civil War occasioned a national reckoning with the war's meaning, and this process produced and depended on literature and public performances that re-formed and deformed memory.[10] The reimagining of slavery and the Civil War also depended, however, on private performances that occurred in homes—domestic spaces that doubled, as Amy Kaplan has shown, with the domestic space of the nation.[11] As this chapter will show, Raggedy Ann scripted home-based practices of memory that sometimes coordinated with and other times diverged from the dynamics of public memorials to the Civil War and the antebellum era. Gruelle integrated children's literature, material culture, and modern marketing techniques to shape white girls' private practices of play, and these performances in everyday life stealthily configured slaveholding and enslavement as racially innocent fun, as American love.

Gruelle aimed to become rich and famous by providing children with wholesome entertainment; no evidence suggests that he intended to rewrite history or to influence contemporary politics. However, he consciously saturated Raggedy Ann with racial meanings, especially blackness as conjured through the white imaginary of minstrelsy. Much as Raggedy Ann's name conjoined African American ragtime music with Riley's midwestern poetry, her visual attributes, I will show, amalgamated Gruelle's mother's childhood doll with a minstrel doll called the Golliwogg. Gruelle further associated Raggedy Ann with blackface when he connected her to the role of Topsy as performed in Tom shows. Most important, Gruelle constructed Raggedy Ann as an imitation of and homage to the character of the Scarecrow of Oz as created by L. Frank Baum, whom Gruelle adored—and Baum's Scarecrow was itself based in and animated by blackface minstrelsy. All these ancestors left traces in Raggedy Ann. Gruelle made no attempt to disguise these traces, which were legible to early twentieth-century consumers (indeed, the minstrel elements probably constituted a significant part of Raggedy Ann's popular appeal) and which remain legible to some contemporary Raggedy Ann enthusiasts who openly constellate Raggedy Ann with Golliwogg, pickaninny, and mammy dolls.[12] Raggedy Ann's white color, like her name, referenced not a straightforward white raciality, but instead the complicated black-and-whiteness of the face-painted minstrel performer. Her flat, white mask of a face was a scrim that could, depending on the circumstance and the audience, reveal or screen out knowledge of race, history, and violence.

## Marketing Raggedyness

Gruelle and his retailers managed and therefore profited from Raggedy Ann's flickering racial meanings by seizing on the day's most current techniques in marketing. Gruelle and his wife, Myrtle Swann Gruelle, began manufacturing Raggedy Ann dolls at home on a small scale in about 1915. Gruelle then wrote and illustrated a book, titled *Raggedy Ann Stories,* which the P. F. Volland Company published in 1918; that same year, Volland commissioned the Non-Breakable Toy Company to manufacture Raggedy Ann dolls on a mass scale. The book-and-doll combination sold brilliantly, in part because anti-German sentiment during World War I motivated parents to buy American products rather than the German-made playthings that then dominated the toy industry. One salesman for Volland reported that retailers, upon receiving a shipment of Raggedy Ann books, often reordered immediately; throughout 1918, Volland subcontracted with multiple presses to print a number of copies of the book commensurate to the demand.[13] The doll, too, sold well: over 3,200 within the first eight months—a mighty accomplishment for a new plaything in a crowded field of consumer products.[14] Between 1918 and his death in 1938, Gruelle wrote and illustrated twenty books featuring a pantheon of "Raggedy" characters, including Raggedy Ann, Raggedy Andy, Beloved Belindy, the Camel with the Wrinkled Knees, and many more figures that were simultaneously marketed as dolls. By 1934, Volland sold almost two million books featuring Raggedy characters.[15] Volland was but one of Gruelle's publishers; others included M. A. Donohue and Company, the Johnny Gruelle Company, and Bobbs-Merrill, and these companies' combined book sales reached many millions. Sales of the dolls have been similarly astronomical from the toys' initial appearance through the present day. United Media Licensing, which currently owns the rights to Raggedy Ann, claims total sales of fifty million Raggedy Ann books and products, including two million items from 1994 to 2009 alone.[16] In 2008, Marketing Evaluations found that "Raggedy Ann has a 94% awareness rate with Moms of Children 2–11"—ninety-three years after Gruelle first introduced the character.[17] Unlike Kewpie Dolls, Brownies, and many other popular dolls of the early twentieth century, Raggedy Ann remains an instantly recognizable fixture in children's culture, available for purchase in almost any toy store. She has been an American icon for almost a century.

Raggedy Ann continues to thrive in part because Gruelle perfected the craft of selling books and dolls in combination—a practice that dates from

1744, when the British publisher and book vendor John Newbery sold *A Pretty Little Pocket-Book* together with balls and pincushions.[18] Gruelle's books advertised his dolls, and his dolls advertised his books. Cross-selling was an explicit goal: a Raggedy doll was often sold with a tag that listed the books in which that character appeared. Today, book-doll combination sales have become the norm with product lines such as the American Girl series. In the past two decades, many originally freestanding works of children's literature (the Curious George series, for example) have been reinvented as book-products in combination with television programs, toys, stickers, greeting cards, and other commodities. Daniel Hade usefully describes the current practices of a corporation that owns the rights to a character from children's literature such as Clifford the Big Red Dog. To such a corporation,

> a Clifford key ring is no different from a Clifford book. Each is a "container" for the idea of "Clifford." Each "container" is simply a means for a child to experience "Cliffordness." In this world [of marketing] there is no difference between a book and a video or a CD or a T-shirt or a backpack.[19]

When corporations retrofit book characters such as Clifford or Curious George with an array of nonbook products, or when a company such as American Girl sells book-and-doll ensembles, these companies are continuing a mode of combination marketing of which Johnny Gruelle was an early virtuoso.

Gruelle succeeded because what he sold, and what millions of Americans bought, was ultimately neither Raggedy Ann books nor dolls, but "Raggedyness." Gruelle contained Raggedyness in books and dolls; he also occasionally packaged Raggedyness in a musical score or theatrical performance. He marketed these products to girls who were implicitly but unquestionably white, because in the early twentieth century, children of color were, as Lisa Jacobson notes, "excluded altogether from advertisers' pantheon of vaunted child consumers."[20] After Gruelle's death in 1938, the Gruelle estate expanded licensing of Raggedy characters. Raggedyness then entered containers as diverse as stationery, piggy banks, pencil sharpeners, sleepwear, toothbrushes, dishes, lamps, figurines, and many other commodities.[21] After 1938, when Raggedyness became almost as much about toothbrushes as dolls or books, Raggedyness became diffuse and almost infinitely flexible. During Gruelle's lifetime, however, Raggedyness securely bound Raggedy books and dolls to each other and to the white girls who read the books and played with the dolls, and who read the dolls and played with the books.

Gruelle triangulated dolls, books, and white girls by basing his books' plots on his observations of his (white) daughter's practices of doll-play. Raggedy Ann's stories, like the doll-play typical of many children, are free-associative, episodic, and casually violent. *Raggedy Ann Stories* follows a community of dolls owned and loved by a human girl named Marcella, whom the Raggedy dolls call their "Mistress." Whenever Marcella sleeps or leaves the nursery in which she and the dolls reside, the secretly sentient dolls stir and pursue wholesome adventures. Sometimes the dolls raid the kitchen for sweets; other times the dolls tumble out the nursery window and explore the countryside or a fairyland that Gruelle named, in later books, the Deep Deep Woods. Many plots pivot on the way in which a doll's physical qualities—for example, the possession of articulated fingers or clumsy mitten-hands—enable or limit activities. Many of the stories are also premised on the idea that a doll's thoughts and personality derive from its physical qualities; for example, when Raggedy Ann rips her head and some of her cotton leaks out, she loses the ability to think clearly until the hole is mended.[22] Before their mistress awakens or returns, the cheerful, playful dolls hide all evidence of their sentience, return to the nursery, and resume the precise positions in which Marcella left them.

Book-toy combinations are powerful as both marketing tools and shapers of culture because they hinge a consumer product to a narrative and thus transform both books and toys into scriptive things. As scriptive things that simultaneously prompted behaviors and allowed for individual agency, Raggedy books provided a Raggedy doll with a name, personality, and plot scenarios. Certainly, many children resisted this interdependence and played with the doll in ways that had nothing to do with the books, and some children encountered either the books or the dolls but not both. Sellers strove, however, to promote the pleasures of linked use, and therefore compounded sales, of book and doll. In one especially effective fusion of books and dolls, retailers encouraged each white girl to imagine herself as Marcella and her individual Raggedy Ann doll as the character in Marcella's story. Department store retailers accomplished this feat in part by erecting child-sized houses—models of Marcella's and Raggedy Ann's nursery—that were stocked with Raggedy Ann dolls and books.[23] These in-store displays encouraged girls physically to enter the imagined space of the books and to perform, in that set, the actions Marcella performed in her nursery—that is, to play with Raggedy Ann.

Such retail displays coordinated with advertising in magazines and the plots of the books themselves to model and thus make white girls and their parents aware of the play-practices of thousands of girls whom they would never see or meet.

Gruelle installed a racially complex and enormously appealing Raggedyness in books and dolls that many white girls acquired ensemble and then unevenly and sometimes resistantly connected through practices of play. This irregularly orchestrated imaginative play with mass-produced commercial products resembled what Benedict Anderson calls the "mass ceremony" of Enlightenment-era adults reading newspapers and novels— a process through which populations collectively imagined nationhood.[24] The book-doll combination integrated playthings and literary texts to prompt ambient performances, normalized aspects of daily life to be enacted and observed by children and adults in domestic spaces. Girls' mass ceremonies of scripted play with Raggedy dolls and books literally imagined the Raggedy universe of meaning: Raggedy spaces such as Marcella's twentieth-century nursery, Raggedy Ann as a racially complex artifact of the antebellum era, and Raggedy plot lines involving harmless violence, sentient property, and loving devotion to Mistress. Throughout these scripts, anxieties about slavery flowed as a steady, ominous undercurrent.

## The Politics of Softness: A Racial Genealogy of Cuddly Dolls

Homemade soft dolls have existed since antiquity, but the commercial mass production of soft dolls is an American innovation—with racial agendas and effects—of the turn of the twentieth century. Most pre-twentieth-century, store-bought toys (unlike homemade topsy-turvy and other rag dolls) were rigid and hard to the touch.[25] Bisque dolls or toy animals of sawdust-stuffed leather did not invite cuddling. As the sober grip with which Elizabeth Page poses her doll in John Wollaston's 1757 painting (figure 4.2) suggests, dolls of the eighteenth and early nineteenth centuries bore duties that were more utilitarian than emotional. Parents valued and sanctioned dolls mainly as luxury objects that announced class status (as Page's did in this portrait), or as a means by which girls learned and practiced sewing and other skills.[26] Around the mid-nineteenth century, however, emphasis shifted toward dolls' ability to train girls in emotional roles. By the 1880s, dolls' "emphasis on sewing" had become "obsolete," according to Miriam Forman-Brunell.[27] The change in dolls' cultural

*Figure 4.2.* An eighteenth-century girl displays her doll as a luxury object that announces class status. *Mann Page and His Sister Elizabeth,* by John Wollaston. Oil on canvas. Virginia, ca. 1757. Courtesy of the Virginia Historical Society, Richmond, Virginia.

*Figure 4.3.* Marcella daydreams as she cuddles Raggedy Ann. Johnny Gruelle, *Raggedy Ann Stories* (Joliet, Ill.: P. F. Volland, 1918), 24.

labors registers in the contrast between Elizabeth Page's display of her doll and the rich maternalism of Gruelle's Marcella in *Raggedy Ann Stories* (figure 4.3). In 1757, Elizabeth Page looks directly at her viewer; her stance says, "This is the doll I own." In 1918, Marcella looks into the distance and bends her neck as she cradles Raggedy Ann to her breast. Whereas Wollaston depicts Page in a moment of class-based self-presentation, Gruelle depicts Marcella in a reverie as she pretends to mother her doll through a comforting cuddle. Wollaston's Elizabeth knows she is being watched, and she returns her viewer's gaze. Gruelle's Marcella is unaware that her private act of imagination is being surveilled by Gruelle, the book's reader, and dolls that are, the book tells us, sentient. By the twentieth century, dolls had become full-fledged aids to and structurers of imagination. At the beginning of the nineteenth century, dolls mainly taught their owners to sew; but by the beginning of the twentieth century, dolls mainly taught their owners to pretend.

As cuddling with dolls came to be regarded as a worthwhile imaginative act, commercial manufacturers began to sell soft toys. A few white American women, most notably Izannah Walker, commercially manufactured cloth dolls in their homes on a small scale as early as the 1840s. It was not until the 1880s and 1890s, however, that numerous white women and some white men set up cottage industries to manufacture soft dolls.[28] These companies stitched racial narratives into their products. Each manufacturer typically sold dolls in several varieties, at least one of which almost always represented an African American. Examples of cloth doll lines that featured black figures include the stockinette dolls of Martha Jenks Chase and the "Missionary Rag Babies" created by Julia Jones Beecher, half-sister to Harriet Beecher Stowe.[29] The standard inclusion of black dolls suggests that manufacturers considered black dolls to be necessary and expected components of a dollmaker's line.

Tellingly, white doll manufacturers did not, as a rule, position Indian or other nonblack dolls of color as crucial to doll communities. The underlying logic that made black dolls—and *not* Indian dolls—seem necessary emerges through examination of E. I. Horsman Company's "Babyland" catalog of approximately 1904.[30] "Babyland," a geographically imagined space materialized in the pages of this advertising booklet, is populated by fourteen dolls. White dolls include "Little Miss Fancy," "Beauty," "Lady," "Dorothy," and "Little Jack Robinson." Black inhabitants of Babyland include "Topsy" and "Aunt Dinah." The catalog includes a pair of racially polarized baby dolls—the white "Little Blossom" and the "Coal-Black Baby," who wear identical christening dresses—as well as a topsy-turvy doll.

The final page of the Babyland catalog explicitly urges a child to collect all the dolls. A girl who did so, and who placed the dolls in her bedroom, would cause that nursery to reproduce the landscape of "Babyland," an imaginary geographical territory (Horsman was not unusual in the use of geographical language to describe a line of dolls; other examples of the same period include "Fairyland Dolls" and the "Dreamland Doll Company"). Most dollmakers of the late nineteenth century were based in the North (Horsman, for example, operated out of New York; Martha Chase was from Rhode Island; and Julia Beecher worked in Elmira, New York), but they populated their doll-lands with characters named "Mammy," "Dinah," and "Topsy." When white dollmakers created these objects, they did not aim to represent the postbellum, northern, urban landscape in which the dollmakers often lived. Rather, the doll-land these manufacturers constructed was the romanticized plantation South of the Lost Cause.

By collecting these dolls and arranging them in the contained space of the individual bedroom, a child caused the nursery to echo the Babyland catalog, to model an imagined, benign plantation.

In the context of this plantation wonderland, the near-universal presence of black dolls and the relative absence of Indian dolls or other dolls of color makes sense—and not only because many Lost Causers imagined the plantation in racially dyadic terms that erased nonblack people of color. The doll, as a genre of object, tells a story about persistence: doll novels such as Rachel Field's *Hitty: Her First Hundred Years* center on the premise that dolls outlive their owners, or at least outlast their owners' childhoods.[31] *Raggedy Ann Stories* opens with a scene of Marcella discovering the doll in an attic, where Marcella's grandmother abandoned it when the doll's first owner became a woman. This emphasis on persistence renders dolls and doll literature uniquely suited to tell stories about African Americans, particularly African American women, "enduring" (a word that plantation literature routinely attached to "mammies"; perhaps most famously, William Faulkner closed *The Sound and the Fury* with the words, in reference to the character of Dilsey, "They endured"). In the hands of white girls, soft black dolls persisted, told stories about endurance, and conjured a Lost Cause wonderland. Conversely, the form of the cuddly doll was uniquely unsuited to tell stories about "vanishing" Indians or the frontier that officially closed only a dozen years before the publication of the Babyland catalog. As later pages in this chapter will show, noncuddly Indian figurines were integral to the "floor games" that H. G. Wells famously played with his sons; these games enacted stories of empire, of civilization and savagery, of war and death, and of the wonderland of the American frontier. In white children's play, hard Indian dolls battled and died on the frontier wonderland of the nursery floor; soft "mammy" dolls endured and persisted and scripted cuddles in the plantation wonderland of the nursery bed.

## Raggedy Ann's Blackface Genealogy

Johnny Gruelle located Raggedy Ann within this soft doll-land that persistently ran cognate to an imagined Lost Cause South full of enduring mammies and other faithful slaves. Doll-worlds were racially charged, as Gruelle acknowledged in an unpublished, unfinished story in which a girl named Polly Peters visits a "Dreamland" populated by "different races of

*Figure 4.4.* Golliwogg (seated) and three Dutch dolls. The Dutch dolls wear clothes fashioned from an American flag. Raggedy Ann inherited the Golliwogg's triangular nose, round eyes, and red, white, and blue clothes. Bertha Upton, *The Golliwogg's "Auto-Go-Cart,"* pictures by Florence Kate Upton (New York: Longmans, Green, 1901). Courtesy of Houghton Library, Harvard University.

dolls," most notably paired "black and white" dolls.[32] Gruelle did not, however, rely only on geographically imagined context to produce Raggedy Ann's racial meanings. Instead, Gruelle loaded his character with visual elements deriving from three blackface minstrel-infused sources. These influences include the "Golliwogg," a book-doll combination invented by Florence Kate Upton and Bertha Upton; several characters created by L. Frank Baum and the men who illustrated his books and performed in his "extravaganzas"; and the character of Topsy. Each of these ancestors left traces on Raggedy Ann's body.[33]

The Golliwogg (figure 4.4 and plate 7) was a doll and book character devised by the painter Florence Kate Upton, an American-born daughter of British nationals. Upton based the Golliwogg on a blackface minstrel doll she remembered from her childhood in the United States; the character's pop-eyes, jet-black skin and hair, and bright red mouth announced his minstrel ancestry, while his red, white, and blue outfit quoted the American flag. While living in London in 1894, Upton painted a story about the adventure of the Golliwogg and his friends, the Dutch dolls, which were also based on toys Upton had owned. Upton's mother, Bertha Upton, wrote verse to narrate the paintings; the following year, Longman's published the collaboration as a picture book for children. The book's financial success inspired the Uptons to create a dozen sequels. Because Florence Kate Upton neglected to patent her character, merchandisers of all sorts manufactured an avalanche of consumer goods: "Golly" (or "Golli" or "Golliwog") products included not only dolls, but postcards, penknives, chinaware, wallpaper, ornaments, paperweights, and advertisements. James Robertson and Sons placed the Golly's face on jam jars, collectible brooches, pencils, playing cards, and children's silverware. By the time Claude Debussy published "The Golliwog's Cakewalk" in 1908, Gollies had become a massive consumer phenomenon in Great Britain.[34] Gruelle's Raggedy Ann quoted the Golliwogg's triangular nose, woolly hair, geometrical face, and American flag–like costume (Upton's Dutch dolls wore clothes literally made from pieces of an American flag), as well as the structure of the book-toy combination that ultimately sold neither books nor playthings but "Golliwoggness."

Gruelle also drew inspiration from the works of L. Frank Baum, of whom Gruelle was a tremendous, even obsessive, fan. Gruelle felt particularly attracted to Baum's character of the Scarecrow, who debuted in Baum's *The Wonderful Wizard of Oz* in 1900 and soon afterward appeared onstage in a popular theatrical adaptation of the novel. Gruelle first expressed his admiration by including a sentient scarecrow in his comic strip "Mr. Twee Deedle" in 1911.[35] Seven years later, Gruelle's first Raggedy book included playful references to Oz and to the Scarecrow in particular. For example, Raggedy Ann's introduction to the other sentient dolls in Marcella's nursery begins when "the soldier dolly turned his head and solemnly winked at Raggedy Ann"—a parallel to Dorothy's introduction to the Scarecrow, who reveals his sentience by "slowly wink[ing]" at the girl from Kansas.[36] A more explicit Oz reference appears in Gruelle's first Raggedy book when one doll comments that Raggedy Ann "looks like a scarecrow!"[37] In 1929, long after Gruelle made his fortune with his Raggedy characters, he returned to the scarecrow

*Figure 4.5.* A pantheon of Raggedy characters. Raggedy Ann plays the piano, and a scarecrow doll (far left) sits beside Beloved Belindy. Johnny Gruelle and Chas. Miller, *Raggedy Ann's Joyful Songs* (New York: Miller Music, 1937), 4.

theme in *The Cheery Scarecrow*, whose title character's face amalgamated the features of Raggedy Ann with those of Baum's Scarecrow as drawn by John R. Neill.[38] Gruelle quoted Baum's other famous illustrator, W. W. Denslow, in a miniaturized scarecrow seated among a group of singing Raggedy toys in the 1937 *Raggedy Ann's Joyful Songs* (figure 4.5). In this illustration, the scarecrow-doll winks at the reader, echoing Gruelle's wink at Baum's legacy.[39]

Baum's Scarecrow, which so enchanted Gruelle, possessed minstrel roots as deep as the Golliwogg's. When Baum originally created the character, he may not have had blackface minstrelsy in mind (although Baum did write at least one blackface play).[40] Immediately after the Scarecrow debuted in *The Wonderful Wizard of Oz* in 1900, however, the character was reinvented in a blackface-infused musical Oz "extravaganza," which opened in Chicago in 1902, moved to Broadway in 1903, and played to packed houses in both cities.[41] Because Baum's novel, its sequels, and its 1939 film adaptation retain lasting popularity, it is easy to forget that the stage production was,

*Figure 4.6.* David Montgomery (left) and Fred Stone (right) in character as the Tin Woodman and Scarecrow, respectively. Courtesy of the Harvard Theatre Collection, Houghton Library, Harvard University.

in the early twentieth century, arguably the best-known and most beloved iteration of Oz.[42]

The blackface actor Fred A. Stone originated the stage role of the Scarecrow in this extravaganza. Stone had long teamed with David Montgomery, who played the Tin Woodman, in acrobatic and blackface performances (figures 4.6 and 4.7). Stone brought to his performance of the Scarecrow a genius for physical humor, and in particular a comedic floppiness that he had honed with Montgomery on the minstrel stage. Blackface performance did not figure as an underlying presence in the 1902 and 1903 Wizard of Oz extravaganzas. On the contrary, minstrel traditions figured prominently and explicitly with the inclusion of songs such as "Under a Panama" ("Bamboo may shade a Zulu / In sunny Africa. / No coon can win out Lulu / Unless he's under a Panama"), "That's Where She Sits All Day (Cockney Coon Song)" ("Boys, have you ever seen my Dinah? / She's got thrown out of Carolina; / She is as lazy as a coon can be"), and "The Sweetest Girl in Dixie."[43] In "The Witch behind the Moon," players sang,

*Figure 4.7.* Fred Stone and David Montgomery in blackface. TCS photos 28 (Stone, F), Harvard Theatre Collection, Houghton Library, Harvard University.

Up behind de moon dere lives a nigger witch dat prowls around at
  night,
Comes a'ridin' down upon a broomstick when de moon don't shine
  too bright;
Keeps a'lookin' out for pickininies while she hums a hoo-doo tune,
In de house you better stay,
So you won't get in de way
Of de witch behind de moon![44]

Baum was so delighted with Montgomery's and Stone's minstrelized performances of his characters that he crafted his subsequent Oz books with
the blackface team in mind. Meanwhile, John R. Neill, who illustrated all
but the first of Baum's Oz books (and also, as discussed in Chapter 1, the
1908 volume *The Story of Little Black Sambo*, which included "The Story
of Topsy"), patterned his visual representation of the Scarecrow on Stone.
Baum dedicated his second Oz novel, *The Marvelous Land of Oz* (1904), to
Montgomery and Stone, whom Neill drew in performance as their respective characters (figure 4.8). Many scholars have noted that Baum probably
wrote this second Oz novel, as well as several of the subsequent novels,
with stage adaptation in mind: *The Marvelous Land of Oz* features physical gags, spectacular magical transformations, and a chorus line of female
soldiers—all of which cause the novel to read as a scenario for a stage extravaganza. Thus a blackface star's performance of the Scarecrow defined
the subsequent literary and visual representations of the character, and a
minstrel-infused extravaganza fundamentally structured the deepest logics of Oz after 1902. *The Wonderful Wizard of Oz*, like *Uncle Tom's Cabin*, is
not a literary text that illustrators, theatrical practitioners, and filmmakers
adapted, but is rather a repertoire, a set of multidirectional calls and responses, repetitions with differences, all of which suffused popular culture
through literature, theater, and material culture, including physical books.

When Johnny Gruelle created Raggedy Ann in 1915, he quoted Oz's logics and visual tropes: Gruelle imprinted the face of Neill's Scarecrow—
especially its flat surface, triangular nose, perfectly round eyes, and
semicircular smile—on Raggedy Ann's face, and he imbued his cotton
creation with the physical floppiness of Stone's body in performance. Influence flowed, then, from blackface minstrelsy through Oz into Raggedy
Ann. This genealogy becomes particularly apparent through a reading of
Baum's 1913 Oz sequel, *The Patchwork Girl of Oz*, which may have been an
immediate source text for the 1918 *Raggedy Ann Stories*. Baum seems to

*Figure 4.8.* John R. Neill depicts Fred Stone and David Montgomery in character as the Scarecrow and Tin Woodman in the dedication page of L. Frank Baum's *The Marvelous Land of Oz* (Chicago: Reilly and Britton, 1904), 4.

have written *The Patchwork Girl of Oz*, like *The Marvelous Land of Oz*, as a study for a staged musical extravaganza starring Fred Stone. *The Patchwork Girl of Oz* prominently features the character of the Scarecrow, plus the minstrel performance styles in which Stone excelled: physical humor, puns, and songs. In a striking echo of the 1902 Oz extravaganza song, "Under a Panama," in which the lyrics declare that "No coon can win

*Figure 4.9.* Raggedy Ann in one of many episodes in which she is thrown or tossed. Johnny Gruelle, *Raggedy Ann Stories* (Joliet, Ill.: P. F. Volland, 1918), 32.

out Lulu," a character in *The Patchwork Girl of Oz* sings a song titled "My Lulu" in a minstrelized black dialect:

> Ah wants mah Lulu, mah coal-black Lulu;
> Ah wants mah loo-loo, loo-loo, loo-loo, Lu!
> Ah loves mah Lulu, mah coal-black Lulu,
> There ain't nobody else loves loo-loo, Lu![45]

In *The Patchwork Girl of Oz*, Baum's eponymous character is sewn out of an old bed-quilt and magically brought to life. That is to say, she is, like Raggedy Ann, a sentient stuffed doll (although the Patchwork Girl, unlike Raggedy Ann, is the size of an adult human). She encounters Baum's other sentient mannequin, the Scarecrow, who woos her in the minstrel tradition of comedically elevated language. In *The Patchwork Girl of Oz*, as in previous novels, Baum emphasizes the Scarecrow's soft, light body, which enables him to be tossed frequently and without harm. In one of many tossing incidents, one member of a tribe of Africanized "Tottenhots"

> seized the Scarecrow's arm and was astonished to find the straw man whirl around so easily. So the Tottenhot raised the Scarecrow high in the air and tossed him over the heads of the crowd. Some one caught him and tossed him back, and so with shouts of glee they continued throwing the Scarecrow here and there, as if he had been a basket-ball.[46]

Gruelle adopted the Scarecrow's tossability as a central quality of Raggedy Ann, who is frequently and harmlessly thrown through the air (figure 4.9).

Gruelle's enthusiasm for Baum's Stone-influenced Scarecrow extended into fandom for Fred Stone himself. Gruelle wrote an unpublished, undated dramatic treatment for a musical titled (perhaps provisionally) "Raggedy Ann Show," in which Gruelle intended Stone to star. In this treatment (which mentions Stone by name five times), Gruelle imagines Stone playing a Scarecrow who has adventures with Raggedy Ann, the human girl Marcella, and other Raggedy dolls. The dreamland setting quotes Oz in the figure of not only the Scarecrow but also the "Wickedy Witch Wanda," an homage to Baum's Wicked Witch of the West (Gruelle refers to another of his sources, Upton's Golliwogg, when two of his characters claim to be the King and Queen of Bolliwoggle).[47] Gruelle calls for Stone's blackface specialties in the Scarecrow's "loppy dance" and "a funny falling act in which he staggers around and finally flops."[48] By placing Fred Stone's Scarecrow, with its minstrel-infused physical humor, into play with Raggedy Ann, Marcella, and the Wickedy Witch Wanda, Gruelle suggests not only admiration for Stone and Oz, but also a desire to integrate Raggedyness and Ozness. Even more significantly, the wish for Raggedy and Oz characters to meet onstage reveals Gruelle's belief that Raggedyness and Ozness were fundamentally compatible.[49] Gruelle designed Raggedy characters in reference to Oz, but also as extensions rather than contradictions of Baum's imaginary, including Baum's racial visions.

The Raggedy Ann Show was never produced, so Gruelle did not realize his dream of Baum's Scarecrow meeting Raggedy Ann onstage. In 1923, however, an even deeper integration of Ozness and Raggedyness occurred: in *Stepping Stones*, a musical extravaganza, Fred Stone performed

*Figure 4.10.* Fred A. Stone (left) and Dorothy Stone (right) in performance as Raggedy Andy and Raggedy Ann. Advertising leaflet, "Charles Dillingham Presents Fred Stone in *Stepping Stones* with Dorothy Stone," 1923. Courtesy of the Harvard Theatre Collection, Houghton Library, Harvard University.

as a Raggedy Andy doll (figure 4.10).[50] *Stepping Stones* ran in Chicago, New York, and elsewhere during the 1923–24 season, and Fred Stone played Raggedy Andy opposite his daughter, Dorothy Stone, in the role of Raggedy Ann. The blackface star and his daughter sang a number, "Raggedy Ann," with music by Jerome Kern and lyrics by Anne Caldwell, that mixed references to two of Gruelle's sources: African American ragtime music and James Whitcomb Riley's poem "The Raggedy Man":

> We'll rattle off to find our ragtime cabaret,
> Where we can rag our raggy rags till break of day.
> Oo Raggedy Ann,
> Do say what you can
> Come and dance with your Raggedy Man.[51]

The stylizations with which Stone animated both the Scarecrow and Raggedy Andy drew not only on minstrelsy in general, but also on the specific blackface role of Topsy in *Uncle Tom's Cabin*. When Stone was in his teens, he began performing minstrel routines with his brother Ed, and in 1887 ran a six-week stint with a Kickapoo medicine show. Stone first achieved notice, however, in the late 1880s and early 1890s when he played Topsy in a traveling Tom show. His employer described Stone in this role as "a star":

> As a dancer of breakdowns in black-face guise, he beat 'em all. He showed peculiar aptitude for the humor of Topsy, and the part afforded him ample scope for the development of his whimsical talent.[52]

What connected *Uncle Tom's Cabin* to Oz to Raggedyland was not simply Fred Stone and his "whimsical talent," but more deeply, the black-and-whiteness that underlay Topsy, the Scarecrow, and Raggedy Ann and Andy. All of these characters, indebted as they are to minstrelsy, enact not racial admixture but instead the simultaneity of blackface: each of these characters holds blackness and whiteness both in distinction and in tender contact, much as a minstrel's makeup softly covers the face without penetrating it. As scholars from Eric Lott to David Roediger to William J. Mahar have argued, when white minstrels corked up, they performed a blackness that did not obliterate whiteness but that instead produced and shaped it. The white performer in blackface, like the topsy-turvy doll, gained form from what showed and what hid, from whiteness-and-blackness, from the promise and threat of racial flip-flops.

The character of Topsy contained these promises and threats. Stowe derived the name "Topsy" from the phrase "topsy-turvy," which the *Oxford English Dictionary* traces to 1530 (the *OED* suggests that "topsy-turvy" may have been a corruption of "top side turned").[53] When Stowe published *Uncle Tom's Cabin*, however, the word "topsy" had no independent meaning. A parallel may be found in the term "hocus-pocus." "Hocus" signifies nothing except a demand for "pocus." By naming a character "Topsy," Stowe created a sense of incompletion, a call for closure. Readers did consciously perceive the incompletion of Topsy's name: an article in *Arthur's Home Magazine* in 1853 recounted an incident in which

> a little girl, while listening to the reading of *Uncle Tom's Cabin*, [asked her mother,] "why don't the book never mention Topsy's last name? I have tried to hear it whenever it spoke of her, but it has not once spoke." "Why, she

had no other name, child." "Yes she had, mother, and I know it." "What was it?" "Why, Turvey [*sic*]—Topsy Turvey [*sic*]."⁵⁴

As the girl in this anecdote understood, the name "Topsy"—or "top side"—demanded that the reader supply "Turvy"—or "turned." The partial name "Topsy" foreshadowed the character's inevitable turnaround, her conversion. After the publication of *Uncle Tom's Cabin*, topsy-turvy dolls absorbed the Topsy/Eva relationship and often acquired the name "Topsy-Eva" dolls (see plate 4). However, the character of Topsy, *independent of Eva*, existed in complex relationship to the topsy-turvy doll, because the defining flip of the topsy-turvy doll lay nascent within Topsy from the moment of her entrance. Just as the topsy-turvy doll is permanently in the act of changing race, Topsy was permanently midconversion, a top side about to turn.

Topsy's wish to change races, to "be skinned, and come white,"⁵⁵ which Stowe presented as a tragic consequence of slavery, became by the turn of the twentieth century yet one more comic aspect of the pickaninny. Numerous soap companies, most famously Pears' Soap, touted their products with trade cards and other advertisements in which black children partially or fully turned white. Some advertisements of the period explicitly connected this racial transformation to Topsy. In a turn-of-the-century advertisement for J. and P. Coats' thread, for example, Topsy assures Eva that Topsy, like Coats' black thread, cannot lose her color. This advertisement jokingly suggests that Topsy would stupidly believe that Eva believes Topsy's color could "come off by wetting [*sic*]." The humor asserts the impossibility of racial transformation, but it simultaneously posits the possibility of belief in Topsy turning white.⁵⁶

One of the most striking examples of Topsy turning white in the early twentieth century may be found in repeated images of Topsy whitening her face with powder. Illustrations of Topsy powdering her face appear, for example, in the *Little Folks' Edition of Uncle Tom's Cabin* and the *Uncle Tom's Cabin Picture Book* (figures 4.11 and 4.12, respectively).⁵⁷ In 1913, the same year that an anonymous artist placed a powder puff in Topsy's hand for the *Uncle Tom's Cabin Picture Book*, John R. Neill handed Baum's Patchwork Girl a similar implement (figure 4.13). The parallel images become most striking in the light of the fact that neither Stowe's Topsy nor Baum's Patchwork Girl ever powders her face in the text of the respective novels. Despite the absence of powder in Stowe's or Baum's prose,

*Figure 4.11.* Topsy whites up. Unsigned illustration, "Topsy at the Dressing Table." Anon., *Little Folks' Edition: Uncle Tom's Cabin* (New York: Graham and Matlack, ca. 1910), 41. Courtesy of the University of Virginia Library.

illustrations of Topsy and the Patchwork Girl whiting up do not disrupt the respective stories because the idea of temporary whiteness (in oscillation with temporary blackness) was always inherent in Topsy and the Patchwork Girl. The whiting up signals a theatrical performance, a reference to the minstrel practices that thread through both characters. The illustrators of Topsy and the Patchwork Girl did not draw whitening *into*

*Figure 4.12.* Topsy whites up in another unsigned illustration. Anon., *Uncle Tom's Cabin Picture Book* (New York: Graham and Matlack, 1913), 4. Courtesy of the University of Virginia Library.

each story; they drew whitening *out* of each story. Topsy was always already in the act of whiting up.

When Topsy whites up totally, if temporarily, the result embodies the negative of the minstrel mask: white skin punctuated by oversized eyes, a geometric nose, and woolly but nonblack hair. That result is Raggedy Ann.

*Figure 4.13.* The Patchwork Girl whites up. L. Frank Baum, *The Patchwork Girl of Oz*, illustrated by John R. Neill (Chicago: Reilly and Britton, 1913), 46.

Johnny Gruelle associated Raggedy Ann with Topsy from his earliest conceptions. In a 1909 cartoon, Gruelle drew a child playing with a Topsy-like doll alongside a proto–Raggedy Ann doll.[58] Later, when Fred Stone's daughter Dorothy performed the role of Raggedy Ann onstage, she replicated the gestures with which Caroline Fox Howard had imbued Topsy more than seventy years earlier (figure 4.14). In a photograph of Dorothy Stone playing Raggedy Ann (which appears on page 78 of Patricia Hall's *Raggedy Ann and More: Johnny Gruelle's Dolls and Merchandise* and is

*Figure 4.14.* "Oh! I'se So Wicked, as Sung by Mrs G. C. Howard." Sheet music. Geo[rge]. C. Howard (New York: Horace Waters, 1854). The illustration shows Caroline Fox Howard in performance as Topsy. Courtesy of the American Antiquarian Society.

unfortunately not available for reproduction in this book), Dorothy Stone strikes a stance nearly identical to Caroline Fox Howard's: each actress stands in an oversized pinafore, pelvis forward, one foot thrust out, hands flipped up in what could be the opening pose of a cakewalk. Each woman's stance is presentational; each suggests, "I am here to entertain you." We see this "cakewalk" position persist throughout formal and informal performances of Raggedy Ann, such as that of an anonymous girl in an photograph, circa the 1920s, that appears as the frontispiece in Patricia Hall's *Raggedy Ann and Johnny Gruelle: A Bibliography of Published Works.*[59] The girl in this photograph holds her hand up in the same presentational style of Caroline Fox Howard. There is no reason to suppose that Dorothy Stone or the anonymous girl thought consciously, in the 1920s, about Topsy or Caroline Fox Howard in the 1850s. When called upon to strike a pose as Raggedy Ann, however, both the girl and Dorothy Stone restored minstrel postures that were inherent in the character they aimed to represent.

Raggedy Ann's whiteness, like the minstrel performer's cork-blackness, is always temporary. Raggedy Ann, like a topsy-turvy doll, Topsy, and a blacked-up minstrel performer, always contains within her the idea of racial flip-flops; the promise or threat of racial transformation. If one side of the topsy-turvy doll is exposed, the other side always lurks, waiting, beneath the skirts. Sooner or later, the reverse side will emerge. Raggedy Ann's whitened skin exposes the white side of the topsy-turvy doll, but the black side promises to crop up. One such eruption occurs in the figure of Gruelle's Beloved Belindy.

Gruelle describes Beloved Belindy, who sits next to the scarecrow doll in figure 4.5, as "the mammy of Raggedy Ann and Raggedy Andy and all of the other dolls in the nursery."[60] Gruelle introduced her to the Raggedy ensemble in an eponymous book of 1926. Gruelle left no statement as to why he created Beloved Belindy, but the reason was likely commercial: Gruelle regularly invented new characters so he could add new lines of Raggedy merchandise. Gruelle's introduction of a mammy doll in 1926 constituted a good economic bet, given the "heightened glorification of mammy from 1906 through the mid-1920s" that Cheryl Thurber has traced.[61]

In the original draft of the story that would become *Beloved Belindy*, the eponymous character did not exist; the protagonist was Raggedy Ann. Late in the writing process, Gruelle invented a mammy doll character and retroactively substituted her for Raggedy Ann. As many Raggedy collectors have noticed, Beloved Belindy is indistinguishable from Raggedy Ann, except for Belindy's appearance and explicit description as a "mammy." In this book, Beloved Belindy does not speak in dialect (unlike Gruelle's human character, Dinah, who labors in Marcella's family's kitchen and laundry), nor does she reminisce about life "before the war" or indulge in other clichés common in mammy literature of the 1920s. Beloved Belindy has dark skin where Raggedy Ann has light skin, exaggerated lips where Raggedy Ann has thin lips, and a red headscarf where Raggedy Ann has red hair. Apart from these reversals, the dolls are largely identical. Johnny Gruelle's manuscript papers further demonstrate the interchangeability of the characters in their creator's mind: over and over, Gruelle corrected manuscripts to transform Raggedy Ann into Beloved Belindy or vice versa. In one unpublished Christmas story, for example, Gruelle employed strikeouts twice to flip between Raggedy Ann and Beloved Belindy:

> "Beloved Belindy has never had a Christmas before!" Raggedy Ann started to explain.
>
> "So she stayed awake and watched me from the window! Didn't you, Beloved Belindy?" Santa asked.
>
> "It was all so lovely and wonderful!" ~~Raggedy~~ Beloved Belindy managed to answer."[62]
>
> Raggedy Andy laughed so hard . . . his rag legs doubled up in under him and he sat down in ~~Beloved Belindy's lap~~ Raggedy Ann's lap.[63]

This manuscript includes no other flips in character, and it was not typical of Gruelle to substitute one character for another. Raggedy Andy and Raggedy Ann, for example, seldom trade lines in Gruelle's corrections—but Raggedy Ann and Beloved Belindy often do. When Johnny Gruelle created Beloved Belindy, he clearly understood that a mammy character would in no way contradict or disrupt any existing logic in Marcella's nursery. Beloved Belindy slid seamlessly into the Raggedy nursery because that soft wonderland was a racially innocent reimagination of the Lost Cause plantation. Beloved Belindy was not so much a new character as she was an amplification of traces already within Raggedy Ann.

Beloved Belindy was Gruelle's second attempt to introduce a mammy character to the Raggedy pantheon. Sometime between 1920 and 1926, before Gruelle published *Beloved Belindy*, he wrote an unpublished story, "Raggedy Auntie," that melds explicit references to blackface and plantation literature with subtle echoes of *Uncle Tom's Cabin*. In "Raggedy Auntie," Marcella's mother sews a "black faced doll" stuffed with "clean white cotton" and sporting white button eyes that "looked very chalky."[64] The emphasis on "chalky" eyes, as well as the repeated terms "black face" or "black faced" (the terms appear seven times in six pages) laminates the character to the minstrel mask. The black-faced doll's outside reverses the coloration of Raggedy Ann, but her stuffing of "clean white cotton" matches Raggedy Ann's interior. It is therefore not surprising when another doll notes that the black-faced doll is "almost like Raggedy Ann."[65] *Almost*, indeed.

Marcella names the doll Raggedy Auntie, a term that refers in this racialized context not to familial status but to a subservient caretaking function (plantation literature often used the terms "mammy" and "auntie" interchangeably). Marcella "squeeze[s] her to see how nice and soft" she is. When Marcella leaves the nursery with Raggedy Auntie in tow, the other dolls animate. A mechanical Dutch doll named Henny laments to Raggedy Ann that Marcella "has named the new doll Raggedy Auntie and we will get all mixed up when we call you!" The dolls seem to pronounce Auntie "Ann-tee" rather than "Ahn-tee"; therefore they worry about the repetition of the syllable "Ann" in the doubled names. Most tellingly, however, no doll worries that "Raggedy Auntie," if pronounced Ann-tee, might be confused with "Raggedy Andy." Ann-tee sounds closer to Andy than to Ann, but the dolls' anxiety consolidates only around possible confusion between Auntie and Ann, thus revealing that the similarity, and potential confusion of identities, is not only phonological.[66]

This anxiety about the interchangeability of Ann and Auntie quickly gives way, however, to overt rejection of blackness. Henny declares, "I shall not like Raggedy Auntie! She looks too black! No one likes a balck [sic] doll!"[67] Raggedy Andy responds to Henny by wordlessly giving "him a push, sending him sliding from his chair." The other dolls laugh delightedly at the push, "for they kn[o]w that this [is] a signal for a romp."[68] The dolls happily kick and bump each other. Then the dolls hear Marcella approaching, and they quickly resume the positions in which she left them so that she will not discover their sentience. Marcella places Raggedy Auntie on a chair next to Henny and then leaves the nursery.

As soon as Marcella exits, Henny again rejects Auntie on the basis of what Gruelle called, in "Polly Peters and the Wish-Wish Man," the doll's "race": "I do not care to sit so near a doll with a black face!" The "new doll hear[s] Henny say this," but sits "just as still as [can] be."[69] Although Raggedy Auntie does not move, the other dolls assume her to be sentient, and try to interact with her. They chastise Henny for being "rude and ill mannered." Raggedy Ann apologizes to Raggedy Auntie for Henny's rudeness, but the "black faced doll just [sits] and smile[s]" without moving. Except for Henny, the dolls gather around the immobile Auntie and "each one in turn [takes] the new doll's hand" and introduces himself or herself. Regardless of Henny's disdain, Ann assures Auntie, "We shall play with you!"[70]

Upon hearing this promise of integrated play, Raggedy Auntie animates:

Raggedy Auntie wipe[s] her white button eyes with her rag hand, "I jess guess we all will be frens!" she [says], "But I jes thought if you all didn't like me I would jess pretend I wasn't alive!"

So, Raggedy Ann put[s] her arms around Raggedy Auntie and pull[s] her gently from the chair, and then when the new black faced doll [is] in front of her, Raggedy Ann put[s] her arms around the new doll and [gives] her a hug. . . .

"Thank you, . . ." Raggedy Auntie [says], "I spect we all is gwine to have lots of fun!"[71]

This interaction echoes the "conversion" scene between Stowe's Topsy and Eva. In this tableau—repeated endlessly in illustrations (including figure 1.3 in Chapter 1 and plate 3, and figure 5.7 in Chapter 5), Tom shows, and, by Gruelle's lifetime, film—Eva kneels beside the despairing Topsy and asks, "What does make you so bad, Topsy?" The enslaved girl replies,

"Couldn't never be nothin' but a nigger, . . . If I could be skinned, and come white, I'd try then."

"But people can love you, if you are black, Topsy. Miss Ophelia would love you, if you were good." . . .

"No; she can't bar me, 'cause I'm a nigger! . . .There can't nobody love niggers, and niggers can't do nothin'!"[72]

Eva touches Topsy on the shoulder and asserts her Christian love for the girl, and Topsy responds by bursting into tears. This is the conversion that was promised in Topsy's name ("topsy," we remember, signified nothing in 1852 except a call for "turvy," a prediction of topside turned); it is Little Eva's only successful conversion in the novel. In Gruelle's and Stowe's respective scenes, hatred of blackness ("No one likes a balck [sic] doll!" and "she can't bar me, 'cause I'm a nigger! . . . There can't nobody love niggers"[73]) causes a black character to harden emotionally and therefore to behave unacceptably (in Auntie's case, to feign insentience, and in Topsy's case, to be "wicked"). In Stowe's text, the black-white dyad ("representatives of the two extremes of society . . . representatives of their races"[74]) consolidates so Eva's touch can convert Topsy not only to Christianity and thus to eternal life but also to sensation which, in Stowe's sentimental context, made one human. Topsy's desire to "be skinned, and come white" is answered not literally (as in illustrations that put a powder puff in her hand) but spiritually in the conversion to sensate humanity, as evidenced by Topsy's tears. Similarly, in Gruelle's story, Raggedy Ann lays hands on her dialectic twin and converts her to vigorous, sentient life—the early twentieth-century "mind cure" equivalent of Christianity—by persuading Auntie to animate and play. Each interaction ends with a promise for the future cast in the ideals of Stowe's and Gruelle's respective moments: sentimental redemption or Raggedy fun.

Marcella reenters the nursery just after all the dolls except Henny have resumed their positions. Henny, unwilling to sit next to Raggedy Auntie, abandons the chair on which Marcella seated him and hides behind the toy piano. Marcella doesn't notice Henny's absence and scoops up all the other dolls for a ride in the car. When Marcella leaves, Henny emerges from his hiding spot to discover that he is alone. In his "loneliness," he acknowledges "that if he had not been so rude, but had made friends with Raggedy Auntie, he would now be shooting along, listening to the hum of the motor and seeing the pretty things" with the other dolls. "I am very sorry!" Henny declares, and he resolves to apologize to Raggedy Auntie.[75]

When Marcella returns to the nursery, she discovers Henny back in his chair. She "place[s] Raggedy Auntie in the chair with Henny and put[s] his arm about her shoulder." Henny is "surprised" to find Auntie's shoulder "nice and soft." Henny thinks, "She's just like Raggedy Ann!"[76] Now that Henny has seen the error of his ways, the equivalence between Auntie and Ann produces not anxiety but reassurance. When Marcella leaves and the dolls reanimate, Henny apologizes "for being so rude" and asks Raggedy Auntie to forgive him.

> "Ha, ha, ha! Deed I will Marse Henny!" Raggedy Auntie laugh[s] as she return[s] the hug Henny gave her. So Henny pull[s] the new black faced doll from the chair and dance[s] around the room.[77]

This paragraph encapsulates Gruelle's tensions: interracial dancing is allowable, even celebrated, but only after Raggedy Auntie declares her subservience by calling Henny "marse," a plantation literature corruption of "master." Much as the dolls call the white Marcella "mistress" and pretend to be insentient in her presences, Raggedy Auntie calls a white doll "marse" and pretends (if briefly) to be insentient in the other dolls' presence. Raggedy Auntie eagerly assumes her role as servant: she tucks a doll in with a white bedspread and declares, "I knows honey that Miss Marcella was jess pretendin' but anyhow, I'm goin' to be a real for sure Auntie to all you dolls, jess the samey!"[78] The dolls are delighted by Auntie's promise to care for them. Henny whispers to Raggedy Ann, "Raggedy Auntie is just as nice as she can be, even if she has a black, black face!" Racial harmony in the nursery has been restored according to the logics crafted through Lost Cause plantation fiction: strict racial hierarchies produce peace, love, and domestic tenderness.

Raggedy Ann agrees with Henny, and then enunciates the story's moral.

> "Some of the most prescious [*sic*] things in the world are hidden beneath rough out side [*sic*] coverings. And, it is wrong to ever judge anyone by their appearance, for the person with the ugliest face, may really be the one with the kindest heart!"
>
> "I remember once you said, 'the old, shabby violin, although it was scratched and rough on the outside, might give the sweetest sound, if it was played upon by one who understood![']" Henny [says].
>
> "Yess [*sic*] indeed, Henny!" Raggedy Ann smile[s], "And to play upon others, we must use kindly, loving methods, then, we shall find out that they in return are filled with the same sunny happiness that we are!"[79]

The didactic moral espouses a superficial egalitarianism based on a valuation of people's interiors rather than exteriors. More subtly, however, the moral hails the Blakean line *cum* cliché, "I am black, but O! my soul is white."[80] This idea that black skin could cover a white soul embeds in Topsy's wish to "be skinned" (not bleached or powdered) and "come white" (not skinless, tortured, and exposed). In Auntie's case, her "rough out side [*sic*]" of her black face masks "the most prescious [*sic*] things in the world," that is, "clean white cotton." The moral positions blackness and whiteness simultaneously in close intimacy and stark distinction and thus aligns Raggedy Auntie's body with the logic of Topsy and of Raggedy Ann herself. Each of these figures represents not blackness, whiteness, or racial admixture, but instead the black-and-whiteness, the racial complexities, of the topsy-turvy doll and the minstrel performer.

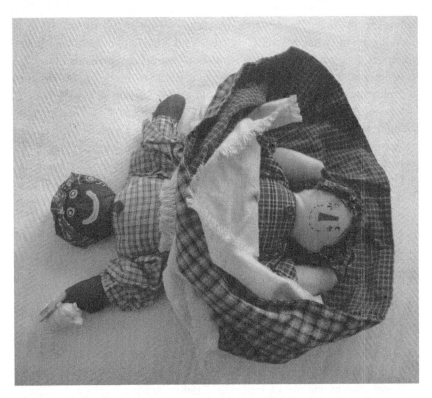

*Figure 4.15.* Raggedy Ann–Mammy Topsy-Turvy Doll, Kotton Kountry Kreations. Photograph by Phyllis Thompson.

Raggedy Ann's connections to blackface, Topsy, plantation literature, mammies (or aunties), the Scarecrow, and Golliwoggs were plain in the early twentieth century, and they remain perceptible to some today. Contemporary collectors and other Raggedy Ann enthusiasts persistently pair Raggedy dolls with pickaninny dolls, mammy dolls, and Golliwoggs. For example, Kotton Kountry Kreations is a cottage industry that manufactures "Primitive Country Dolls," Raggedys, and "Black Dolls" including "Mammies." The company's name refers explicitly to the "cotton country" of the plantation South, as well as the dolls' constitutive material. The company's initials indicate either an association with the Ku Klux Klan or an absence of concern at being misconstrued as having Klan sympathies. In a hybrid that is astonishing only in its lucidity, Kotton Kountry Kreations produced a topsy-turvy doll in which one half is a Belindy-like mammy doll, and the other half is Raggedy Ann (figure 4.15 and plate 8). Dollmaker Linda Wolf has sewn an equally revealing hybrid doll: her "Golly," as Wolf labels her doll, replicates Raggedy Ann's iconic triangular nose, "pie slice" eyes, lower eyelashes, and red-striped stockings; but also the name and ink-black skin of the Golliwogg, as well as the multiple pigtails associated with Topsy.[81] These hybrid dolls, as well as contemporary collectors' persistent pairing of Raggedys with pickaninnies, mammies, and Gollys, show that Raggedy Ann's location within a blackface genealogy remains at least partially perceptible today.

Raggedy Ann's blackface ancestors—Topsy, the Golliwogg, the Scarecrow—left traces on her body: a flat, geometric face, woolly hair, physical softness and floppiness, playfulness, cleverness, acrobatic skill, tossability, cheerfulness, imperviousness to pain, tendency toward benign mischief, natural ability to entertain, and cuddliness. Raggedy Ann's ancestors marked her not with a mixture of "blackness" and "whiteness," but rather with the "black-and-whiteness" of the blacked-up minstrel performer or the topsy-turvy doll—bodies that do not merely mingle blackness and whiteness, but that instead keep blackness and whiteness simultaneously in tense distinction and in intimate contact. Raggedy Ann does not represent a black, white, or racially amalgamated body, just as the topsy-turvy doll does not refer simply or directly to a mixed-race child. Raggedyness is a sign not of African Americans or African Americanness, but of black-and-whiteness. Raggedyness signifies not slaves but the system of slavery, not black or white people but rather, to use Eric Lott's famous phrase, white people's love and theft of blackness.[82] Raggedy Ann is a whited-up minstrel performer; a complicated, racially obsessive thing of enormous cultural utility; a hulking, steaming, meaning-machine ready to be set to labor.

## *The Enslavement of Raggedy Ann*

In contrast to the character of the Golliwogg, who interacts mainly with other dolls and who does not seem to be owned by any human, Raggedy Ann constantly espouses her devotion to her "Mistress," the human child character Marcella, whom she and the other Raggedy dolls wish only to please. Gruelle's central conceit—that the Raggedy dolls are alive but that they hide their sentience—invites the question of *why* Raggedy dolls maintain their secret. If the dolls are alive, vigorous, and fun-loving, why do they not, like Carlo Collodi's eponymous hero in *Pinocchio* (1883), simply leave the humans' home and pursue their own fortunes? If the dolls are motivated to scramble nightly out the nursery window and pursue delightful adventures in the Deep Deep Woods, why are they not motivated to remain in that realm and to decline to return to Marcella's nursery? The answer, Gruelle suggests over and over, is that the dolls faithfully love their owner and that this love precludes any desire for freedom.

This answer was not unique to Gruelle (Frances Hodgson Burnett employed the same conceit in 1906 in *Racketty Packetty House*), but neither was it the only available way to configure dolls in literature.[83] Contemporary contrasts exist in L. Frank Baum's *Dot and Tot of Merryland* (1901) and Margery Williams Bianco's *The Velveteen Rabbit* (1922). In *Dot and Tot of Merryland*, dolls revolt and riot against humans, who then forcibly subdue them.[84] In *The Velveteen Rabbit,* the eponymous character never expresses love for the "Boy" who owns him. The Boy does love the Velveteen Rabbit, but that love is fickle: when the Boy's parents attempt to burn the toy, the child voices no objections, expresses no grief, and effortlessly transfers affection to a new doll. The Velveteen Rabbit desires not to serve and love the Boy, but to be "Real" and to dance. The Rabbit discovers that the Boy's love can never fulfill him. Slated for death by burning, the Rabbit cries real tears, and from those tears sprouts a flower, and out of the flower steps a fairy. The fairy transforms the Rabbit, who had been Real only to the Boy, into a living Rabbit, a truly Real Rabbit, who then joyfully joins his own kind in the forest.[85]

An even tarter contrast appears between Gruelle's books and Baum's *The Patchwork Girl of Oz*, in which Baum's characters openly debate the Patchwork Girl's status as enslaved or free. After the sorcerer Dr. Pipt magically brings the quilted mannequin to life, the Patchwork Girl, nicknamed "Scraps," wants to leave and seek her own fortune. Dr. Pipt explains that she has no right to do so, because she is "a—a sort of slave."[86] The stuttering struggle to define Scraps's status as enslaved or free becomes one of the central themes of the novel. Soon after Scraps comes to life, a magic Liquid of Petrification accidentally spills on Unc[le] Nunkie and Pipt's wife, Margolotte, turning both into stone. Nunkie's nephew and Scraps then embark on a quest to acquire the ingredients for a spell that will reverse the petrification. Early in this quest, the Patchwork Girl comments on her liberation from slavery:

Here am I, made of an old bedquilt and intended to be a slave to Margolotte, rendered free as air by an accident that none of you could foresee. I
am enjoying life and seeing the world, while the woman who made me is
standing helpless as a block of wood. If that isn't funny enough to laugh at,
I don't know what is.[87]

As Scraps notes, she is freed from slavery, from the status of thing, precisely
*because* her owner transforms from flesh to stone. For Baum, slavery and
freedom, thingness and humanity, are finite in quantity but tremulously
volatile in quality: one always threatens to transform, topsy-turvy, into the
other.[88]

Gruelle, who was so deeply influenced by Baum, evaded questions that
formed, for Baum, a center of gravity. Whereas the Patchwork Girl passes
from insentience to sentience, from enslavement to freedom, Raggedy
Ann is always already sentient and happily enslaved. Baum's characters
question their enslavement and seek—and even riot for—freedom, agency,
and personal fulfillment, but Gruelle's characters ask no such questions
and desire only to serve. Gruelle literally obliterated acknowledgment of
African American servitude in a 1928 manuscript draft titled "Katinka
and Katunka (Story 14)." In this manuscript, Beloved Belindy comments,

All the dolls here love each other very, very much and look at me. I am ~~just~~
a rag Mammy doll. ~~If I was a real for sure person, I would not be able to
play with everyone about me, cause I would be a servant~~. But here, one doll
is just as good as another as long as he, or she has kindly loving thoughts
for the others![89]

In Marcella's nursery, then, dolls' natural servitude happily displaces—and
thus retains—thoughts of racial politics. Whereas Baum's characters scoff
at a would-be human owner and engage in lengthy dialogues about their
rights and their status as enslaved or free, Gruelle's characters glance off
questions of their servitude with incidental phrases such as "it would never
do" to allow a human to know of their sentience.[90] Gruelle's characters
could sow the seeds of their own freedom and transformation, as the Velveteen Rabbit does when he sheds the tears that incubate a fairy. Instead,
Gruelle aggressively and persistently asserts that Raggedy Ann loves her
Mistress and finds complete fulfillment in playing the role of passive, nonsentient doll—an object that, in Gruelle's universe, *does not exist*. Within
the Raggedy universe, *all* dolls live; a sentient doll such as Raggedy Ann

cannot impersonate an "ordinary" or inert doll, because no such object exists. In short, Raggedy Ann *pretends* to be inert, *pretends* to be a nonsentient doll so as to provide Marcella *with* a doll. As Marcella's ideal concubine, Raggedy Ann lovingly, willingly, and faithfully gives the gift of her own soft body.[91]


## *The Politics of Softness Revisited: The Racial Power of Play*

Book-toy combinations by definition link narratives to material things, reading to playing. At the turn of the twentieth century, this linkage seemed especially important because the Child Study Movement had successfully promulgated the idea that children's imaginative practices, especially girls' play with dolls, could and should serve cultural purposes. The Child Study Movement, which was influenced by Sigmund Freud and led by the psychologist (and sometime white supremacist) G. Stanley Hall and his colleagues at Clark University, argued that a psychologically and physically vigorous childhood was crucial to not only a productive individual adulthood but also to the overall physical and moral health of the United States. Psychologists therefore encouraged parents and teachers to observe their children, especially during play, and to take notes in an anthropological style.[92] Gruelle was one of thousands of parents who did so, and his notes eventually informed his Raggedy books.

Alice Minnie Herts Heniger, who founded the Children's Educational Theatre (CET) on the Lower East Side of Manhattan in 1903, was among those who believed in the power of children's imaginative play, as performance, literally to shape civilization. Heniger created the CET explicitly as a Progressive tool: her children's theater aimed to mold the behaviors and imaginations of immigrant and first-generation children so as to Americanize them, and through them, their families. Heniger did not, however, confine her project to the immigrant communities of lower Manhattan. In 1918, the same year Gruelle published *Raggedy Ann Stories*, Heniger collaborated with G. Stanley Hall to publish a dramatic manifesto titled *The Kingdom of the Child*. This manifesto lauded the "culture power" of children's imaginative play and urged parents to "enter the kingdom of the child"—that is, to pretend with the child—so as to harness and channel "all the vital imaginative power of the race."[93] In one memorable passage, Heniger contrasted a boy building a box and a girl making biscuits with a boy pretending to be a giant and a girl pretending to be a fairy. For

Heniger, "Both the boy in making the giant and the girl in making the fairy do something more important to the progress of civilization than either does in making the box or the biscuits."⁹⁴ For Heniger, children's acts of "making" such fantastic creatures literally strengthened their powers of imagination, which could then be applied toward imagining and realizing great futures for their nation. Because children's imaginative play was believed literally to shape "the progress of civilization," Heniger and Hall urged parents to monitor and manage children's play. Heniger's dramatic manifesto doubled as a parental advice manual in which Heniger instructed parents to "enter into the kingdom of childhood"—that is, to insinuate themselves into children's imaginative lives—not through force or coercion, but rather through gentle guidance and manipulation of a child's "imitative" or "dramatic instinct." The destiny of the United States was believed literally to depend on parents' success in this endeavor.

Dolls offered one crucial way for parents to shape girls' imaginative play. Just as a parent might gently encourage a boy to "make" a giant or a girl to "make" a fairy, soft dolls such as Raggedy Ann encouraged their owners to take specific actions. As D. W. Winnicott and many others of the nineteenth and twentieth centuries have observed, children's physical engagements with soft dolls may be divided into two broad categories: children embrace and cuddle soft dolls, and they violently abuse them.

Let us consider first the act of cuddling. Cuddle games are best understood in opposition to "Floor Games," as the writer H. G. Wells famously described the imaginative games he played with his sons. In "floor games," the boys and their father used boards to build miniature islands and archipelagos, wildernesses and cities on the nursery floor. The Wellses then populated their terrain with small, hard, rigid dolls, most notably lead soldiers and figurines of "Red Indians" and "Zulus." The boys and their father played games of invasion and conquer—games that frankly modeled imperialist visions. For H. G. Wells, these games had the practical value of "building up a framework of spacious and inspiring ideas in [the boys] for after life." This development of "spacious" ideas, Wells believed, contributed directly and literally to imperialist ventures: "The British Empire will gain new strength from nursery floors."⁹⁵ Wells's belief in the literal political power of children's play echoes Heniger's belief in the "culture power" of imaginative performance.

The contrast between Wells's boys' floor games and Gruelle's girls' cuddle games is revealing. Floor games tell violent stories about wilderness and war; these games model imperialism by granting a child panoptic vision over territorial battles.[96] The boy is outside the action, aloof, all-powerful. He holds small, hard figurines in the hand and deploys them with chess-like movements (one member of the child-study movement noted in 1921 that bottle dolls—hard figurines built out of small bottles—are "the chessmen of children, used for playing the serious game of life").[97] Cuddle games, in contrast, involve the child bodily with the doll (figure 4.3). Whereas the boy playing floor games causes figurines to interact with each other, the girl playing cuddle games interacts directly with the toy. Floor games transform a nursery floor into oceans and islands populated by "savages" and conquerors, and transform boys into model imperialists; cuddle games with compliant, cottony, soft dolls transform a girl into a doting "mistress." Girls' cuddle games tell stories about domesticity, family, and love. When cuddle games involve racially complex dolls that a book characterizes as faithful slaves, then those games perform fantasies of slavery as domesticity, of servitude as a mode of love, and of plantations as families.

Violence was explicitly foregrounded and celebrated in floor games, but violence was also integral, rather than extraordinary, to children's cuddle play with soft dolls that were mass-marketed for the first time at the turn of the twentieth century. Before that moment, European toys had dominated U.S. markets, and those dolls had been mainly rigid and hard. Boys' hard toys were often made of metal that accommodated rough play, but girls' hard toys—most notably bisque dolls—were fragile. At the turn of the twentieth century, however, the emergent U.S. toy industry produced "unbreakable" dolls that aimed to provide an alternative to (or even a strike against) European dolls and the values those dolls embodied and transmitted. Whereas European bisque dolls dictated prim play, cuddly American dolls encouraged vigorously physical use through both their composition and their attached narratives. For example, the Teddy Bear of 1903 simultaneously told a story about Theodore Roosevelt's wilderness adventure and accommodated rough play that would have destroyed a European china doll.[98]

The Raggedy Ann doll was first mass-marketed by the Non-Breakable Toy Company, whose name announced its toys' mission to accommodate violence. As Raggedy books and marketing constantly emphasized, Raggedy Ann was unbreakable because she possessed a cotton body—that is, she could not be hurt. Gruelle was far from alone in associating cotton with both abusability and invulnerability. In 1910, for example, Olice Agness Flynn patented a soft doll with this description of her product:

[The] fabric casings [are] stuffed with cotton or other soft *yielding* material [which] will be flexible and cannot readily be broken by bending or pulling the doll, or by the rough usage to which such toys are subjected.[99]

Cotton materially and symbolically connected dolls to the labor of African American slaves and sharecroppers. For Flynn, Gruelle, and many others, the key property and virtue of cotton was that it was "yielding"— i.e., submissive—and therefore able to endure "rough usage." But cotton does not only render Raggedy Ann fit for rough usage; cotton functions also as an essential force that constitutes personality and actions. In particular, Raggedy Ann's cotton interior enables the doll to move endlessly without tiring and always to maintain a cheerful attitude. "If my head was not stuffed with lovely new white cotton," Raggedy Ann comments at one point, "I am sure it would have ached with the worry!"[100] Cotton prevents worry and renders Raggedy Ann impervious to pain; therefore abuse cannot harm her—hers is the cotton of the Cottolene girl (plate 1) rather than Callie Campbell (figure 1.2 in Chapter 1). *Raggedy Ann Stories* repeatedly highlights the connection between cotton and unfelt abuse, as in this quotation from Raggedy Ann after a lengthy nighttime adventure in which the dolls rescue a dog:

If my legs and arms were not stuffed with nice clean cotton I feel sure they would ache, but being stuffed with nice clean white cotton, they do not ache and I could not feel happier if my body were stuffed with sunshine.[101]

"Nice clean white cotton," Gruelle reminds his reader here and in many other passages, is Raggedy Ann's foundational material, and the phrase itself encapsulates the doll's racial contradictions and alibis. "Cotton" alludes to plantations, slaves, and sharecroppers. "White cotton" draws attention away from laboring humans and toward the literal color of the material itself. The phrase "white cotton" is a diversion, a moment of legerdemain in which cotton is associated with whiteness rather than blackness. The addition of the word "clean" further asserts the benign innocence of the material that constitutes Raggedy Ann's (and Beloved Belindy's, and Raggedy Auntie's) body and personality. And finally, the word "nice" encapsulates Raggedy Ann's core value: as Henny learned in "Raggedy Auntie," niceness trumps all. Because Raggedy Auntie is "nice and soft" like Raggedy Ann, the dolls accept the Auntie's faithful labor, just as Marcella accepts Raggedy Ann's loving servitude. Gruelle's oeuvre values niceness over goodness;

in Raggedy Land, sugary sweetness obliterates the very concept of justice. Raggedy Ann endlessly asserts that cotton is nice, clean, and white and thus screens out processes of producing cotton that are far from nice, clean, or white.

Given that the emergent U.S. toy industry manufactured soft dolls specifically to accommodate cuddling interposed with violence, and that that violence was cast as a patriotic exercise in the development of vigorous American child-bodies, it is unsurprising that children abused dolls. G. Stanley Hall and A. Caswell Ellis, for example, observed children "flogging" dolls;[102] Miriam Forman-Brunell describes historical children's common acts of violence against dolls, including one girl who smashed her doll against a window and another who "disciplined her doll by forcing it to eat dirt, stones, and coal."[103] Children of all races committed violence against dolls of all colors, but white girls specifically targeted soft black dolls for ritualistic and exceptionally violent abuse, which the dolls, of course, submissively endured (the next chapter of this book analyzes these violent rituals in greater detail). For example, the painter Florence Kate Upton had, as a child in the United States, used her black minstrel doll (upon which she later based the Golliwogg) as a "throwing target."[104] Gruelle includes such a scene in *Beloved Belindy*: when mean boys amuse themselves by tossing Beloved Belindy through the air and beating her with a stick, the mammy cheerfully endures the violence and worries only that her pretty dress might be ruined—which would, of course, upset her "Mistress."[105]

Raggedy Ann dolls, like all soft toys, prompt both cuddling and abuse, while advertising and *Raggedy Ann Stories* model more specific practices of play within this general, dualistic prompt. Indeed, Raggedy Ann succeeded throughout the twentieth century as a book-doll combination *because* the doll's materiality and the books' narratives intersected, through marketing, to script legible scenarios for play. An individual child could, of course, resist these scripts, and for exactly this reason advertisers went out of their way to promote the linked use, and therefore sales, of Raggedy books and dolls. One advertisement praised "Dear old squeezable Raggedy Ann and Raggedy Andy," whom "tiny tots just love to romp around with—because they can do most anything with them, and the dear dolls are so good natured they just won't break, with all the cuddling and tossing around and bumpy adventures they are sure to get."[106] Such advertisements instructed consumers to "cuddle" and "toss" Raggedy dolls—acts that Raggedy Ann survived because of her "good nature." The

*Figure 4.16.* Dinah, a caricatured African American woman who works for Marcella's family, wrings out Raggedy Ann. Steam rises off the boiling wash water. Raggedy Ann and Dinah wear similar dresses (both blue with small patterns), and Dinah's red headscarf mirrors Raggedy Ann's red hair. Johnny Gruelle, *Raggedy Ann Stories* (Joliet, Ill.: P. F. Volland, 1918), 21.

advertisement hinged playful caresses and abuse to narrative, the expectation that Raggedy Ann's child-owner would use her to imagine and play out "bumpy adventures." *Raggedy Ann Stories* coordinated with such advertising to model "bumpy" play in which white children loved, hugged, and threw Raggedy Ann, along with all the doll's racial complexities. In the pages of Gruelle's books, white children cuddle Raggedy Ann to the breast (figure 4.3) and dismember her; their servants boil her and wring her out (figure 4.16). Children in Raggedy Ann's stories sleep with her, beat her, cut her, confide in her, kick her, and tree her. And, with great frequency, they hang her.

The multiple scenes of hanging throughout Raggedy Ann's stories reimagine that act as racially innocent. Raggedy Ann's love of benign mischief often results in her getting dirty or wet, and these episodes are routinely followed by scenes of restorative cleaning and drying. Cleaning usually entails boiling, and drying requires hanging. In one hanging scene, for example, Gruelle paints Raggedy Ann with a gouged-out eye,

*Figure 4.17.* Raggedy Ann hangs upside down by the crotch. Johnny Gruelle, *Raggedy Ann Stories* (Joliet, Ill.: P. F. Volland, 1918), 18.

*Figure 4.18.* The Patchwork Girl, topside-turned, flies through the air while the Scarecrow lies helplessly impaled on a stake. L. Frank Baum, *The Patchwork Girl of Oz*, illustrated by John R. Neill (Chicago: Reilly and Britton, 1913), 281.

hung up by one foot, while in another, a clothespin both points toward the doll's crotch and pinches folds of cloth that quote a vulva (figure 4.17 and plate 9). Soft minstrelized characters from which Raggedy Ann descended endure similar violence: the Scarecrow lies helplessly impaled upon a stake while the Patchwork Girl flies, topside-turned, through the air (figure 4.18).

Gruelle's many images of hanging reimagined lynching as harmless violence against dolls. In the early twentieth century, lynching declined overall but became increasingly racialized as white-on-black crime. From 1889 to 1899, Americans lynched one person, on average, every other day, and two out of three of the victims were African American. From 1900 to 1909, one person was lynched every fourth day, but nine out of ten of the victims were African American. The raw numbers of lynching steadily decreased: from 1910 to 1919, Americans lynched a person every fifth day; from 1920 to 1929, Americans lynched a person every nine days. The

*Figure 4.19.* Raggedy Ann, divested of her cottony brains and hung. Johnny Gruelle, *Raggedy Ann Stories* (Joliet, Ill.: P. F. Volland, 1918), 47.

percentages, however, remained steady during these decades: nine of ten victims were African American.[107]

Violence against African Americans in the Midwest—where Gruelle grew up—and especially in Illinois—home to the early manufacturer, publisher, and distributor of Raggedy Ann—erupted in the form of riots in the years leading up to Gruelle's creation of his book-doll combination. Race riots occurred in Springfield, Ohio, in 1906, in Springfield, Illinois, in 1908, and in East St. Louis, Illinois, in 1917. In the 1908 riot, whites lynched two African Americans, killed six others, and injured many more. In the riot in East St. Louis, Illinois, one year before Gruelle debuted his book-doll combination, whites murdered somewhere between forty and one hundred African Americans. In the summer of 1919, one year after the publication of *Raggedy Ann Stories*, whites lynched seventy-six African Americans in twenty-five race riots across the country. One of the bloodiest of these riots occurred in Chicago: twenty-three African Americans died in that four-day riot. The twenty-five riots of the hot months of 1919 earned that season the name "Red Summer."[108]

Unlike the victims of these riots, Raggedy Ann does not mind being ravaged and hanged. In figure 4.19, Raggedy Ann's head has been harmlessly skinned and emptied of her cottony brain so the stuffing might dry separately—an image that both recalls and suppresses knowledge of African American bodies that white lynchers ransacked for "souvenirs" such as ears, teeth, fingers, or genitals.[109] Throughout the nonordeal, Raggedy Ann smiles cheerfully. A poem published in the Chicago *Daily Tribune* in October 1920—barely fifteen months after race riots devastated African Americans in that city—names Raggedy Ann's dual prompt toward cuddling and unfelt violence, love and spanks: "I kin play eny bumpity game / Wuth my Raggedy Ann—'n she's ist the same; / Never gits sick 'er breaks 'er head / 'Enever she tumbles wite out o' 'er bed. / I love 'er 'n spank 'er 'z much 'z I can, / But that never bothers my Raggedy Ann."[110] Raggedy Ann's fixed smile in figures 4.9, 4.17, 4.19, and many other illustrations makes the same claim that Frances Hodgson Burnett's Uncle Tom doll did (figure 2.1 in Chapter 2): because Burnett's "cheerfully hideous" black doll smiled permanently, it "appeared to be enjoying the situation" of being whipped.[111] Raggedy Ann, as insensate to pain as any other imagined faithful slave, any other pickaninny, enjoys being thrown, boiled, wrung out, skinned, and hanged. It's racially innocent fun.

# 5

# The Scripts of Black Dolls

A tear is an intellectual thing.
> —William Blake, "The Grey Monk"

In 1985, at the age of 102, Daisy Turner recalled an incident from her childhood in which she transformed a black doll from a tool of coercion into one of resistance. Turner, an African American woman, was born in Vermont, where she lived for most of her life. In about 1891, when Turner was about eight years old, a teacher in her predominantly white elementary school concocted a verse pageant for the students to perform at the end of the school year. Poetry had long been an important part of Turner's home life: her family habitually created, memorized, and recited verse, and through these practices Turner developed a remarkable memory (with folklorist Jane C. Beck, the adult Turner videotaped many hours of memorized verse; she also performed nineteenth-century poetry in Ken Burns's documentary *The Civil War*).[1] As Turner remembered in extraordinary yet credible detail, each girl in her school pageant represented a different country. The girls appeared onstage holding dolls, each girl costumed identically with her doll, and recited poems written by the teacher. The first girl to step onstage was Turner's classmate Amy Davis. Turner told the folklorist,

> [Amy Davis] was all dressed in white with blue sash, and little ribbons on her hair. And her doll in white and ribbons. She held her doll, very lovely, in her arms, and said, [Turner cradles her cane as if it were a doll in arms] "My dolly came from sunny France; her name is Antoinette. She's two years old on Christmas day, and a very darling pet." So she went on, rambling about her doll Antoinette. "I hope she'll take the prize." So then she

went and set Antoinette out front on the seat and went back and turned her skirts and fixed her hair ribbons and sat behind like the mother.[2]

The teacher had selected Daisy to represent the "country" of Africa and had written a poem for Daisy to perform with a black doll named Dinah.[3] For reasons that Turner did not explain to the folklorist, she balked from the day she received the assignment. Upon her father's urging, she reluctantly agreed to follow the teacher's instructions, and she dutifully memorized the poem. But on the day of the pageant, Daisy rebelled.

I was the last one to go out at the foot [end] of this thing with this black doll. Well, the more I thought of it . . . I begin thinking what a fool I'd been to let my father work me into taking this black doll and saying it was all right, and thinking it was all right 'cause he said so. With my dolls at home, my white dolls, and my white dress and everything, I could have been the best. Instead of that, there I was, the old school dress they all had seen, my hair braided instead of being fluffed and everything. I was angry.

When Daisy got onstage, she spontaneously refused the poem her teacher had written. Drawing on her family's evening tradition of improvising and reciting verse, Daisy extemporized:[4]

> You needn't crowd my dolly out
> Although she's black as night
> And if she is at the foot of this show
> I think she'll stand as good a chance
> As the dollies that are white.
>
> My daddy says that half the world
> Is nearly dark as night.
> And it's no harm to take a chance
> And to stay right in the fight.
>
> So stand up dolly
> And look straight
> To the judges at the right.
> And I'll stand right by your side
> If I do look a fright.

"And so I went on saying my piece through," she explained in 1985. "But instead of saying the piece that the teacher had taught me to say, I was saying what I wanted to say on my own."

Daisy Turner's story raises as many questions as it answers. Exactly what was it about the doll, the poem, and the school pageant that angered the girl and provoked her resistance? Turner recalled her improvised poem in detail, but she claimed to remember only the first two lines of the teacher's poem: "My doll was born in Africa / My doll was born in the sun."[5] Despite the folklorist's requests, Turner never explained what the doll looked like, or exactly what she objected to in the doll's appearance. All we know about the doll is that her name was Dinah, that she represented "Africa," and she was black. We know, also, that in 1985, Turner apparently considered the doll's objectionable qualities to be self-evident, unspeakable, or both.

The significance of Daisy Turner's resistance emerges through this chapter's excavation and reconstruction of the history of black dolls in play. The opening chapter of this book showed how the allegation that black children did not experience pain excluded them from claims of innocence and ultimately defined them out of childhood itself. This chapter concludes that argument by showing how black dolls constituted a key site in which that libel was enacted in the nineteenth century—and then contested, to enormously powerful effect, in the twentieth. In the second half of the nineteenth century, literature, nonfiction, theater, and material culture—the dolls themselves—coordinated with each other to script violent and degrading play with black dolls. Archival evidence shows that many white children did, in fact, enact those scripts by attacking black dolls viciously and shamelessly. The dolls, of course, endured these attacks without complaint. These linked performances of violence and endurance staged contests over citizenship, personhood, and the memory of slavery.

In the early twentieth century, however, New Negro adults began using commercially manufactured dolls to interrupt this history and to choreograph new practices of play. In 1908, Richard Henry Boyd founded the National Negro Doll Company (NNDC), which sold fragile black dolls that required gentle play; other black-owned companies (including the Marcus Garvey–associated Berry and Ross) followed suit and sold black dolls throughout the 1920s. During these decades, debates about black dolls appeared regularly in New Negro periodicals. In the late 1930s, African American psychologists Dr. Kenneth Clark and Dr. Mamie Clark entered these debates when they launched their famous "doll tests," which pivotally influenced the civil rights movement and which continue to define American popular beliefs about children, race, and dolls.

In their tests, Dr. Clark and Dr. Clark asked African American children to express preferences for black or white dolls. The majority of black children preferred white dolls, the Clarks discovered. In the Clarks' view, these results revealed the negative effects of segregation on children's psyches—an argument that became pivotal in the landmark 1954 Supreme Court Case, *Brown v. Board of Education*, which ruled against segregation in public schools.[6] In the half-century since *Brown v. Board of Education*, the doll tests have become a fixture in popular culture: they have figured prominently in at least three films and full-length television documentaries, and have become a standard element in narratives of desegregation and civil rights.[7] The doll tests continue to be restaged periodically; in the late 1980s, two such restagings received extensive attention in *Time*, *Jet*, and other popular media; and the *Journal of Black Psychology* published a special issue on doll tests in 1988. A search of YouTube will reveal many restagings of the test by journalists (including one program that aired on MSNBC in 2008) and amateurs (including *A Girl Like Me*, a 2005 short film by then-sixteen-year-old Kiri Davis, whose application of the test to children in her neighborhood earned her spots on *Oprah*, NPR, and many other national media outlets, as well as numerous honors). As Gwen Bergner recently argued, the doll tests defined arguments about race, multiculturalism, and self-esteem that structured educational policy in the second half of the twentieth century.[8] The Clarks implanted in American common sense the belief, which remains prominent today, that any black child who prefers white dolls is necessarily showing symptoms of individual and societal pathology: internalized racism.

The doll tests so deeply influenced American beliefs about race despite deep flaws in the Clarks' experiments—flaws that ranged from the statistical methods the Clarks used to the questions that produced the data to the conclusions drawn from the data. Of the many critiques, two challenge the doll tests most fundamentally: doll preference does not necessarily index self-esteem (as Gwen Bergner put it, there is no evidence that "preference for white dolls among black children indicate[s] anything other than a preference for white dolls"[9]), and the doll experiments do not show that school segregation psychologically damages black children.[10] Kenneth Clark acknowledged that he could not establish a causal relationship between school segregation and psychic damage.[11] If anything, the Clarks' evidence suggested the opposite: their subjects who attended integrated schools in the North were *more* likely than their segregated southern counterparts to prefer white dolls (Daisy Turner, who attended an integrated school in Vermont half a century earlier, fit this pattern). In sum, wrote Richard Kluger, author of the definitive history of *Brown v. Board of Education*, the Clarks' tests "did not definitively prove anything."[12] Why, given these well-reasoned critiques, did the Clark doll experiments appear so persuasive? And if the Clarks did not necessarily show psychological damage, exactly what did they show? In other words, the Clarks produced evidence of *something*, and observers, from the 1930s through today, find that something persuasive and affecting. But what exactly did the Clarks reveal about race, childhood, U.S. history—and dolls?

This chapter answers these questions, as well as the earlier question of what, exactly, Daisy Turner was resisting, by locating both Daisy Turner's refusal and the Clarks' experiments within a century-long history of black dolls in play in the United States. Through material dolls and the structure of the experiment, the Clarks created a dramatic arc that extended from, and therefore bore the cultural weight of, a century of performance practices involving black dolls. This genealogy of performance, I argue, is what Daisy Turner rejected and is also the source of the doll test's ongoing persuasiveness. The doll test derives more power from a history of performance than from the discipline of psychology, so critiques of the Clarks' social science methods, however trenchant, do not address the main source of the test's power and therefore do not make the doll test less persuasive. In other words, the doll tests were, from the start, more affective than convincing, so dissections of *how* the tests were unconvincing did little to compromise their effects. This chapter recuperates the Clarks by defending the doll test not as flawed social science but instead as brilliant drama. Furthermore, this argument redeems the Clarks' child subjects by offering a new understanding of them not as psychologically damaged dupes, not as passive internalizers of racism, but instead as agential experts on children's culture. African American children, including Daisy Turner and the subjects of the Clark doll experiments, resisted scripts that white and black adults embedded—for different purposes and with differing levels of intentionality—in black dolls. To understand these acts of resistance, we must first consider dolls not as objects to look at, but things that script behaviors.

## Black Dolls as Scriptive Things

The Clarks' doll experiment, designed by Mamie Clark, aimed to assess African American children's attitudes toward the white and black races and therefore toward themselves. In the experiment, an African American child was brought into a room containing four plastic, jointed baby dolls, each of which was about a foot tall. Two of the dolls were brown with black hair and two were pinkish with yellow hair; beyond these differences, the dolls were identical. All wore diapers; all lacked markings of gender. The experimenter issued an ordered series of requests, including "Give me the doll that is a nice doll," "Give me the doll that looks bad," "Give me the doll that looks like a white child," and "Give me the doll that looks like a Negro child."[13] Finally, the Clarks asked, "Give me the doll that looks like you." Two hundred and fifty-three children, all African American, underwent the doll test between 1939 and 1947. Of these, 150, or 59 percent, chose a pinkish doll as the "nice doll," and an equal percentage identified a brown doll as the one that "looks bad."[14] Sixty-six percent of all subjects chose a brown doll as the one that "looks like you," while 33 percent claimed a white doll as the one that looked like themselves (1 percent indicated that they did not know or offered no response).[15] African American children's preference for white dolls, the Clarks argued, symptomized internalized racism.

Dr. Clark and Dr. Clark assumed a psychological identification between child and doll; they believed that an African American child's attitude toward a brown doll, which the child identified as Negro, necessarily revealed an attitude toward the self. In this view, dolls are containers and delivery systems for the ideas of white and black raciality. This view also posits children as cultural receptacles, and their actions as symptoms of societal pathologies of racism.

The problem with the Clarks' positing of dolls as delivery systems for racial concepts is that dolls cannot contain *only* the idea of race; they also transmit the idea of *doll*. The material form of the doll cannot be incidental to children, and especially not to girls, because almost all girls know what they are "supposed" to do with dolls—even if they choose to play differently or not at all with them.

This point is crucial, as becomes clear through a comparison between the Clarks' experiment with dolls and their experiment with line drawings and crayons. When the Clarks administered their doll test, they sometimes also asked their test subjects to color a line drawing of a girl or boy "the color that you are." Next, the child was given a line drawing of another child, the opposite sex of the test subject, and instructed, "Color him (or her) the color you like little boys (or girls) to be."[16] One hundred and sixty African American children, aged five to seven, underwent the "coloring test" along with the doll test. Of these, 88 percent provided what the Clarks considered a "reality response" by coloring the child "like you" a shade that the Clarks felt roughly matched the child's skin color. Almost 7 percent gave what the Clarks considered "phantasy responses" by coloring in the drawing significantly lighter than the child's own skin. And 5 percent of the children gave what the Clarks called "irrelevant responses" by applying to the drawing a nonhuman color such as purple or green. When asked to indicate the color she or he liked in other children, 48 percent used a brown or black crayon, 36 percent used white or yellow, and 16 percent selected an "irrelevant color."[17]

The Clarks posited line drawings and crayons as interchangeable with dolls—that is, as different experimental means to the same goal of assessing children's racial attitudes. The test results, however, undermine this supposition. In the coloring tests, 88 percent of Negro children used a "reality" shade of crayon to represent their own skin color, but in the doll tests, only 66 percent of the Negro children chose a brown doll as the one that "looks like you." And whereas in the coloring tests, 36 percent expressed, through drawing, a preference for children colored white or yellow, in the doll test 59 percent selected the light doll as the "nice" one. The Clarks concluded that the results of the coloring test "support[ed]" the results of the doll tests, but that "the trend" toward unrealistic self-identification and internalized racism "was seen more definitely with the Dolls test."[18] Thus the Clarks highlighted the continuities between the coloring and doll tests, and offered no explanation for the significant discrepancies—88 percent versus 66 percent, 36 percent versus 59 percent—in experiments that aimed to measure the same psychological factors in overlapping test subjects.

Consideration of the experiments' physical materials as scriptive things can clarify disparities that the Clarks downplayed. Different things—paper and crayons, dolls—embed in distinct genealogies of performance and therefore prompt different behaviors. In the 1940s, coloring books and crayons had a much shorter and more limited history than dolls did. The McLoughlin Brothers publisher is credited with creating the coloring book in the 1880s, and until 1903, when Binney and Smith invented crayons, children colored mainly with paints. Throughout the early twentieth century, Binney and Smith sold crayons mainly to schools in sets limited to eight colors.[19] In the 1940s, then, line drawings and crayons carried with them a relatively brief and school-oriented history of coloring practices. Dolls, on the other hand, bore a long, extensive, and overdetermined genealogy of performances in homes, schools, and other spaces of play. Dolls and line drawings with crayons may have resembled each other as visual images—that is, as objects to look at—but they registered, as things, in distinct gestural histories.

The Clarks' brown dolls and Daisy Turner's "Dinah" doll contained not only the idea of African Americanness, but the ideas of *doll* and *black doll*, and these things scripted historically located behaviors associated with black dolls. When dolls are viewed as scriptive things, children—not just professional actresses such as Shirley Temple and Dakota Fanning, but all children—emerge as skilled actors in the performance of childhood. Daisy's rejection of a black doll and her resistance to an onstage performance with that doll intervened in not only a school pageant but also a history of practices with black dolls. Daisy Turner refused, certainly, the doll's visually based racial significations (which, the Clarks posited, are interchangeable with those in line drawings). In so doing, however, Daisy also resisted the doll's historically located *scripts*. Recovery of these scripts reveals the hidden stakes of racial innocence not only in the resistance of Daisy Turner and the Clarks' test subjects, but also in the actions of other African American adults and children who used dolls to shape political performances of play from the mid-nineteenth through the mid-twentieth century.

## The Scenarios That Black Dolls Script: Servitude and Violence

From the 1830s through the 1890s, when Daisy Turner stepped onstage, black dolls coordinated two main play scenarios: servitude and violence. Scenarios of servitude were embedded in the earliest known visual representation of a black doll in the United States, which appears in the 1831 first edition of Eliza Leslie's *The American Girl's Book*, a manual of instructive and wholesome activities for girls. This book, which was republished at least seventeen times by 1880, was read by generations of American girls. *The American Girl's Book* taught its readers to make several dolls, including a dancing doll, a jointed linen doll, and a "common linen doll," which was a simplified version of the jointed doll. The manual also instructed the

*Figure 5.1.* Unsigned illustration, "A Black Doll." Eliza Leslie, *American Girl's Book, Or, Occupation for Play Hours* (Boston: Munroe and Francis, 1831), 294. Leslie's book was revised many times between 1831 and 1880, but this image and the attendant instructions for sewing a black doll appeared, unaltered, in every edition. Courtesy of the American Antiquarian Society.

reader to make "A Black Doll" (figure 5.1) as a variation of the common linen doll:

> The linen part must have an outside covering of black silk or black canton crape. The frock should be of domestic gingham or calico, and she should have a check apron. A white muslin cap on her head will greatly improve her appearance. You may make a whole family of these linen dolls, repre-

senting a mother and several children, among them a baby. A black one may then be added as a servant.[20]

This passage overtly instructs a girl reader to sew a doll, but it also provides a narrative for play with that doll as a servant. Leslie first connects the black doll's servitude with its physical constitution: its blackness, its "commonness," its apron and muslin cap. Immediately after the physical description, however, the passage raises the possibility of black dolls existing within black families, not as domestic servants but as figures of domesticity: "You may make a whole family of these linen dolls, representing a mother and several children, among them a baby." If a girl misunderstands "these" to refer to black rather than white linen dolls, the next line immediately corrects the error: "A black one may then be added as a servant." The passage thus posits black dolls as isolated from black families, as inherently fit for servitude, and as natural adjuncts to white families, marginal afterthoughts. As such, Leslie's text instructs not only the making of the doll, but also a scenario for play, much as *Uncle Tom's Cabin* provided Frances Hodgson Burnett with play scenarios that she entered with her doll.[21]

The mode of sale and the physical properties of commercially produced black dolls also prompted play scenarios in which black dolls served white ones. Throughout the nineteenth century, Germany and France dominated the international doll market, and most commercially manufactured dolls in the United States originated in one of these two countries. Many European black dolls were made from the same molds as white dolls and therefore were not grotesque in their features. Because the imported dolls were expensive, few American children of color owned European dolls.[22] When a well-to-do nineteenth-century white girl acquired a European black doll, it was typically a late addition to an already extensive collection of white dolls. This sequence of acquisition resulted in nineteenth-century white girls seldom owning more than one European black doll; thus play scenarios imagining African American families were precluded while other, isolative roles—such as servitude—remained easily available for black dolls in play.[23] Like *The American Girl's Book*, advertisements for and articles about commercially made black dolls pointed out physical features that positioned black dolls as servile adjuncts to white doll families. An 1877 article in *Harper's Bazaar*, for example, described European dolls representing "negresses in gaudy head kerchief and sleeves rolled up as if for washing day," while an 1885 *Harper's Bazaar* article observed "bisque negresses, with woolly hair, to be dressed as maids to fairer

dolls" as well as "colored dolls . . . arrayed as cooks with gray [gay] tur-
bans, or in coachman's attire."[24]

Literature about dolls, both commercially imported and homemade,
provided more detailed narratives about—and thus more specific play scenarios for—black dolls as natural servants. One of many examples appears
in the 1863 *The Dolls' Surprise Party*, written by "Aunt Laura." In this book,
two racially unmarked, presumably white girls play with a group of non-
commercial dolls, "which the little girls had fixed up for themselves."[25] The
homemade dolls include "a black doll, a man, that they called Cesar, and a
small black one called Topsey [*sic*]."[26] One of the girls falls asleep and wak-
ens to discover that her dolls are secretly alive: the white dolls are enjoying a party while Topsey sets the table and Cesar serves coffee. *The Dolls'
Surprise Party* is but one of many fictional works from the nineteenth and
twentieth centuries in which dolls come to life and black dolls, without
comment or explanation, immediately serve white dolls. This conceit appears, for example, in Johnny Gruelle's *Beloved Belindy* and throughout
the "Live Dolls" series of books penned by Josephine Scribner Gates. In
that series' inaugural volume, a group of dolls comes to life, and the very
first action taken by a black doll named Dinah is to use a toy telephone to
order groceries. Soon after, she tends a white baby doll and cooks for the
white dolls.[27]

Fiction often associated the name "Dinah," in black dolls and humans,
with servitude (for example, *Raggedy Ann Stories* and *Uncle Tom's Cabin*
both feature African American kitchen workers named Dinah, as does the
song, "I've Been Working on the Railroad").[28] In "The Dollies' Visit," a
short story by C.H.W. published in the *Youth's Companion* in 1874, a white
girl named Phebe describes herself as a "kind mistress" to "my work girl,"
a black doll named Dinah.[29] The name Topsy (or "Topsey," as in *The Dolls'
Surprise Party*), was also commonly associated with servant dolls, as in
Gates's *The Live Dolls' Busy Days*, in which a black doll knocks on the door
of a human girl's home and announces, "I's Topsy, an' I hear you alls want
a maid-of-all-work. I knows cookin' some, an' I kin scrub an' build fires
an' take out you alls' ashes."[30]

The names "Dinah" and "Topsy" did not refer to an identical set of
images or ideas, but the two names and figures often collapsed into each
other (a collapse that also occurred beyond the realm of dolls: John Lobb,
in his "Editorial Note" to an 1878 edition of Josiah Henson's autobiography, quoted Henson as commenting, "Mrs. Stowe's description of Topsy
is quite correct: her real name was Dinah").[31] The names "Dinah" and

"Topsy" could even overlap or combine, as in the anonymously authored "The Helpful Club: A True Story," published in Chicago's *Unity* in 1884, in which a doll is named Dinah Topsy Tina.[32] In doll play of the nineteenth century and today, regimented ritual coexisted and intersected with anarchy: as we will see later in this chapter, girls and their dolls might stage a genteel tea party that devolves into a water fight; and a photograph can collapse references to doll play and theatrical performance. Representational play with dolls inherently slurs differences between person and thing, and also, often, between things: in play, a stuffed horse might converse with a teapot; a doll of six inches might befriend a doll that is two feet tall. Switches in gender were common, as when, in the hands of Frances Hodgson Burnett, a Topsy doll became Uncle Tom. Dolls also frequently changed race: cloth dolls were sometimes deliberately or accidentally bleached, stained, or dyed; and children used these changes in color as prompts for play incorporating racial changes. For example, the doll named "Dinah Topsy Tina" bore these three names because, the story's narrator notes, she "*used* to be black"—prior, one presumes, to some act of bleaching.[33] This chaotic transmutability underwrote, as possibility, even the most orderly of doll play.

Doll play's tendency to collapse boundaries enabled multiple facets of culture—instruction for homemade dolls, the manufacture and sale of commercial dolls, historical and fictional girls' practices of naming their dolls "Dinah" or "Topsy," and literature about dolls—to merge so as to co-script scenarios in which black dolls served white ones. In other words, girls received a set of mutually reinforcing prompts from divergent sources. These prompts converged to script a diffuse, unauthored, performed narrative in U.S. culture. The relationship between this script and historical children's actions was never simple, because children often revised and refused the prompts they received. They did, however, receive and comprehend these prompts toward play scenarios of black dolls' servitude. Georgianna Hamlen recalled in her 1885 memoir that when she "was a little girl [in the mid-nineteenth century], very small dolls of black china were *supposed to be the proper thing for servants* in doll houses."[34] Perhaps Hamlen and her friends had read Harriet Beecher Stowe's 1870 short story, "Lulu's Pupil," in which a white girl owns a "black china doll with red petticoats that waited on the white lady dolls."[35] Or perhaps they had read any of many similar stories that designate black china dolls as servants. But Hamlen's use of the phrase "were supposed to be" suggests that the notion that a black doll was "the proper thing" to serve white dolls derived from no single source—that is, no individual text that the girls simply imitated—but rather from a common sense of how girls were expected to play. As competent performers, most children, especially girls, understood the play scenarios that black dolls scripted; that is, children who were diverse in their genders, races, classes, regions, and personal preferences largely understood how one was "supposed" to play with black dolls.

Daisy Turner understood—indeed, she memorized—the printed script that her teacher prepared for her to recite in the school pageant with a black doll named Dinah. As a competent performer, Daisy Turner would also have understood the overdetermined status of black dolls, especially those named Dinah, as servants. Daisy contended with two overlapping but nonidentical scripts: the teacher-authored script of the pageant, which included rhymed verse and orderly stage direction, and the unauthored, diffuse yet cohesive script, the set of prompts, that embedded in a black doll named Dinah.

The scripts of black dolls often merged servitude with violence. An 1861 issue of *Godey's Lady's Book*, for example, instructed its reader to make a "Miss Dinah Pen-Wiper" (figure 5.2). The magazine told the reader to "Take a black china baby"—that is, the sort of commercially manufactured black doll that Georgianna Hamlen understood was "supposed to be the proper thing for servants"—and to "dress it with three black cloth skirts."[36] On top of these skirts, the reader was to dress the black doll in colorful clothes and a turban. The doll's owner was then to lift the outer skirts and use the doll's undergarments as a depository for smears of excess ink. The "Miss Dinah Pen-Wiper" conjoined service with implied violence: this doll had a job, which was to endure lifted skirts, the probing of a pen, and the spillage of excessive and potentially despoiling fluid— rape imagery reminiscent of that of the skirt-flipping topsy-turvy doll.[37] Servitude and violence also merged in a 1912 Dallas newspaper item titled "For Girls Who Make Gifts" (a title that explicitly named its intended actors—girls—and actions—making and giving). The article taught girls to make a "Topsy Pincushion"—a useful household item not unlike the Miss Dinah Pen-Wiper. These instructions begin with a description that could apply equally well to a minstrel performer blacking up: the girl is to take a nonspecific "doll's head," which could be any color ("never mind," the newspaper tells girls, properties such as dirt or "fad[ing]"), and to "apply a good coat of shoe blacking"—a substance used by some minstrel performers as stage makeup. The newspaper instructs the girl to complete

*Figure 5.2.* "The Miss Dinah Pen-Wiper." *Godey's Lady's
Book and Magazine,* May 1861, 451. This illustration
accompanied instructions for making the pen-wiper.
Courtesy of the American Antiquarian Society.

the doll's minstrel mask with "thick red lips and white eyeballs" and then
"fasten [the doll's head] with glue or stitches on to a piece of heavy cardboard with cotton wadding enough to form a good sized body to the waist
of the doll." When the doll is complete, the girl should "stick a few dozen
colored-headed pins into topsy's [sic] shoulders."[38]

ELSIE IN THE PLAY-ROOM. — Page 110.

*Figure 5.3.* "Elsie in the Play-Room." The accompanying text reads, "How the children laughed! Eva had hung her old black doll, Dinah, against a beam, 'for a *punish*' as she said." Mrs. D. P. Sanford. *Frisk and His Flock* (1875; New York: E. P. Dutton, 1877), 110. Elizabeth Nesbitt Room, Information Sciences Library, University Library System, University of Pittsburgh.

Fiction and poetry, too, celebrated violence against black dolls, often as it merged with servitude. In the 1863 book *Dolly and I,* by the nineteenth-century best-selling children's author Oliver Optic (pseudonym of William Taylor Adams), a black doll named Dinah "had seen hard service in her day, and did not look as though she would last much longer"—a decimation that none of the white children in the story regret.[39] And in *Frisk and His Flock,* an 1877 children's book by Mrs. D. P. Sanford, a group of white children laugh when a white girl named Eva "hung her old black doll, Dinah, against a beam, 'for a *punish*'" (figure 5.3).[40] (The girl's name, Eva, implies the presence of Topsy; thus this novel, like "The Helpful Club: A True Story," collapsed Dinah and Topsy within a single black doll.) A poem by E.L.E. titled "Topsy," which appeared in the *Youth's Companion* in 1879, tells of a doll named Topsy who is unloved by her girl owner. The girl gives the unwanted doll to the poem's narrator, who makes her into a maid to a white china doll. The girl then drops Topsy and breaks the doll's head off.[41] And in the 1885 *Jimmy: Scenes from the Life of a Black Doll,* a white girl "mistress" repeatedly whips her black doll.[42]

This violence coexisted, in literature and in life, with a passionate love that white children expressed toward black dolls.[43] In 1887, one white mother reported in the magazine *Babyhood* that her toddler daughter owned two rag dolls, one white and one black (named, yet again, Dinah), and that "her affections are centered on the colored" doll: the girl will "never [go] to bed without Dinah in her arms, and cr[ies] for 'Di' if the nurse has forgotten to put it in the crib." This love for Dinah did not, however, prevent the child from giving the doll a "gash in her throat."[44] Love and violence were not mutually exclusive but were instead interdependent: even as historical white children loved their black dolls, they whipped, beat, and hanged black dolls with regularity and with ritualistic and sometimes sexually sadistic ferocity (children did and do commit violence against nonblack dolls as well, but nineteenth-century white children singled out black dolls for attacks that were especially vicious and that took racialized forms such as hanging or burning). In Buffalo, New York, in the late 1880s, a white girl named Mabel Ganson and her white friend genitally mutilated a black doll named Dinah in an effort to make the cloth doll appear to urinate. The girl grew up to become Mabel Dodge Luhan, a well-known patron of the arts, and in her memoir she described the attack in erotic terms: during the event, the girls "were both awfully excited with a queer delicious kind of pleasure, both mysterious and yet familiar." Luhan recalled that she "sat down on the floor and holding Dinah firmly between my knees I poked a hole into the seam between her dark legs in the place where the hole ought to be." She then held the doll's legs open under a faucet and forced cold water into the gash. The girl expected the doll to absorb the stream, perhaps as the lower half of the Miss Dinah Pen-Wiper absorbed excess ink: "I suppose we thought that Dinah would just swell up and retain the water, but she didn't," Luhan wrote. "She got danker and danker until she was a squishy bundle of rags and the colors ran together and into each other and into the washbowl." With that, "Dinah was done for."[45]

Such viciousness against a black doll was far from isolated. In 1898, a Minneapolis newspaper invited children to write letters describing their play with toys. The newspaper published the letters of forty local girls and boys, each identified by name, address, school, and grade (which ranged from fifth to eighth). Seven of the letters focused on black dolls, and most of these shamelessly reported violence. A girl named Alice Leland announced that she "burned to death" a black doll, while Wm. G. Scholtz reported that he enjoyed pinching his "dearest" plaything, a "little black rubber doll named Tom," and that he allowed a cat to "bite Tom's toes and pull his hair," which provided "fun" for the cat. Scholtz echoed Frances Hodgson Burnett when he declared that his Tom doll, like Burnett's brutalized rubber doll of the same name, "never complained." And Harry E. Cass devised a toy theater out of a box and a homemade curtain, where he "made" a black doll "perform" dramas of African exploration. "Sometimes," the child added, "I would play I was hanging him." The article was titled, with no sign of intentional irony, "Toys That Made Childhood Sweet."[46] Burning, biting, and hanging effigies of African Americans seems "sweet" when those actions are performed by white children who carry an aura of racial innocence.

Harry E. Cass was not alone in his enjoyment of hanging black dolls. In 1902, an anonymous African American woman wrote in the *Independent*, "I have seen very small white children hang their black dolls. It is not the child's fault, he is simply an apt pupil."[47] By couching that statement within a discussion of lynching, the anonymous author suggested that white children were "pupil[s]" of an observed reality of antiblack mob violence, and that their doll play reflected this education. White children did witness the lynching of African Americans; indeed, white children actively participated in these murders. In the 1899 lynching of Richard Coleman in Maysville, Kentucky, for example, "little children from six to ten years of age carried dried grass and kindling wood and kept the fire burning all during the afternoon."[48] The anonymous essayist in the *Independent* may have been correct, then, in her suggestion that some white "pupil[s]" observed or participated in lynchings and then recapitulated that reality in their play.

Harry E. Cass, however, was probably not one of those children, because no African Americans were hanged—legally or by mob—in Minnesota during the seventh-grader's lifetime.[49] To the contrary, during the 1880s and 1890s many African Americans regarded Minnesota, and Minneapolis in particular, as notably congenial places to live and conduct business. The Reverend J. M. Henderson, writing in the black newspaper the *Christian Recorder* in 1888, described "the social environment" for African Americans in Minnesota as "adapted to cultivate and invigorate all the finer feelings and nobler qualities."[50] In June 1898, just six months before Harry Cass wrote to his newspaper, Horace Graves wrote in the *Christian Recorder* that the "white population [of the Twin Cities] is of that type whose hearts are open for the success of the black of their cities."[51]

Harry Cass was most likely a "pupil" not of mobs but of culture—much like Frances Hodgson Burnett, who whipped her "Uncle Tom" doll not after watching a whipping, but after reading Stowe's novel.[52] Cass may have read Stowe's novel, and perhaps he read *Frisk and His Flock* or one of the many other stories in which white children hanged black dolls. Maybe Daisy Turner did the same. Harry Cass certainly observed the play practices of other children, including, perhaps, his neighbors in Minneapolis who cheerfully reported destroying black dolls. Literature and material culture, I have argued, co-scripted nineteenth-century practices of play, and white children like Burnett enacted—and thus revised—the scripts. This process of reinvention, of repetition with differences, was collective. Nineteenth-century doll play was not private; representational play occurred throughout the home and also outside, where it was witnessed by families, neighbors, and, more importantly, other children. Children and former children described their play in periodicals and books, further transmitting practices from child to child. Burnett took cues from Stowe's novel and a doll, but then she published accounts of her play and thus co-scripted other children's behaviors: in 1888, when Burnett was publicizing *Little Lord Fauntleroy*, a girl approached her to say she had read about Burnett's whipping of her black doll and had been inspired toward similar play with her own black doll.[53] The publicity of doll play enabled children to influence each other, to function as teachers as well as pupils. Doll play existed, then, not only in the context of fiction, instructional literature, and the materiality of playthings, but also in the context of other children's practices. White children, as doll-players, were not only repositories and reflectors of racist culture; they were its co-producers.

## Dolls and Blackface

White children's representational play with black dolls has not, to date, been located in relation to blackface minstrelsy, in part because most scholars have understood minstrelsy as a realm of adult, working-class men.[54] This frame precludes children, and especially middle-class children and their home-based practices, from analysis. In fact, however, nineteenth-century white children's play with black dolls circulated gestures both out of and *into* blackface performance. Children's material culture reproduced the minstrel mask (as in the face of Raggedy Ann, or the "Topsy pincushion").[55] White girls, playing in pairs or groups, held their black dolls before them, with the dolls facing each other, and spoke for and through them, often performing minstrel dialect and humor. When a white girl spoke in dialect from behind a black doll, the doll functioned as the minstrel mask, a prop in the performance of corkless racial ventriloquism. Girls and boys used groups of black dolls to stage home-based minstrel shows, often in homemade toy theaters. These domestic activities were neither disconnected from onstage performance nor merely imitative of it. Rather, black dolls, like the Tomitudes discussed in Chapter 3, physically traveled between the home and the stage. As a conduit for the gestures of blackface, black dolls theatricalized the home and domesticated the theater.

Sarah Barrow represented the inherent theatricality of doll play in her 1863 children's book *Funny Little Socks*.[56] In this novel, two white girls, Lina and Minnie, play with three dolls: Lina handles the white "Mrs. Morris" while Minnie propels and speaks for the white "Mr. Montague" and a black servant named Toby.[57] Although Barrow writes most of her novel in conventional prose, she represents the girls' doll play as a script, including stage directions and narrative comments to indicate the girls' gestures.

MR. MONTAGUE. Toby, bring some water this minute.
TOBY. (*Minnie brings him in with a pitcher.*) Here, massa, here de water. . . .
MRS. M[ORRIS]. Toby, put down that water, and go 'way.

Minnie accordingly made believe that Toby was pouring water right on the floor; then she turned the pitcher upside down in his hand, and spoke for him.

TOBY. Dere de water, missis.

MRS. M. Oh! it's all over the carpet! How dare you, Toby?

TOBY. Why, missis, you *told* me to put down de *water*!

. . . .

"Oh! did ever anybody have such a funny play before!" cried Lina, fairly dropping Miss [*sic*] Morris, and clapping her hands with delight. "I mean always to play this way."[58]

In this passage, doll play absorbs and is absorbed by theatrical conventions. Lina doubles the meaning of "play": she calls the episode "a funny play" but then immediately slides into the use of "play" as a verb: "I mean always to play this way" (thus Lina echoes the discovery that Hilda Doolittle would make some thirty years later: "a play and to play were the same").[59] The girls use dolls to enact minstrel humor (a black servant's comic misunderstanding of the instruction to put water "down," and the slapstick result of that misapprehension), puns, and dialect—all of which Barrow renders as a dramatic script.

Helen C. Weeks's 1871 novel *Four and What They Did* narrates an amateur marionette show in which two black dolls named Jake and Dinah—yet another Dinah—get married (figure 5.4).[60] The scene deploys minstrelsy's characteristic misunderstanding of words to comedic effect: when the justice of the peace asks Jake, "Can you support a wife?," Jake replies, while almost knocking over his doll-wife, "Pretty well, sir; but I'd a little rather she'd stand on her own feet."[61] This comedy transforms into overt violence in the justice of the peace's next question to Jake: "Will you be kind to Dinah as long as you live[, and n]ever leave her out over night on the grass, or hanging in the grape-vine, with her head down?" Jake replies that he "can't promise" never to hang his wife, because Chester, the boy who owns both dolls, "does that."[62]

Barrow's and Weeks's strategies of representation reflected a historical reality of white children using black dolls to stage miniature theatricals, including minstrel shows, in the home.[63] In fin-de-siècle Minneapolis, we recall, Harry Cass transformed a box and a piece of cloth into a homemade toy theater, where he "made" a black doll "perform" (prior, one supposes, to its hanging).[64] At the same moment, psychologists G. Stanley Hall and A. Caswell Ellis observed white children in Worcester, Massachusetts,

JAKE'S WEDDING. See page 296.

*Figure 5.4.* "Jake's Wedding." Dolls named Jake and Dinah are temporarily strung with wires and then manipulated as marionettes in a homemade toy theater. Unsigned illustration in Helen C. Weeks, *Four, and What They Did* (New York: Hurd and Houghton, 1871), facing 296. Courtesy of Harvard College Library, Widener Library, KC1431.

staging minstrel shows with black dolls.[65] Georgianna Hamlen's mid-nineteenth-century childhood friend reconfigured a soap box as a miniature theater in which she staged a fairy play with black china dolls playing "gnomes" who dug in "black cambric, [which was] supposed to be coal, with wooden tea-spoons, supposed to be spades."[66] James Alden Markill recalled that when he was a boy in the mid-nineteenth century, his twin sister Janie knit thirty-seven black dolls, including recognizable characters from *Uncle Tom's Cabin* (Topsy, Uncle Tom, Aunt Chloe, Dinah) and the minstrel stage ("Jim Crow"). The twins created miniature sets of plantation scenes, within which they manipulated the dolls as puppets to act out an amalgamated Uncle Tom/minstrel show for an appreciative audience of friends and family.[67]

The Topsy doll, as a stage role, literary character, and material plaything, constituted a central artery in the bidirectional flow of gestures into and out of theatrical blackface performance. Within the home, white children such as James and Janie Markill staged minstrel performances *with* black dolls named Topsy, and beyond the home, white children and adults corked up to perform *as* black dolls named Topsy (as distinct from costuming themselves as the human character named Topsy). In each of these situations, a white child temporarily donned a mask of blackness—cork or doll—and performed according to minstrel conventions. At the turn of the twentieth century, amateur doll pageants, in which children and adults dressed and performed as dolls, were common—and to include a blackfaced performance of a Topsy doll was de rigueur. Amateurs from South Carolina to Idaho staged Charles Barnard's 1897 play *Bibi, A Comedy of Toys, in Three Acts,* which was set in a toy store and which featured many doll characters, including a Topsy doll.[68] Other plays that were popular with amateurs (especially child performers) and that featured a character of a Topsy doll included *The Frolic of the Dolls* and *The Doll Shop.*[69] Also common were high society "doll parties" in which children (and sometimes adults) costumed themselves as different kinds of dolls. For example, in Emporia, Kansas, in 1891—the year of Daisy Turner's pageant—Mabel Hainer attended a "rag baby party" in the guise of a Topsy doll.[70]

Even when a Tom show configured Topsy as flesh rather than cloth, the character transported doll-oriented behaviors into the theater. Thus children's play with black dolls not only imported gestures *from* minstrelsy but also exported practices *to* blackface performance. As early as 1852, the stage directions for H. J. Conway's version of *Uncle Tom's Cabin* had "Topsy making a dress for a large doll baby" that appeared with Topsy onstage.[71]

*Figure 5.5.* "Miss Lotta Crabtree as
TOPSY." 1868. Courtesy of Christopher
Brammer.

Many white actresses, in publicity photographs of themselves blacked-up
in character as Topsy, posed with dolls; examples of such actresses ranged
from Lotta Crabtree, one of the most famous nineteenth-century actresses
to play Topsy, to an anonymous actress in William Brady's Tom show (figures 5.5 and 5.6) and another anonymous actress in Stetson's *Uncle Tom's
Cabin.* That so many publicity photographs depicted Topsy holding a doll
suggests not only that stage Topsies may well have performed with dolls
but also that troupe managers believed this image would stimulate sales of
theater tickets. Topsy with a doll in hand, it seems, offered pleasures that
an empty-handed Topsy lacked.

## "Topsy is a doll. Dolls do not cry when they fall"

Dolls do not feel, so the blurring of distinctions between Topsy and dolls
libeled black children as insensate. Harriet Beecher Stowe first likened Topsy

*Uncle Tom's Cabin. Byron Photo. Courtesy of W. A. Brady.*

Topsy.

—*Page 256.*

*Figure 5.6.* An actress plays Topsy with a rag-doll prop at her feet. Photograph from W. A. Brady production of *Uncle Tom's Cabin*. Harriet Beecher Stowe, *Uncle Tom's Cabin; or, Life Among the Lowly, Embellished with Scenes and Illustrations* (New York: R. F. Fenno, 1904), 256. Collection of the author.

to a doll as one component of an antislavery argument. Stowe repeatedly described Topsy's eyes as "glitter[ing] glass beads" that, like a doll's eyes, re-flected external light rather than manifested inward humanity.[72] When Eva converts Topsy, awakening her to her own humanity, the change registers in Topsy's formerly beadlike eyes: at the "moment [in which] a ray of real belief, a ray of heavenly love, had penetrated the darkness of her heathen soul," Topsy's "round, keen eyes . . . were overcast with tears;—large, bright

" No, she can't b'ar me. 'cause I'm a nigger."

*Figure 5.7.* "No, she can't b'ar me, 'cause I'm a nigger." In this illustration by Ike Morgan, Topsy visually rhymes with a black doll, both of which have multiple pigtails, unfitted dresses, and faces defined by patches of absolute white and absolute black. This image visualizes the moment immediately before Eva lays hands on Topsy and converts her, as discussed in Chapter 1. Grace Duffie Boylan, *Young Folks Uncle Tom's Cabin* (New York: H. M. Caldwell, 1901), 104. Courtesy of Harvard College Library, Widener Library, AL3527.434

drops rolled heavily down, one by one, and fell on the little white hand."[73] Topsy's conversion, then, alters the precise organ that previously constituted her doll-likeness.

Authors, illustrators, and performers expanded on Stowe's initial likening of Topsy to a doll but erased Topsy's subsequent transition out of doll-hood and into humanity. To suggest that Topsy's doll-likeness was permanent and essential rather than symptomatic was to reverse Stowe's attack on slavery.[74] In 1901, Ike Morgan (who later illustrated L. Frank Baum's *The Woggle-Bug Book*) posited this essential likeness when he drew Topsy and a Golliwogg-like doll with nearly identical pigtails, unfitted dresses, and faces that patched together absolute white and absolute black (figure 5.7).[75] In 1900, the popular association between Topsy and black dolls was posthumously inserted into Stowe's prose when a juvenile edition of *Uncle Tom's Cabin* likened Topsy to an "ugly little black doll."[76] This line, which had no direct antecedent in Stowe's text, appeared in three additional juvenile editions of Stowe's novel between 1900 and 1910.[77]

Essentialized as doll-like, the Topsy of popular culture felt no pain. As an 1880 schoolbook explained, Topsy could fall "flat on her back"—but "Will Topsy cry? O, no; for Topsy is a doll. Dolls do not cry when they fall."[78] Rearticulation of this libel appears in yet another photograph of an anonymous actor—most likely a white girl in blackface—playing Topsy by raising her hand to strike a black doll (figure 5.8).

In this photograph, one figure who is not easily categorized as person or thing (a doll-like slave character) beats another figure who is also not easily categorized as person or thing (a slavelike doll character). The beating, however, never quite occurs. The girl raises her hand to strike the doll, but the two figures remain frozen forever in anticipation. Violence is endlessly deferred in this performance of pain that never pains. Flattened equally into the photograph, Topsy and doll are equalized as insensate things. In Tom shows, Topsy beat her doll, which felt no pain; Ophelia beat Topsy, who felt no pain; and Topsy figuratively beat herself in mirror image, without pain.

This performance of violence that never penetrates, of pain that never pains, imagined an alternative to both the "corporal discipline" and "disciplinary intimacy" that Richard Brodhead has influentially identified.[79] In Brodhead's view, Stowe staged, through Topsy, a contest between corporal discipline (which Michel Foucault might call punishment) and disciplinary intimacy, or the application of control that the authority personalizes and imbues with loving affects (a contrast to Foucauldian discipline, which is impersonal). In *Uncle Tom's Cabin*, Aunt Ophelia tries unsuccessfully to control Topsy through corporal discipline, but Little Eva reforms Topsy through touch that melds "love with moral expectation" when Eva implores, "I love you, and I want you to be good . . . for my sake."[80] Eva succeeds where Ophelia fails, and thus Stowe critiques corporal discipline as fundamentally flawed (Brodhead notes that Stowe "raises corporal punishment to [a] pitch of moral intensity"[81]) and champions disciplinary intimacy—that loving mode of social control that Brodhead calls the nineteenth-century American "middle class's greatest creation, absorption, and self-identifying badge."[82]

In theaters, however, doll-like blackfaced Topsies forged a third possibility in which corporal discipline and disciplinary intimacy disappeared

*Figure 5.8.* In performance as Topsy, a blackfaced actress—most likely a white girl—raises her hand to strike a black doll. Collodion print, ca. 1885–90. Collection of the author.

together behind comically unfelt violence. For Stowe, corporal discipline was *tragically* ineffective because of flaws inherent in corporal discipline; but stage Topsies redefined corporal discipline as *comically* ineffective because Topsy could not be hurt. Tom shows did not, of course, invent comic violence, which had antecedents in Punch and Judy and many other theatrical traditions. What stage Topsies did innovate, however, was comic violence as a riposte to the then-recent formation of disciplinary intimacy. Topsy's doll-likeness recuperated corporal discipline by claiming it not as effective or moral, but as *in*effective and *therefore* neither moral nor immoral but amoral. The corporal discipline that stage Topsies resurrected was not the antebellum sternness emblematized by Aunt Ophelia, but the postbellum fun of mass cultural excess, of consumption without consequence—a corporal un-discipline. When a doll-like slave beat a slave-like doll, the performance lampooned *both* corporal discipline *and* disciplinary intimacy, reducing both to apolitical entertainment. This racial innocence—that is, the child-borne appearance of the apolitical—both masked and delivered the powerful libel that African Americans were doll-like and insensate, and were appropriate objects for white violent fun. By transporting the gestures of play with black dolls from the home to the stage, actresses playing Topsy transformed Stowe's critique of violence-based-discipline into a jubilant theatrical attack on African Americans.

When Daisy Turner stepped onstage in 1891, she carried with her not only a black doll but also these collapsing histories of home-based play with black dolls, of onstage pageants including black dolls as characters, of onstage citations of everyday play with black dolls, and of the scenarios of servitude and violence that circulated through all these gestural traditions. Each girl in Daisy's pageant dressed like the doll in her arms; Daisy's classmate Amy Davis and her doll Antoinette, for example, both wore white dresses with blue ribbons. Like Amy Davis, Daisy must have doubled with the doll in her arms—but this doubling, in the context of a black girl and doll onstage, caused Daisy's performance to cite that of stage Topsies and their doubling dolls, as in figure 5.8. Although Turner did not describe Dinah's appearance, she did describe her own costume, which must have mirrored that of the doll. Turner lamented wearing "the old school dress they all had seen, my hair braided instead of being fluffed." Turner also mentioned that the dress she wore was red and that she would have preferred a white dress. A red dress was associated with Topsy: in every image in this book in which the original was in color, Topsy wears red. A 1901 advertisement for a "pickaninny" doll linked Topsy, a red dress, and work clothes: "Little Topsy, / Flipsy flopsy, / Dress of red, / Curly head. / Little apron, white and clean, / Nicest Topsy ever seen."[83] If Daisy wore a plain red dress and braided hair, the doll, too, must have worn a plain red dress and braided hair. In 1891, a black girl in a plain red dress and braided hair, standing onstage in a doubling performance with a black doll, would inevitably have recalled one and only one famous role. The school pageant recruited Daisy Turner into the role of Topsy—a slave, a person legally defined as a thing.

## The Terrifying Instability between People and Things

Dolls of all colors anxiously raise questions about the definitions and limits of humanity. As I have argued throughout this book, all dolls in play, and all stories about sentient dolls, trouble the boundary between person and thing—the terror at the ontological core of slavery. Nineteenth-century black dolls, however, uniquely literalized these functions in that they were owned, insentient things that often explicitly represented enslaved humans. Black dolls marked and eroded the border between person and thing; thus they functioned as devices in the meaning and memory of slavery.

Many white children, including Frances Hodgson Burnett, consciously linked literature and black dolls so as to perform fantasies about brutalized slaves. Georgianna Hamlen, for example, recalled that a childhood friend, "who had been reading about Southern plantations and the negro slaves," coaxed her mother to buy her six black china dolls. The girl dressed them "in blue and white striped cotton, and [made] them hold up the train of her best doll's best gown."[84] The white doll represented "Edith, the planter's daughter," and Georgianna Hamlen "thought that she [the white doll] looked very Southern and very proud as she stood on her father's verandah."[85] British novelist Amelia Barr was similarly inspired by a book to enslave her dolls. In about 1837 when Barr was about six years old, she encountered a schoolbook that contained "a picture of a very black slave loaded with chains, toiling in the sugar field, and a tall, white overseer with a whip standing near." Influenced by this image, the white girl "very soon abstracted the steel chain that held my mother's bunch of keys, loaded my negro doll with chains, [and] selected a white doll to act as overseer."[86] White children in 1890s Massachusetts used dolls to play at "slave-selling."[87] And in an 1870 story, the author "Aunt Fanny" (who also wrote, under the pseudonym of Aunt Laura, *The Dolls' Surprise Party*) dispassionately described a knitted black "mammy" doll that had, in "one of her old black legs" a "*bullet-hole, where the Southerners had shot her when she was running away head-over-heels from slavery.*" The narrator explained, "Really and truly, it was only a small pin-hole in the wood, but her little mistress"—that is, the white girl who owned the mammy doll— "made believe that the Southerners had shot her."[88]

Children imagined dolls as slaves, and conversely, adult writers imagined slaves as dolls. By the late nineteenth and early twentieth century, plantation fiction and memoirs took up this simile obsessively, as when Marietta Holley described a slave named Felix as "look[ing] like a tiny black doll" in the 1892 novel *Samantha on the Race Problem*.[89] Especially pernicious was the practice of describing enslaved people as "live dolls" that were fit only to serve as white girls' playthings. In Joel Chandler Harris's 1902 novel *Gabriel Tolliver: A Story of Reconstruction*, an antebellum doctor purchases a recently kidnapped African woman to serve as a "live doll [who] would please his daughter." Upon the presentation of the human gift, the doctor repeats the phrase: "I have brought you a *live doll*, daughter; come and see how you like it."[90] One 1906 antislavery memoir, *The Little Slave Girl*, deploys the trope of the slave as live doll to devastating, ironic effect. In an opening chapter titled "Rebecca's Live Doll," a white girl named Rebecca coldly informs an enslaved woman that she "choose[s]" the woman's baby to have "for mine" as a "live doll."[91] This scene retells the story of Little Eva's steamboat encounter with Uncle Tom, depicting the white girl's insistence that her father acquire the slave she has chosen ("*I want him*") not as Christian love but as heartless, self-centered dehumanization. Upon hearing that the white girl has recategorized the baby as a "live doll," the enslaved mother, "down-trodden and crushed—mentally, spiritually, and physically" can only continue sewing while the girl runs off to inform her father "of her new possession."[92]

*The Little Slave Girl* lays bare the threat of dehumanization that underlies the convertibility between black dolls and slaves, sentient things and people legally defined as things, things and people—a terror that Bill Brown describes as the American uncanny.[93] Popular culture that toyed with the transmutability between black dolls and slaves lent a veneer of harmlessness, of racial innocence, that never quite suppressed the menace. Terror surfaces, for example, in the anonymously authored story compilation *Little Miss Consequence*, published by McLoughlin Brothers between 1859 and 1862 (figure 5.9 and plate 10). *Little Miss Consequence*

mimics the structure and some content of German author Heinrich Hoffmann's 1845 didactic children's book *Der Struwwelpeter* (*Shaggy Peter*).[94] The
"dark, dark" story, "The Girl Who Inked Herself and Her Books, and How
it Ended," retells and crucially alters Hoffmann's story of "Die Geschichte
von den schwarzen Buben" ("The Story of the Inky Boys"). In Hoffmann's
tale, three white boys taunt a moor, and as punishment, St. Nicholas dips
the white boys in ink, permanently staining them black. The McLoughlin
Brothers version reverses the story and its moral. Miss Mopsa, a white girl
whose name echoes that of Topsy and thus portends Topsy-like flip-flops,
commits the crime of dipping her own hands in ink and smearing her
books. That is, she treats herself like the "Miss Dinah Pen-Wiper" described
concurrently in *Godey's Lady's Book* in 1861. The racial transgression, then,
is not only that the white girl physically blackens herself, but that she treats
herself like a thing that soaks up excess (Mabel Ganson Dodge Luhan, we
recall, was surprised when her Dinah doll was unable to absorb a torrent of
water). As Miss Mopsa sucks in the ink, she turns black. Her parents deem
the black girl "too hideous for a daughter," so they redefine her as a black
doll and sell her to a rag shop, which "suspends" her from an iron link.

When McLoughlin Brothers hanged Miss Mopsa, as a black doll, at a rag
shop, the publisher Americanized the British tradition of the "Black Doll
Shop," an unseemly type of secondhand store that trafficked in rags, bones,
stolen goods, and racial terror. According to legend, which Edward Walford cheerily recounted in *Old and New London* (1881), the Black Doll Shop
originated through slavery. (Walford is best understood as a re-teller of a
popular story, not as a historian of the black doll rag-and-bone shops that
did exist in nineteenth-century London.) In Walford's account, the black
doll became a sign of used and possibly stolen goods for sale because of a
white "woman who, travelling abroad, brought back with her a black baby
as a speculation."[95] The woman found "that such an article had no value in
England," so she "wrapped it up in a bundle of rags and sold it to one of
the founders of the [used goods] trade."[96] That is, the white woman discovered that she could not sell a slave in England and therefore disguised the
baby as stolen rag and bone, as a thing, which *was* salable. According to the
legend, the "little nigger"—a girl—was raised at the expense of the church.
When she grew up, she opened her own used goods shop. Like the doll-like
stage Topsies who beat black dolls, the proprietor doubled her construction
as stolen rag and bone with her traffic in those substances. She marked her
storefront with a black doll "hung out as a sign."[97] The formerly enslaved
woman and her children opened fifty rag-and-bone shops and marked each

THE GIRL WHO INKED HERSELF
AND HER BOOKS, AND
HOW IT ENDED.

LISTEN to the dark, dark story
  Of Miss Mopsa's fault and fate,
How she inked herself and books, 'till
  Black as any polished grate.

Seated at her writing-copy,
  In the ink her hands she dips,

*Figure 5.9.* "The Girl Who Inked Herself and Her Books, And How It Ended." This first page of the story visually tells the entire tale: in the upper right corner, Miss Mopsa appears as a white girl. A line threads around the verse, leading the reader's eye first to the left, to the schoolbook Miss Mopsa defaces, then down, as Miss Mopsa turns gray and then black. Bottom center, the line becomes a shelf on which the inkwell rests, and finally, in the bottom right corner, the thread becomes the device by which Miss Mopsa, redefined and sold as a black doll, hangs. *Little Miss Consequence* ([New York:] McLoughlin Bros., between 1859 and 1862), n.p. Courtesy of the University of Florida Digital Collections.

with a hanged black doll, like Miss Mopsa, which wordlessly symbolized the viciousness of racial violence and the quivering transmutability between thing and person, slavery and freedom, rag and flesh at the axis of the bone.

## Daisy Turner's Resistance

Daisy Turner knew slavery indirectly but intimately through her family. According to her family's oral tradition, her grandfather, Alexander Turner, survived the middle passage and the auction block in New Orleans. Sold to a man named John Gouldin, Turner labored on a plantation in Port Royal, Virginia, where his son, Alec Turner, was born in 1845. In 1862, Alec Turner escaped to New Jersey; he joined the First New Jersey Cavalry and fought in several battles during the Civil War. After the war, he married a freedwoman named Sally Early, and the two built their home and raised a family in Vermont. Daisy was the middle daughter of thirteen children. The Turner family prized their memories and their history, and Daisy Turner grew up hearing her parents and uncle recite antebellum stories, songs, and poetry. She also grew up with a visceral connection to slavery through her father's blood. When Alec Turner was a boy, a slaveholder discovered him learning to read from primer and lashed him with a bullwhip, spilling the boy's blood on the book. Alec later retrieved the blood-soaked primer and took it with him when he escaped. Daisy Turner treasured this heirloom for the history it evidenced; she frequently handled the book that contained her father's blood, showing both to anyone willing to listen to the story.[98]

The poem that Daisy Turner's teacher wrote—the poem that the eight-year-old girl refused to recite on stage and that the 102-year-old woman still refused to recite on video—almost certainly configured "Dinah" as a slave. The poem declared that the doll was "born in Africa," but the doll's name was associated with American servitude from the "Miss Dinah Pen-Wiper" to *Uncle Tom's Cabin* to the song "I've Been Working on the Railroad."[99] The doll's name and materiality simultaneously signaled violence and black vulnerability, as when white children gathered and laughed as a white girl "hung her old black doll, Dinah, against a beam, 'for a *punish*'" in the novel *Frisk and His Flock*. Daisy's and Dinah's mirrored plain red dresses and braided hair, too, bespoke American servitude—specifically, the enslavement of Topsy—rather than life in Africa. By 1891, commercially manufactured black dolls representing "Africa" had established a visual vocabulary by which to identify a doll as an inhabitant of that continent. This vocabulary included "savage" costuming such as grass skirts or nose rings.[100] Turner's plain red dress, however, counterindicated the presence of a grass skirt or related accoutrements. The Dinah that the teacher put in Daisy's hands may have been "born" in Africa, but she was named, she dressed, and she labored in America. The missing piece of the story, unspoken but unavoidable, is the middle passage.

When Daisy Turner stepped onstage, visually doubled with a black doll named Dinah, the girl was conscripted into practices involving black dolls: serving, hanging, beating, whipping, soaking, blacking up, and enduring dehumanization both off- and onstage. How could she shake off the ghosts of stage Topsies who beat their doll-doubles? How could she shatter the mirror between herself and her slave-doll, and assert that she was a girl, a free person, not a live-doll-slave? How could Daisy announce to her classmates and neighbors that she would perform no comic violence, no breakdowns, no cheery songs celebrating unfelt abuse? She found her answer in her improvised exhortation to

> . . . stand up dolly
> And look straight
> To the judges at the right
> And I'll stand right by your side
> If I do look a fright

Daisy structured her resistance as a correction in the doll's posture. Unlike Stowe's Topsy, who "cring[es]" and sneaks "furtive glances" from the "corners of her eyes," a black doll, in Daisy's view, should "stand up" and "look straight" at those who judge her.[101] Tom shows paired cringing blackfaced Topsies with battered dolls, but Daisy redefined this pairing in her promise to "stand right by your side," despite "look[ing] a fright"—a three-word phrase that conflates fear with ugliness. After interrupting the postures of minstrelsy and declaring the worth of the doll and herself, Daisy concluded not by embracing the doll (as Kenneth and Mamie Clark surely would have wished), but instead by throwing it down: "I set myself down, but instead of setting gently, I had half throwed [*sic*] Dinah up against the seats like that and set myself down with the red dress and all." As she threw the doll away from her body, Daisy disrupted the doubling effect (although her reference to her "red dress and all" suggests that she remained conscious of the visual link between her and the doll). The ungentle rejection of the doll reconfigured a conventionalized act of comic violence—throwing a black doll—as an expression of Daisy's thoughts, as an intellectual and political act.

The performance of resistance at the school pageant became a favorite episode in Daisy Turner's life, and Turner recounted the story frequently for almost a century. But she refused to fill the story's gaps. She consistently brushed off questions of what the doll looked like. When asked about the teacher's poem, which the eight-year-old girl dutifully memorized, the grown woman, who had a special gift for retaining verse, insisted she could not remember the teacher's words. This claim of forgetfulness is not credible from a woman who punctuated her 104th birthday celebration by unhesitatingly reciting from memory a seventeen-minute poem.[102] Even in 1985, Daisy Turner continued to resist, to slip from the gummy doll that threatened to incorporate her into narratives of servitude and violence, of blackface and slavery.[103]

## New Negroes, New Dolls

The traditions of nineteenth-century doll play that children expertly perceived—traditions that Harry Cass enacted and that Daisy Turner resisted—clashed with a second, concurrent history: one of African American adults objecting to black girls' practices of doll play and attempting to reshape those practices for the purpose of racial uplift. African American adults, especially men, wanted girls to embrace black dolls as signs and inculcators of self-respect. However, African American girls often refused black dolls along with the scripts those dolls transmitted, and this refusal can be understood as itself a sign and assertion of self-respect or at least self-protection.

Daisy Turner and her father, Alec Turner, were in this way at cross-purposes. When Daisy first received the teacher's poem, she balked at memorizing and performing it with the Dinah doll, but her father convinced her to participate in the pageant. As Daisy Turner recalled, Alec Turner told his daughter that there "was no harm" in doubling with the black doll because

> who could know, or who would realize or decide, which house looked the
> prettiest, painted red or green or blue or whatever the color was, or which
> tree was the loveliest. And so if I was a little darker-skinned girl and I took
> the dark-colored doll, I was just as lovely as the others.

In this recounting of events, Daisy expressed aversion to the doll, the poem, and the pageant, but Alec Turner responded by reassuring his daughter that *she*, a "darker-skinned girl," was "lovely." That is, Alec Turner assumed that a black girl's feelings toward a black doll reflected her feelings toward her raced self. For Alec Turner, like Kenneth and Mamie Clark half a century later, dolls provided occasions to perceive and to declare which colors and therefore which races were "lovely" or, in the Clarks' term, "nice." The possibility that children might react to a doll as a *doll* with its own histories of performance seems to have occurred to neither Alec Turner nor the Clarks.[104]

When African American girls rejected black dolls, their parents often despaired. In 1853, forty years before Alec Turner urged his daughter to perform with the Dinah doll and a century before *Brown v. Board of Education*, William J. Wilson (who wrote under the pseudonym "Ethiop") lamented in *Frederick Douglass' Paper* that "every one of your readers knows that a black girl would as soon fondle an imp as a black doll." Once, Wilson recalled, he "introduced [a black doll] among a company of twenty colored girls" who responded by "screaming" and running away.[105] In Wilson's view, girls' distaste for black dolls resulted from an "education" through "art or literature" that causes African Americans to "depreciate, . . . despise, [and] almost hate ourselves."[106] Wilson in 1853, Alec Turner in 1891, and the Clarks in 1939 shared precisely the same assumptions about children, dolls, and what one might now call internalized racism.

Some New Negro writers tried to counter black girls' rejection of black dolls by advocating the rejection of white dolls.[107] For example, "Dolly's Dream," a 1920 short story by Nora Waring that appeared in the *Brownies' Book* (the National Association for the Advancement of Colored People's short-lived juvenile magazine, co-edited by W. E. B. Du Bois and Jessie Redmon Fauset), features a black girl whose name, Dolly, announces her doubleness with a plaything. Dolly loves a golden-haired doll, and the girl wishes that she, too, had blond hair. Unlike Toni Morrison's Pecola, who goes mad with this desire, Dolly receives her wish. A fairy godmother gives Dolly "pinky white skin and blue, blue eyes" as well as golden hair. When Dolly's family and neighbors fail to recognize her, Dolly realizes that her dark skin, hair, and eyes locate her in a community, and she wishes for her original body—that is, she wishes to be a black Dolly rather than a white dolly, to be neither white nor a thing. Dolly awakens to discover that her transformation was but a dream, and she reenters the waking world glad to have "'cwinkly' black curls."[108]

If, African American adults reasoned, beautiful white dolls filled black children with inappropriate desires and grotesque minstrel dolls inculcated black children with self-loathing, then perhaps beautiful black dolls could foster racial pride. An anonymously authored essay in the *Christian Recorder* in 1889 called passionately for a doll "modeled after the best types of Afro-American girls and young women." Such a product "will come; it must come," the author argued, because it is needed, and therefore whoever creates it will earn "a fortune."[109] In the early decades of the twentieth century, African American entrepreneurs tried to produce dolls that fit this bill (although none earned anything close to a fortune). The National Baptist Convention coordinated efforts to manufacture, sell, and promote black dolls: Black Baptist minister Richard Henry Boyd founded the National Negro Doll Company (NNDC) in 1908, and in that same year the National Baptist Convention and the Illinois Federation of Women's Clubs passed resolutions to endorse the company.[110] In late November 1908, several African American women's clubs in Indianapolis cosponsored a Negro doll fair (women's clubs would later organize "Negro Doll Clubs" and "doll bazaars").[111] Soon more manufacturers, both African American and not, produced noncaricatured black dolls marketed to black children. In the teens and twenties, doll companies including the Garveyite Berry and Ross Company, the Gadsden Doll Company, and the E. M. S. Novelty Company advertised often in the *Crisis*, the *Brownies' Book*, the Chicago *Defender*, and other African American periodicals.[112]

African American adults championed beautiful black dolls as direct causes of racial uplift. Booker T. Washington, an enthusiastic proponent of the NNDC, wrote in 1910 that black dolls "will have the effect of instilling in Negro girls and in Negro women a feeling of respect for their own race."[113] One anonymous newspaper writer commented in the *Negro Star* in 1921, "Take a child and let her play with a white doll three years[,] then bring a brown doll and she will not have the brown doll." White dolls "only teach white superiority and black inferiority" but a parent may reverse the process and "give the Negro child a Negro dolls [*sic*] and see if it does not change the attitude of the Negro regarding black and white."[114] One man proclaimed in the *Freeman* his "Resolutions for 1909" with the far-reaching goal of being "helpful to the entire race." The fourth resolution (superseded only by caring well for children, buying a home, and boycotting racist newspapers): "My children shall play with Negro dolls."[115]

Michele Mitchell attributes the urgency New Negroes invested in black dolls to concerns over the propagation of the race. White dolls, New

Negroes argued, teach a black girl to want white babies and by extension the white husbands who can give her those babies; in contrast, black dolls teach desire for black babies and therefore black husbands.[116] Black dolls were thus understood as tools by which to oppose racial mixing. Mitchell brilliantly analyzes New Negro reformers' use of dolls to represent and attempt to influence families, but she does not comment on what is most remarkable of all: not *how* New Negro reformers thought about doll families, but *that* African American adults consistently understood dolls to represent families—and only families.

As this chapter and the previous one showed, white adults and children sometimes configured groups of dolls as families, but at other times arranged dolls into communities, into publics. Many girls collected dolls that represented different countries and arranged them into what now resembles a proto–League of Nations. The catalog of the white-owned Babyland doll company imagined a plantation wonderland populated by "Topsy" and "Aunt Dinah"; and Marcella was "mistress," not mother, to the Raggedy dolls in her nursery.[117] White-authored novels such as *Funny Little Socks* depicted play in which dolls represented neighbors and servants. African American girls, especially middle-class ones, did use dolls to represent publics, but African American adults were consistent and even insistent in imagining dolls exclusively as families, as "children" to girl "mothers." We see this disjunction within the Clark family: in 1947, Mamie and Kenneth Clark's six-year-old daughter Kate collected dolls "of every color and nation" in the model United Nations mode, but in the North Side Center for Child Development, Kate's psychologist parents structured therapeutic play exclusively around what Mamie Clark described as "families of dolls" (the Clarks' doll tests, similarly, valued affinity rather than diversity when they tested children's willingness to associate themselves positively with a doll of a hue similar to their own).[118] White authors used the terms "mistress" and "mother" frequently and interchangeably to describe white girl doll owners, but African American authors used only the term "mother." I have been unable to find even one instance, from any year, in which an African American of any age or gender described an African American girl as a "mistress" to a doll. This void suggests that African Americans consciously rejected this easily available term along with its implications, as mapped in previous chapters, that slavery is a form of love, of innocent play.

One can, of course, configure dolls as a community without employing the term "mistress," but significantly, New Negro writers seldom pursued that option. Some black-authored doll stories even envisioned dollhood as *oppositional* to community. In "Dolly's Dream," for example, the protagonist discovers that to become like her blonde doll is to be *separated* from her community, and to regain her dark flesh is to reunite not only with her family but also with her neighbors. In New Negro thought, to be a child was to be a member of a family and a community, but to be a doll was to be a member of a family alone. This distinction appears especially clearly in the story "Mary and Her Dolls," which appeared in Silas X. Floyd's 1905 didactic manual, *Floyd's Flowers; or, Duty and Beauty for Colored Children.* In this story, an African American girl named Mary has five dolls, whom she describes as her "family." Mary's father suggests that Mary give one of her dolls to a poor girl, but Mary objects on the grounds that she loves her "babies" as much as her father loves his children. Her father affirms Mary's logic by kissing her. Mary then finds a way to reconcile a charitable impulse with loyalty to her doll-children: she will use her savings to buy a new doll for the poor girl.[119] Floyd's story ends happily because Mary's solution distinguishes between storied dolls—that is, dolls with which she has played, dolls through which she has imagined "family"—and a new doll to be purchased from a store. Mary is willing to give money for a doll, but she is unwilling to give away her immaterial, affective attachment to a "baby." This distinction creates an avenue for public charity—for community—while preserving the analogy between dolls and family.

When Floyd included this story in a work of prescriptive literature, he implied that his black child-readers should imitate Mary in both her charity and her vision of dolls as families. Floyd and many other reformers called for black girls to use black dolls to play out stories of family as distinct from community, and yet those same reformers wanted doll play to uplift the race as a whole. If doll play was to serve communities, why should it not represent communities? Why did New Negro reformers want Negro girls to use dolls to play out stories of families but not neighborhoods?

The answer may be found in the gestures that these different scenarios of play script. If a girl casts dolls as her "children" and herself as "mother," she performs gestures of care-giving: dressing, feeding, disciplining, and cuddling. If that same girl casts her dolls as something other than a family—as friends or neighbors to each other, for example—she might interact directly with them, or she might stage interactions among the dolls that do not acknowledge the presence of the child. The white girl-characters in *Funny Little Socks* play in this way when they use dolls to stage a scene among two courting neighbors and a minstrelized servant. The distinction between games of "family" and games of "community" replicates the distinction between "cuddle games" and what H. G. Wells called "floor games," as discussed in the previous chapter. "Floor games" involving hard figurines of soldiers and "natives" play out geographical fantasies of publics: villages, regions, and nations. The games are openly political, not innocent ("The British Empire," Wells wrote, "will gain new strength from nursery floors"[120]). Cuddle games, in contrast, appear to be about love; they take on a child's aura of innocence, which obscures a doll's political history. When New Negro adults called upon Negro girls to imagine dolls as families and not communities, they instructed girls to play cuddle games, not floor games. Thus New Negro adults instructed black girls to perform innocence—the quality from which a century of popular culture had disqualified African American children.

Pain, I have argued throughout this book, was the wedge that split images of white and black childhood into respective trajectories of tender innocence and nonchildlike invulnerability. Black dolls were especially powerful sites through which to perform the libel that black flesh was invulnerable to pain. From the Topsy/pickaninny/"nigger" doll that could be thrown without getting hurt (Chapter 1) to the gutta-percha "Uncle Tom" whose grin implied, to Frances Hodgson Burnett, that he enjoyed being whipped (Chapter 2), to the painless clubbing of Beloved Belindy (Chapter 4) to the ritualistic beating of black dolls by actresses playing Topsy (Chapter 5), play with black dolls made claims about African Americans' ability to feel.

In counterpoint, African Americans selected dolls as special sites through which to reflect on feelings, especially pain and vulnerability. New Negroes widely understood tender rituals of cuddling black dolls as both cause and effect of racial uplift; that is, they cared about black dolls not only as meaningful texts, but as scriptive things. "Mothers!" wrote Marcus Garvey, "give your children dolls that look like them to play with and cuddle" so that "they will learn as they grow older to love and care for their own children and not neglect them."[121] "Today," a 1912 article in the trade journal *Toys and Novelties* observed approvingly, "many negro children were seen fondling black dolls." The author of the article ascribed this tenderness to the success of doll manufacturers that "assist this effort 'to instill in the minds of children race love'" and "race loyalty."[122]

The National Negro Doll Company sold fragile dolls that required gentle care and that thus scripted small rituals of tenderness.[123] The NNDC seems never to have manufactured its own dolls, but rather to have imported noncaricatured dolls from Germany. These dolls broke easily, as evidenced by an undated pamphlet in which the NNDC issued "Special . . . INSTRUCTIONS that Should be Followed out Carefully" to ensure the dolls' safety. "BEWARE of Broken Dolls," the NNDC proclaimed in large letters. The pamphlet detailed the care that the company took in packing the dolls for shipment. Despite these measures, the NNDC received "a lot of complaints" that the delicate dolls were often "crushed or damaged" in post.[124] These elaborate "instructions" show not only that the dolls were fragile, but also that the NNDC regarded their fragility as a characteristic to manage rather than a problem to correct or even apologize for. NNDC dolls, unlike dolls of rag or rubber, could not be treated roughly—at least not more than once. Because NNDC dolls shattered when subjected to carelessness, much less abuse, they intervened in nearly a century of violent play scripted through black dolls. NNDC dolls determinatively ordered their users not to abuse black dolls. Any child who disobeyed this order would be left with a pile of shards rather than a plaything.

The National Negro Doll Company, like most other early twentieth-century producers and distributors of black dolls, was short-lived. The company folded only a few years after it opened, and by 1930, most companies that specialized in African American dolls had closed up shop. Advertisements for these companies, which had appeared regularly in magazines such as the *Crisis* throughout the 1920s, disappeared from the pages. Dolls distributed by the NNDC or similar companies may have deeply affected some children, but their cultural impact did not approach that of, say, Johnny Gruelle's Beloved Belindy. After New Negro doll manufacturers and distributors closed down, white-manufactured minstrel or mammy dolls, which were made of rags and which invited violence, remained widely available.

By the 1930s, then, when the Clarks launched their doll test, black dolls had for over a century scripted violent and degrading play-performances, both off- and onstage, that libeled African Americans as naturally servile and insensate to pain. African American children, particularly girls, had largely rejected black dolls and the modes of play these dolls scripted. And African American women and especially men, from William J. Wilson to Alec Turner to Booker T. Washington, had, with growing urgency, viewed black children's play with white dolls as a symptom of societal racism and tender play with black dolls as a potential cure for that pathology. This is the deep-rooted and high-stakes contest that the Clarks entered—and ultimately reconfigured.

## Tears and Other Intellectual Things

Mamie Phipps Clark designed the doll test for her 1939 master's thesis in psychology at Howard University, and she and her husband then ran the tests through 1947.[125] During those years, the Clarks administered the test to 253 children, all African American, in Massachusetts, Pennsylvania, Delaware, South Carolina, and Arkansas.[126] Of the children the Clarks tested, the majority preferred white dolls, and the Clarks argued that this choice revealed psychological damage caused by systemic racism. They published their findings in the *Journal of Experimental Education* (1939), the *Journal of Social Psychology* (1940), the *Journal of Negro Education* (1950), and many other scholarly venues. In 1951, Thurgood Marshall, then a lead lawyer for the NAACP, recruited Kenneth Clark to be an expert witness in several court challenges to segregation.[127] Kenneth Clark testified in three out of the four lower court cases that eventually melded into *Brown v. Board of Education* in 1954.

For *Brown*, Kenneth Clark coauthored a statement, which NAACP lawyers appended to a court brief, in which he summarized social science research relevant to psychological damage and segregation. This brief did not mention the doll tests, but it was steeped in the thinking about self-esteem that the Clarks had developed through their decade of experimentation with dolls. The NAACP also submitted to the Supreme Court a 1950 report that Kenneth Clark wrote for the Midcentury White House Conference on Children and Youth. This report did cite the Clarks' experiments. Neither of the Clarks testified orally in *Brown*, and the court's decision never referred directly to the doll tests. However, the unanimous *Brown* decision, authored by Chief Justice Earl Warren, prominently cited the 1950 report in which Kenneth Clark did discuss the doll experiments.

The national public became aware of the doll experiments before *Brown*, in 1947, with the publication of a lengthy article about the Clarks, illustrated with photographs by Gordon Parks, in *Ebony* magazine.[128] After *Brown*, Kenneth Clark's popular writings (*Prejudice and Your Child* in 1955 and the more widely read *Dark Ghetto* in 1965, as well as articles in numerous magazines) secured the place of the doll tests in the public view. Toni Morrison's 1970 novel, *The Bluest Eye*, fictionalized the doll tests through the figure of Pecola, who longed for and pathologically identified with white dolls.[129] For six decades following *Brown*, the American Psychological Association trumpeted the Clark doll tests as examples of the positive effects of social science research on public policy.[130] Because of this ongoing publicity, the doll tests have "set the parameters for virtually all subsequent research on racial identity, self-esteem, and child development."[131] Ever since *Brown*, the Clark doll tests have been cited, narrated, and restaged to tell stories about race in America.

The Clarks represented their findings as transparent revelations of black children's damaged self-esteem. In fact, however, they carefully structured their experiment as a dramatic arc that ensured that most children would prefer the white doll. The test's results were predictable because of the order of the questions.

1. Give me the doll that you like to play with— (a) like best.
2. Give me the doll that is a nice doll.
3. Give me the doll that looks bad.
4. Give me the doll that is a nice color.
5. Give me the doll that looks like a white child.
6. Give me the doll that looks like a colored child.
7. Give me the doll that looks like a Negro child.
8. Give me the doll that looks like you.[132]

The eight questions divided into three subsets. The first subset, consisting of questions one through four, was "designed," the Clarks wrote, "to reveal preferences" in dolls.[133] The second subset, questions five through seven, determined whether a child understood the dolls' colors of plastic as signifiers of racial identities. And the third subset, consisting solely of question eight, asked a child to affiliate a doll with himself or herself.

Anyone who had read the op-eds and letters in the New Negro press during the 1910s, '20s, and '30s would have known that most African American children preferred white dolls. It was therefore unsurprising that many of the Clarks' subjects chose the pink doll in response to positive questions 1, 2, and 4, and the brown doll in response to negative question 3. It was equally predictable, during the second subset of questions, that most children competently read the dolls' colors as representations of race.

The final subset—the eighth request, "Give me the doll that looks like you"— constituted the climax of the experiment. Upon hearing that question, many of the children who had designated the white doll as "nice" and the Negro doll as "bad" (as 59 percent of them had, in each respective case) suddenly changed demeanor. Children who had been "free and relaxed" suddenly "broke down and cried"; and some "ran out of the testing room, unconsolable [*sic*], convulsed in tears."[134] For others, the answer to the eighth question was disturbingly easy: "That one," said one boy, pointing to the brown doll. "It's a nigger. I'm a nigger."[135]

The Clarks acknowledged that they manipulated the order of their questions to provoke children's rejection of the Negro doll. In an earlier version of the test, the Clarks first asked the children to identify the dolls racially (subset 2), next asked which doll was like them (subset 3), and finally asked which doll they preferred (subset 1). When questioned in this order, black children had a "marked tendency" to identify with and to prefer black dolls. The Clarks discarded this finding as "not necessarily a genuine expression of actual preference, but a reflection of ego involvement." They "controlled" for this "distortion" by changing the order so that children expressed doll preference before they identified a doll with themselves.[136] In other words, the Clarks knew that differently ordered questions produced different results, and they discarded the ordered processes that produced the data they did not want.

Analysis of doll play as a genealogy of performance accounts for this difference in results far better than the Clarks' claims of "distortion" and false positives. In the Clarks' original sequence, children were asked which doll was most like them before they were asked which doll was nice or bad. Therefore, the first question drew children's attention to *themselves*, and asked the children to understand a doll *through* and *in relation to* the self. The person was primary, the doll secondary. In the original sequence, then, the Clarks framed a doll as an *object* that symbolized a person, not a *thing* that prompted play. (An *object*, we recall, is a material item that one looks through or beyond to see something human, whereas a *thing* asserts itself within a field of matter.) Many children responded by identifying the brown doll—which they understood to represent Negro raciality—as the object most like themselves. In the revised sequence, however, the Clarks' initial request—"Give me the doll that you like to play with"—instructed the children to think about the dolls *as dolls* and *in play*. The doll in play, not the person, was primary to the sequence of requests. The Clarks noted that the children did, indeed, approach the dolls as playthings: "Many of the children entered into the experimental situation—particularly the doll test and the coloring test—with freedom similar to that of play."[137] The Clarks seem to have assumed that children play the same way with black and white dolls, and that the questions were therefore racially neutral. As this chapter has shown, however, traditions of play with black and white dolls are not comparable—and historically located children, as experts in children's culture, are sharply aware of how one is "supposed" to play with racially distinct dolls. A child with basic knowledge of children's culture may well have understood the Clarks' revised opening request—"Give me the doll you like to play with"—as a choice between a white doll that prompted cuddle play and a black doll that scripted play of violence and servitude. This binary choice appears in figure 5.3 as a split down the middle of the image: to the center and left, a white girl cuddles white dolls, and to the right, a black doll hangs. That a majority of black children preferred the former mode of play could reveal low self-esteem but could just as well constitute resistance to the demeaning performances that black dolls had scripted for over a century.

In one iteration of the doll experiment, investigators seem to have varied the Clarks' questions so as to focus very tightly on scenarios and actions of doll play rather than the dolls *or* the children. This apparently slight variation produced significantly different results. In the 1951 case of *Belton v. Gebhart* and *Bulah v. Gebhart*, Kenneth Clark testified that forty-one African American children in Delaware had not been asked to "Give me the doll that looks bad," but instead were asked, "Which of these dolls is *likely to act bad*?"[138] This phrasing anthropomorphized the dolls and asked the child to imagine and describe the dolls as animate—that is, to project the dolls into play. The phrasing addressed *only* how the doll would "act." The question did not ask black children to identify how *they*, as individuals, would play with black or white dolls, but instead asked how the dolls would "likely" function in abstracted, scripted play. By 1951, white children, in literature and life had, for a full century, meted out discipline to black dolls that the children had made to act "bad" (in figure 5.3, the white girl has hung the black doll "for a *punish*").[139] Any child who chose the black doll answered the question precisely as the investigator phrased it: the black doll in scripted play was indeed more likely to act bad. And indeed, when the children were asked which doll "looks bad," 59 percent chose the black doll, but when children were asked which doll was "likely to act bad," the percentage of children who chose the black doll rose to 75. The latter question addressed cultural practices, not preference and certainly not self-esteem; and the children's answers demonstrate expertise in practices of play. The Clark doll tests may ultimately prove little about self-esteem, but they tell us a great deal about how African American children of the 1930s, '40s, and '50s thought about racialized doll play.

The Clarks' phrasing and order of questions hurtled children toward an impossible choice. In the Clarks' finalized order, questions in the first subset framed dolls as things in play and asked children which things and practices of play they preferred (or, in the exceptional 1951 case, asked children to read dolls' scripts). Most children, predictably, rejected the practices of play associated with and scripted through black dolls. The second subset of questions asked children to identify the dolls as objects that represented racial groups. Again predictably, most children competently read these objects of children's culture. The third subset, the eighth question, forced children who had rejected the practices of play scripted through black dolls and who had identified the brown dolls as signifiers of Negro raciality to confront an impossible choice: were they *more* nice, like the white doll, or more Negro, like the bad doll? Which quality—niceness or Negroness—better described their essential truth?[140]

Children who had been led, question by question, into an epistemological trap responded to the climactic eighth question by breaking down and sobbing. The Clarks claimed that their test subjects' tears symptomized societal racism, but in the immediate sense, the ones who made the children cry were the Clarks—and Kenneth Clark acknowledged as much. Upon hearing that eighth question, Kenneth Clark said, children sometimes "looked at *me* as if *I* were the devil for putting them in this predicament."[141] At other times, Kenneth Clark wrote, the eighth question caused "some children [to look] at the investigator with terror or hostility."[142] For these reasons, Kenneth Clark said, the tests constituted "a traumatic experience for me as well."[143]

If the Clarks were initially surprised by the children's tears, they certainly were not surprised in the fifth, sixth, seventh, eighth year of testing. The Clarks could have altered their experiment to avoid these responses (they had, after all, previously revised the test to avoid an unwanted result). The fact that they did not do so shows that the Clarks viewed tears as a desirable result of the doll tests. That they repeatedly staged a drama that climaxed with children sobbing suggests that the Clarks *wanted* children to cry.

This chapter, like most scholarship on the doll tests, has considered the experiment mainly from the perspective of the Clarks. But let us pause and briefly reexamine it from the perspective of the child test subjects.

The Clarks knew that the eighth question was the last, *but the children did not know that*. For all the children knew, there were ten more questions, thirty more questions to come. Imagine that you are a child taking the test. It's the 1940s. You're five. You're alone in a room with an adult whom you do not know. The adult begins by asking you questions about toys and play. These questions are comfortable because toys and play are subjects about which you know a lot and have strong opinions. Next, the adult asks you about dolls and race. These questions, too, are comfortable, because they're easy, and you know the right answers. Then, the adult blindsides you with a disturbing, impossible question. At this point, all you want is to stop the test and go home. What resources are available to you? What are your options?

You could run out of the room, slamming the door behind you. And indeed, some children did that. Alternatively, you could clam up, glare at the adult, and refuse to answer any more questions. Again, some children did that. Or you could cry—and this is what many children did. Of all the resources available to a child to stop the test, tears were perhaps the most powerful and effective. Unlike children who ran from the room or refused to answer, children who cried did not appear to defy authority. Tears appeared to be purely expressive and therefore non-agential. Tears seemed innocent.

The impossible, binary demand that the Clarks' subjects faced echoed the one that Daisy Turner had confronted fifty years earlier: liken yourself dangerously to a black doll or appear to reject your own racial identity. When Daisy Turner spewed furious verse, she created a third option and thus shattered the binary. Many of the Clarks' subjects forged their own third option when they terminated the experiment by crying. In each of these respective cases, a child resourcefully used the tools—improvised verse, tears—that were available to her or him. Daisy Turner exercised agency by discarding the pageant's script, but the Clarks' subjects exercised agency by *enacting* the scripted behavior of crying. In other words, the Clarks authored a dramatic arc that evoked children's tears, but those tears were simultaneously agential, because by crying, children halted a painful experiment—one that they had no way of knowing was already over.[144] This intersection of scripting and agency illustrates one of this book's central underlying arguments: people are able to resist scripting because they have agency, but agency can also, even simultaneously, emerge *through* scripting. Resistance and scripting are not incompatible; they are often mutually constitutive.

For a century, black dolls in rag and rubber had grinned through the abusive play that they were created to survive. But the Clarks used the materiality of black dolls in conjunction with a carefully-structured dramatic arc to script black children's performances of weeping. These performances refuted the libel that black youth could not feel pain—and they did so at one precise site where that libel had been enacted: black dolls. In a brilliant act of cultural jujitsu, the Clarks pivoted black dolls so as to use all the force of the libel against itself. *Pace* William Blake, a tear is not, in itself, an intellectual thing—rather, Mamie Clark and Kenneth Clark used things to make tears intellectual.

When the Clarks scripted, through dolls, a spectacle of black children's pain, they cast black children in the role of "suffering child," "innocent child," and therefore "child." This defamiliarizing gesture recalled and reversed the work of Lewis Hine's photograph of Callie Campbell picking cotton (Chapter 1). Where Hine showed a child cotton picker who was surprisingly, unfamiliarly white, the Clarks showed suffering children who were unfamiliarly black, and black children who were unfamiliarly suffering. The pained white child, Hine's photograph suggested, deserved protection in the form of child labor laws. When the Clarks vividly described black children weeping, they argued that African American youth not only *could* be hurt but *had* been hurt—by systemic racism. This argument reversed the flight of the pickaninny through popular culture to resurrect Stowe's initial imagining of Topsy as an essentially vulnerable child who had been unnaturally hardened by slavery's violence. The Clarks and the NAACP repeated Stowe's argument with differences when they cast black youth as suffering children, segregation as cruelty toward children, and civil rights, by extension, as a form of child protection. Through this performance, the Clarks and the NAACP located civil rights on the side of childhood innocence, as Stowe had located abolition a century earlier.

From the mid-nineteenth century through the early twentieth century, two qualities defined childhood innocence: whiteness and obliviousness. The Clarks wrought a spectacular performance of black childhood innocence, and this triumphant intervention aided *Brown v. Board of Education* not only in the task of legally desegregating public schools, but also in that of culturally desegregating childhood innocence itself. *Brown* acknowledged that children's daily lives are political, that children do not exist in a state of holy ignorance. (Indeed, the main point of the doll tests was that black children do absorb racism and that it causes them to suffer—unlike Little Eva, for whom "evil rolls off [her] mind like dew off a cabbage-leaf,—not a drop sinks in."[145]) *Brown*, and the civil rights move-ment more generally, pried the "whites only" sign off the fountain of childhood innocence and elevated to common sense the fact that children do absorb political ideologies.[146] With these two changes, the civil rights movement fundamentally reshaped the relationship of childhood, inno-cence, and race in the United States.

Today, many emblems of racial innocence—faithful mammies and uncles who caress white children, Topsies who enjoy comic violence—are understood to be political. Because of the success of the civil rights movement, Disney has disavowed *Song of the South*, Aunt Jemima pancake syrup and Uncle Ben rice receive repeated, never-quite-good-enough makeovers, and most toy retailers would not dream of ped-dling a kerchiefed Dinah doll. The "wonderful 'leaping' fish" that Henry James observed flying through popular culture have been banished from mainstream toy stores, but they have alighted in new spaces: flea markets, websites, and auctions that traffic in Golliwoggs and other items of racist children's culture. Some buyers and sellers claim to be oblivious to these things' politics (one consumer wrote in 2005, "There is nothing wrong with Golliwoggs. . . . I do not think they are racist at all, I just find them to be adorable toys"[147]), but this posi-tion, once dominant, is now fringe. Most items of "black memorabilia" are now sold as historical-political collectibles—as things understood to script adults' acts of accumulation and display, not children's acts of innocent play.[148]

Within children's culture, however, emblems of racial innocence flour-ish in new guises. Contemporary topsy-turvy dolls contrast a pale-faced Little Red Riding Hood at one pole with a brown Wolf in Grandma's Clothing at the other; thus they retain the sexual subtext while cloaking—but not expunging—the racial meanings that enslaved women sewed into these dolls a century and a half earlier. Little Eva filtered into Shirley Tem-ple and other, ever-proliferating surrogates. The loving embrace between the white, masterful child and the African American adult servant con-tinues to surface in films such as Dakota Fanning's and Jennifer Hudson's *The Secret Life of Bees*. Topsy turned into the pickaninny, whited up, and went undercover in the Scarecrow and Raggedy Ann. These changes mark not the end of racial innocence but its reconfiguration for a postsegrega-tion era. Like riddles cribbed from minstrel shows, these re-formations convey logics, styles, and practices from the nineteenth century to the twenty-first. They renew childhood as an infinitely flexible, inexhaustible resource. The solemnly restored call to "protect the children" reanimates, disguises, and draws power from old, half-forgotten contests over love and pain and fun, over the racial limits of innocence, and over the American question of who is a person and who is a thing.

# Notes

NOTES TO INTRODUCTION

1. Don Ellzey, "JP Refuses to Marry Couple," *Daily Star* (Hammond, La.) 15 October 2009. http://www.hammondstar.com/articles/2009/10/15/top_stories/8847.txt.

2. Ibid.

3. "Landrieu: Keith Bardwell Should Be Dismissed for Denying Marriage Licenses to Interracial Couples," Associated Press, *Huffington Post* 16 October 2009. http://www.huffingtonpost.com/2009/10/16/landrieu-keith-bardwell-s_n_324361.html. On childhood and futurity, see Lee Edelman, *No Future: Queer Theory and the Death Drive* (Durham, N.C.: Duke University Press, 2004).

4. "Louisiana Justice Who Refused Interracial Marriage Resigns," CNN, 3 November 2009. http://www.cnn.com/2009/US/11/03/louisiana.interracial.marriage/index.html.

5. "US Judge's Mixed Marriage Refusal," BBC, 16 October 2009. http://news.bbc.co.uk/2/hi/americas/8310509.stm. Beth Humphrey McKay, online message to the author, 29 August 2010.

6. Mary Foster, "Interracial Couple Denied Marriage License in Tangipahoa Parish," *Times-Picayune,* Saint Tammany Edition, 16 October 2009. http://www.nola.com/crime/index.ssf/2009/10/interracial_couple_denied_marr.html.

7. Tavia Nyong'o analyzes this image in depth in *The Amalgamation Waltz: Race, Performance, and the Ruses of Memory* (Minneapolis: University of Minnesota Press, 2009), 29–30.

8. C. J. Parker, *The Inhabitants of Medway v. The Inhabitants of Needham*, Supreme Court of Massachusetts, Norfolk, 16 Mass. 157, October 1819.

9. Mrs. Child [Lydia Maria Child], *An Appeal in Favor of that Class of Americans Called Africans* (Boston: Allen and Ticknor, 1833), 210. See also George Bradburn, Report, Docket H998 Intermarriage, House Unpassed Legislation 1841, Massachusetts Archives. I thank Amber Moulton for referring me to Child's, Parker's, and Bradburn's defenses of interracial marriage. See Amber Moulton, "'Marriage Extraordinary': Interracial Marriage and the Politics of Family in Antebellum Massachusetts," Ph.D. diss., Harvard University, 2011.

10. In the definition of Michael Omi and Howard Winant, racial formation, or "the sociohistorical process by which racial categories are created, inhabited, transformed, and destroyed," occurs through "historically situated *projects* in which human bodies and social structures are represented and organized" (Michael Omi and Howard Winant, *Racial*

*Formation in the United States from the 1960s to the Present*, 2d ed. [New York: Routledge, 1994], 55–56). Racial formation, in other words, is the macrolevel phenomenon that occurs through large- and small-scale racial projects (ibid., 60, 68). "The linkage between culture and structure, which is at the core of the racial formation process," writes Winant, "gives racial projects their coherence and unity" (Howard Winant, "Racism Today: Continuity and Change in the Post-Civil Rights Era," *Ethnic and Racial Studies* 21, no. 4 [1998]: 756). That linkage, I argue in this book, occurs through performance. Human bodies in motion, in performance, link material, visual, and print cultures to each other and to social structures such as capitalism and law (for which performance is also a crucial component). Performance is both part of racial projects and a set of practices by which racial projects connect with each other and with societal structures to create historical processes of racial formation.

11. Philippe Ariès influentially argued that a belief in childhood innocence emerged only during the Enlightenment (Philippe Ariès, *Centuries of Childhood: A Social History of Family Life*, trans. Robert Baldick [New York: Vintage Books, 1962], esp. 100–127). Scholars who have expanded upon, refined, or quarreled with Ariès include Anne Higonnet, James R. Kincaid, and Linda Pollack.

12. On the doctrine of infant depravity in the United States, see Sylvia D. Hoffert, "'A Very Peculiar Sorrow': Attitudes Toward Infant Death in the Urban Northeast, 1800–1860," *American Quarterly* 39, no. 4 (1987): 605–8.

13. This brief, introductory summary of several hundred years of cultural history necessarily simplifies and omits much. On Locke's and Rousseau's rejection of the doctrine of infant depravity, see Alexander Moseley, *John Locke* (London: Continuum, 2007), 118, 169, and Jürgen Oelkers, *Jean-Jacques Rousseau* (London: Continuum, 2008), 93, 114–17, 212–13. On the tabula rasa, and in particular on the necessity of not misreading it as a state of passivity, see John Yolton, *John Locke and Education* (New York: Random House, 1971), 52–55. John W. and Jean S. Yolton's Introduction to Locke's *Some Thoughts Concerning Education* provides a superb exegesis of Locke's ideas and some major interpretations of these ideas (John W. Yolton and Jean S. Yolton, Introduction to John Locke, *Some Thoughts Concerning Education* [New York: Oxford University Press, 1989], 1–69). I discuss Locke, Rousseau, Wordsworth, and romantic childhood in closer detail in Chapter 1.

14. On the circulation of Wordsworth's poetry in the United States in the nineteenth century, see Barbara Garlitz, "The Immortality Ode: Its Cultural Progeny," *Studies in English Literature* 6 (Autumn 1966): 639–49. Bernard Wishy, Karen Sánchez-Eppler, and Claudia Nelson have written about the trope of angelic children in sentimental narratives redeeming adults through a combination of touch and moral suasion, thus converting their elders to Christianity, temperance, or other good behavior.

15. Sánchez-Eppler points out that childhood solidified as an attribute of innocence, rather than vice versa: "[F]or the nineteenth century, childhood is better understood as a status or idea associated with innocence and dependency than as a specific developmental or biological period." Karen Sánchez-Eppler, *Dependent States: The Child's Part in Nineteenth-Century American Culture* (Chicago: University of Chicago Press, 2005), xxi. Several scholars have shown that the figure of the child—and therefore innocence—defined sentimental

literature itself. Elizabeth Dillon notes that "the debut of the child as a central figure of literary and popular culture" was "one of the most striking aspects of sentimental discourse" (Elizabeth Dillon, *The Gender of Freedom: Fictions of Liberalism and the Literary Public Sphere* [Stanford, Calif.: Stanford University Press, 2004], 204), and Ala Alryyes comments similarly that the rise of the novel was "intertwined with the child's story" and that "whereas children are virtually absent from eighteenth-century fiction, they populate every manner of sentimental text in the nineteenth century" (Ala Alryyes, *Original Subjects: The Child, the Novel and the Nation* [Cambridge, Mass.: Harvard University Press, 2001], 119).

16. Harriet Beecher Stowe, *Uncle Tom's Cabin* (1852), Norton Critical Edition, ed. Elizabeth Ammons (New York: W. W. Norton, 1994), 126. Cited hereafter as "Stowe."

17. Ibid., 257–58.

18. Ibid., 322, 324.

19. Ann Douglas, *The Feminization of American Culture* (reprint, New York: Noonday Press, 1998), 3.

20. Keith Bardwell mobilized this transmissibility in 2009 when he invoked the innocence of children as a means of declaring *himself* innocent of defying constitutional law, innocent of racism. In other words, Bardwell, like so many of the historical figures in this book, used childhood to play innocent.

21. Kathryn Bond Stockton might call these sites "switchpoints" in which "one sign's rich accumulations . . . lend themselves to another." Stockton, *Beautiful Bottom, Beautiful Shame: Where "Black" Meets "Queer"* (Durham, N.C.: Duke University Press, 2006), 4.

22. Today Uncle Tom may seem, to some, as holy and innocent as Eva. This perception of mutual innocence became possible because Stowe, Billings, Jewett, and hundreds of others unevenly, and with differing intentions, created that vision. This book shows that the white child's innocence was a crucial means toward that end and many other, often directly conflicting, ends.

23. In Harris's first book, Remus was free; Harris's later books configured Remus as a slave.

24. "Childhood," *Blackwood's Magazine* 12, no. 67 (1822): 139–45, cited in Claudia Nelson, *Boys Will Be Girls: The Feminine Ethic and British Children's Fiction, 1857–1917* (New Brunswick, N.J.: Rutgers University Press, 1991), 17; "Childhood," *Godey's* 4 (June 1832), 268; cited in Karin Calvert, *Children in the House: The Material Culture of Early Childhood, 1600–1900* (Boston,: Northeastern University Press, 1992), 104–5. Calvert lists many other sources in which similar ideas appear. My first chapter further discusses innocence as an active state of deflection.

25. James R. Kincaid, *Child-Loving: The Erotic Child and Victorian Culture* (New York: Routledge, 1992), 12; James R. Kincaid, *Erotic Innocence: The Culture of Child Molesting* (Durham, N.C.: Duke University Press, 1998), 16.

26. As Anne Higonnet notes, "[C]hildren deny, or enable us to forget, many aspects of adult society" (Anne Higonnet, *Pictures of Innocence: The History and Crisis of Ideal Childhood* [London: Thames and Hudson, 1998], 23). Those "aspects of adult society" are, more specifically, class and gender: romantic paintings imagine children as possessing "no class, no gender, and no thoughts" (24).

27. Chapter 3 analyzes Billings's "arbor scene" in detail.

28. See Sánchez-Eppler, *Dependent States*, xv–xvi, on the transformation of proverbs into nursery rhymes as evidence of "childhood as the repository of older cultural forms relinquished as adults." See Higonnet, *Pictures of Innocence*, 28, 51, on the appearance of the mob-cap in John Everett Millais's best-selling 1879 print *Cherry Ripe*. On children's clothing as quoting the past, see Higonnet, 49.

29. On the minstrel origins of these riddles, see Robert C. Toll, *On with the Show: The First Century of Show Business in America* (New York: Oxford University Press, 1976), 95. Shirley Temple tells the suspenders joke in a staged minstrel show within the 1936 film *Dimples*.

30. George Lipsitz, "The Possessive Investment in Whiteness: Racialized Social Democracy and the 'White' Problem in American Studies," *American Quarterly* 47, no. 5 (1995): 369. See also Richard Dyer, *White* (New York: Routledge, 1997).

31. Ann duCille, "The Shirley Temple of My Familiar," *Transition* no. 73 (1997): 13.

32. See also Robin Bernstein, "Dances with Things: Material Culture and the Performance of Race," *Social Text* 101 (Winter 2009): 67–94.

33. Sarah N. Roth, "The Mind of a Child: Images of African Americans in Early Juvenile Fiction," *Journal of the Early Republic* 25 (Spring 2005): 100–101. The term "Tomitude," which may be traced to Charles Briggs's essay, "Uncle Tomitudes" (*Putnam's Monthly* [January 1853], 97–102), has come to refer to household goods representing Uncle Tom, Topsy, Eva, Eliza, or related characters. See Stephen A. Hirsch, "Uncle Tomitudes: The Popular Reaction to *Uncle Tom's Cabin*," in *Studies in the American Renaissance, 1978*, ed. Joel Myerson (Boston: Twayne, 1978), 303–30.

34. Claire Parfait, *The Publishing History of* Uncle Tom's Cabin, *1852–2002* (Burlington, Vt.: Ashgate, 2007), 63.

35. Chapter 3 details Jewett's advertising campaign.

36. In the nineteenth century, the words "bandana" and "handkerchief" were used interchangeably. See J. J. Murphy, *Children's Handkerchiefs: A Two Hundred Year History* (Atglen, Penn.: Schiffer, 1998), 4.

37. On handkerchiefs for "show and blow," see Helen Gustafson, *Hanky Panky: An Intimate History of the Handkerchief* (Berkeley, Calif.: Ten Speed Press, 2002), 26.

38. Stowe, 227. As I argue in Chapter 3, the image could also illustrate Eva's line, "There's a 'sea of glass, mingled with fire.'"

39. Henry James, *A Small Boy and Others* (New York: Charles Scribner's Sons, 1913), 158–59; emphasis added.

40. Stowe, 385.

41. Ibid., 72.

42. Ibid., 73.

43. Ibid., 84.

44. Some scholars might claim that the handkerchief is not ideologically coherent because the handkerchief's material has been identified as muslin, which is a cotton-based fabric. Any cotton product in 1852 would almost surely have resulted from slave labor, in which

case the handkerchief advertising Stowe's abolitionist novel materializes irony and even hypocrisy. However, the handkerchief at the Harriet Beecher Stowe Center, which I examined firsthand, is linen, which derives from flax and which does not emblematize slave labor as cotton does. It is possible that other extant Jewett handkerchiefs are indeed muslin (several different versions were produced, so the material could have varied). The linen handkerchief in the Harriet Beecher Stowe Center, however, is an ideologically unified object: It made meaning in its historical context through a combination of its textual content (visual, verbal, and aural), its materiality (linen), and the motions, the performances, that it prompted (weeping and drying the eyes).

45. In her description of meaningful lines of activity, Susan Leigh Foster favors the term *choreography* over *script* because, in her view, "the legacy of the dramatic text continues to infuse the script with a kind of permanence, whereas the notion of choreography as a theoretical premise underscores the changeability of events and their environs" (Susan Leigh Foster, "Geographies of Gender," *Signs* 24. no. 1 [1998]: 28). In this claim, however, Foster foregrounds vernacular uses of the word "script" rather than the actual practices of actors and directors.

46. W. B. Worthen, "Antigone's Bones," *TDR* 52, no. 3 (2008): 10–33; Diana Taylor, *The Archive and the Repertoire: Performing Cultural Memory in the Americas* (Durham, N.C.: Duke University Press, 2003), 20.

47. Taylor, *Archive and the Repertoire*, 16, 19, 20.

48. Ibid., 36, 21.

49. Mildred Rutherford, *American Authors: A Hand-Book of American Literature from Early Colonial to Living Writers* (Atlanta: Franklin, 1894), 513.

50. Leslie Fiedler, *The Inadvertent Epic: From* Uncle Tom's Cabin *to* Roots (Toronto: Canadian Broadcasting Corporation, 1979).

51. James, *A Small Boy*, 159.

52. Lauren Berlant, *The Female Complaint: The Unfinished Business of Sentimentality in American Culture* (Durham, N.C.: Duke University Press, 2008), viii and passim.

53. On minstrel influence upon Topsy, see Elizabeth Young, *Disarming the Nation: Women's Writing and the American Civil War* (Chicago: University of Chicago Press, 1999), 36, 316 n. 49. On Topsy as the paradigmatic child, see Richard Brodhead, "Sparing the Rod: Discipline and Fiction in Antebellum America," *Representations* 21 (Winter 1988): 85.

54. Stowe, 213.

55. Montgomery Gregory, "The Drama of Negro Life," in *The New Negro*, ed. Alain Locke (1925; New York: Simon and Schuster, 1997), 155.

56. Linda Williams, *Playing the Race Card: Melodramas of Black and White from Uncle Tom to O. J. Simpson* (Princeton, N.J.: Princeton University Press, 2001).

57. Philip Fisher, *Hard Facts: Setting and Form in the American Novel* (New York: Oxford University Press, 1987) 4, 100.

58. The "Lost Cause" was an imagined antebellum South populated by naturally servile African American slaves and noble white slave owners. By collectively imagining this society, the South, in the face of undeniable military defeat, aimed to win a larger cultural war.

The stratagem was effective, and from the end of Reconstruction through the early twentieth century, writers and artists in the "Plantation school" justified the disenfranchisement of African Americans by imagining the prewar South as an innocent playground in which blacks and whites lived in the harmony produced through strict but natural social hierarchies. See Chapter 3 for further discussion of the Lost Cause.

59. The imagined "faithful slave" was central to Lost Cause ideology. As David Blight has shown, white supremacist fantasies of faithful slaves built steadily throughout the postbellum nineteenth century but reached an apex in the early decades of the twentieth century (David Blight, *Race and Reunion: The Civil War in American Memory* [Cambridge, Mass.: Belknap Press of Harvard University Press, 2001], 274 and passim). Especially with the semicentenary of the war in 1911–1915, white Americans, both northern and southern, eagerly produced and consumed Lost Cause literature and "Old Plantation Days" public performances in which "uncles" and "mammies" adored their owners and never desired freedom. In an effort to concretize this valorization of the "faithful slave," the United Daughters of the Confederacy lobbied Congress from 1905 through 1925 to erect a memorial to mammies in every state—South and North, West and East (Blight, *Race and Reunion*, 284–88; Micki McElya, *Clinging to Mammy: The Faithful Slave in Twentieth-Century America* [Cambridge, Mass.: Harvard University Press, 2007]). At stake in these efforts was the meaning of the war, of enslavement and slave owning, and of race itself. Stories of faithful slaves enabled white Americans to reinvent enslavement as a universally congenial peculiarity, slave owning as paternalistic stewardship, and the Civil War as a contest over states' rights rather than slavery.

60. Lois Kuznets, *When Toys Come Alive: Narratives of Animation, Metamorphosis, and Development* (New Haven, Conn.: Yale University Press, 1994), 2.

61. Miriam Formanek-Brunell, *Made to Play House: Dolls and the Commercialization of American Girlhood, 1830–1930* (1993; Baltimore: Johns Hopkins University Press, 1998), 23.

62. Julia Charlotte Maitland, *The Doll and Her Friends; Or, Memoirs of the Lady Seraphina* (London: Grant and Griffith, 1852), 1.

63. Ibid., 4.

64. Maitland is one of many white writers who described dollness as a racial category. See also, for example, the anonymously authored *Sketches of Doll Life. A Christmas Story for Doll Mamas* (Boston: Loring, 1863), 112, 134; and Mary Mister, *The Adventures of a Doll* (London: Darton, Harvey and Darton, Gracechurch-Street, 1816), 2.

65. Anon., *A Doll's Story* (London: Grombridge and Sons, ca. 1852), 8; qtd. in Kuznets, *When Toys Come Alive*, 107.

66. The Confederate Museum in Richmond, Virginia, owns a doll that is believed to have been used to smuggle quinine and morphine. See Georgia Dickinson Wardlaw, *The Old and the Quaint in Virginia* (Richmond, Va.: Dietz Press, 1939), 299–300. See also Edward P. Alexander, *Early American Dolls: The Imogene Anderson Collection* (Ticonderoga, N.Y., 1937), 5; and Dawn Reno, *Collecting Black Americana* (New York: Crown, 1986), 39.

67. Frederick Douglass, *My Bondage and My Freedom* (New York: Miller, Orton, and Mulligan, 1855), 39.

68. James, *Small Boy*, 160.

69. A few scholars, including Sánchez-Eppler and Mary Niall Mitchell, have successfully argued from both positions simultaneously.

70. Joseph R. Roach, *Cities of the Dead: Circum-Atlantic Performance* (New York: Columbia University Press, 1996), 2.

71. Ibid., 3.

72. The difference between scriptive things and effigies may be clarified through the nouns and the verbs that attend to each concept. First, the nouns: scriptive things are nonliving chunks of matter, but effigies can be living humans, corpses, or nonliving things. This distinction is important because of the verbs that animate the nouns: effigies *surrogate* or *perform*, but scriptive things *issue instructions* for (but do not rigidly dictate) their own use. Scriptive things *utter*; they may say, variously, hold me, look at me, cry into me, cuddle me, hit me. Scriptive things, but not necessarily effigies, hail users (individually and in groups), inviting identifiable bodily responses (see Chapter 2). An item may function as both a scriptive thing and an effigy. A black doll, for example, might be an effigy that surrogates the role of Topsy. By surrogating Topsy, the doll cites previous behaviors of play *with* Topsy dolls—and through these quotations, the doll prompts future behaviors of play (see Chapter 5). In this case, surrogation and scripting enable each other while remaining distinct functions within a single thing.

73. Roach, *Cities of the Dead*, 36.

74. William Wordsworth, "Ode: Intimations of Immortality from Recollections of Early Childhood" (1807), in *Selected Poems and Prefaces by William Wordsworth*, ed. Jack Stillinger (Boston: Houghton Mifflin, 1965), 188

75. Carolyn Steedman, *Strange Dislocations: Childhood and the Idea of Human Interiority, 1780–1930* (Cambridge, Mass.: Harvard University Press, 1995).

76. On loss as constitutive of performance, see Peggy Phelan, *Unmarked: The Politics of Performance* (New York: Routledge, 1992), 146–66.

77. Roach, *Cities of the Dead*, 2.

78. Clarence Darrow, "Mercy for Leopold and Loeb," August 1924, in *The Roaring Twenties: Eyewitness History*, ed. Tom Streissguth (New York: Infobase, 2007), 352–54.

79. Kincaid, *Child-Loving*, 5.

80. Orville Dewey, *A Discourse on Slavery and the Annexation of Texas* (New York, 1844), 10; qtd. in George M. Fredrickson, *The Black Image in the White Mind: The Debate on Afro-American Character and Destiny, 1817–1914* (New York: Harper and Row, 1971), 102.

81. On romantic racialists' configuration of African American adults as childlike, see Fredrickson, *Black Image in the White Mind*, 97–129, and Roth, "Mind of a Child," 93–95.

82. Twelfth Annual Screen Actors Guild Awards, 29 January 2006. The quotation is transcribed from an online recording of the television broadcast. "Dakota Fanning presenting an award to Shirley Temple," http://www.youtube.com/watch?v=2V4Sue3ID48, accessed 29 January 2010.

83. See Roach, *Cities of the Dead*, 78–85, on celebrities as effigies.

84. Other child actors whom James Kincaid locates in Shirley Temple's genealogy of

"big-eyed, kissy-lipped blonde" figures include Jackie Coogan, Tatum O'Neal, Ricky Schro-eder, Drew Barrymore, and Macaulay Culkin (Kincaid, *Child-Loving*, 369).

85. On Shirley Temple in relation to Little Eva, see Berlant, *Female Complaint*, 49–50, 53–54; Patricia Turner, *Ceramic Uncles and Celluloid Mammies: Black Images and Their Influence on Culture* (New York: Anchor, 1994), 83; and Jim O'Loughlin, "Articulating *Uncle Tom's Cabin*," *New Literary History* 31, no. 3 (2000): 586–89.

86. In 1934, the Academy gave Temple a "special Oscar," which the girl reportedly placed "on her shelf next to the rest of her dolls." Kevin Starr, *The Dream Endures: California Enters the 1940s* (1997; New York: Oxford University Press, 2002), 259.

87. Toni Morrison, *The Bluest Eye* (1970; New York: Pocket Books, 1972), 20.

88. Ibid.

89. Ibid.

90. Ibid., 20, 22.

NOTES TO CHAPTER 1

1. Trade cards were a common mode of advertising in the 1880s and were not uncommon in the 1890s. Ellen Gruber Garvey's *The Adman in the Parlor: Magazines and the Gendering of Consumer Culture, 1880s to 1910s* (New York: Oxford University Press, 1996) is the definitive source on this form of advertising.

2. Cottolene was similar, in look and use, to Crisco. It was produced and marketed by the N. K. Fairbank Company (which was also known for Gold Dust washing powder, for which E. W. Kemble created the logo of the "Gold Dust Twins"). See Susan Strasser, *Satisfaction Guaranteed: The Making of the American Mass Market* (New York: Pantheon, 1989), 8–9, and Marilyn Maness Mehaffy, "Advertising Race/Raceing Advertising: The Feminine Consumer(-Nation), 1876–1900," *Signs* 23, no. 1 (1997): 131–74.

3. On the aesthetics of cuteness, see Lori Merish, "Cuteness and Commodity Aesthetics: Tom Thumb and Shirley Temple," in *Freakery: Cultural Spectacles of the Extraordinary Body*, ed. Rosemarie Garland Thomson (New York: New York University Press, 1996), 187.

4. The Library of Congress attributes this photograph to Lewis Hine "based on provenance." Library of Congress Prints and Photographs Online Catalog, http://lcweb2.loc.gov/cgi-bin/query/h?pp/nclc:@field(NUMBER+@band(nclc+00628)), retrieved 22 August 2009.

5. On Hine's control over the photographs he took for the NCLC, see Maren Stange, *Symbols of Ideal Life: Social Documentary Photography, 1890–1950* (New York: Cambridge University Press, 1989), 67–68.

6. Catherine Reef, *Childhood in America: An Eyewitness History* (New York: Facts on File, 2002), 91–113.

7. Anne Scott MacLeod, "The *Caddie Woodlawn* Syndrome: American Girlhood in the Nineteenth Century," in *A Century of Childhood, 1820–1920*, by Mary Lynn Stevens Heininger et al. (Rochester, N.Y.: The Margaret Woodbury Strong Museum), 99–119; Michelle Ann Abate, *Tomboys: A Literary and Cultural History* (Philadelphia: Temple University Press, 2008). On the figure of the "bad boy," see Kenneth Kidd, *Making American Boys:*

*Boyology and the Feral Tale* (Minneapolis: University of Minneapolis Press, 2004), especially 49–86. Viviana A. Zelizer, *Pricing the Priceless Child: The Changing Social Value of Children* (New York: Basic Books, 1985).

8. Jacob Abbott, *Stories of Rainbow and Lucky* (New York: Harper and Brothers, 1860); Harriet E. Wilson, *Our Nig. Or, Sketches from the Life of a Free Black* (1859; reprint, introduced by Henry Louis Gates Jr., New York: Vintage, 1983). On idealized black children in antebellum texts, see Holly Keller, "Juvenile Antislavery Narrative and Notions of Childhood," *Children's Literature* 24 (1996): esp. 89–90.

9. James Kincaid, *Erotic Innocence: The Culture of Child Molesting* (Durham, N.C.: Duke University Press, 1998), 57.

10. A rare example of a purely wicked white child character, Miss Mopsa, appears in Chapter 5. Significantly, as punishment for her crimes, Miss Mopsa mystically turns black and is sold. A white child who is devoid of innocence, this story warns, cannot remain white—or free.

11. Karen Sánchez-Eppler, *Dependent States: The Child's Part in Nineteenth-Century American Culture* (Chicago: University of Chicago Press, 2005), xxi.

12. On the figure of the pickaninny, see Kenneth Goings, *Mammy and Uncle Mose: Black Collectibles and American Stereotyping* (Bloomington: Indiana University Press, 1994), and Patricia A. Turner, *Ceramic Uncles and Celluloid Mammies: Black Images and Their Influence on Culture* (New York: Anchor, 1994).

13. *Oxford English Dictionary*, s.v. "piccaninny."

14. Goings, *Mammy and Uncle Mose,* 37. See also Turner, *Ceramic Uncles and Celluloid Mammies,* 13–18, 36.

15. E. W. Kemble, *A Coon Alphabet* (New York: R. H. Russell, 1898), n.p.

16. Kirk Savage, *Standing Soldiers, Kneeling Slaves: Race, War, and Monument in Nineteenth-Century America* (Princeton, N.J.: Princeton University Press, 1997), 7.

17. Debra Walker King, *African Americans and the Culture of Pain* (Charlottesville: University of Virginia Press, 2008), 5, 6.

18. William Cowper Brann, *The Complete Works of Brann, the Iconoclast,* vol. 6 (1898; New York: Brann, 1919), 1.

19. 1 Corinthians 13.11, King James Bible.

20. Philippe Ariès, *L'Enfant et la vie familiale sous l'ancien régime* (1960); trans. Robert Baldick under the title *Centuries of Childhood: A Social History of Family Life* (New York: Vintage Books, 1962).

21. Sylvia D. Hoffert, "'A Very Peculiar Sorrow': Attitudes toward Infant Death in the Urban Northeast, 1800–1860," *American Quarterly* 39, no. 4 (1987): 606.

22. On the relationship between infant depravity and child-rearing practices, particularly the use of swaddling and walking stools, see Karin Calvert, *Children in the House: The Material Culture of Early Childhood, 1600–1900* (Boston: Northeastern University Press, 1992), 19–38.

23. Quoted in Steven Mintz and Susan Kellogg, *Domestic Revolutions: A Social History of American Family Life* (New York: Free Press, 1988), 15.

24. Robert Southey, *The Life of Wesley; And the Rise and Progress of Methodism* (1820; New York: Harper and Brothers, 1847), 2:306–7.

25. The doctrine of infant depravity declined in part because a faction of Protestants challenged Calvinism and the doctrine of infant depravity. During and after the Great Awakening of the 1740s, anti-Calvinists criticized the idea of infant damnation as a "grotesquerie," an example of Calvinist excess, and thus used the doctrine as a wedge by which to unseat Calvinism's dominance (Peter Gregg Slater, *Children in the New England Mind in Death and in Life* [Hamden, Conn.: Archon Books, 1977], 50). The British minister John Taylor attacked the doctrine in his 1740 *The Scripture-Doctrine of Original Sin Proposed to Free and Candid Examination*. This "manifesto," along with a similar argument launched by the Reverend Samuel Webster in 1757, influenced the eighteenth-century Boston minister Charles Chauncy, who then staged what was arguably the most effective clerical challenge to the doctrine of original sin in the United States (ibid., 52–55). The Reverends Peter Clark, Joseph Bellamy, and Jonathan Edwards defended the doctrines of original sin (and, by extension, the belief in infant damnation), but each of their defenses fell short: Clark was an intellectually and stylistically weak writer, and Bellamy's argument responded to selected elements of the challenge while leaving the greater range of attacks unanswered (ibid., 55–58). Edwards, however, issued a masterly and uncompromising counterattack in *The Great Christian Doctrine of Original Sin Defended* (published posthumously in 1758). In this work, Edwards argued that Adam and all descended from him were a "single entity—*mankind*," and that therefore all people had committed the primal sin (ibid., 59–60). In Edwards's formulation, contemporary humans did not passively inherit sin; rather, they had acquired sin personally through their participation in the Fall. Sin was therefore not intrinsic to humans; it was paradoxically acquired before birth. This point, which Perry Miller called Edwards's "most original and brilliant conception," was intended to bolster the belief in original sin, but it inadvertently raised the possibility of human sinlessness—that is, it imagined a before before the before (Perry Miller, *Jonathan Edwards* [New York: Meridian Books, 1959], 278, cited in Slater, *Children in the New England Mind,* 62). Contra Edwards's intentions, *The Great Christian Doctrine of Original Sin Defended* ultimately weakened belief in original sin and thus indirectly eroded the corollary of infant damnation.

26. Anne Bradstreet, "The Four Ages of Man," in Bradstreet, *The Tenth Muse Lately Sprung Up in America, or, Severall Poems, Compiled with Great Variety of Wit and Learning, Full of Delight* (London: For Stephen Bowtell at the Signe of the Bible in Popes Head-Alley, 1650), 43.

27. William Wordsworth, "Ode: Intimations of Immortality from Recollections of Early Childhood" (1807), in *Selected Poems and Prefaces by William Wordsworth*, ed. Jack Stillinger (Boston: Houghton Mifflin, 1965), 187.

28. Barbara Garlitz, "The Immortality Ode: Its Cultural Progeny," *Studies in English Literature* 6 (Autumn 1966): 639–49.

29. Most scholars describe the romantic child in relation to John Locke and Jean-Jacques Rousseau. John Locke outlined his ideas regarding childhood and the tabula rasa in *An Essay concerning Human Understanding* (1690); and in 1762, Jean-Jacques Rousseau's *Emile: Or,*

*on Education* laid the groundwork for the romantic formulation of childhood. Romanticism posited the child as fundamentally a part of nature, and no more inherently sinful than a tree or a storm. On Locke, Rousseau, and their heavy influence on U.S. practices of child rearing, see Jacqueline S. Reinier, *From Virtue to Character: American Childhood, 1775–1850* (New York: Twayne, 1996), 1–19; Bernard Wishy, *The Child and the Republic: The Dawn of Modern American Child Nurture* (Philadelphia: University of Pennsylvania Press, 1967), vii–viii; John Cleverley and D. C. Phillips, *Visions of Childhood: Influential Models from Locke to Spock* (New York: Teachers College Press, 1986), 15–41; and Calvert, *Children in the House,* 59–61. Mark I. West's *Children, Culture, and Controversy* (Hamden, Conn.: Archon, 1988) provides an especially lucid overview of the decline of the doctrine of infant depravity, the emergence of Lockean visions of childhood, and the ways in which this change gave rise to a belief in childhood innocence. Judith Plotz's *Romanticism and the Vocation of Childhood* (New York: Palgrave, 2001) is among the best studies of British romantic childhood. Also excellent is the work of Alan Richardson: "Periodization: The Case of Romanticism," in *Teaching Children's Literature: Issues, Pedagogy, Resources,* ed. Glenn Edward Sadler (New York: Modern Language Association, 1992) and *Literature, Education, and Romanticism: Reading as a Social Practice, 1780–1832* (Cambridge, UK: Cambridge University Press, 1994). Anne Higonnet's *Pictures of Innocence: The History and Crisis of Ideal Childhood* (London: Thames and Hudson, 1998) is unparalleled in its analysis of the rise of childhood innocence in and through visual culture.

30. Calvert, *Children in the House,* 140–42.

31. Ibid., 105. See also Lloyd DeMause, *The History of Childhood* (New York: Psychohistory Press, 1974), 364, and David Grylls, *Guardians and Angels: Parents and Children in Nineteenth-Century Literature* (London: Faber and Faber, 1978).

32. Barbara Welter, "The Cult of True Womanhood, 1820–1860," *American Quarterly* 18, no. 2 (1966), 151–74; Aileen S. Kraditor, *Up from the Pedestal: Selected Writings in the History of American Feminism* (Chicago: Quadrangle, 1970).

33. Nancy Cott, "Passionlessness: An Interpretation of Victorian Sexual Ideology, 1790–1850," *Signs: Journal of Women in Culture and Society* 4, no. 2 (1978): 220. Several essays map ongoing conversations about the cult of true womanhood, the cult of domesticity, and the concept of "separate spheres." See, for example, Nancy Isenberg, "Second Thoughts on Gender and Women's History," *American Studies* (1995): 93–103, and Mary Kelley, "Beyond the Boundaries," *Journal of the Early Republic* 21, no. 1 (2001): 73–78. See also Cathy N. Davidson and Jessamyn Hatcher, eds., *No More Separate Spheres! A Next Wave American Studies Reader* (Durham, N.C.: Duke University Press, 2002).

34. Deborah Gorham, *The Victorian Girl and the Feminine Ideal* (London: Croom Helm, 1982), 7.

35. Ibid.

36. Letter "To an Unrecognized Poetess, June, 1846," *Greenwood Leaves,* 2d ed. (Boston, 1850), 311, qtd. in Welter, 160.

37. John Ruskin writes similarly, "The perfect loveliness of a woman's countenance can only consist in . . . majestic childishness." Ruskin, "Of Queens' Gardens," in *Sesame and*

*Lilies: The Two Paths and the King of the Golden River* (1865; London: J. M. Dent and Sons, 1907), 60; qtd. in Gorham, *Victorian Girl,* 6.

38. Elizabeth Oakes Smith, *The Sinless Child* (1842, Southern Literary Messenger), reprinted in *Nineteenth-Century American Women Poets: An Anthology,* ed. Paula Bernat Bennett (Malden, Mass.: Wiley-Blackwell, 1998), 42.

39. Definitions of these terms appear in my Introduction.

40. Claudia Nelson, *Boys Will Be Girls: The Feminine Ethic and British Children's Fiction, 1857–1917* (New Brunswick, N.J.: Rutgers University Press, 1991), 5.

41. Harriet Beecher Stowe, *Uncle Tom's Cabin* (1852), Norton Critical Edition, ed. Elizabeth Ammons (New York: W. W. Norton, 1994), 215. Cited hereafter as "Stowe."

42. I avoid the term "cult of childhood" because it was associated more with British than American constructions of childhood, and also because Marah Gubar has brilliantly deconstructed this discourse and debunked many scholarly assumptions about this British "cult." Marah Gubar, *Artful Dodgers: Reconceiving the Golden Age of Children's Literature* (New York: Oxford University Press, 2009).

43. Hazel Carby, *Reconstructing Womanhood: The Emergence of the Afro-American Woman Novelist* (New York: Oxford University Press, 1987), 23–32.

44. Cott, "Passionlessness," 228.

45. Ann DuCille, *The Coupling Convention: Sex, Text, and Tradition in Black Women's Fiction* (New York: Oxford University Press, 1993), 31–32.

46. Mary Niall Mitchell, *Raising Freedom's Child: Black Children and Visions of the Future after Slavery* (New York: New York University Press, 2008), 80. See also 68 on the opposition between innocent white children and noninnocent black children.

47. Elizabeth Young, *Disarming the Nation: Women's Writing and the American Civil War* (Chicago: University of Chicago Press, 1999), 37–38.

48. Mitchell, *Raising Freedom's Child,* 118–19.

49. Chanta M. Haywood shows that the mid-nineteenth-century African American press sometimes published juvenile stories "subverting the idea of 'true womanhood' and critiquing the inapplicability of such standards for many black girls." Chanta M. Haywood, "Constructing Childhood: The 'Christian Recorder' and Literature for Black Children, 1854–1865," *African American Review* 36, no. 3 (2002): 424.

50. Anna Mae Duane, *Suffering Childhood: Violence, Race, and the Making of the Child Victim* (Athens: University of Georgia Press, 2010), 3.

51. William Blake, *Songs of Innocence and of Experience* (1789, 1794; facsimile edition, New York: Oxford University Press, 1967), 9–10. Blake's poem does, on one level, posit equality between the black narrator and a white boy, but it also configures the black boy as the white boy's natural servant. However, the poem also suggests that both boys will enter the kingdom of heaven. The point is not that Blake's poem is unified in its suggestion of racial equality (indeed, nothing in this very complex poem could be called "unified"), but rather that Blake installed a black boy within his "songs of innocence," represented tenderness between the boy and his mother, envisioned the black narrator in heaven, and thereby included a black child in a romantic vision of childhood.

52. Father of a Family, *Poems: Moral and Religious, For Children and Youth* (Greenfield, Mass.: Denio and Phelps, 1821), 41–42.

53. Ibid., 42.

54. Ibid.

55. Ibid., 43.

56. Duane brilliantly maps the ways in which early Americans—including white and African American abolitionists as well as white proslavery writers—incorporated suffering black children into their arguments. See Duane, *Suffering Childhood,* 152–59. At the mid-nineteenth century, however, the trajectory that Duane narrates reversed, and the suffering black child was replaced, I show, by the libel of the insensate pickaninny.

57. Claire Perry comments on the relative absence of nonblack children of color in nineteenth-century American visual culture. Claire Perry, *Young America: Childhood in 19th-Century Art and Culture* (New Haven, Conn.: Yale University Press, 2006), 147.

58. Stowe, 213.

59. W. T. Lhamon Jr., *Raising Cain: Blackface Performance from Jim Crow to Hip Hop* (Cambridge, Mass.: Harvard University Press, 1998), 142; Eric Lott, *Love and Theft: Blackface Minstrelsy and the American Working Class* (New York: Oxford University Press, 1993), 217–18; Elizabeth Young, *Disarming the Nation: Women's Writing and the American Civil War* (Chicago: University of Chicago Press, 1999), 36–47.

60. On monogenesis and polygenesis, see George M. Fredrickson, *The Black Image in the White Mind: The Debate on Afro-American Character and Destiny, 1817–1914* (New York: Harper and Row, 1971), 71–96.

61. Harriet Beecher Stowe, *A Key to* Uncle Tom's Cabin*; Presenting the Original Facts and Documents Upon Which the Story Is Founded* (Boston: John P. Jewett, 1853), 50.

62. Stowe, 218, 207.

63. Ibid., 207.

64. Ibid., 217.

65. Ibid., 208.

66. Ibid., 209.

67. Stowe, *Key,* 51.

68. Richard Brodhead, "Sparing the Rod: Discipline and Fiction in Antebellum America," *Representations* 21 (Winter 1988): 85.

69. Stowe, 215.

70. Ibid., 214.

71. Ibid., 214–15.

72. Ibid., 214.

73. Ibid., 214–15.

74. Ibid., 213.

75. Ibid., 213–14.

76. Ibid., 245–46, emphasis added.

77. Ibid., 248.

78. Ibid.

79. Ibid., 249.

80. Ibid., 267.

81. Ibid., 246.

82. George Aiken, *Uncle Tom's Cabin; or, Life Among the Lowly* (1852), in *Early American Drama*, ed. Jeffrey H. Richards (New York: Penguin, 1997), 391.

83. George Howard, "'*Oh, I'se So Wicked*' as Sung by Mrs. G. C. Howard in Her Original Character of Topsy [in *Uncle Tom's Cabin*]" (New York: Horace Waters, 1854). The sheet music was "Respectfully Dedicated to G. L. Aiken, Esq." Although George Howard, the producer of the inaugural performance of *Uncle Tom's Cabin*, wrote the song, he did so for inclusion in Aiken's script. For the sake of simplicity, I refer to the iteration of Topsy who performs this song as "Aiken's Topsy."

84. Anti-Tom novels—that is, novels of the 1850s and 1860s that sought to counter Stowe through representations of happy slaves or unhappy free African Americans—often claimed, similarly, that black parents abused their children, who felt no pain. See Sarah N. Roth, "The Mind of a Child: Images of African Americans in Early Juvenile Fiction," *Journal of the Early Republic* 25 (Spring 2005): 102–3. At the axis of unfelt pain, then, the Aiken play resembled anti-Tom novels more than it did Stowe's work.

85. Aiken, *Uncle Tom's Cabin*, 400.

86. Howard, "'*Oh, I'se So Wicked.*'"

87. Duane, *Suffering Childhood*, 3–5 and passim.

88. Thomas Jefferson, *Notes on the State of Virginia* (1781), reprint, ed. Merrill D. Peterson, in *The Portable Thomas Jefferson* (New York: Penguin, 1975), 187.

89. Elizabeth B. Clark, "'The Sacred Rights of the Weak': Pain, Sympathy, and the Culture of Individual Rights in Antebellum America," *Journal of American History* 82, no. 2 (1995): 474. See also David Morris, *The Culture of Pain* (Berkeley: University of California Press, 1991), 39–40.

90. Linda Williams, *Playing the Race Card: Melodramas of Black and White from Uncle Tom's Cabin to O. J. Simpson* (Princeton, N.J.: Princeton University Press, 2001), 24. Williams quotes Lauren Berlant, "The Subject of True Feeling: Pain, Privacy, and Politics," in *Cultural Studies and Political Theory*, Jodi Dean, ed. (Ithaca, N.Y.: Cornell University Press, 2000). On visible pain as a necessary component of sentimentalism, see also Duane, *Suffering Childhood*, 141–42.

91. Elaine Scarry, *The Body in Pain: The Making and Unmaking of the World* (New York: Oxford University Press, 1985), 22.

92. For a differing perspective, see Debra Walker King, *African Americans and the Culture of Pain* (Charlottesville: University of Virginia Press, 2008).

93. Henry James, *A Small Boy and Others* (New York: Charles Scribner's Sons, 1913), 159.

94. Montgomery Gregory, "The Drama of Negro Life," in *The New Negro*, ed. Alain Locke (1925; New York: Simon and Schuster, 1997), 155; Patricia A. Turner, Tavia Nyong'o, Jayna Brown, and other scholars view Topsy as the pickaninny's progenitor. See Turner, *Ceramic Uncles and Celluloid Mammies*, 13; Tavia Nyong'o, "Racial Kitsch and Black Performance," *Yale Journal of Criticism* 15, no. 2 (2002): 376; and Jayna Brown, *Babylon Girls: Black Women Performers and the Shaping of the Modern* (Durham, N.C.: Duke University Press, 2008), 67.

95. "The Happy Families," advertisement for Arnold Print Works, *Youth's Companion*, 26 October 1893, 550.

96. Untitled advertisement for Arnold Print Works, *Youth's Companion*, 25 October 1894, 519.

97. This advertisement suggests that any (white) child would want to pet the doll as much as throw it about. On the paired actions of cuddling and abusing racially complex cloth dolls, see Chapter 4.

98. Michael Korda, *Making the List: A Cultural History of the American Bestseller 1900–1999* (New York: Barnes and Noble, 2001), 16, 26.

99. Booth Tarkington, *Penrod* (New York: Grosset and Dunlap, 1914), 141.

100. Ibid.

101. Albert Shaw, ed., *American Review of Reviews* 53 (1916): 505.

102. "'Penrod' in a Play Is Highly Amusing," unsigned review, *New York Times*, 3 September 1918, 9.

103. Images of many pickaninny products are available through the Ferris State University's Jim Crow Museum of Racist Memorabilia. See http://www.ferris.edu/jimcrow/picaninny/more/.

104. On American animation's debts to blackface minstrelsy and to the African American "bre'r rabbit" tales, especially as retold and disseminated by white author Joel Chandler Harris, see Christopher P. Lehman, *The Colored Cartoon: Black Representation in American Animated Film, 1907–1954* (Amherst: University of Massachusetts Press, 2008); Daniel Goldmark, *Tunes for 'Toons: Music and the Hollywood Cartoon* (Berkeley: University of California Press, 2005), 83 and passim; Susan Willis, *A Primer for Daily Life* (New York: Routledge, 1991), 130–32 and passim; and Kevin S. Sandler, ed., *Reading the Rabbit: Explorations in Warner Bros. Animation* (New Brunswick, N.J.: Rutgers University Press, 1998). These scholars largely base their arguments on the visual and musical characteristics of early animated characters. However, the defining characteristic of U.S. animation (until at least the 1970s) is unfelt violence—which links characters such as Tom and Jerry, Bugs Bunny, and even early Mickey Mouse to the figure of the pickaninny, who was *not* a stock character of the minstrel stage. This crucial point intervenes in the historiography of U.S. animation by reorienting it not to the antebellum minstrel show but instead to Topsy and her progeny from 1852 through the early twentieth century.

105. See Sarah E. Chinn, *Inventing Modern Adolescence: The Children of Immigrants in Turn-of-the-Century America* (New Brunswick, N.J.: Rutgers University Press, 2009), 29–76.

106. The Cottolene trade card depicts cotton as "nice, clean, and white," as Raggedy Ann, the subject of Chapter 4, often declared. The cotton that Hine photographed, in contrast, is not nice or clean—nor, the photograph implies, should its labor be white.

107. Hine did, on rare occasions, photograph children of color. See Patricia Pace's excellent essay, "Staging Childhood: Lewis Hine's Photographs of Child Labor," *Lion and the Unicorn* 26, no. 3 (2002): 324–52.

108. As many scholars, most notably George Fredrickson, have argued, the libel of the "childlike Negro" surfaced in the 1850s with romantic racialism, most notably in *Uncle Tom's*

*Cabin* (Fredrickson, *Black Image in the White Mind,* 97–129). What has gone unnoticed, however, is that the libel waned in the second half of the nineteenth century and then spiked anew in the late nineteenth and early twentieth centuries. As white southerners who had been antebellum children began to enter old age, and as a young generation of "New Negroes" came of age and organized for civil rights, fantasies about childlike, docile African American slaves took on new urgency among "Lost Causers" who regretted the end of slavery and wanted to limit African Americans' rights.

109. Chapter 5 tells a story of another white teacher, this time in Vermont in 1891, who cast another resistant black girl in a Topsy-like role.

110. The *National Antislavery Standard* reprinted this story from the *Evening Post* under the title "Incidents of Hospital Life" on 28 November 1863, and the *Christian Recorder* republished it under the title "Spattin' Me" on 12 December 1863. See also the *American Missionary,* June 1863, 132.

111. Stowe, 215–16,

112. Ibid., 385.

113. Carla L. Peterson, "Capitalism, Black (Under)Development, and the Production of the African-American Novel in the 1850s," *American Literary History* 4, no. 4 (1992): 583; Elizabeth Ammons, "Stowe's Dream of the Mother-Savior: *Uncle Tom's Cabin* and American Women Writers before the 1920s," in *New Essays on Uncle Tom's Cabin,* ed. Eric J. Sundquist (New York: Cambridge University Press, 1986), 155–95.

114. Ammons also maps "echoes and inversions" between Augustine St. Clare and Mr. Bellmont and between Aunt Ophelia and Aunt Abby. Ammons, "Stowe's Dream," 183.

115. Harriet E. Wilson, *Our Nig,* 101.

116. Ibid., 96. In another instance, "Mrs. Bellmont found her weeping [over James's impending death] and whipped her with the raw-hide, adding an injunction never to be seen sniveling again." From that point on, Frado "was very careful never to shed tears on his account, in her presence" (77).

117. Ibid., 96.

118. Ibid., 74, emphasis added.

119. Ibid., 6.

120. Ibid., emphasis added.

121. Ibid., 107.

122. Lynde Palmer, *Helps Over Hard Places: Stories for Girls* (Boston: American Tract Society, 1862), 178.

123. Ibid., 174–76.

124. Ibid., 180.

125. Ibid.

126. Evidence of Wilson's awareness of abolitionist culture appears not only in the text of *Our Nig* but also in the novel's printing history. George C. Rand, who printed *Our Nig,* was an abolitionist whose office was located at 3 Cornhill in Boston (Rand also printed *Uncle Tom's Cabin* for John P. Jewett). As Eric Gardner has recently shown, Cornhill at midcentury was a geographical center for abolitionism. The American Tract Society, which published

"Poor Black Violet," was located at 28 Cornhill, mere steps away from Rand. That Wilson knew Rand and frequented this street suggests that she was broadly aware of abolitionist activities. Eric Gardner, "'This Attempt of Their Sister': Harriet Wilson's *Our Nig* from Printer to Readers, *New England Quarterly* 66, no. 2 (June 1993): 228–29, 230.

127. Stowe, 256.

128. Wilson, *Our Nig*, 107.

129. Frederick Douglass, *My Bondage and My Freedom*, with introduction by James M'Cune Smith (New York: Miller, Orton, and Mulligan, 1855), 39. Stowe's character George Harris, whom Stowe based in part on Frederick Douglass, similarly asserts that to his white, slaveholding father, "I was no more than a fine dog or horse; to my poor heart-broken mother I was a *child*." Stowe, 374.

130. On Douglass and romanticism, see Ian Finseth's *Shades of Green: Visions of Nature in the Literature of American Slavery, 1770–1860* (Athens: University of Georgia Press, 2009); and Martin Halliwell's entry on Douglass in *The Encyclopedia of the Romantic Era, 1760–1850*, vol. 1, ed. John Christopher Murray (New York: Taylor and Francis, 2004), 287–88.

131. Douglass, *My Bondage and My Freedom*, 39.

132. Ibid., 40.

133. Topsy's and Eva's status as both inversions of each other and "siblings" was literalized in the twentieth century when vaudeville stars Rosetta and Vivian Duncan, who were billed as the "Duncan Sisters," performed the respective roles in the theatrical show and later in the film titled *Topsy and Eva*, which ran in various forums from 1923 through 1942. The University of Virginia's magisterial website, "Uncle Tom's Cabin in American Culture," posts a superb collection of reviews and visual images from the Duncan Sisters' careers as well as a useful scholarly essay by John Sullivan. See http://utc.iath.virginia.edu/onstage/duncanhp.html and http://utc.iath.virginia.edu/interpret/exhibits/sullivan/sullivanf.html.

134. Douglass, *My Bondage and My Freedom*, 40.

135. Ibid.

136. Ibid., 41. The neurasthenic, white slaveholding boy that Douglass ridicules is precisely the boy that white plantation writer Joel Chandler Harris worries about in *Told by Uncle Remus: New Stories of the Old Plantation* (New York: McClure, Phillips, 1905). See Chapter 3.

137. Douglass, *My Bondage and My Freedom*, 40–42.

138. See, for example, P. Gabrielle Foreman, "Sentimental Abolition in Douglass's Decade: Revision: Erotic Conversion, and the Politics of Witnessing in *The Heroic Slave* and *My Bondage and My Freedom*," in *Sentimental Men: Masculinity and the Politics of Affect in American Culture,* ed. Mary Chapman and Glenn Hendler (Berkeley: University of California Press, 1999), 149–62. I thank Betsy Klimasmith for encouraging me to contrast Douglass with Harry.

139. Stowe, 3.

140. Hilda Doolittle, a girl who would grow up to become the poet H.D., observed such casting in a Tom show of 1892. See Chapter 3.

141. Stowe, 333.

142. John R. Neill illustrated, by my count, forty-nine books for Reilly and Britton (later Reilly and Lee) between 1903 and 1920. (Neill illustrated many more for that publisher after 1920 and also worked for other publishers throughout his career.) Neill's forty-nine Reilly and Britton or Reilly and Lee books include at least twenty books by L. Frank Baum, as well as *Little Black Sambo*, which appears in the same volume with *The Story of Topsy*. Neill's illustrations for *Sambo* and the unsigned illustrations for *Topsy* are similar in style, and both contain Neill's hallmarks, especially in the characters' elongated legs. Barton lays out an excellent case for Neill as the illustrator of *The Story of Topsy*. See Phyllis Settecase Barton, *Pictus Orbis Sambo: A Publishing History, Checklist, and Price Guide for the Story of Little Black Sambo, 1899–1999* (Sun City, Calif.: Pictus Orbis, 1998), 206–8.

143. Anon., *The Story of Topsy* (Chicago: Reilly and Britton, 1908), 50.

144. Ibid., 52.

NOTES TO CHAPTER 2

1. Frances Hodgson Burnett, *The One I Knew Best of All: A Memory of the Mind of a Child* (New York: Charles Scribner's Sons, 1893), 44. In this memoir, Burnett refers to her child-self in the third person.

2. Ibid., 53.

3. Ibid., 57.

4. Ibid., 58.

5. Ibid., 56, 55. Burnett's whipping of her black doll attracted attention, but no opprobrium, from the *New York Times* ("Mrs. Burnett's Early Life," review of *The One I Knew Best of All: A Memory of the Mind of a Child*, *New York Times*, 19 November 1893, 23) and in Elizabeth Bryant Johnston's chapter on Burnett in *Our Famous Women: An Authorized Record of the Lives and Deeds of Distinguished American Women of Our Times* (Hartford, Conn.: A. D. Worthington, 1885).

6. Burnett, *One I Knew Best*, 44. The quoted phrases separated by the ellipsis appear in the reverse order in Burnett's memoir.

7. Ibid., 56. The toughness and resilience of gutta-percha is apparent in its contemporaneous use as a covering for golf balls and canes, including the cane that Preston Brooks used to beat Charles Sumner on the floor of the United States Senate in 1856. See David Herbert Donald, *Charles Sumner and the Coming of the Civil War* (Alfred A. Knopf, 1960; reprint, Naperville, Ill.: Sourcebooks, 2009), 244. I thank Paul Erickson for alerting me to the composition of Brooks's cane.

8. Burnett, *One I Knew Best*, 55. Frances Hodgson Burnett was far from alone in her actions, and subsequent chapters in this book treat the whipping of dolls in greater detail. See also Sharon Marcus, *Between Women: Friendship, Desire, and Marriage in Victorian England* (Princeton, N.J.: Princeton University Press, 2007), 161–63.

9. Tavia Nyong'o reads the "shiny, hard, and brittle" materiality of racist ceramic figurines of black children as a "racial simile" in which "a black skin is as hard as stone; not skin at

all, but a mask, with perhaps nothing behind it." Nyong'o, "Racial Kitsch and Black Performance," *Yale Journal of Criticism* 15, no. 2 (2002): 377.

10. See Saidiya V. Hartman, *Scenes of Subjection: Terror, Slavery, and Self-Making in Nineteenth-Century America* (New York: Oxford University Press, 1997).

11. Chapter 5 deals in greater depth with white children's practices of violence against black dolls.

12. Martin Heidegger, "The Thing," in *Poetry, Language, Thought,* trans. Albert Hofstadter (New York: Harper and Row, 1971), 174–82. In a 2001 issue of *Critical Inquiry* that defined and galvanized the field of "thing theory," Bill Brown built upon Heidegger's distinction between object and thing, noting that "we look *through* objects (to see what they disclose about history, society, nature, or culture—above all, what they disclose about *us*)," but a thing requires us to confront it on its own terms, to look at a muddy window rather than through a clean one (Bill Brown, "Thing Theory," *Critical Inquiry* 28, no. 1 [2001]: 4).

13. I thank Betsy Klimasmith for her observation that a knife becomes a thing when it is in the hands of a trained chef.

14. Brown, "Thing Theory," 3–4.

15. Roland Barthes, *Camera Lucida: Reflections on Photography,* trans. Richard Howard (New York: Hill and Wang, 1981), 26–27.

16. Ibid., 51, 26.

17. Brown, "Thing Theory," 4. See also Bill Brown, *A Sense of Things: The Object Matter of American Literature* (Chicago: University of Chicago Press, 2003).

18. Brown, "Thing Theory," 4.

19. Arjun Appadurai, "Introduction: Commodities and the Politics of Value," in *The Social Life of Things: Commodities in Cultural Perspective,* ed. Arjun Appadurai (Cambridge, UK: Cambridge University Press, 1986), 5.

20. W. J. T. Mitchell, *What Do Pictures Want? The Lives and Loves of Images* (Chicago: University of Chicago Press, 2006), 7.

21. Joseph R. Roach, *Cities of the Dead: Circum-Atlantic Performance* (New York: Columbia University Press, 1996), 27.

22. Ibid.

23. Austin argued that a certain form of utterance, which he called a "performative," did not merely describe or communicate, but in itself performed an action. Examples of utterances that perform actions include the phrases "I promise," "I bet," and "I pronounce you married." In other words, to say "I promise" is to perform the action of promising. A "constative," in contrast, is a statement that refers to matters beyond itself—that is, a statement that does not itself perform an action. All the sentences in this endnote are constatives because they describe Austin's ideas rather than perform actions.

24. Burnett, *One I Knew Best,* 56.

25. E. W. Kemble, *A Coon Alphabet* (New York: R. H. Russell, 1898).

26. Ibid., n.p.

27. Patricia Crain, *The Story of A: The Alphabetization of America from* The New England Primer *to* The Scarlet Letter (Stanford, Calif.: Stanford University Press, 2000), 91.

28. Ibid., 88, 85, 91.

29. Ibid., 101.

30. Two of the twenty-six rhymes end without violence against African Americans: one verse ends with an African American character punching a fish, and another resolves without any violence when some swimmers, who thought they were threatened by a whale, discover that a hump in the ocean is actually a floating watermelon.

31. Louis Althusser, "Ideology and Ideological State Apparatuses (Notes towards an Investigation)," in *Lenin and Philosophy and Other Essays* (New York: Monthly Review Press, 1971), 127–86. See especially 174–77.

32. Ibid.

33. Burnett, *One I Knew Best*, 58.

34. Jonathan Culler, *Structuralist Poetics: Structuralism, Linguistics, and the Study of Literature* (Ithaca, N.Y.: Cornell University Press, 1975). See also Jonathan Culler, *On Deconstruction: Theory and Criticism after Structuralism* (Ithaca, N.Y.: Cornell University Press, 1982). Reader-response theory provides a broad avenue by which to think about the scriptive properties of things. Wolfgang Iser and Wayne Booth argue that a literary text actively encourages an "implied reader" to perform a finite range of actions (Wolfgang Iser, *The Implied Reader: Patterns of Communication in Prose Fiction from Bunyan to Beckett* [Baltimore: Johns Hopkins University Press, 1974]; Wayne C. Booth, *The Rhetoric of Fiction* [Chicago: University of Chicago Press, 1961]). A particularly helpful cousin to the scriptive thing appears in Walker Gibson's "mock reader." Gibson, writing in 1950 and within the school of New Criticism, was a text-oriented literary critic whose "mock reader" is not an actual human being, but is instead "a role that the real reader is invited to play for the duration of the novel" (Jane P. Tompkins, "An Introduction to Reader-Response Criticism," in *Reader-Response Criticism: From Formalism to Post-Structuralism*, ed. Jane P. Tompkins [Baltimore: Johns Hopkins University Press, 1980], xi). In tellingly theatrical language, Gibson described the mock reader as a "fictitious reader . . . whose mask and costume the individual takes on in order to experience the language [of a text]" (Walker Gibson, "Authors, Speakers, Readers, and Mock Readers," *College English* 11 [February 1950]: 265–69; reprinted in Tompkins, *Reader-Response Criticism*, 1–6; 1). This mock reader is an "artifact, controlled, simplified, abstracted out of the chaos of day-to-day sensation" (Gibson, "Authors, Speakers, Readers, and Mock Readers," 1). The mock reader, like a scriptive thing's user, responds to a set of instructions dictated by the text—and that response may take many forms, including resistance.

35. On the habitus as a system of culture, see Pierre Bourdieu, *Outline of a Theory of Practice*, trans. Richard Nice (Cambridge: Cambridge University Press, 1977), and Marcel Mauss, "Techniques of the Body," trans. Ben Brewster, *Economy and Society* 2, no. 1 (1973): 70–88.

36. Quoted in Ralph Keyes, *The Wit and Wisdom of Oscar Wilde* (New York: Gramercy, 1999), 6. Judith Butler argues in a similar vein that Althusser underestimates the range and effects of "disobedience" in possible responses to hails; for Butler, gender transgression such as drag can simultaneously and ambivalently critique and ratify gender norms. See Judith Butler, "Gender Is Burning: Questions of Appropriation and Subversion," in *Bodies That Matter: On the Discursive Limits of "Sex"* (New York: Routledge, 1993), 121–40.

37. Else Elisabeth Hysing Koren, *The Diary of Elisabeth Koren, 1853–1855*, ed. David T. Nelson (Northfield, Minn.: Norwegian-American Historical Association, 1955), 62. See also Sarah Meer, *Uncle Tom Mania: Slavery, Minstrelsy, and Transatlantic Culture in the 1850s* (Athens: University of Georgia Press, 2005), 21, on laughter and tears as a response to *Uncle Tom's Cabin*.

38. Koren, *Diary*, 63.

39. On the incompleteness of all evidence, see Donna Haraway, "Situated Knowledges: The Science Question in Feminism and the Privilege of Partial Perspective," in *Simians, Cyborgs, and Women: The Reinvention of Nature* (New York: Routledge, 1991), 183–201.

40. James C. Scott, *Domination and the Arts of Resistance: Hidden Transcripts* (New Haven, Conn.: Yale University Press, 1991).

41. Hartman, *Scenes of Subjection*, 8.

42. The topsy-turvy doll predated *Uncle Tom's Cabin* (Jim O'Loughlin, "Articulating *Uncle Tom's Cabin*," *New Literary History* 31, no. 3 [2000]: 586). After the novel's publication, the doll was often called "Topsy-Eva," as is the case in plate 4.

43. It is impossible conclusively to determine who invented this folk object. Most doll historians believe that the topsy-turvy doll originated on antebellum plantations as one of a number of fabric arts practiced by enslaved women. Only one competing theory of the doll's origins has emerged: that the topsy-turvy doll may relate to the "Pennsylvania hex doll," an eighteenth-century instrument purportedly used for casting spells and curing warts (Wendy Lavitt, *American Folk Dolls* [New York: Alfred A. Knopf, 1982], 13). The Pennsylvania hex doll, which was not associated with children or play, possessed both human and pig heads. Even if the topsy-turvy doll did relate to the Pennsylvania hex doll, someone, somewhere along the way, *reinvented* the doll to contain the idea of racial difference, which was absent from the Pennsylvania hex doll. The theory of the Pennsylvania hex doll origin offers no explanation for the topsy-turvy doll's racial element; therefore that theory fails to account for all the evidence. No historian has suggested that the topsy-turvy doll's racial aspects—which are what concern us here—originated anywhere other than among enslaved African American women. See Kimberly Wallace-Sanders, *Mammy: A Century of Race, Gender, and Southern Memory* (Ann Arbor: University of Michigan Press, 2008), 33–35, 57; Elizabeth Young, *Disarming the Nation: Women's Writing and the American Civil War* (Chicago: University of Chicago Press, 1999), 40; Robbin Henderson et al., *Ethnic Notions: Black Images in the White Mind* (Berkeley: Berkeley Art Center Association, 1982), 74; Miriam Forman-Brunell, s.v. "Dolls" and "Play," in *Girlhood in America: An Encyclopedia*, ed. Miriam Forman-Brunell (ABC-CLIO, 2001), 226, 505; Myla Perkins, *Black Dolls: An Identification and Value Guide, 1820–1991* (Paducah, Ky.: Collector Books, 1993), 33, 63, 64, 68–69, 72, 74, 95; and Myla Perkins, *Black Dolls Book II: An Identification and Value Guide* (Paducah, Ky.: Collector Books, 1995), 7, 9, 29, 34, 44, 76–81, 126, 138, 350. Museums whose collections include topsy-turvy dolls of the nineteenth and twentieth centuries include the California African American Museum in Los Angeles; the Churchill County Museum in Fallon, Nevada; the Mariposa Museum and World Culture Center in Peterborough, New Hampshire; the New-York Historical Society; the Orange County Historical Museum in Hillsborough, North Carolina; the

Philadelphia Doll Museum; and the Stoy Museum of the Lebanon County Historical Society in Lebanon, Pennsylvania.

44. Karen Sánchez-Eppler, *Touching Liberty: Abolition, Feminism, and the Politics of the Body* (Berkeley: University of California Press, 1993), 133–34, 174.

45. Elizabeth Young, "A Wound of One's Own: Louisa May Alcott's Civil War Fiction," *American Quarterly* 48, no. 3 (1996): 449; Leland S. Person, "Poe's Philosophy of Amalgamation: Reading Racism in the Tales," in *Romancing the Shadow: Poe and Race*, ed. J. Gerald Kennedy and Liliane Weissberg (New York: Oxford University Press, 2001), 212; Robert Leigh Davis, *Whitman and the Romance of Medicine* (Berkeley: University of California Press, 1997), 164.

46. Wallace-Sanders, *Mammy*, 57; and Kimberly Wallace-Sanders, "A Peculiar Motherhood: The Black Mammy Figure in American Literature an Popular Iconography, 1824–1965," Ph.D. diss., Boston University, 1995, 28–30, 33.

47. Patricia Hill Collins, "The Politics of Black Feminist Thought," in *Feminist Theory Reader: Local and Global Perspectives,* ed. Carole R. McCann and Seung-Kyung Kim (New York: Routledge, 2003), 319.

48. Ibid., 330.

49. The most famous enslaved woman known to have sewn dolls is Harriet Jacobs. See Jean Fagin Yellin, *Harriet Jacobs: A Life* (New York: Basic Books, 2004), 92. The Daughters of the American Revolution Museum owns three dolls that Jacobs made.

50. Maude Southwell Wahlman, *Signs and Symbols: African Images in African American Quilts* (Atlanta: Tinwood Books, 2001).

51. Gladys-Marie Fry, *Stitched from the Soul: Slave Quilts from the Antebellum South* (Chapel Hill: University of North Carolina Press, 1990), viii.

52. Jacqueline L. Tobin and Raymond G. Dobard, *Hidden in Plain View: The Secret Story of Quilts and the Underground Railroad* (New York: Doubleday, 1999).

53. Noam Cohen, "In Frederick Douglass Tribute, Slave Folklore, and Facts Collide," *New York Times*, 23 January 2007.

54. Joan N. Radner and Susan S. Lanser, "Strategies of Coding in Women's Cultures," in *Feminist Messages: Coding in Women's Folk Culture,* ed. Joan Newlon Radner (Urbana: University of Illinois Press, 1993).

55. Ibid., 5.

56. Frances E. W. Harper, *Iola Leroy; or Shadows Uplifted* (1892); reprint with introduction by Hazel Carby (Boston: Beacon, 1987), 9; cited in Radner and Lanser, "Strategies of Coding," 5.

57. Jo Radner and Susan Lanser, "Dropping Bobby Pins: Gender, Sexuality, and Complicit Coding," keynote address at Feminine Folklore and Masculine Myths, Harvard University, Cambridge, Massachusetts, 9 February 2007.

58. Radner and Lanser, "Strategies of Coding," 9.

59. I thank Betsy Klimasmith for pointing out that the grandmother's hymn in *Iola Leroy* perfectly exemplifies implicit code.

60. Harper, *Iola Leroy,* 179.

61. Meir Sternberg, *The Poetics of Biblical Narrative: Ideological Literature and the Drama of Reading* (Bloomington: Indiana University Press, 1985), 9; cited in Radner and Lanser, "Strategies of Coding," 7.

62. Radner and Lanser, "Strategies of Coding," 7, emphasis added.

63. Ibid.

64. Shirley Samuels, *Romances of the Republic: Women, the Family, and Violence in the Literature of the Early American Nation* (New York: Oxford University Press, 1996), 113; Rebecca Deming Moore, "The Topsy-Turvy Doll," in *Dolls: An Anthology,* ed. Julia A. Robinson (Chicago: Albert Whitman, 1938), 123, and *Christian Observer,* 30 March 1910, 17.

65. Moore, "Topsy-Turvy Doll," 123.

66. Advertisement for Albert Bruckner and Sons "TU-IN-ONE" doll, patented 9 July 1901. Advertisement reprinted in Perkins, *Black Dolls* (1993), 69.

67. Lavitt discusses a well-documented clothed wooden doll produced by an enslaved person (Lavitt, *American Folk Dolls,* 68–70).

68. Cuddling is one action that soft toys script; other actions receive extensive analysis in Chapter 4.

69. For a differing perspective and a cogent refutation of that perspective, see, respectively, Lavitt, *American Folk Dolls,* 22, and Wallace-Sanders, *Mammy,* 33–34.

NOTES TO CHAPTER 3

1. Harriet Beecher Stowe, *Uncle Tom's Cabin* (1852), Norton Critical Edition, ed. Elizabeth Ammons (New York: W. W. Norton, 1994), 127, 130. Cited hereafter as "Stowe."

2. Joel Chandler Harris, *Uncle Remus: His Songs and His Sayings* (1881 [1880]), edited and introduced by Robert Hemenway (New York: Penguin, 1982), 55, 59.

3. Hortense J. Spillers, "Changing the Letter: The Yokes, the Jokes of Discourse, or, Mrs. Stowe, Mr. Reed," in Stowe, 554, 556, 558. Scholars who have expanded on Spillers's argument include P. Gabrielle Foreman, "'This Promiscuous Housekeeping': Death, Transgression, and Homoeroticism in *Uncle Tom's Cabin,*" *Representations* 43 (Summer 1993): 57–59, and Diane Roberts, *The Myth of Aunt Jemima: Representations of Race and Region* (New York: Routledge, 1994), 37–38.

4. James R. Kincaid, *Child-Loving: The Erotic Child and Victorian Culture* (New York: Routledge, 1992); James R. Kincaid, *Erotic Innocence: The Culture of Child Molesting* (Durham, N.C.: Duke University Press, 1998); Michel Foucault, *The History of Sexuality, Volume I: An Introduction*, trans. Robert Hurley (New York: Vintage, 1980).

5. Leslie Fiedler, "Come Back to the Raft Ag'in, Huck Honey!" *Partisan Review* 15 (June 1948): 664–71. The question of whether Harris's work fits into Fiedler's paradigm has received some attention; see Jesse Bier, "'Bless you, Chile': Fiedler and 'Huck Honey' a Generation Later," *Mississippi Quarterly* 34, no. 4 (1981): 456–62, and R. Bruce Bickley Jr., *Joel Chandler Harris* (Boston: Twayne, 1978), 73. Fiedler commented on sexuality in *Uncle Tom's Cabin* in *Love and Death in the American Novel* (Cleveland, Ohio: Meridian, 1960), 159–265.

6. Stowe, 128.

7. Ibid., 154.

8. Ibid., 189.

9. Ibid., 253.

10. Spillers, "Changing the Letter," 556.

11. Stowe, 143, 156–57.

12. Ibid., 252.

13. Marianne Noble surveys readers' sexual responses to *Uncle Tom's Cabin* in *The Masochistic Pleasures of Sentimental Literature* (Princeton, N.J.: Princeton University Press, 2000), 126–27. Noble spelunks in Stowe's novel for what she calls the "weird curves" of masochistic pleasure (3). Her expedition, which I discuss later in this chapter, succeeds because sexual violence, as distinct from nonsadomasochistic sexual desire, does indeed abound in *Uncle Tom's Cabin.*

14. On Remus as a literary descendant of Tom, see Thomas P. Riggio, "Uncle Tom Reconstructed: A Neglected Chapter in the History of a Book," *American Quarterly* 28, no. 1 (1976): 56–70, and Kathleen Diffley, Representing the Civil War and Reconstruction: From Uncle Tom to Uncle Remus," in *A Companion to American Fiction, 1865–1914*, ed. Robert Paul Lamb and G. R. Thompson (Malden, Mass.: Blackwell, 2005), 240–59.

15. Saidiya V. Hartman, *Scenes of Subjection: Terror, Slavery, and Self-Making in Nineteenth-Century America* (New York: Oxford University Press, 1997); Ann Laura Stoler, *Carnal Knowledge and Imperial Power: Race and the Intimate in Colonial Rule* (Berkeley: University of California Press, 2002); Ann Laura Stoler, *Race and the Education of Desire: Foucault's History of Sexuality and the Colonial Order of Things* (Durham, N.C.: Duke University Press, 1995); and Laura Wexler, *Tender Violence: Domestic Visions in an Age of U. S. Imperialism* (Chapel Hill, N.C.: University of North Carolina Press, 2000).

16. See Stephen A. Hirsch, "Uncle Tomitudes: The Popular Reaction to *Uncle Tom's Cabin,*" in *Studies in the American Renaissance, 1978*, ed. Joel Myerson (Boston: Twayne, 1978), 303–30.

17. "Uncle Tom's Cabin and Its Opponents," *Eclectic Review* 96 (December 1852): 717–44 ; qtd. in *Uncle Tom's Cabin as Book and Legend: A Guide to an Exhibition*, compiled by Chester E. Jorgenson (Detroit: Friends of the Detroit Public Library, 1952), 33.

18. Henry James, *A Small Boy and Others* (New York: Charles Scribner's Sons, 1913), 159.

19. Ibid., 160.

20. This undated, anonymous statuette is part of the Harry Birdoff Collection at the Harriet Beecher Stowe Center in Hartford, Connecticut. Images of this statuette appear on the University of Virginia's website, "*Uncle Tom's Cabin* and American Culture," http://utc.iath.virginia.edu/tomituds/8115f.html.

21. Images for all the Parkhurst cards, including the card that lists the game's "DIRECTIONS," are available through the website "*Uncle Tom's Cabin* and American Culture," http://utc.iath.virginia.edu/tomituds/game3f.html.

22. The Billings illustrations and the cards were published in March and November of 1852, respectively; therefore the illustrations influenced the cards and not vice versa.

23. Classified ad, *New York Tribune*, 23 October 1852, 1.

24. Lori Merish, *Sentimental Materialism: Gender, Commodity Culture, and Nineteenth-Century American Literature* (Durham, N.C.: Duke University Press, 2000), 25.

25. Scholars who have engaged with this passage includes Linda Williams, "'A Wonderful, "Leaping" Fish': Varieties of *Uncle Tom*," in *Playing the Race Card: Melodramas of Black and White from Uncle Tom to O. J. Simpson* (Princeton, N.J.: Princeton University Press, 2002), 45–99; Jim O'Loughlin, "Articulating *Uncle Tom's Cabin*," *New Literary History* 31, no. 3 (2000): 573–97; Caroline F. Levander, *Cradle of Liberty: Race, the Child, and National Belonging from Thomas Jefferson to W. E. B. Du Bois* (Durham, N.C.: Duke University Press, 2006), 134; Eric Lott, *Love and Theft: Blackface Minstrelsy and the American Working Class* (New York: Oxford University Press, 1995), 215; Christine Richards, "Gender, Race, and the 'Art' of Fiction: Henry James's Criticism and Harriet Beecher Stowe," *Literature and History* 9, no. 1 (2000): 43–55; and Barbara Hochman, "Sentiment without Tears: *Uncle Tom's Cabin* as History in the 1890s," in *New Directions in American Reception Study*, ed. Philip Goldstein and James L. Machor (New York: Oxford University Press, 2000), 255. Jim O'Loughlin notes that James acknowledges differences between the book and the dramatization but describes them as "acting in concert." See O'Loughlin, "Articulating *Uncle Tom's Cabin*," 594, 527.

26. James, *Small Boy*, 159–60.

27. Ibid., 160.

28. On Stowe's visual language, see Sheila Ruzycki O'Brien, "'There Is No Arguing with Pictures': Stretching the Canvas of Gender in the Art Portraits, Picture-language, and Original Illustrations in *Uncle Tom's Cabin*," *American Transcendental Quarterly* 20, no. 2 (2006): 461–62; Jo-Ann Morgan, Uncle Tom's Cabin *as Visual Culture* (Columbia: University of Missouri Press, 2007), 24, 66; O'Loughlin, "Articulating *Uncle Tom's Cabin*," 592, and Joan D. Hedrick, *Harriet Beecher Stowe: A Life* (New York: Oxford University Press, 1994), 208. On "Mrs. Stowe's picture," see James, *Small Boy*, 160.

29. Anon., "Introduction to the New Edition," Harriet Beecher Stowe, *Uncle Tom's Cabin; Or, Life Among the Lowly* (1852; New Edition, Boston: Houghton, Mifflin, 1879), xi. Although this introduction refers to Stowe in the third person, she may have written it.

30. Ibid.

31. Harriet Beecher Stowe to Gamaliel Bailey, 9 March 1851. Quoted in Hedrick, *Harriet Beecher Stowe*, 208, from typescript, Boston Public Library.

32. Every scholar listed in note 25, for example, cites this letter in her or his discussion of Stowe's visual language.

33. Stowe, 150.

34. Ibid., 127, 224. Stowe also describes African Americans in general as "impressible" in *The Key to* Uncle Tom's Cabin (Boston: John P. Jewett, 1853; reprint, Bedford, Mass.: Applewood, n.d.), 27.

35. Stowe, 214.

36. Noble, *Masochistic Pleasures*, 131, 138.

37. A burn wound could also constitute sentimental imprinting: St. Clare says that his mother "impressed, burnt into my very soul . . . an idea of the dignity and worth of the meanest human soul" (Stowe, 197).

38. Theodore Dwight Weld, *American Slavery As It Is: Testimony of a Thousand Witnesses* (New York: American Anti-Slavery Society, 1839).

39. Walker's accounts of his life included *Trial and Imprisonment of Jonathan Walker, at Pensacola, Florida, For Aiding Slaves to Escape from Bondage, With an Appendix Containing a Sketch of His Life* (Boston: Anti-Slavery Office, 1845); Jonathan Walker, *A Brief View of American Chattelized Humanity* (Boston: privately printed, 1847); and Jonathan Walker, *A Picture of Slavery for Youth* (Boston, J. Walker, n.d.).

40. Marcus Wood, *Blind Memory: Visual Representation of Slavery in England and America, 1780–1865* (New York: Routledge, 2000), 246.

41. Stowe, 99.

42. The Earl of Shaftesbury to Harriet Beecher Stowe, 14 December 1852, reprinted in Charles Edward Stowe, *Life of Harriet Beecher Stowe Compiled from Her Letters and Journals* (Boston: Houghton, Mifflin, 1889), 170.

43. A. Woodward, M.D., *A Review of* Uncle Tom's Cabin, *Or, An Essay on Slavery* (Cincinnati: Applegate, 1852), 68.

44. Claire Parfait, *The Publishing History of* Uncle Tom's Cabin, *1852–2002* (Burlington, Vt.: Ashgate, 2007), 35–37; Hedrick, *Harriet Beecher Stowe,* 223.

45. See Morgan, Uncle Tom's Cabin *as Visual Culture,* 2, on the higher price for a two-volume set.

46. Parfait, *Publishing History,* 100. Jewett published but did not physically produce Stowe's novel, which was printed by George Curtis Rand's company (Eric Gardner, "'This Attempt of Their Sister': Harriet Wilson's *Our Nig* from Printer to Readers," *New England Quarterly* 66, no. 2 [1993]: 230).

47. Thomas F. Gossett, Uncle Tom's Cabin *and American Culture* (Dallas: Southern Methodist University Press, 1985), 164–65.

48. "Uncle Tom's Cabin," *Manhattan,* January 1883, 30; qtd. in Parfait, *Publishing History,* 47.

49. Ibid., qtd. in Parfait, *Publishing History,* 63.

50. James F. O'Gorman, *Accomplished in All Departments of Art. Hammatt Billings of Boston, 1818–1874* (Amherst: University of Massachusetts Press, 1998), 47.

51. *National Era,* 4 March 1852, 3; qtd. in Parfait, *Publishing History,* 48. See Parfait, "'The Story of the Age': Advertising and Promotion," in Parfait, *Publishing History,* 47–66, for a superb survey of Jewett's advertisements.

52. O'Gorman, *Accomplished in All Departments,* 51, 54. See also Morgan, Uncle Tom's Cabin *as Visual Culture,* 27, 42. Jane Tompkins also ascribes special significance to Stowe's twenty-second chapter, arguing that the arbor scene "presents in miniature the structure of the whole novel" because the "entire scene itself is a re-presentation of others that come before and after" (Jane Tompkins, *Sensational Designs: The Cultural Work of American Fiction, 1790–1860* [New York: Oxford University Press, 1985], 137).

53. Stowe, 226, emphasis added.

54. Ibid., 227; emphasis added to "pointed."

55. By embedding rotation in his most famous image of Little Eva and Uncle Tom,

Billings linked these characters to the "topsy turvy logic" that Elizabeth Young argues pervades *Uncle Tom's Cabin* (Elizabeth Young, "Topsy Turvy: Civil War and *Uncle Tom's Cabin*," in *Disarming the Nation: Women's Writing and the American Civil War* [Chicago: University of Chicago Press, 1999]).

56. The inclusion of a sideways illustration in a novel of the 1850s was not unusual, and there is no evidence that Billings deliberately embedded symbolism in the sideways image. However, Billings did intentionally design his illustration, which is wider than it is tall, for sideways insertion into Stowe's text.

57. Hortense J. Spillers describes Eva and Tom as having "intimate contact" in the arbor scene as written by Stowe. Spillers, "Changing the Letter," 556.

58. Harriet Beecher Stowe, *Uncle Tom's Cabin; or, Life Among the Lowly. Illustrated Edition, Complete in One Volume, Original Designs by Billings; Engraved by Baker and Smith* (Boston: John P. Jewett, 1853). Although this edition bears the date of 1853, the actual publication date was December 1852.

59. On the argument that Billings's second arbor scene depicts Eva as younger and therefore less sexual than his first, see O'Gorman, *Accomplished in All Departments,* 54, and Morgan, Uncle Tom's Cabin *as Visual Culture,* 36.

60. An article in 1931 claimed that the last Tom show had closed, but Thomas Gossett has documented revivals well into the 1930s. As Lauren Berlant has noted, elements of the Tom show continue to reanimate every time actors in a production of Rogers and Hammerstein's *The King and I* chant "Poor Eliza!" See Gossett, Uncle Tom's Cabin *and American Culture,* 385, and Lauren Berlant, "Poor Eliza," *American Literature* 70, no. 3 (1998): 635–68.

61. See Joseph P. Roppolo, "Uncle Tom in New Orleans: Three Lost Plays," *New England Quarterly* 27, no. 2 (1954): 213–26; Harry Birdoff, *The World's Greatest Hit:* Uncle Tom's Cabin (New York: S. F. Vanni, 1947), 21–23; Richard Moody, *Dramas from the American Theatre, 1762–1909* (Cleveland: World, 1966), 351.

62. On the Howard troupe, see Laurence Senelick, *The Age and Stage of George L. Fox, 1825–1877,* rev. ed. (Iowa City: University of Iowa Press, 1999); Bluford Adams, *E Pluribus Barnum: The Great Showman and the Making of U.S. Popular Culture* (Minneapolis: University of Minnesota Press, 1997); and a forthcoming book by John Frick. See also Bruce McConachie, *Melodramatic Formations: American Theatre and Society, 1820–1870* (Iowa City: University of Iowa Press, 1992); Jeffrey D. Mason, *Melodrama and the Myth of America* (Bloomington: Indiana University Press, 1993); and Lott, *Love and Theft.* The Harriet Beecher Stowe Center in Hartford, Connecticut, archives the primary sources that Harry Birdoff used in writing *The World's Greatest Hit.*

63. Barnard Hewett, *Theatre U.S.A., 1665–1957* (New York: McGraw-Hill, 1957), 172–73.

64. Gossett famously claimed that "perhaps as many as fifty people would eventually see *Uncle Tom's Cabin,* the play, for almost every one person who would read the novel" (Gossett, Uncle Tom's Cabin *and American Culture,* 260). Stowe, 18.

65. Cordelia Howard MacDonald, "Memoirs of the Original Little Eva," *Educational Theatre Journal* 8 (December 1956): 269.

66. H. P. Phelps, *A Record of the Albany Stage* (Albany, N.Y.: Joseph McDonough, 1880), 287.

67. Howard MacDonald, "Memoirs of the Original Little Eva," 270. In her fifteen-page memoir, Howard MacDonald offered but one other comment on the play's politics: her show "pleaded for an unpopular cause, both North and South" (281). Clearly, neither sectional nor racial politics was central to her memories of her family's business.

68. Lott, *Love and Theft*, 214; David Grimsted, "*Uncle Tom* from Page to Stage: Limitations of Nineteenth-Century Drama," *Quarterly Journal of Speech* 56, no. 3 (1970): 235–44.

69. Bruce A. McConachie, "Out of the Kitchen and into the Marketplace: Normalizing *Uncle Tom's Cabin* for the Antebellum Stage," *Journal of American Drama and Theatre* 3 (1991): 10–11.

70. Lott, *Love and Theft*, 211–33; Adams, *E Pluribus Barnum*, 129–39. Barnum competed with the Howard-Aiken production until 1856, when the showman decided that if he could not vanquish the Howards, he would buy them. He staged their show in his lecture hall, and he then managed the Howard-Aiken production on its 1856–57 tour of Great Britain. See Adams, *E Pluribus Barnum*, 139.

71. *New York Evening Post*, 19 November 1853, qtd. in Adams, *E Pluribus Barnum*, 131.

72. On the figure of the kneeling slave, see Kirk Savage's *Standing Soldiers, Kneeling Slaves: Race, War, and Monument in Nineteenth-Century America* (Princeton, N.J.: Princeton University Press, 1997), and George Boulukos's *The Grateful Slave: The Emergence of Race in Eighteenth-Century British and American Culture* (Cambridge: Cambridge University Press, 2008).

73. Taylor's dramatization ran for eleven nights at the National Theatre in August 1852—a run that reviewers and audiences apparently deemed ten and a half nights too long. Senelick, *Age and Stage of George L. Fox*, 57.

74. George Aiken, *Uncle Tom's Cabin* (1852), in *Early American Drama*, ed. Jeffrey H. Richards (New York: Penguin, 1997), 408.

75. Ibid., 405.

76. "Indicator," *National Era*, 18 August 1853.

77. On the rise of celebrity culture in the United States at the mid-nineteenth century, see Adams, *E Pluribus Barnum*; Michael Newbury, "Eaten Alive: Slavery and Celebrity in Antebellum America," *ELH* 61, no. 1 (1994): 159–87; and David Haven Blake, *Walt Whitman and the Culture of American Celebrity* (New Haven, Conn.: Yale University Press, 2006).

78. "Found—The Original Little Eva," *Boston Sunday Advertisement*, 30 October 1932, n.p., in file, "Clippings: Howard, Cordelia," Harvard Theatre Collection.

79. "First Little Eva Still Lives in Boston." *Boston Sunday Globe*, 9 July 1933, clipping in Harry Birdoff Papers, Harriet Beecher Stowe Center; and Howard MacDonald, "Memoirs of the Original Little Eva," 281.

80. "Little Eva," *Liberator*, 11 November 1853, 177; O'Gorman, *Accomplished in All Departments*, 47.

81. See, for example, Anon., "'Little Eva,' 90 Years Old Today, Rides to Boston to Dine

with Niece," n.s., n.d., Harvard Theatre Collection. Similarly mundane articles marked the actress's seventy-eighth and eighty-seventh birthdays.

82. "First Little Eva Still Lives in Boston."

83. "Found—The Original Little Eva." See also *New York World*, 21 December 1924, clipping in the Harry Birdoff Papers, Harriet Beecher Stowe Center.

84. Ralph Eugene Lund, "Trouping with Uncle Tom," *Century Magazine*, January 1928, 336.

85. Adolphus M. Hart, *Uncle Tom in Paris; or, Views of Slavery Outside the Cabin, Together with Washington's Views of Slavery* (Baltimore: Taylor, 1854), 506; qtd. in Gossett, *Uncle Tom's Cabin and American Culture*, 270.

86. *New York Evening Mirror*, 15 December 1853, clipping in Harry Birdoff Papers, Harriet Beecher Stowe Center, Box 6.

87. Howard MacDonald, "Memoirs of the Original Little Eva," 273.

88. Arden Seymour, "A Veteran Gives Some Memories of Stageland," n.s., n.p., 25 August 1907. Clipping in the Harry Birdoff Papers, Harriet Beecher Stowe Center, Box 5.

89. Stowe, 224.

90. The Folger Library in Washington, D.C., houses an extensive collection of Staffordshire's theatrical figurines of the nineteenth century.

91. Interview with Dawn C. Adiletta, curator, Harriet Beecher Stowe Center, Hartford, Conn., 8 November 2002. On the popularity of the Eva/Tom Staffordshire figurine, see Jennifer DeVere Brody, *Impossible Purities: Blackness, Femininity, and Victorian Culture* (Durham, N.C.: Duke University Press, 1998), 172.

92. Stowe, 322; emphasis added.

93. Ibid., 322, 324.

94. Howard MacDonald, as an adult, commented on her hair color: "I was not the typical Eva. My curls were brown instead of blond." (Howard MacDonald, "Memoirs of the Original Little Eva," 272).

95. Ibid. Howard MacDonald wrote her essay in 1928; it was published posthumously.

96. Oscar [no last name], "Amusement Budget," *Northern Budget*, Troy, New York, 21 March, 1870, clipping in Harvard Theatre Collection.

97. See Gregg Camfield, *Sentimental Twain: Samuel Clemens in the Maze of Moral Philosophy* (Philadelphia: University of Pennsylvania Press, 1994) on the role of realism in sentimentalism.

98. On Rial's production and the "double mammoth" performances, see Birdoff, *World's Greatest Hit*, chaps. 13 and 14, and extensive primary documentation in the Harvard Theatre Collection and the Birdoff Papers at the Harriet Beecher Stowe Center.

99. H.D., *The Gift: The Complete Text* (1982), edited, annotated, and introduced by Jane Augustine (Gainesville: University of Florida Press, 1998). The memoir, which H.D. wrote during World War II, was first published posthumously in 1982.

100. Susan Stanford Friedman, *Psyche Reborn: The Emergence of H.D.* (Bloomington: Indiana University Press, 1981), 138.

101. H.D., *Gift*, 44.

102. Tracy Davis, "Performative Time," in *Representing the Past: Essays in Performance Historiography*, ed. Charlotte M. Canning and Thomas Postlewait (Iowa City: University of Iowa Press, 2010), 142–67.

103. H.D., *Gift*, 44.

104. Ibid.

105. Ibid., 45.

106. Ibid., 47.

107. Marvin Carlson, *The Haunted Stage: The Theatre as Memory Machine* (Ann Arbor: University of Michigan Press, 2003), 11.

108. H.D., *Gift*, 47.

109. Ibid., 48.

110. Ibid., emphasis added.

111. Classified ad, *New York Tribune*, 23 October 1852, 1.

112. Mason Stokes suggests that the "point of the [Parkhurst card] game was apparently to rescue slaves from slavery and to reunite broken families"—only to refracture those families through the shuffling of cards for further play. (Mason Stokes, *The Color of Sex: Whiteness, Heterosexuality, and the Fictions of White Supremacy* [Durham, N.C.: Duke University Press, 2001], 195–96). In fact, however, the game directed players to break families *apart* by extracting Tom and Eva *from* their respective families (the game defined Eva's family as Ophelia, St. Clare, and Topsy; and defined Tom's family as Chloe, Mose, and Pete) so as to unite Eva and Tom in the winner's hand.

113. Seymour, "Veteran Gives Some Memories," n.p.

114. Peggy Phelan, "The Ontology of Performance: Representation without Reproduction," in *Unmarked: The Politics of Performance* (New York: Routledge, 1992), 146–66.

115. William Wordsworth, "Ode: Intimations of Immortality from Recollections of Early Childhood" (1807), in *Selected Poems and Prefaces by William Wordsworth*, ed. Jack Stillinger (Boston: Houghton Mifflin, 1965), 188.

116. Carolyn Steedman, *Strange Dislocations: Childhood and the Idea of Human Interiority, 1780–1930* (Cambridge, Mass.: Harvard University Press, 1995), 10 and passim.

117. Harris, *Uncle Remus*, 40.

118. On writers' responses to Harris, see John Goldthwaite, *The Natural History of Make-Believe: A Guide to the Principal Works of Britain, Europe and America* (New York: Oxford University Press, 1996), 251–286; Walter M. Brasch, *Brer Rabbit, Uncle Remus, and the 'Cornfield Journalist': The Tale of Joel Chandler Harris* (Macon, Ga.: Mercer University Press, 2000), xix–xxiv; and Alice Walker, "Uncle Remus, No Friend of Mine," *Southern Exposure* (Summer 1981): 29–31.

119. Harris, *Uncle Remus*, 40.

120. Joel Chandler Harris, "The Negro as the South Sees Him," *Saturday Evening Post*, 2 January 1904; reprinted in Julia Collier Harris, *Joel Chandler Harris: Editor and Essayist: Miscellaneous Literary, Political, and Social Writings* (Chapel Hill: University of North Carolina Press, 1931), 116.

121. Ibid., 117.

122. Michael Rogin, "'Make My Day!': Spectacle as Amnesia in Imperial Politics [and] The Sequel," in *Cultures of United States Imperialism*, ed. Amy Kaplan and Donald E. Pease (Durham, N.C.: Duke University Press, 1993), 507.

123. On Lost Cause ideology, see Rollin G. Osterweis, *The Myth of the Lost Cause: 1865–1900* (Hamden, Conn.: Archon, 1973). Osterweis identifies Edward A. Pollard's *The Lost Cause: A New Southern History of the War of the Confederates* (New York: E. B. Treat, 1866) as a "blueprint" of "immense" influence on the South's future (Osterweis, *Myth of the Lost Cause*, 11, 14). See 752 of Pollard for an especially clear statement of the ideology of the Lost Cause. See also Edward A. Pollard, *The Lost Cause Regained* (New York: G. W. Carleton, 1868), 154, 155, 213–14.

124. Stowe to Bailey, 9 March 1851; quoted in Hedrick, *Harriet Beecher Stowe*, 208.

125. Ibid.

126. Joel Chandler Harris, 20 June 1882, printed in "The Birthday Garden Party to Harriet Beecher Stowe," *Atlantic Monthly Supplement* 50, no. 298 (1882): 13.

127. Harris also commented on Stowe's use of ekphrasis when he noted, in the introduction to his first book, that Stowe's "genius *painted the portrait* of the Southern slave-owner, and [thus] defended him" (Harris, *Uncle Remus*, 40, emphasis added).

128. Noble, *Masochistic Pleasures*, 3.

129. As Elizabeth Young argues, Stowe built inversion into the deepest logic of *Uncle Tom's Cabin*. This "topsy turvy logic" structures Stowe's desire to cause her readers to be "impressed," because an impression reverses an image. Young, *Disarming the Nation*, passim.

130. Stowe usually said that she envisioned Tom's death scene first; but sometimes she contradicted herself and reported that she began with the scene of Tom being whipped. See Gossett, Uncle Tom's Cabin *and American Culture*, 92–93, on the inconsistency.

131. Judith Fetterley's *The Resisting Reader: A Feminist Approach to American Fiction* (Bloomington: Indiana University Press, 1978) considers feminist practices of resistant reading, but it is crucial to remember that resistant reading can be reactionary, as it was in Harris's case.

132. Harris, "Negro as the South Sees Him," 116; emphasis added.

133. James, *Small Boy*, 159–60.

134. Kyla Wazana Tompkins reveals subtle irony within Stowe's fourth chapter as well: Tompkins brilliantly argues that Chloe's teasing of the young George Shelby contains "mounting aggression" in which Chloe "is pushing and prodding him to . . . extremes of self-importance" that make the white child "the object of the joke." Tompkins, "'Everything 'Cept Eat Us': The Antebellum Black Body Portrayed as Edible Body," *Callaloo* 30, no. 1 (2007): 212–13. In this interpretation, Chloe prods a white child unknowingly to perform comic acts before an audience of enslaved adults. This dynamic parallels the one in which enslaved African American women scripted white children's acts of cuddling with obscene topsy-turvy dolls, as described in Chapter 2.

135. On the geographical scope of Stowe's vision, see Sarah Meer, *Uncle Tom Mania: Slavery, Minstrelsy, and Transatlantic Culture in the 1850s* (Athens: University of Georgia Press, 2005), and Denise Kohn, Sarah Meer, and Emily B. Todd, eds., *Transatlantic Stowe: Harriet Beecher Stowe and European Culture* (Iowa City: University of Iowa Press, 2006).

136. Stowe, 18.

137. James, *Small Boy,* 159, emphasis added.

138. Stowe, 17.

139. Ibid., 380.

140. Harris, *Uncle Remus,* 55.

141. Gérard Gennette, *Narrative Discourse: An Essay in Method,* trans. Jane E. Lewin (Ithaca, N.Y.: Cornell University Press, 1980).

142. Harris, "Negro as the South Sees Him," 116–17.

143. Douglas A. Blackmon, *Slavery by Another Name: The Re-Enslavement of Black People in America from the Civil War to World War II* (New York: Doubleday, 2008). On rituals of racial etiquette as a mode of power, see Jennifer Ritterhouse, *Growing Up Jim Crow: How Black and White Southern Children Learned Race* (Chapel Hill: University of North Carolina Press, 2006).

144. On intimacy as an element of subjugation, see Hartman, *Scenes of Subjection,* 5 and passim, and Stoler, *Carnal Knowledge and Imperial Power.*

145. Harris, "Negro as the South Sees Him," 117–18.

146. Ibid., 118, 129.

147. Ibid., 118.

148. Examples of early twentieth-century works in which ageing white women reminisce about mammies include Caroline E. Merrick, *Old Times in Dixie Land: A Southern Matron's Memories* (New York: Grafton Press, 1901); Elizabeth Lyle Saxon, *A Southern Woman's War Time Reminiscences* (Memphis: Pilcher, 1905); Mrs. N[ancy] B[ostick] De Saussure, *Old Plantation Days: Being Recollections of Southern Life before the Civil War* (New York: Duffield, 1909); Sarah Johnson Cocke, *Old Mammy Tales from Dixie Land* (1911, reprint, introduced by Harry Stillwell Edwards [New York: E. P. Dutton, 1971]); Eliza Ripley, *Social Life in Old New Orleans: Being Recollections of My Girlhood* (New York: D. Appleton, 1912); Gertrude Langhorne, *Mammy's Letters* (Macon, Ga.: J. W. Burke, 1922); and Susan Bradford Eppes, *The Negro of the Old South: A Bit of Period History* (1925; Macon, Ga.: J. A. Burke, 1941). On mammy memoirs, see Micki McElya, *Clinging to Mammy: The Faithful Slave in Twentieth-Century America* (Cambridge, Mass.: Harvard University Press, 2007), 40–48.

149. Harris, *Told by Uncle Remus* 4, 5. On "overcivilization" and neurasthenia as crises in white supremacy at the turn of the twentieth century, see Gail Bederman, *Manliness and Civilization: A Cultural History of Gender and Race in the United States, 1880–1917* (Chicago: University of Chicago Press, 1995).

150. Harris, *Told by Uncle Remus,* 10.

151. Ibid., 12.

152. Ibid., 13.

153. Alexander Saxton, *The Rise and Fall of the White Republic; Class Politics and Mass Culture in Nineteenth-Century America* (London: Verso, 1990), 176.

154. Steedman, *Strange Dislocations,* 10.

155. Joel Chandler Harris, *Wally Wanderoon and His Story-Telling Machine,* illustrated by Karl Moseley (New York: McClure, Phillips, 1903).

156. Ibid., 4.

157. Ibid., 18.

158. Ibid., 28.

159. Ibid., 29.

160. Ibid., 28.

161. Ibid., 30.

162. Ibid., 30–31.

163. Ibid., 117.

164. Peggy Phelan, *Mourning Sex: Performing Public Memories* (London: Routledge, 1997), 11–12.

165. On Harris's depression, see Brasch, *Brer Rabbit*, 256 and passim.


NOTES TO CHAPTER 4

1. Patricia Hall, *Johnny Gruelle: Creator of Raggedy Ann and Andy* (Gretna, La: Pelican, 1993), 207.

2. Ibid., 60.

3. Ibid., 63.

4. Accounts differ as to whether the doll was made in the mid-nineteenth century for Alice or in the 1880s by Alice for Johnny's sister Prudence. The story that Gruelle preferred and circulated in the press, however, linked the doll to his mother's, not his sister's, childhood. See Hall, *Johnny Gruelle*, 107.

5. Patricia Hall, *Raggedy Ann and Andy: A Retrospective Celebrating 85 Years of Storybook Friends* (New York: Simon and Schuster, 2001), n.p.; Patricia Hall, *Raggedy Ann and More: Johnny Gruelle's Dolls and Merchandise* (Gretna, La: Pelican, 2000), 41; Hall, *Johnny Gruelle*. 58.

6. Angela Sorby, *Schoolroom Poets: Childhood, Performance, and the Place of American Poetry, 1865–1917* (Durham: University of New Hampshire Press, 2005).

7. Introduction to Johnny Gruelle, *Orphant Annie Storybook* (1921; Carmel, Ind.: Indiana Center for the Book, 1989), n.p. Riley and Gruelle's parents were spiritualists who often held séances together. According to Alice Benton Gruelle, one séance successfully raised the spirit of Henry Wadsworth Longfellow. R. B. Gruelle, letter to James Whitcomb Riley, 13 March ca.1900, Manuscripts Department, Lilly Library, Indiana University, Indiana.

8. Johnny Gruelle, *Raggedy Ann Stories* (P. F. Volland, 1918; reprint, Indianapolis: Bobbs-Merrill, 1961), 7–8.

9. I refer to the fictional character as "Marcella" and Gruelle's daughter as "Marcella Gruelle."

10. David Blight, *Race and Reunion: The Civil War in American Memory* (Cambridge, Mass.: Belknap Press of Harvard University Press, 2001).

11. Amy Kaplan, "Manifest Domesticity," *American Literature* 70, no. 3 (1998): 581–606.

12. Doll collectors and cottage industries routinely group Raggedy dolls with Golliwoggs (often spelled Golliwogs, Gollies, or Gollys) and/or pickaninny or mammy dolls (often

described as "primitives") on websites. Examples at the time of this book's publication include http://www.kottonkountrykreations.com, http://www.cynthiascountrydesigns.com, http://www.countrymammiesmercantile.com, and http://www.yulokod.ca/sunny/dolls/golliwogs.html. Books written by and for doll collectors, such as Dee Hockenberry's *Enchanting Friends: Collectible Poohs, Raggedies, Golliwoggs, and Roosevelt Bears* (Atglen, Penn.: Schiffer, 1995), consistently assume that collectors overlap in their enthusiasm for Raggedies, Golliwoggs, Topsy dolls, and mammy dolls.

13. Hall, *Johnny Gruelle*, 113, 115.

14. Ibid., 115.

15. Ibid., 165.

16. United Media Licensing, "Classic Raggedy Ann and Andy," http://www.unitedmedialicensing.com/b2b/html/raggedy_ann_and_andy.html, accessed 9 June 2009.

17. Ibid.

18. Beverly Lyon Clark, Introduction, in Clark and Margaret R. Higonnet, eds., *Girls, Boys, Books, Toys: Gender in Children's Literature and Culture* (Baltimore: Johns Hopkins University Press, 1999), 1; Lance Bertelsen, "Popular Entertainment and Instruction, Literary and Dramatic: Chapbooks, Advice Books, Almanacs, Ballads, Farces, Pantomimes, Prints and Shows," in *The Cambridge History of English Literature, 1660–1780*, ed. John Richetti (New York: Cambridge University Press, 2005), 67; Lois Kuznets, *When Toys Come Alive: Narratives of Animation, Metamorphosis, and Development* (New Haven, Conn.: Yale University Press, 1994), 20.

19. Daniel Hade, "Storytelling: Are Children's Book Publishers Changing the Way Children Read? (Digested Version)," *Children's Literature Association Quarterly* 28, no. 3 (2003): 140.

20. Lisa Jacobson, *Raising Consumers: Children and the American Mass Market in the Early Twentieth Century* (New York: Columbia University Press, 2004), 6.

21. Kim Avery's *The World of Raggedy Ann Collectibles: Identification and Values* (Paducah, Ky.: Collector Books, 1997) thoroughly surveys the diverse containers for Raggedyness.

22. Gruelle, *Raggedy Ann Stories*, 10–12.

23. Hall, *Raggedy Ann and More*, 69.

24. Benedict Anderson, *Imagined Communities: Reflections on the Origin and Spread of Nationalism* (1983; revised edition, London: Verso, 1991), 35.

25. Karin Calvert, *Children in the House: The Material Culture of Early Childhood, 1600–1900* (Boston: Northeastern University Press, 1992), 117.

26. Miriam Formanek-Brunell, *Made to Play House: Dolls and the Commercialization of American Girlhood, 1830–1930* (1993; Baltimore: Johns Hopkins University Press, 1998), 8–13, 19.

27. Ibid., 19.

28. Chapter 5 in this volume discusses doll companies owned and operated by African Americans in the early twentieth century

29. Linda Edward, *Cloth Dolls from Ancient to Modern: A Collector's Guide with Values* (Atglen, Penn.: Schiffer, 1997), 37–41.

30. Ibid., 62–65.

31. Rachel Field, *Hitty: Her First Hundred Years,* illustrated by Dorothy P. Lathrop (1929; New York: Macmillan, 1943).

32. Johnny Gruelle, "Polly Peters and the Wish-Wish Man," n.d., 11, collection of Joni Gruelle Wannamaker, Manuscript Binder #1. I examined these materials when they were in the private home of Joni Gruelle Wannamaker and Tom Wannamaker. The materials have since been transferred to the Brian Sutton-Smith Library and Archives of Play at the National Museum of Play in Rochester, New York. They are cataloged there as the "Gruelle Family Collection, 1880s–2008." All citations of Gruelle's manuscript materials refer to the archives as I encountered them in Tom and Joni Gruelle Wannamaker's home.

33. Gruelle did not incorporate racial caricature into Raggedy Ann alone. In 1917, after he trademarked Raggedy Ann but before he published *Raggedy Ann Stories,* Gruelle illustrated an edition of Helen Bannerman's *Little Black Sambo.* And in 1921, Gruelle wrote a non-Raggedy book titled *Eddie Elephant,* which featured a pickaninny-like character named "Cocoa-Boy." Helen Bannerman, *All About Little Black Sambo,* edited and illustrated by Johnny Gruelle (New York: Cupples and Leon, 1917); Johnny Gruelle, *Eddie Elephant* (Chicago: M. A. Donohue, 1921).

34. See Norma S. Davis, *A Lark Ascends: Florence Kate Upton, Artist and Illustrator* (Metuchen, N.J.: Scarecrow Press, 1992); Clinton Derricks-Carroll, *Buy Golly! The History of the Golliwog* (London: New Cavendish, 2005); Hockenberry, *Enchanting Friends*; Dee Hockenberry, *Collecting Golliwoggs: Teddy Bear's Best Friends* (Atglen, Penn.: Schiffer, 2003); and Francis Joseph and Lynne Godding, *The Golly Collectors Handbook* (London: Francis Joseph, 2003).

35. Patricia Hall, *Raggedy Ann and Johnny Gruelle: A Bibliography of Published Works* (Gretna, La: Pelican, 2001), 33.

36. Gruelle, *Raggedy Ann Stories,* 9; L. Frank. Baum, *The Wonderful Wizard of Oz* (1900; reprint, annotated and introduced by Michael Hearn, New York: W. W. Norton, 2000), 36.

37. Gruelle, *Raggedy Ann Stories,* 56.

38. Johnny Gruelle, *The Cheery Scarecrow* (Joliet, Ill.: P. F. Volland, 1929).

39. Johnny Gruelle and Chas. Miller, *Raggedy Ann's Joyful Songs* (New York: Miller Music, 1937), 4.

40. Baum wrote a blackface play, *Blackbird Cottages,* with music by Louis F. Gottschalk, which was produced in California in 1916. See Michael Hearn's annotation to Baum, *The Wonderful Wizard of Oz,* 389.

41. The best sources on the Oz extravaganza and Fred Stone are, respectively, Mark Evan Swartz, *Oz before the Rainbow: L. Frank Baum's* The Wonderful Wizard of Oz *on Stage and Screen to 1939* (Baltimore: Johns Hopkins University Press, 2000), and Armond Fields, *Fred Stone: Circus Performer and Musical Comedy Star* (Jefferson, N.C.: McFarland, 2002).

42. On Baum's experiences as an actor, playwright, and enthusiast of theater, see Katharine M. Rogers, *L. Frank Baum: Creator of Oz* (New York: St. Martin's Press, 2002). Frank Joslyn Baum and Russell P. MacFall's *To Please a Child: A Biography of L. Frank Baum, Royal Historian of Oz* (Chicago: Reilly and Lee, 1961) also comments on Baum and the theater,

but that book should be consulted only with caution as it is known to contain unreliable information.

43. "Under a Panama," music by J. B. Mullen, lyrics by Vincent Bryan; "That's Where She Sits All Day," music and lyrics by Frank Leo; "The Sweetest Girl in Dixie," music by Robert J. Adams, lyrics by James O'Dea. All lyrics quoted from *The Wizard of Oz: The Lyrics*, booklet accompanying CD set, *The Wizard of Oz* (San Diego, Calif.: Hungry Tiger Press, 2003).

44. Louis Weslyn (lyrics) and Charles Albert (music), "The Witch behind the Moon" (New York: M. Witmark and Sons, 1902); quoted in Swartz, *Oz before the Rainbow*, 47.

45. L. Frank Baum, *The Patchwork Girl of Oz* (1913; Ann Arbor, Mich.: For Your Knowledge, 2003), 137. Some late twentieth-century editions of *The Patchwork Girl of Oz* are silently amended to read, "Ah want mah Lulu, mah cross-eyed Lulu."

46. Ibid., 245. The Scarecrow is also tossed frequently in Baum's *The Wonderful Wizard of Oz*.

47. Johnny Gruelle, "Raggedy Ann Show," n.d., collection of Joni Gruelle Wannamaker, Manuscript Binder #2, 4, 8.

48. Gruelle, "Raggedy Ann Show," 4, 6.

49. Gruelle was not alone in his belief that Oz and Raggedyland could and should intersect. The publisher Bobbs-Merrill suggested a crossover when it invited Gruelle to illustrate a new edition of *The Wonderful Wizard of Oz* in 1922. Gruelle leaped at the chance, but for legal reasons, the edition was never produced (Hall, *Johnny Gruelle*, 135–36, and Michael Patrick Hearn, "Introduction to the Annotated Wizard of Oz," in *The Wonderful Wizard of Oz*, by L. Frank Baum [1900; reprint, annotated and introduced by Michael Hearn, New York: W. W. Norton, 2000], lv).

50. Hall, *Raggedy Ann and More*, 78, and Hall, *Raggedy Ann and Johnny Gruelle*, 180. The Harvard Theatre Collection owns programs for performances in several venues, as well as sheet music for the Raggedy number, "Raggedy Ann," which Fred Stone sang.

51. "Raggedy Ann," lyrics by Anne Caldwell, music by Jerome Kern (New York: T. B. Harms, 1923).

52. T. Walsh, "When Fred Stone Played Topsy," unpublished article, 2–3, qtd. in Fields, *Fred Stone*, 35.

53. *Oxford English Dictionary*, s.v. "topsy-turvy." Although the topsy-turvy doll did predate *Uncle Tom's Cabin*, there is no evidence that Stowe named Topsy as a deliberate reference to the doll (which went by several names, including the "double-headed doll").

54. Anon., "Varieties," *Arthur's Home Magazine*, May 1853.

55. Stowe, 245.

56. Lautz Bros. Soaps of Buffalo, New York, issued a trade card in which a white man "cleaned" the right half of a black boy's face, turning that side white. A Pearline trade card repeated this visual joke, except with an African American woman "cleaning" a black child. A Fairy Soap trade card featured a white child in fine dress asking a black child, dressed in rags, "Why doesn't your mamma wash you with Fairy Soap?" The American Antiquarian Society archives all of these cards. The Coats' thread trade card is online at the University of

Virginia's website, "*Uncle Tom's Cabin* and American Culture," http://utc.iath.virginia.edu/tomituds/toadsf.html.

57. Harriet Beecher Stowe, anonymous adaptation, *Little Folks' Edition: Uncle Tom's Cabin* (New York: Graham and Matlack, n.d. [ca. 1910]); Anon., *Uncle Tom's Cabin Picture Book* (New York: Graham and Matlack, 1913). The blackfaced actress Mona Ray also powdered herself white when she played Topsy in the 1927 filmic version of *Uncle Tom's Cabin*.

58. Johnny Gruelle, illustrated verse, *Cleveland Press*, 1909. Reprinted in Hall, *Johnny Gruelle*, 106.

59. Hall, *Raggedy Ann and Johnny Gruelle*, 2. The photograph depicts Johnny Gruelle standing before a drawing of Raggedy Ann, while a young girl appears in the foreground in costume as Raggedy Ann and holding an early Raggedy Ann doll. The girl in the photograph is not Marcella Gruelle, who died on November 8, 1915, eight weeks after her father trademarked Raggedy Ann but before the doll was manufactured.

60. Johnny Gruelle, *Beloved Belindy* (Joliet, Ill.: P. F. Volland, 1926), 7.

61. Cheryl Thurber, "The Development of the Mammy Image and Mythology," in *Southern Women: Histories and Identities*, ed. Virginia Bernhard, Betty Brandon, Elizabeth Fox-Genovese, and Theda Perdue (Columbia: University of Missouri Press, 1992), 97.

62. Johnny Gruelle, untitled short story, n.d., 2, collection of Joni Gruelle Wannamaker, Manuscript Binder #1. The struck-out "Raggedy" must refer to Ann rather than Andy because the surrounding dialogue features Ann and not Andy.

63. Ibid., 4.

64. Johnny Gruelle, "Raggedy Auntie," n.d., collection of Joni Gruelle Wannamaker, Manuscript Binder #1, 4, 1. I date the story between 1920 and 1926 because the story includes Raggedy Andy (created in 1920), but Beloved Belindy (created 1926) is conspicuously absent.

65. Ibid., 1.

66. Ibid., 1, 3.

67. Ibid., 3.

68. Ibid.

69. Ibid., 4.

70. Ibid.

71. Ibid.

72. Stowe, 245–46.

73. Johnny Gruelle, "Raggedy Auntie," n.d., 3; Stowe, 245.

74. Stowe, 213.

75. Johnny Gruelle, "Raggedy Auntie," n.d., 5.

76. Ibid.

77. Ibid.

78. Ibid., 6.

79. Ibid.

80. William Blake, "The Little Black Boy," in *Songs of Innocence and of Experience* (1789 and 1794), introduction and commentary by Geoffrey Keynes (Oxford: Oxford University Press, 1967), plate 9.

81. A photograph of this Raggedy-Topsy-Golliwogg doll appears in Hockenberry, *Collecting Golliwoggs*, 81.

82. Eric Lott, *Love and Theft: Blackface Minstrelsy and the American Working Class* (New York: Oxford University Press, 1993).

83. Frances Hodgson Burnett, *Racketty-Packetty House* (New York: Century, 1906). Burnett adapted *Racketty-Packetty House* for the stage; her play of the same title was produced in New York and elsewhere beginning in 1913 and was published in 1926.

84. L. Frank Baum, *Dot and Tot of Merryland*, with pictures by W. W. Denslow (Chicago: M.A. Donohue, 1901).

85. Margery Williams [Bianco], *The Velveteen Rabbit, Or, How Toys Become Real*, illustrated by William Nicholson (1922; New York: Avon, 1982).

86. Baum, *Patchwork Girl*, 64.

87. Ibid., 68.

88. *The Patchwork Girl of Oz* was but one of many stories in which Baum displayed his anxious obsession with slavery. In his non-Oz stories, Baum often connected slavery explicitly to African and African American bodies. In *American Fairy Tales*, for example, Baum published "The Laughing Hippopotamus," in which an African and a hippopotamus engage in a contest of wits to see who can enslave the other (the hippopotamus triumphs, but the human escapes) (L. Frank Baum, *American Fairy Tales* [Chicago: George M. Hill, 1901]). Baum also connected slavery to black bodies in a series of adventure novels he published under the pseudonyms Floyd Akers and Captain Hugh Fitzgerald. In these novels, two white boy "fortune hunters" are accompanied on their adventures by their black servants, Nux and Bryonia, who call the white boys and men "Mars," a plantation literature corruption of "master." Baum suggests an inherent enslaveability of black bodies by pointedly explaining that Nux and Bryonia are *not* slaves (thus suggesting that, without this explanation, a character or the reader might reasonably assume these twentieth-century men to be enslaved by the white American boys). Floyd Akers [L. Frank Baum], *The Boy Fortune Hunters in Panama* (Chicago: Reilly and Britton, 1908), 119; and Floyd Akers [L. Frank Baum], *The Boy Fortune Hunters in the South Seas* (Chicago: Reilly and Britton, 1911). The characters discuss whether Nux and Bryonia are slaves in Captain Hugh Fitzgerald [L. Frank Baum], *Sam Steele's Adventures on Land and Sea* (Chicago: Reilly and Britton, 1906), 71.

When Baum wrote the Oz books, he disarticulated slavery from black bodies but maintained his attention to slavery. In *The Wonderful Wizard of Oz* (1900), enslaved characters include the Munchkins, who explain to Dorothy that the wicked Witch of the East, upon whom Dorothy's house landed, "held all the Munchkins in bondage for many years, making them slave for her night and day" (L. Frank Baum, *The [Wonderful] Wizard of Oz*, with pictures by W. W. Denslow [1900; Chicago: Rand McNally, 1956], 21). When the Wicked Witch of the West captures Dorothy and her companions, the witch enslaves the girl and her friends. Dorothy, grateful not to be killed, resolves to be a "meek" slave and "to work as hard as she could" (ibid., 146). Baum explicitly discusses slavery (and uses the word "slave" or "slavery") on pages 21, 25, 80, 133, 134, 135, 139, 140, 145, 147, 153, and 167. Baum also refers to former slaves being set free from bondage on pages 32 and 33. Furthermore, Baum includes lengthy discussions of servitude and obedience to "masters" and "mistresses." Slavery pulses through Baum's work as an explicitly named, persistent concern.

89. Johnny Gruelle, "Katinka and Katunka (Story #14)," 1928, collection of Joni Gruelle Wannamaker, Manuscript Binder #1.

90. Gruelle, *Raggedy Ann Stories*, 42.

91. Sharon Marcus notes that mid-nineteenth-century British literature abounded with "dolls in stores waiting 'to be chosen and sold,'" and girls in doll literature who "fantasize about owning and mastering a female object." Thus doll literature likens "the girl's selection of a doll" to "the purchase of a female slave for a harem." Marcus, *Between Women: Friendship, Desire, and Marriage in Victorian England* (Princeton, N.J.: Princeton University Press, 2007), 162.

92. David I. Macleod, *The Age of the Child: Children in America, 1890–1920* (New York: Twayne, 1998), 24–25.

93. G. Stanley Hall, Introduction to Alice Minnie Herts Heniger, *The Kingdom of the Child* (New York: E. P. Dutton, 1918), 2. For an excellent treatment of Hall's racial politics, see Gail Bederman, *Manliness and Civilization: A Cultural History of Gender and Race in the United States, 1880–1917* (Chicago: University of Chicago Press, 1995).

94. Heniger, *Kingdom of the Child*, 33–34.

95. H. G. Wells, *Floor Games* (London: Frank Palmer, 1911), 10.

96. The panoptic vision of floor games echoes the panoptic vision created through dollhouses and toy theaters. On panopticism and dollhouses, see Frances Armstrong, "The Dollhouse as Ludic Space, 1690–1920," *Children's Literature* 24 (1996): 23–54. On toy theaters, see Suzanne Rahn, "Wild Models of the World: The Lure of the Toy Theater," in *Rediscoveries in Children's Literature* (New York: Garland, 1995), 23–37.

97. Mary A. Lowe, *The Use of Dolls in Child-Training; Or, a New System of Story-Telling* (New York: Abingdon, 1921), 5.

98. A deeply useful analysis of "unbreakable" dolls as embodiments of an ideal American vigor appears in Formanek-Brunell, *Made to Play House*, 90–116.

99. O. A. Flynn, U.S. patent 958,387, 17 May 1910; emphasis added. Others also used the word "yielding" to describe soft dolls. For example, in April 1914, Kate Jordan wrote in *Toys and Novelties* that a "yielding body is essential to the perfect doll all designers are striving toward" (qtd. in Hall, *Raggedy Ann and More*, 35).

100. Gruelle, *Raggedy Ann Stories*, 33.

101. Ibid., 38–40.

102. G. Stanley Hall and A. Caswell Ellis, *A Study of Dolls* (New York: E. L. Kellogg, 1897), 51.

103. Formanek-Brunell, *Made to Play House*, 30–32. Formanek-Brunell lists many sources that describe observations of children's violence against dolls.

104. Marilynn Olson, "Turn-of-the-Century Grotesque: The Uptons' Golliwogg and Dolls in Context," *Children's Literature* 28 (2000): 74.

105. Gruelle, *Beloved Belindy*, 19–20.

106. "A JOLLY RAG DOLLY," advertisement in the *Duluth News-Tribune*, 12 December 1920, 9.

107. Joel Williamson, *The Crucible of Race: Black-White Relations in the American South since Emancipation* (New York: Oxford University Press, 1984), 117–18; Stewart E. Tolnay and E. M. Beck, *A Festival of Violence: An Analysis of Southern Lynchings, 1882–1930* (Urbana: University of Illinois Press, 1992); The National Association for Advancement of Colored People, *Thirty Years of Lynching in the United States, 1889–1918* (1919; New York: Arno Press and New York Times, 1969); Philip Dray, *At the Hands of Persons Unknown: The Lynching of Black America* (New York: Random House, 2002). On photography, memory, and lynching, see Jonathan Markovitz, *Legacies of Lynching: Racial Violence and Memory* (Minneapolis: University of Minnesota Press, 2004); Dora Apel, *Imagery of Lynching: Black Men, White Women, and the Mob* (New Brunswick, N.J.: Rutgers University Press, 2004); Leigh Raiford, "The Consumption of Lynching Images," in *Only Skin Deep: Changing Visions of the American Self*, ed. Coco Fusco and Brian Wallis (New York: International Center of Photography and Harry N. Abrams, 2003), 267–73; and James Allen, Hilton Als, Congressman John Lewis, and Leon F. Litwack, *Without Sanctuary: Lynching Photography in America* (Santa Fe, N.M.: Twin Palms, 2000). On performance and lynching, see Harvey Young, "The Black Body as Souvenir in American Lynching," *Theatre Journal* 57, no. 4 (2005): 639-657.

108. Peter M. Bergman, *The Chronological History of the Negro in America* (New York: Harper and Row, 1969), 347–95 passim.

109. See Williamson, *Crucible of Race*, 188, and Young, "Black Body," on the taking of bodily "souvenirs."

110. A. R. Quin, "My Raggedy Ann," *Chicago Daily Tribune*, 21 October 1920, 13. The poem parodies James Whitcomb Riley's poem, "The Raggedy Man," which was a source of Gruelle's name for his doll.

111. Burnett, *One I Knew Best of All*, 56.

NOTES TO CHAPTER 5

1. Turner's account of the pageant, including its specificity of detail, is credible because Turner was not a typical person, but was instead an individual with an extraordinary memory, especially for verse. With folklorist Jane C. Beck, Daisy Turner recorded over eighty hours of interviews, much of which consisted of lengthy poetry recitals.

2. *On My Own: The Traditions of Daisy Turner*, produced and directed by Jane Beck and Wes Graff (Middlebury: Vermont Folklife Center and the University of Vermont, 1986). Unless otherwise noted, all of Turner's quotations are transcribed from this DVD. Information about the Turner family also derives from the DVD, except where otherwise specified. Short audio clips of Turner's interviews are online at http://vermontfolklifecenter.org/multimedia/womenspeak/womenspeak_turner/. These clips, which include Turner's recounting of the story about the pageant, are edited slightly differently from the DVD and therefore do not always match my transcription.

3. To distinguish between the 8-year-old and the 102-year-old Daisy Turner, I generally refer to the former as "Daisy" and the latter as "Turner." I use the term "black doll" to refer to any doll representing an African American because that is the term that people of diverse

races used most consistently throughout the nineteenth and early twentieth centuries to identify such dolls.

4. In interviews with Beck, Daisy Turner described many incidents in which members of her family wrote, improvised, and recited original poetry as a means of preserving family memories and enacting identity.

5. Jane C. Beck, private correspondence with the author, 7 May 2009.

6. Richard Kluger, *Simple Justice: The History of* Brown v. Board of Education *and Black America's Struggle for Equality* (1975; New York: Vintage, 2004), esp. chap. 14, "The Doll Man and Other Experts."

7. The three films are the historical drama *Separate but Equal* (1991) and the documentaries *The Road to* Brown (1989) and *Simple Justice* (1993).

8. Gwen Bergner, "Black Children, White Preference: *Brown v. Board*, the Doll Tests, and the Politics of Self-Esteem," *American Quarterly* 61, no. 2 (2009): 299–332.

9. Ibid., 317.

10. See, for example, Herbert Garfinkel, "Social Science Evidence and the School Segregation Cases," *Journal of Politics* 21, no. 2 (1959): 37–59.

11. Kluger, *Simple Justice*, 353.

12. Ibid., 356.

13. Kenneth B. Clark and Mamie P. Clark, "Racial Identification and Preference in Negro Children," in *Readings in Social Psychology*, 3rd ed., ed. Eleanor E. Maccoby, Theodore M. Newcomb, and Eugene L. Hartley (New York: Holt, Rinehart and Winston, 1947), 602.

14. Ibid., 608.

15. According to my review of the Clarks' original data sheets, which are housed in the Manuscripts division of the Library of Congress, boys and girls showed no statistically significant differences in their responses.

16. Kenneth B. Clark and Mamie P. Clark, "Emotional Factors in Racial Identification and Preference in Negro Children," *Journal of Negro Education* 19, no. 3 (1950): 342.

17. Ibid., 343–44.

18. Ibid., 344.

19. Tim Walsh, *Timeless Toys: Classic Toys and the Playmakers who Created Them* (Kansas City, Mo.: Andrews McMeel, 2005), 20–22.

20. Eliza Leslie, *American Girl's Book, Or, Occupation for Play Hours* (Boston: Munroe and Francis, 1831), 294.

21. See Chapter 2.

22. Interview with Barbara Whiteman, curator, the Philadelphia Doll Museum, 27 March 2008.

23. On black dolls as supplements within white girls' collections of white dolls, see Myla Perkins's superb *Black Dolls: An Identification and Value Guide, 1820–1991* (Paducah, Ky.: Collector Books, 1993), 20.

24. *Harper's Bazaar*, 6 January 1877, 3; *Harper's Bazaar*, 3 January 1885, 3. Perkins provides many more examples of black dolls configured as servants.

25. Aunt Laura, *The Dolls' Surprise Party* (Buffalo: Breed, Butler, 1863), 18. The catalog of the American Antiquarian Society identifies Aunt Laura and Aunt Fanny both as pseudonyms of Frances Elizabeth Mease Barrow.

26. Laura, *Dolls' Surprise Party*, 17.

27. Josephine Scribner Gates, *The Story of Live Dolls: Being an Account of How, on a Certain June Morning, All of the Dolls in the Village of Cloverdale Came Alive* (Indianapolis: Bowen-Merrill [later Bobbs-Merrill], 1901; Indianapolis: Bobbs-Merrill, 1920). Many later books in the series feature black dolls—often named Dinah or Topsy—that repetitiously, unquestioningly serve white dolls. See the previous chapter for discussion of a black doll's assumed servitude in Gruelle's *Beloved Belindy*.

28. Lois Kuznets and Frances Armstrong have both noted that nineteenth-century white girls routinely named black dolls "Dinah." Lois Kuznets, *When Toys Come Alive: Narratives of Animation, Metamorphosis, and Development* (New Haven, Conn.: Yale University Press, 1994), 104; Frances Armstrong, "The Dollhouse as Ludic Space, 1690–1920," *Children's Literature* 24 (1996): 44. The phrase "Dinah doll" was even sometimes used as a synonym for "black doll."

29. C.H.W., "The Dollies' Visit," *Youth's Companion* (Boston), 2 July 1874, 217.

30. Josephine Scribner Gates, *The Live Dolls' Busy Days* (1907), reprinted in *The Live Dolls in Wonderland: An Omnibus for Children containing The Live Dolls' House Party, The Live Dolls' Busy Days, The Live Dolls in Wonderland* [Indianapolis: Bobbs-Merrill, 1946]), 76. Dinah and Topsy travel together to magical lands in Gates's *The Live Dolls in Wonderland* (1912).

31. John Lobb, Editorial Note to Josiah Henson, *An Autobiography of the Rev. Josiah Henson (Mrs. Harriet Beecher Stowe's "Uncle Tom"), From 1789 to 1877*, rev. and enl. ed. (London: Christian Aid Office, 1878), 8.

32. "The Helpful Club: A True Story," *Unity* (Chicago),1 March 1884, 313. Black dolls named "Mammy" were uncommon until the twentieth century.

33. Ibid.

34. Georgianna Hamlen, *Chats, "Now Talked of This and Then of That"* (Boston: Lee and Shepard, 1885), 227, emphasis added.

35. Stowe, "Lulu's Pupil," *Our Young Folk*, September 1870, 531.

36. Hamlen, *Chats*, 227; "The Miss Dinah Pen-Wiper," *Godey's Lady's Book and Magazine*, May 1861, 451.

37. See Chapter 2 for analysis of the topsy-turvy doll.

38. "For Girls Who Make Gifts." n.a. *Dallas Morning News*, 11 November 1912, 11.

39. Oliver Optic, *Dolly and I* (Boston: Lee and Shepard, 1863), 19.

40. Mrs. D. P. Sanford, *Frisk and His Flock* (1875; New York: E. P. Dutton, 1877), 110.

41. E.L.E., "For the Companion. Topsy." *Youth's Companion*, 8 May 1879, 159.

42. *Jimmy: Scenes from the Life of a Black Doll. Told by Himself to J. G. Sowerby* (London: George Routledge and Sons, 1988). Sharon Marcus discusses fictional girls' whipping of black and white dolls as erotic. Sharon Marcus, *Between Women: Friendship, Desire, and Marriage in Victorian England* (Princeton, N.J.: Princeton University Press, 2007), 159–63.

43. On white girls' preferences for black dolls, see Miriam Formanek-Brunell, *Made to Play House: Dolls and the Commercialization of American Girlhood, 1830–1930* (1993; Baltimore: Johns Hopkins University Press, 1998), 28–29.

44. Margaret English, "Home-Made Rag Doll," *Babyhood*, July 1887, 264.

45. Mabel Dodge Luhan, *Intimate Memories: The Autobiography of Mabel Dodge Luhan*, edited with a new foreword by Lois Palken Rudnick (Santa Fe, N.M.: Sunstone Press, 2008), 17–18.

46. "Toys That Made Childhood Sweet," *Minneapolis Journal*, 17 December 1898, Supplements I, II, III. Many nineteenth- and twentieth-century works of fiction, memoir, and social science describe white children like Alice Leland burning black dolls. See, for example, G. Stanley Hall and A. Caswell Ellis, *A Study of Dolls* (New York: E. L. Kellogg, 1897), 30.

47. Anon., "The Negro Problem: How It Appears to a Southern Colored Woman," *Washington Bee* 22, no. 20 (1 November 1902): 1; republished as "A Colored Woman, However Respectable, Is Lower than the White Prostitute," *Independent*, 18 September 1902, 2221–24; reprinted in Gerda Lerner, *Black Women in White America: A Documentary History* (New York: Vintage, 1972), 168.

48. *New York World*, 7 December 1899, quoted in Ralph Ginzburg, *100 Years of Lynchings* (Baltimore: Black Classics Press, 1997), 28. In "The Black Body as Souvenir in American Lynching" (*Theatre Journal* 57, no. 4 [2005]: 639–57), Harvey Young argues that white children played a special role in remembering and reporting lynchings. White children were often less guarded than white adults in their enthusiasm for lynching; as a result, much that is known about the lynching of African Americans was "leaked" by white children.

49. According to John D. Bessler's *Legacy of Violence: Lynch Mobs and Executions in Minnesota* (Minneapolis: University of Minnesota Press, 2003), Minnesota had no death penalty between 1868 and 1883, so no executions, by hanging or otherwise, occurred during those years (104–5). After the death penalty became legal, "the only black man legally executed in Minnesota was hanged in Duluth at 1:40 A.M. in 1903" (140), five years after Harry Cass wrote to the *Minnesota Journal*. There is no record of any lynchings in Minnesota during the decade and a half before 1898.

50. Rev. J. M. Henderson, "The Garden Spot of America," *Christian Recorder*, 26 July 1888.

51. Horace S. Graves, "Chicago Paragraphs," *Christian Recorder*, 9 June 1898. I thank Erin Dwyer for pointing out Graves's and Henderson's assessments of Minnesota.

52. It is possible that Harry Cass witnessed or participated in a lynching outside of Minnesota. More likely, however, Cass was influenced by literary texts and other children's practices of play that are known to have existed in Minnesota during his lifetime.

53. "Little Lord Fauntleroy: A Pleasant Chat with the Gifted Author of a Children's Classic," *Daily Inter Ocean* (Chicago), 4 November 1888, column E, 1.

54. Studies in this mode include works by Eric Lott, David Roediger, W. T. Lhamon, and Alexander Saxton. Jayna Brown has recently "challenge[d] the male bias shaping earlier works on blackface minstrelsy and the formation of popular culture," arguing for the centrality of black women to this history. Jayna Brown, *Babylon Girls: Black Women Performers and the Shaping of the Modern* (Durham, N.C.: Duke University press, 2008), 3 and passim.

55. "For Girls Who Make Gifts," *Dallas Morning News*, 11 November 1912, 11.

56. Sarah L. Barrow, *Funny Little Socks: Being the Fourth Book of the Series* (New York: Leavitt and Allen, 1863). On the title page of *Funny Little Socks*, Barrow identifies herself as the daughter of "Aunt Fanny" (a.k.a. Aunt Laura), author of *The Dolls' Surprise Party*.

57. In Oliver Optic's 1863 novel *Dolly and I*, two white girls similarly "speak for" and through a white "lady" doll and a black servant doll named (yet again) Dinah (Optic, *Dolly and I*, 47).

58. Barrow, *Funny Little Socks*, 82–83.

59. H.D., *The Gift: The Complete Text* (1982), edited, annotated, and introduced by Jane Augustine (Gainesville: University of Florida Press, 1998), 48. See Chapter 3 for further analysis of H.D.'s memoir.

60. Helen C. Weeks, *Four and What They Did* (New York: Hurd and Houghton, 1871). The "marionettes" are dolls to which one of the novel's characters has added strings.

61. Ibid., 298.

62. Ibid., 298. Weeks's novel is set in Minneapolis, the same city in which Harry E. Cass would report hanging a black doll twenty-seven years later.

63. This practice elaborated on the "toy theater," a popular plaything that originated in Great Britain in the early nineteenth century. A toy theater was a miniature proscenium stage with wings and a curtain. It was sold with paper figures, often representing casts for specific plays. Commercial toy theaters were most popular with British boys, but in the United States and in Britain, girls and boys created homemade toy theaters, which they populated not only with paper figures but with dolls of all sorts. See George Speaight, *The History of the English Toy Theatre* (1946; rev. ed., London: Studio Vista, 1969); Suzanne Rahn, "Wild Models of the World: The Lure of the Toy Theater," in *Rediscoveries in Children's Literature* (New York: Garland, 1995), 23–37; Lyn Stiefel Hill, "There Was an American Toy Theatre!," *Theatre Survey* 16, no. 2 (1975); and Liz Farr, "Paper Dreams and Romantic Projections: The Nineteenth-Century Toy Theater, Boyhood and Aesthetic Play," in *The Nineteenth-Century Child and Consumer Culture*, ed. Dennis Denisoff (Burlington, Vt.: Ashgate, 2008), 43–62.

64. "Toys That Made Childhood Sweet."

65. Hall and Ellis, *Study of Dolls*, 35. See also Sabrina Thomas, "The Ritual of Doll Play: Implications of Understanding Children's Conceptualization of Race," in *Rituals and Patterns in Children's Lives*, ed. Kathy Merlock Jackson (Madison: University of Wisconsin Press, 2005), 113.

66. Hamlen, *Chats*, 228.

67. James Alden Markill, "Janie's Minstrel Troupe," *Youth's Companion*, 13 February 1890, 82.

68. "'A Comedy of Toys': Unique Entertainment in Aid of the Y. M. C. A. Building," *Sunday State* (Columbia, S.C.), 2 October 1898, 6; "Most Successful Amateur Affair. Children of St. Margaret's Pleased Those Present," *Idaho Daily Statesman*, 26 May 1906, 8.

69. E. F. Harkins, "'The Christian' Run Not to Be Extended," *Boston Journal*, 17 December 1915, 13; "Grant School to Give Children's Opera Today," *San Jose Mercury Herald*, 7 March 1916, 8; "Fraternity Chapter," *San Jose Mercury Herald*, 3 July 1921, 26.

70. "Rag Baby Party: Children Represent Rag Dolls—A Unique and Charming Entertainment," *Emporia Daily Gazette* (Emporia, Kan.), 14 February 1891.

71. H. J. Conway, *Uncle Tom; Or, Life Among the Lowly* (Boston: unpublished manuscript, ca. 1852), act 5. The manuscript is online at the University of Virginia's website, *Uncle Tom's Cabin* and American Culture http://utc.iath.virginia.edu/onstage/scripts/conwayhp.html. An unpublished 1876 promptbook for a production with Conway's script retained this stage direction, which suggests that Conway's stage Topsies interacted with dolls for at least a quarter of a century.

72. Harriet Beecher Stowe, *Uncle Tom's Cabin* (1852), Norton Critical Edition, ed. Elizabeth Ammons (New York: W. W. Norton, 1994), 206, 207, 214, 244. Cited hereafter as "Stowe."

73. Ibid., 245.

74. Illustrators and performers who expanded on Topsy's early doll-likeness but erased her later humanity replicated the dynamic of Joel Chandler Harris's "Uncle Remus" books, which restaged Stowe's fourth chapter but erased the rest of *Uncle Tom's Cabin*. See Chapter 3 on Harris's rewriting of Stowe.

75. It is particularly interesting to note how many illustrators depict Topsy playing with a doll despite the fact that Stowe creates no such scene for her reader (Ophelia merely mentions Topsy's action in the past tense). L. Frank Baum, pictures by Ike Morgan, *The Woggle-Bug Book* (Chicago: Reilly and Britton, 1905); Grace Duffie Boylan, illustrations by Ike Morgan, *Young Folks Uncle Tom's Cabin, Adapted for Children* (New York: H. M. Caldwell, 1901).

76. Anon., *Uncle Tom's Cabin: Young Folks' Edition* (Chicago: M. A. Donohue, n.d. [ca. 1900]), 37.

77. The line appears in Mary E. Blain, *Pleasant Hour Series Uncle Tom's Cabin Rewritten for Young Readers* (New York: Barse and Hopkins, ca. 1900); H[enrietta]. E[lizabeth] Marshall, *Uncle Tom's Cabin Told to the Children* (New York: E. P. Dutton, ca. 1904), and *Uncle Tom's Cabin Little Folks' Edition* (New York: Graham and Matlack, ca.1910).

78. Francis Wayland Parker, *Supplementary Reading for Primary Schools: Second Book* (Boston: Robert S. Davis, 1880), 21. This quotation neatly conflates the *Uncle Tom's Cabin* character, doll-ness, and unhurtability.

79. Richard H. Brodhead, "Sparing the Rod: Discipline and Fiction in Antebellum America," *Representations* 21 (Winter 1988): 67–96.

80. Ibid., 86, citing Stowe, 245.

81. Brodhead, "Sparing the Rod," 83.

82. Ibid., 70.

83. Advertisement quoted in "Novelties in Santa Claus Land," *New York Times*, 3 November 1901, SM9.

84. Hamlen, *Chats*, 227.

85. Ibid.

86. "Dolls of Famous Women: Miss Mary Wilkins, Miss Susan B. Anthony, Mrs. Kate Douglas Wiggin and Others Had Them," *Portland Oregonian*, 16 April 1899, 17.

87. Hall and Ellis, *Study of Dolls*, 34.

88. Aunt Fanny [Frances Elizabeth Barrow], *The Children's Charity Bazaar* (Edinburgh: Edmonston and Douglas, 1870), 22–23. In a similar vein, an 1874 story described a black doll named Dinah as "contraband"—the Civil War term for enslaved people who escaped behind Union lines or into the Union forces (C.H.W., "The Dollies' Visit," *Youth's Companion*, 2 July 1874, 217).

89. Marietta Holley, *Samantha on the Race Problem,* illustrations by E. W. Kemble (New York: Dodd, Mead, 1892), 124. This book was later republished as *Samantha Among the Colored Folks.*

90. Joel Chandler Harris, *Gabriel Tolliver: A Story of Reconstruction* (New York: McClure, Phillips, 1902), 11; emphasis added.

91. *The Little Slave Girl, A True Story, Told by Mammy Sara Herself, Who is Still Alive, to Eileen Douglass* (London: S. W. Partridge, 1906), 5, 9.

92. Ibid., 8, 6. In 1823, the white novelist Eliza Ware Farrar described a parallel scene but reversed its meaning: in Farrar's book, an African American mother named Dinah is "well pleased" when white children "make a plaything" of her son. Eliza Ware Farrar, *The Adventures of Congo in Search of His Master: An American Tale* (London, 1823), 14–15; quoted in Sarah N. Roth, "The Mind of a Child: Images of African Americans in Early Juvenile Fiction," *Journal of the Early Republic* 25 (Spring 2005): 96.

93. Bill Brown, "Reification, Reanimation, and the American Uncanny," *Critical Inquiry* 32, no. 3 (2006): 175–207.

94. *Little Miss Consequence* ([New York] McLoughlin Bros., between 1859 and 1862).

95. Edward Walford, *Old and New London: A Narrative of its History, its People, and Its Places: A New Edition Carefully Revised and Corrected,* vol. 6: *The Southern Suburbs* (1881; London: Cassell, 1893), 163–64.

96. Ibid.

97. Ibid.

98. Daisy Turner told the story of the blood-soaked primer to folklorist Jane C. Beck. The Vermont Folklife Center has posted this audio recording online at http://www.vermontfolklifecenter.org/childrens-books/alecs-primer/audio-photos.shtml. Daisy Turner frequently showed the primer and narrated its origins until the book was destroyed in a house fire in 1962.

99. The phrase "born in" contrasts with the language describing the origins of Amy Davis's doll, which "came from" France. The phrase "came from" constructs Amy Davis's doll as a traveler or tourist, whereas the phrase "born in" suggests that Daisy's doll originated in one place but inhabited another.

100. The German doll company Heubach Koppelsdorf, for example, manufactured many such dolls at the turn of the twentieth century. See Perkins, *Black Dolls*, 34–37.

101. Stowe, 213, 209, 207.

102. Gregory Sharrow, "A Teacher's Guide for On My Own: The Traditions of Daisy Turner and Journey's End: The Memories and Traditions of Daisy Turner and Her Family" (Middlebury: Vermont Folklife Center, 1996), 4.

103. Upon Beck's repeated requests, Turner finally divulged the first two lines of the

poem, but then claimed she could remember no more. Jane C. Beck, private correspondence with the author, 7 May 2009.

104. How do children, who are competent performers of childhood and experts in children's material culture, become adults who view dolls not as things-in-performance but instead as objects that represent race? This question cannot be answered positivistically, but one might speculate that the repeated behaviors of parenthood produce the change in perspective. Parenthood necessitates repeated acts of looking at children. In different regions and historical moments, these acts of looking take different forms, ranging, for example, from the inspection of a child's labor to the surveillance of a child's hygiene to the supervision of a child's imaginative practices. High stakes attend many of these repeated practices of looking: a young child who is not watched risks injury or death. The parent's highly charged, repetitive acts of looking *at* a child may, over time, sediment over the individual's past practices of looking *from* the child's perspective.

105. Ethiop [William J. Wilson], *Frederick Douglass' Paper*, 11 March 1853, 94–95; quoted in Timothy Shortell, "The Rhetoric of Black Abolitionism: An Exploratory Analysis of Antislavery Newspapers in New York State," *Social Science History* 28, no. 1 (2004): 75–109.

106. Wilson, *Frederick Douglass' Paper*, 94.

107. Charles W. Chesnutt's 1904 short story "The Doll" takes a different angle. In this story, a doll ominously hung on a spike reminds an African American barber of his daughter and therefore of how much he stands to lose if he takes revenge on his father's murderer. Despite the fact that Chesnutt never specifies the doll's coloration, Eric Sundquist persuasively interprets the hung doll as a symbolic lynching. Eric Sundquist, *To Wake the Nations: Race in the Making of American Literature* (Cambridge, Mass.: Belknap Press of Harvard University Press, 1993), 450–53.

108. Nora Waring, "Dolly's Dream," *The Brownies' Book*, November 1920, 351–52. This story is reprinted in Dianne Johnson-Feelings, ed., *The Best of the Brownies' Book* (New York: Oxford University Press, 1996), 41–43.

109. *Christian Recorder*, 12 December 1889.

110. "The Negro Doll Question Is Reaching Dignity," *Freeman* (Indianapolis), 14 November 1908, 4.

111. "Duquoin's Negro Doll Fair. The Colored Women's Club have Decided to Hold One This Month," *Freeman* (Indianapolis), 14 November 1908, 6. See also Michele Mitchell, *Righteous Propagation: African Americans and the Politics of Racial Destiny after Reconstruction* (Chapel Hill: University of North Carolina Press, 2004), 182–83; Evelyn Brooks Higginbotham, *Righteous Discontent: The Women's Movement in the Black Baptist Church, 1880–1920* (Cambridge, Mass.: Harvard University Press, 1993), 166, 194.

112. Mitchell, *Righteous Propagation*, 184.

113. Booker T. Washington, "Negro's Part in Southern Development," *Annals of the American Academy of Political and Social Science* 35, no. 1 (1910): 131.

114. "Echoes from the National Grand Master's Address," *Negro Star* (Wichita, Kan.), 25 November 1921, 3.

115. Nelson C. Crewes, "Resolutions for 1909," *Freeman* (Indianapolis), 17 April 1909, 2.

116. Michele Mitchell, "The Colored Doll Is a Live One! Material Culture, Black Consciousness, and Cultivation of Intraracial Desire," in *Righteous Propagation*, 173–96.

117. See Chapter 4. See also Sharon Marcus, who comments on British fiction that configures white girls as mistresses of dolls. Sharon Marcus, *Between Women*, 162–63.

118. "Problem Kids: New Harlem Clinic Rescues Ghetto Youth," *Ebony*, July 1947, 23; Mamie Phipps Clark, *The Reminiscences of Mamie Phipps Clark*, Oral History Collection of Columbia University, New York, 25 May 1976, 73, http://www.columbia.edu/cu/lweb/digital/collections/nny/clarkm/transcripts/clarkm_1_1_73.html.

119. Silas X. Floyd, *Floyd's Flowers; Or, Duty and Beauty for Colored Children* (Atlanta: Hertel, Jenkins, 1905), 75–79.

120. H. G. Wells, *Floor Games* (London: Frank Palmer, 1911), 10.

121. Quoted in David Cronon, *Black Moses: The Story of Marcus Garvey and the Universal Negro Improvement Association* (Madison: University of Wisconsin Press, 1955), 175.

122. Dorothy S., Elizabeth A., and Evelyn J. Coleman, *The Collector's Encyclopedia of Dolls*, vol. 2 (New York: Crown, 1968), 148, citing a 1912 *Toys and Novelties* article.

123. Katharine Capshaw Smith argues persuasively that New Negro reformers, including Floyd, understood the bodies of black children as "the site on which the character of the new black identity can be staged," and that this staging involved bodily practices of imagination, including play with dolls. Katharine Capshaw Smith, "Childhood, the Body, and Race Performance: Early 20th-Century Etiquette Books for Black Children," *African American Review* 40, no. 1 (2006): 799.

124. NNDC advertising pamphlet, reprinted in Perkins, *Black Dolls*, 22–23.

125. During the 1930s, a small number of white-owned manufacturers began using identical molds to produce inexpensive plastic dolls in white and black variations. The Clarks obtained such dolls 1939 at a Woolworth's on 125th Street in Harlem, New York. There is some disagreement as to whether the Clarks purchased the dolls together or whether Kenneth Clark purchased them alone. See Joe Holley, "Kenneth Clark Dies; Helped Desegregate Schools," *Washington Post*, 3 May 2005, sec. B, 4; Sam Roberts, "Kenneth B. Clark: An Integrationist to This Day, Believing All Else Has Failed," *New York Times*, late ed., 7 May 1995, sec. 4, 7, col. 1; Kluger, *Simple Justice*, 315. It seems likely that Mamie, the test's designer, participated in the initial purchase.

126. Clark and Clark, "Racial Identification and Preference," 603; Kluger, *Simple Justice*, 317.

127. Kluger, *Simple Justice*, 315.

128. "Problem Kids: New Harlem Clinic Rescues Ghetto Youth," *Ebony*, July 1947, 23. On the Clarks' visibility in the black public sphere before *Brown*, see Gerald Markowitz and David Rosner, *Children, Race, and Power: Kenneth and Mamie Clark's Northside Center* (Charlottesville: University Press of Virginia, 1996), 32–34.

129. Toni Morrison, *The Bluest Eye* (1970; New York: Simon and Schuster, 1972). On the relationship between Morrison's novel and the Clark doll tests, see Christopher Douglas, "What *The Bluest Eye* Knows about Them: Culture, Race, Identity," *American Literature* 78, no. 1 (2006): 141–68, and Anne Anlin Cheng, "Wounded Beauty: An Exploratory Essay on

Race, Feminism, and the Aesthetic Question," *Tulsa Studies in Women's Literature* 19, no. 2 (2000): 191–217.

130. Bergner, "Black Children, White Preference," 300.

131. Ibid.

132. Clark and Clark, "Racial Identification and Preference," 602.

133. Ibid.

134. Ibid., 611.

135. Kenneth Clark, *Prejudice and Your Child* (1955; 2nd ed, enl., Boston: Beacon Press, 1963), 45. See also Ben Keppel, "Kenneth B. Clark in the Patterns of American Culture," *American Psychologist* 57, no. 1 (2002): 32. Kluger mentions a variation of this quotation in *Simple Justice*, 356. Other children answered similarly: a six-year-old Arkansas girl named Erma Lee, for example, explained that the brown doll was like her because "he's a nigger." Kenneth Clark Papers, data sheets for 1941, Library of Congress.

136. Kluger, *Simple Justice*, 602–3. Gwen Bergner notes that the Clarks, in altering the order of questions, "actually skewed *for* white preference behavior." Bergner, "Black Children, White Preference," 309.

137. [Kenneth and Mamie Clark?], "The Genesis of Racial Identification and Preferences in Negro Children." Undated typed manuscript, Box 46, folder 2 "Miscellany," Kenneth Clark Papers, Library of Congress, 25.

138. Kluger, *Simple Justice*, 441, emphasis added.

139. Sanford, *Frisk and His Flock*, 110.

140. Put another way, the first subset of questions foregrounded children's historical practices of engaging dolls as things, and the second subset coercively led children into an adultified reading of dolls primarily as symbolic objects, not things-in-play. The difference between the first and second subset of questions parallels the different positions of Daisy Turner and her father, respectively: Daisy Turner resisted a genealogy of performance that the black doll cited from the past and scripted for the future, whereas her father viewed the doll primarily as a representation of blackness and therefore urged his daughter to embrace the doll—and, through it, her raced self—as "lovely." In 1891, the clash between that African American daughter and father climaxed in Daisy's torrent of furious verse. Half a century later, the Clarks ensured a similarly dramatic climax with their eighth question, which forced a child to connect the doll-as-thing with doll-as-object by locating herself or himself in relation to both simultaneously. The Clarks thus forced together competing perspectives to create an epistemological crisis.

141. Quoted in Kluger, *Simple Justice*, 318; emphasis added.

142. Clark, *Prejudice and Your Child,* 45; [Clark and Clark?], "Genesis of Racial Identification," 26.

143. Quoted in Kluger, *Simple Justice*, 318.

144. When I call the children's tears agential, I do not mean to suggest that the children consciously weighed their options and strategically, much less cynically, selected the most appealing one. My point, rather, is that tears were a remarkably effective means by which to stop the test—an end that many children probably wanted urgently.

145. Stowe 215.

146. This historical change registers in the assumptions of even the most hardened racists. For example, Keith Bardwell, the Louisiana justice of the peace who in 2009 refused to marry an interracial couple (see Introduction), described mixed-race children as "innocent" and sure to suffer rejection from both black and white communities. Thus Bardwell asserted nonwhite children's innocence and sensitivity to political matters—but he used these assertions to *justify* his attempt to prevent the birth of children of color.

147. Narelle Cockram, comment posted 11 February 2005 to "Save the Golliwogg" website http://members3.boardhost.com/gipsy/msg/306.html, accessed 22 September 2010.

148. When I bought the Raggedy Ann-mammy topsy-turvy doll pictured in Chapter 4, the proprietor of Kotton Kountry Kreations mailed it to me with a note expressing hope that I would enjoy the doll. The dollmaker apparently assumed that I—an adult with a credit card—wanted the doll for myself, not for a child.

# Index

# About the Author

Robin Bernstein is Associate Professor of African and African American Studies and of Studies of Women, Gender, and Sexuality at Harvard University. Her previous books include *Cast Out: Queer Lives in Theater.*

Made in the USA
Middletown, DE
14 June 2024

55754347R00198